Niger Delta: The Business of the Oil Curse

Youth in a Globalizing World

Series Editors

Vincenzo Cicchelli, *Ceped, Université Paris Cité/*IRD
Sylvie Octobre, DEPS – DOC, *Ministère de la culture and Centre Max Weber,* ENS *Lyon/*CNRS *(France)*

VOLUME 22

The titles published in this series are listed at *brill.com/ygw*

Niger Delta: The Business of the Oil Curse

By

Marc-Antoine Pérouse de Montclos

BRILL

LEIDEN | BOSTON

Originally published in hardback in 2024.

The translation of this book received support from Ceped (Centre Population Développement) and F3S (Fédération Sciences Sociales Suds).

Cover illustration: © Marc-Antoine Pérouse de Montclos.

The Library of Congress Cataloging-in-Publication Data is available online at https://catalog.loc.gov

Typeface for the Latin, Greek, and Cyrillic scripts: "Brill". See and download: brill.com/brill-typeface.

ISSN 2212-9383
ISBN 978-90-04-70868-6 (paperback, 2025)
ISBN 978-90-04-69734-8 (hardback)
ISBN 978-90-04-69791-1 (e-book)
DOI 10.1163/9789004697911

Contents

Preface   IX
Acknowledgements   X
List of Maps, Figures and Tables   XI
Acronyms   XIV

Introduction   1

PART 1
From Ebony to Black Gold: A Turbulent History

1   **First Stirrings**
     Nigerian Independence and the Niger Delta Republic (1960–1966)   11
     1   From the Slave Trade   11
     2   To Oil Exploration   13
     3   Isaac Boro and the Niger Delta Republic (1966)   16
     4   Toward the Secession of Biafra   19
     5   Controversies Surrounding the Question of Genocide   22

2   **Mirages in the Midst of War**
     The Secession of Biafra (1967–1970)   26
     1   The Great Game of Alliances   27
     2   The Pragmatism of Oil Companies   29
     3   Oil: A Resource for Conflict or an Obstacle to War?   31
     4   Disagreements over Revenue Sharing   34

3   **Boom or Doom?**
     From Prosperity to the Economic and Social Crisis (1971–1989)   40
     1   The Reconstruction Era   40
     2   A Relentless Race to Create New States   43
     3   Centralized Federalism   45
     4   The Uprising of Evangelists, Naked Women and the Youth   49

4   **Shell, the Dictator and the Writer**
     The Ogoni Revolt (1990–1999)   53
     1   The Ogoni, an Emerging Minority   55
     2   MOSOP between Contestations and Divisions   59

3   A Bitter Victory   62
4   The Odi Massacre and the Beginning of the Ijaw Rebellion   67

5   **Militants or Pirates?**
     The Armed Struggle of the Ijaw (2000–2009)   71
     1   Greed or Grievance?   73
     2   The Emergence of MEND (2006–2008)   77
     3   The 2009 Amnesty   80

6   **The Gangster and the Godfather**
     Ordinary Crime and Amnesty in a "Democracy" (2010–2020)   89
     1   An Ijaw President: Goodluck Jonathan (2010–2015)   89
     2   Muhammadu Buhari, or the Dashed Hopes of a Democratic
          Transition (2015–2020)   93
     3   The Business of Amnesty   95
     4   The Institutionalization of Crime   98
     5   Bayelsa and Rivers in Troubled Waters   101

     PART 2
     And What about Oil?

7   **In Search of Lost Oil**
     Dutch Disease under the Tropics   109
     1   Biased Analyses   109
     2   Toward a Pluralistic Interpretation of Nigeria's Problems   114
     3   Godfatherism by Way of Democracy   117
     4   Oil and Violence: A Complex Relationship   119

8   **The End of the Trinity**
     The State, Oil Companies, and "Civil Society"   128
     1   Cult Societies   128
     2   On the "Irresponsibility" of Oil Companies in the Violence   131
     3   The Use of Militias and Security Contracts: Corporate Contributions
          to Crime   132
     4   Three Divided "Blocs"   135
     5   The Trade Unions   138

9   **Majors, Domestic Firms, and the National Company**
     A Multifaceted Industry   142

1   Oil Production: A Wide Range of Actors   143

2   Transnational Corporations   145

3   "Independent" and "Indigenous" Operators   149

4   A Highly Political Nigerianization of the Industry since 1999   151

5   Reforms in Progress   156

10   **Ruling without Governing**
    The Challenges of Acephalous Societies   159

1   An Ethnic Puzzle   161

2   Warrant Chiefs and Indirect Rule   166

3   Political Careers and Crowns   168

4   The Case of Warri   172

11   **Dividing without Ruling**
    Beyond Ethnicity   178

1   The Ibo and the Ijaw: Two Different Agendas   180

2   Discord among the Rebels   183

3   Tribalism and Politics   185

4   Quotas, or the Illusions of Indigeneity   189

PART 3
The Heart of the Matter: The State

12   **Big Business and Political Power**
    An Uneasy Alliance   197

1   Conflicts between Oil Companies and the State   198

2   Corporate Social Responsibility (CSR)   201

3   From Collusion to Separation   206

13   **The Leviathan of the Mangroves**
    A Deficient, Predatory, and Contested State   210

1   A Sense of Alienation   211

2   Land as a Key Bone of Contention   215

3   A Deficient Judicial System   217

4   When Crime Pays: The Reign of Impunity   220

14   **"Authority Stealing"**
    Corruption as a System of Government   227

1   A Model of Maladministration   229

2   The Merits and Drawbacks of Cronyism   232
3   Flexible Perceptions   235
4   The Contradictions of the "Marginalization" Argument   237

15   Pollution
Who Is to Blame?   244
1   A Degraded Environment   247
2   Multinationals in the Eye of the Storm   251
3   Shared Responsibilities   252
4   Between Impotence and Conflicts of Interest: The Role of the
     State   254

16   Incoherence and Fantasy
A Versatile Elite   261
1   On Collusion with Rebels   262
2   Independence, Autonomy, Regionalism, Federalism: An à la Carte
     Menu   266
3   Everyday Arrangements: The Obolo between the Ocean and the Niger
     Delta   267
4   The Balkanization of the Niger Delta   270

Conclusion   275

Annex 1   Overview of "Cult" Societies in Nigeria
           From Students' Fraternities to Street Gangs   281
Annex 2   Three Examples of Domestic Companies   288
Index   293

Preface

Nigeria is an essential link in the global flows of ideas, people and goods. As the most populous country in Africa, it plays a major role in international migration and has a large diaspora overseas. As a cultural laboratory, it also actively contributes to artistic creation thanks, among others, to its writers and a prolific film industry, "Nollywood". With the largest GDP on the continent, Nigeria is one of the world's leading oil and gas producers, a major strategic asset at a time when the war in Ukraine disrupts the geopolitics of fossil fuels. Nigeria has much development potential and some economists see it as one of the four emerging markets of the twenty-first century: the so-called MINT (Mexico, Indonesia, Nigeria, and Turkey).

Yet Africa's giant is also suffering from its strengths. Nigeria is often cited as an emblematic example of the "resource curse". Its oil and gas producing regions in the Niger Delta are torn apart by high levels of political and criminal violence. The youth play a key role in this crisis as activists, militants, gangsters, pirates, "cultists", stooges ... or subalterns.

By analyzing the various factors of conflict in the Niger Delta, this monograph thus sheds new light on oil issues. Based on more than thirty years of fieldwork, it also makes it possible to develop useful comparisons to question the role of youth in other countries affected by the so-called resource curse.

Finally, this book is rooted in reflections that began when I was a young lecturer at the University of Port Harcourt in the late 1980s. I was myself 22 years old when I visited the Niger Delta for the first time. Since then, a lot of water has flowed under the bridge. The following analysis is thus part of a long-term perspective.

Acknowledgements

I would like to thank the anonymous reviewers who helped me finalize the manuscript. My sincere gratitude also goes to all the Nigerian friends and colleagues who facilitated my fieldwork in the Niger Delta. I pay special tribute to the late Ben Akparanta and Kevin Ekeanyanwu in memory of our excursions to Akwete and Azumini River.

The translation of this book received support from Ceped (Centre Population Développement) and F3S (Fédération Sciences Sociales Suds). The French version has been published in Paris in 2024 by the Editions de la Sorbonne under the title *Nigeria: La fabrique de la malédiction du pétrole dans le delta du Niger.*

Maps, Figures and Tables

Maps

1   The 6 states in Nigeria's South-South geopolitical zone   2
2   The 36 states of Nigeria   4
3   Some communities of the Niger Delta   162

Figures

1   Key stakeholders and their relationships in the Niger Delta crisis   6
2   A woman in her canoe at Iko, a village in Akwa Ibom State (2009)   7
3   Aerial view of Port Harcourt (2011)   12
4   Oloibiri, Nigeria's first commercial oil discovery by Shell in 1956 (2011)   16
5   A painting of Isaac Adaka Boro in Bayelsa State (2011)   18
6   A Shell oil well abandoned in Akwa Ibom State (2009)   27
7   A Biafra postal stamp (1967)   35
8   Gas flaring at Bori in Ogoniland near the Eleme Port Harcourt Refinery (1994)   46
9   Mangrove Swamp (2004)   49
10 Ken Saro Wiwa in his office on Aggrey Road, the headquarters of MOSOP in Port Harcourt (1994)   54
11 A MOSOP demonstration at Eeken in Rivers State, following clashes with the Andoni (1994)   54
12 An Ogoni Masquerade (1994)   56
13 An Ogoni Masquerade (1994)   56
14 The president of NYCOP (National Youth Council of the Ogoni People), Goodluck Diigbo, at Eeken in Rivers State (1994)   61
15 Asari Dokubo and his guerrillas of the Niger Delta People's Volunteer Force (NDPVF) at Ogbakiri, Rivers State (2004)   72
16 An illegal refinery at Isaba, near Warri (2011)   74
17 Asari Dokubo at a press conference in Edo State (2011)   77
18 The headquarters of the JTF (Joint Task Force) in Yenagoa, Bayelsa State (2011)   81
19 The red notice of John Togo in Yenagoa, Bayelsa State (2011)   90
20 Goodluck Jonathan during his electoral campaign (2011)   92
21 Muhammadu Buhari during his electoral campaign (2011)   94
22 Timipre Sylva, Bayelsa State Governor (2011)   102

23   Okpoama Beach in Bayelsa State (2011)   110
24   A ghost factory: Brass-LNG (2011)   110
25   Akpo oil field, off the coast of Rivers State (2009)   121
26   A Nigerian policeman (2011)   129
27   The bodyguards of a politician in Edo State (2011)   134
28   Ebikabowei Victor-Ben "Boyloaf", one of the founders of MEND, in Abuja
      (2021)   137
29   Apapa port in Lagos (2010)   143
30   The Brass oil terminal (2011)   147
31   Onne port in Rivers State (2011)   148
32   A gas flare in Nembe, Bayelsa State (2011)   153
33   A traditional chief from Eastern Obolo in Akwa Ibom State (2009)   160
34   The spiritual leader (*pere*) of the Isaba community in Warri South-West in Delta
      State (2011)   164
35   The "king" (*eze*) of the Ikwerre in Port Harcourt (2004)   170
36   The jetty for Brass in Ogbia (2011)   179
37   Yenagoa, the capital city of Bayelsa State (2011)   180
38   A Creek Town chalet in Cross River State (1990)   181
39   Port Harcourt, the largest urban center in the Niger Delta (2011)   187
40   An NDDC (Niger Delta Development Commission) project never completed in
      an Akwa Ibom State village (2009)   198
41   Lagos Port (2010)   202
42   Slums in Port Harcourt (1994)   211
43   Aerial view of the Niger Delta (2011)   214
44   Portrait of Ken Saro-Wiwa in the offices of Environmental Rights Action
      (2011)   228
45   A school in Akwa Ibom State (2009)   230
46   Most people in the Niger Delta depend on the informal economy: A hat seller in
      Yenagoa (2011)   233
47   An illegal refinery near Gbaramatu in Delta State (2011)   245
48   An oil spill caused by the rupture of an Agip pipeline in Bayelsa State
      (2011)   249
49   Emblem of Bayelsa State (2005)   262
50   A PDP supporter in Akwa Ibom State (2009)   265
51   Edowin beach in Eastern Obolo in Akwa Ibom State (2009)   268
52   Canoes in the lagoon (2000)   272
53   A fishing boat off the coast of Bayelsa State (2011)   276
54   Mile 2 Diobu Market in Port Harcourt: Umbrellas provide shelter from both the
      rain and the sun (2011)   279

Tables

1   The regional origin of oil ministers and advisers (1971–2021)   238
2   Conoil, Sapetro and Seplat: Common challenges   291

Acronyms

ACN	Action Congress of Nigeria
AD	Alliance for Democracy
ADEF	Ateke, Dokubo, Egberipapa & Farah (private security firm named after four major beneficiaries of the 2009 amnesty in Rivers State)
AGIP	Any Government In Power
ANPP	All Nigeria People's Party
APC	All Progressives Congress
APP	All People's Party
BAYELSA	BALGA-YELGA-SALGA (a state made up of Brass, Yenagoa and Sagbama LGAs; its first acronym, ABAYELSA, included Ahoada, a Local Government Area currently in Rivers State)
BP	British Petroleum
CLO	Civil Liberties Organisation
Conoil	Consolidated Oil Limited
CSR	Corporate social responsibility
DESOPADEC	Delta State Oil Producing Areas Development Commission
DPR	Department of Petroleum Resources
EFCC	*Economic and Financial Crimes Commission*
ENI	*Ente Nazionale Idrocarburi*
ERA	Environmental Rights Action
FEPA	Federal Environmental Protection Agency
FNDIC	Federated Niger Delta Ijaw Communities
FPSO	Floating Production Storage and Offloading
GTZ	Gesellschaft für Internationale Zusammenarbeit
GWVSNL	*Global West Vessel Specialists Nigeria Limited*
INC	Ijaw National Council
IUCN	International Union for Conservation of Nature
IYC	Ijaw Youth Council
JDZ	Joint Development Zone
JOA	Joint Operating Agreement
JV	Joint Ventures
KAGOTE	Khana, Gokana, Tai, Eleme
KNOC	Korea National Oil Corporation
LGA	Local Government Area
LIMUP	Liberation Movement of the Urhobo People
LNG	Liquefied Natural Gas

MAMSER	Mass Mobilization for Self Reliance, Social Justice, and Economic Recover
MASSOB	Movement for the Actualisation of the Sovereign State of Biafra
MEND	Movement for the Emancipation of the Niger Delta
MOSOP	Movement for the Survival of the Ogoni People
NCNC	National Council of Nigeria and the Cameroons
NDA	Niger Delta Avengers
NDC	Niger Delta Congress
NDEP	Niger Delta Exploration & Production
NDPVF	Niger Delta Volunteer People's Force
NDV	Niger Delta Vigilantes
NDVF	Niger Delta Volunteer Force
NEITI	Nigerian Extractive Industries Transparency Initiative
NGO	Non-Governmental Organization
NIMASA	Nigerian Maritime Administration and Safety Agency
NNOC	Nigerian National Oil Corporation, established in April 1971 and activated in July 1973 to handle government interests in Shell-BP. It is the forerunner of NNPC.
NNPC	Nigerian National Petroleum Corporation, established in April 1977. It became the NNPC Limited in July 2022.
NOSDRA	National Oil Spill Detection and Response Agency
NPDC	Nigerian Petroleum Development Company
NPN	National Party of Nigeria
NUPENG	Nigeria Union of Petroleum and Natural Gas Workers
NYCOP	National Youth Council of Ogoni People
OFSL	Oil Facilities Surveillance Limited (private security firm formed by Ateke Tom, Asari Dokubo and Tom Polo after the 2009 amnesty)
OML	Oil Mining Lease
OMPADEC	Oil Mineral Producing Area Development Commission
ONELGA	Ogba-Ndoni-Egbema Local Government Area (Rivers)
OPC	Oodua People's Congress
OPEC	Organisation of Petroleum Exporting Countries
OPL	Oil Prospecting License
OPTS	Oil Producers Trade Section
PENGASSAN	Petroleum and Natural Gas Senior Staff Association of Nigeria
PIA	Petroleum Industry Act
PIB	Petroleum Industry Bill
PDP	People's Democratic Party
PSA	Production Sharing Agreement

SAFRAP   Société Anonyme Française de Recherches et d'Exploitation Pétrolières,
         the Nigerian branch of ERAP (Entreprise de Recherches et d'Activités
         Pétrolières) which changes its name to Elf in 1975
Sapetro South Atlantic Petroleum
SEPCOL   Shebah Exploration & Production Company Limited
Seplat   Shebah Exploration Platform
UAC   United Africa Company
UNEP   United Nations Environment Programme
WWF   World Wide Fund for Nature

Introduction

Traversed by the Niger River, Nigeria is Africa's largest oil producer and the most populous country on the continent, soon to become the third most populous country in the world. Located on the Atlantic coast, its delta is a labyrinth of creeks and an "ethnic puzzle". The region spans hundreds of miles. It is the third-largest delta in the world and the largest in Africa. Once a center for the global slave trade, it has become a vast oil field. It also borders on the short-lived Republic of Biafra, where a fight for independence between 1967 and 1970 led to one of Africa's bloodiest conflicts in a region now infested with all kinds of armed groups, traffickers, and smugglers.

Who are these young rebels roaming the delta waters with Kalashnikovs on powerful speedboats? Who are these pirates operating on the high seas and launching attacks on oil platforms while claiming to be protected by the Ijaw god of war, Egbesu? Who are the saboteurs who blow up pipelines to steal crude on land: "militants", freedom fighters, terrorists, drunkards, or gangsters? While greed and the lure of power may be the obvious answers, what are they really after? And what role do mineral resources play in all this?

For many observers, oil lies at the root of all the challenges of the Niger Delta. The "black gold" is viewed as a curse that somehow predestined Nigeria to becoming a prime example of financial misuse, industrial waste, endemic corruption, bad governance, exacerbated criminality, and endless violence. Today, Niger Deltans are paying the price for all these predicaments in the form of oil spills, air pollution, underdevelopment, repression, and clashes between rival groups. However, the many conflicts affecting the region cannot be reduced to an opposition between "nice" fishermen, "predatory" soldiers, and the "evil" capitalists of transnational corporations. A thorough analysis rather shows the need to debunk dominant narratives and avoid any form of determinism, as oil production represents just one of the factors contributing to a series of problems that run far deeper into the mangroves of the Niger Delta.

It is always difficult to provide a full picture of a protracted crisis. I lived in Port Harcourt in the late 1980s. Since then, I have returned to the Niger Delta for various assignments, sometimes under armed escort. Hence this book is the result of more than thirty years of investigation in Port Harcourt, Warri, Akassa, Brass, Gbaramatu, Obolo, and Okrika (see Map 1). In the course of my fieldwork, I have conducted interviews with "militants", dedicated ecologists, brilliant intellectuals, "bunkerized" oil workers, politicians, corrupt police and military officers, urban gangsters, and fishermen who, far from the media spotlight, still live peacefully in the creeks. Among others, I have spoken to

Harold Dappa-Biriye, the "patriarch" of Rivers State, Ken Saro-Wiwa, the well-known Ogoni writer hanged by the military junta in 1995, Asari-Dokubo and Ebikabowei Victor-Ben "General Boyloaf", founders of the Ijaw armed rebellion in the following decade, and John Togo, the last rebel to have refused the 2009 amnesty before being killed by the army in 2011.

Of course, fieldwork in the Niger Delta is not enough to analyze the political, economic, and social issues surrounding the so-called resource curse. Nigeria

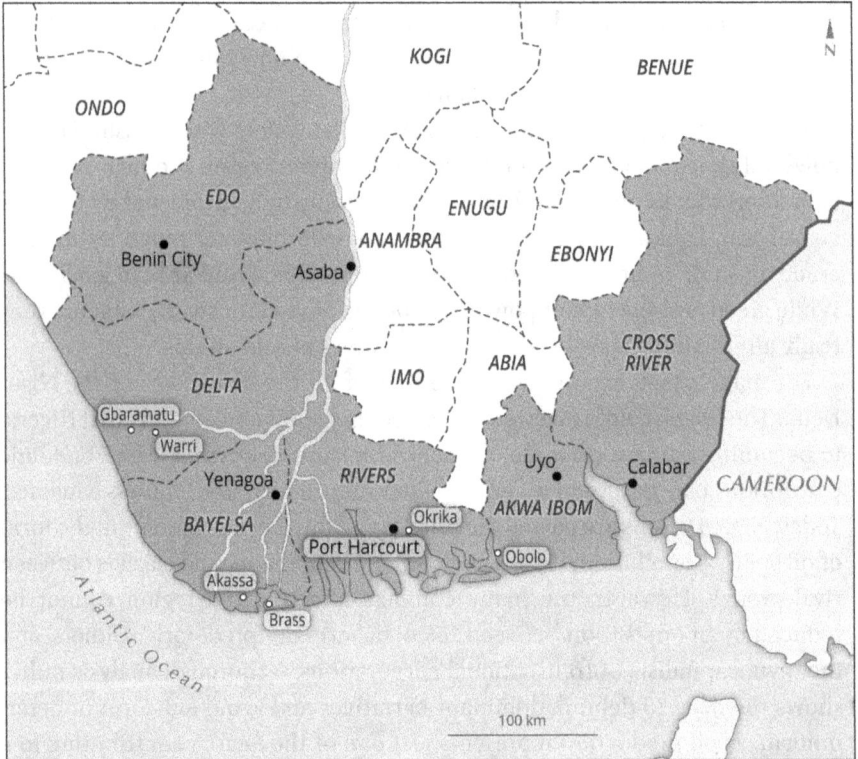

Source: M.-A. de Montclos, IRD-Ceped   Map conception: E. Opigez, IRD-Ceped

RIVERS   State

Asaba ●   State Capital

(Brass)   Area under study

——   International border

- - - - -   Administrative border

▨▨▨▨   South-South geopolitical zone

MAP 1   The 6 states in Nigeria's South-South geopolitical zone

is a huge country and a federation formed of 36 states (see Map 2), with oil production being concentrated in just four of these states: Akwa Ibom, Bayelsa,
Delta, and Rivers. To enrich and complete the research, I therefore conducted
interviews in Abuja, the federal capital, and in Lagos, the country's business
center and the largest city of Africa's most populous country.

In the course of my investigation, I had the opportunity to meet many youths.
Some of them were students, artists, writers, champions of human rights, environmental activists or trade unionists. But others, the so-called "militants",
carried weapons and were members of "cult societies", pirats' groups or gangs
specialized in "bunkering" (the theft of crude oil). This patchwork showed the
diversity and the complexity of the role of the youth in a country which records
a very hight fertility rate and where over half of the population is under 18. It
also revealed the importance of generational dynamics in the fight against the
federal government and international oil companies: from Ken Saro-Wiva to
Asari Dokubo, the leaders of the Niger Delta struggle were young, radical and
opposed to the sense of compromise of the elders. Finally, studying the role of
the youh highlighted the intracy of resource conflicts.

This book thus offers an original understanding of the "oil curse business".
The analysis is based not only on semi-structured interviews and second-
ary sources, but also on a database on violent deaths and lethal incidents as
reported by the local media since 2006 in the Niger Delta and, more generally,
in Nigeria.[1] Combining quantitative and qualitative approaches indeed helps
to cross-check information, deconstruct dominant narratives, and clarify the
impact of oil production on conflicts.

Our findings confirm or, on the contrary, invalidate some of the paradigms of
the academic literature on "weak states" and the "resource curse", especially in
the field of political science.[2] This work is primarily a monograph. Apart from
a few factual points in Chapter 7, it does not venture to make international
comparisons on the "oil curse". But its conclusions will be useful to researchers
who wish to include the case of Nigeria, the giant of Africa, to enrich their
demonstration on a more global scale.

The book is divided into three main sections. Section 1 traces the history
of the Niger Delta from Nigeria's independence in 1960. The chapters are
arranged chronologically, focusing on the key events marking the region: the
Biafran War, the oil boom of the 1970s, the Ogoni uprising of the early 1990s,

---

1   http://www.nigeriawatch.org/index.php?html=4.
2   See, for instance, the seminal works of Auty 1993 and Migdal 1988.

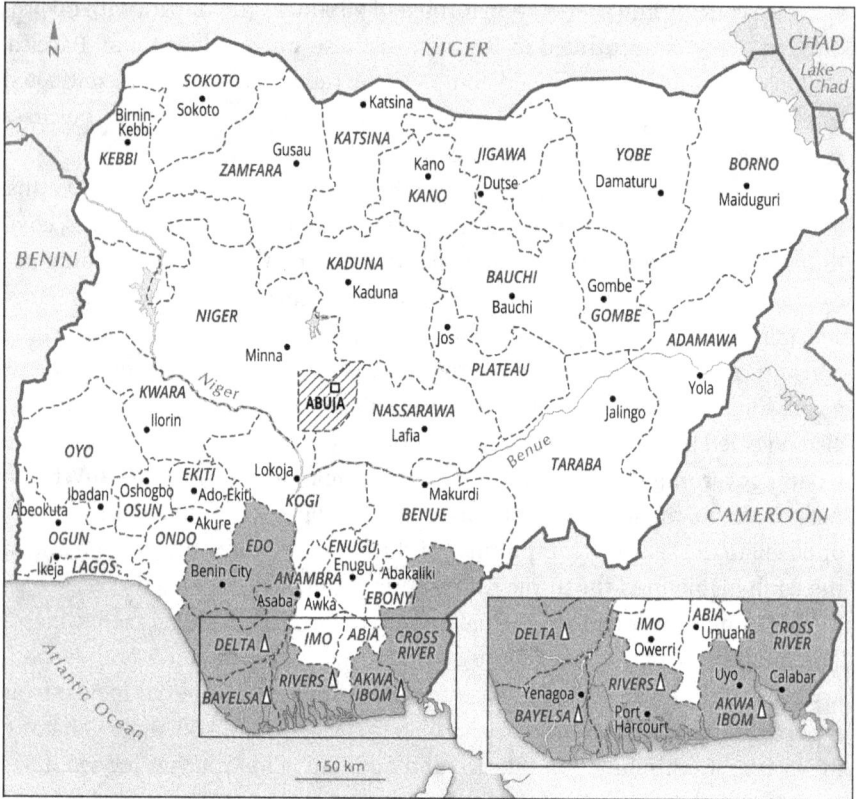

Source: M.-A. de Montclos, IRD-Ceped

Map conception: E. Opigez, IRD-Ceped

Lafia •   State Capital

PLATEAU   State

DELTA Δ   Main Oil Producing State

——   International boundary

-----   State Limit

/////   Federal Capital Territory (Abuja)

▒▒▒   The South-South geopolitical zone

MAP 2   The 36 states of Nigeria

the armed rebellion of the Ijaw in the following decade, the 2009 amnesty, and the fragile status quo that followed.

Section 2 focuses more specifically on the role of oil in conflicts shaped by a multitude of factors. The findings point to a pluralistic interpretation of the

Niger Delta crisis. Unlike proponents of the "oil curse" thesis who tend to focus exclusively on the harmful role of mineral resources, the results show that conflicts cannot be reduced to an economic competition between different communities or multinationals. The relationship between oil and violence is a complex one. We need to go beyond the "trinitarian" vision opposing so-called civil society to an alliance between the Nigerian state and big business. There are many points of convergence and divergence between the various stakeholders in the crisis. It is also important to acknowledge that none of the three main "blocs" involved are monolithic, including the youth (see Figure 1).

For instance, the oil industry is highly competitive, and a distinction should be made between transnational corporations, "independent" companies, domestic firms, and NNPC, a public entity that holds a majority stake in all production joint ventures and a near monopoly over key areas of petro-chemistry and fuel distribution. Consideration should also be given to the role of unions within the sector.

As for the peoples of the Niger Delta, they are very diverse and far from being unanimously opposed to oil companies and the federal government in Abuja. Instead, communities are split along lines involving not just ethnic and linguistic differences, but also conflicts between age groups and social classes—for example, landlords and settlers, coastal fishermen and peasants inland. Undoubtedly, the black gold has often exacerbated communal conflicts aimed to secure larger shares of oil wealth; however, the idea of a volatile "ethnic petro-chemistry" is not sufficient to explain the rising power of young warlords and the modern challenges posed to traditional ceremonial chiefs in acephalous societies.

Part three thus argues that poor governance, the systematic misappropriation of oil revenues, the impunity enjoyed by criminals, and the structural deficiencies of the state lie at the heart of the Niger Delta crisis. Contrary to what is often assumed, multinationals have tense, conflictual relations with the Nigerian government. As for the youth and the common man, they have no illusions about the electoral promises of corrupt, mafia-like politicians. For many people, the Nigerian state is a kind of Leviathan monster in the mangroves. Instead of redistributing oil revenues, doing justice, and regulating land conflicts, it is seen as a predatory power that preserves the impunity of the ruling class and lets citizens fend for themselves to compensate for the lack of basic public services.

The versatility of the elites, the incoherence of the claims made by armed "militants", the contradictions of young activists, generational conflicts, and the collusion between rebels and dubious politicians are all part of the problem. Locals themselves contribute significantly to pollution and oil spills when

Key stakeholders and their relationships in the Niger Delta crisis

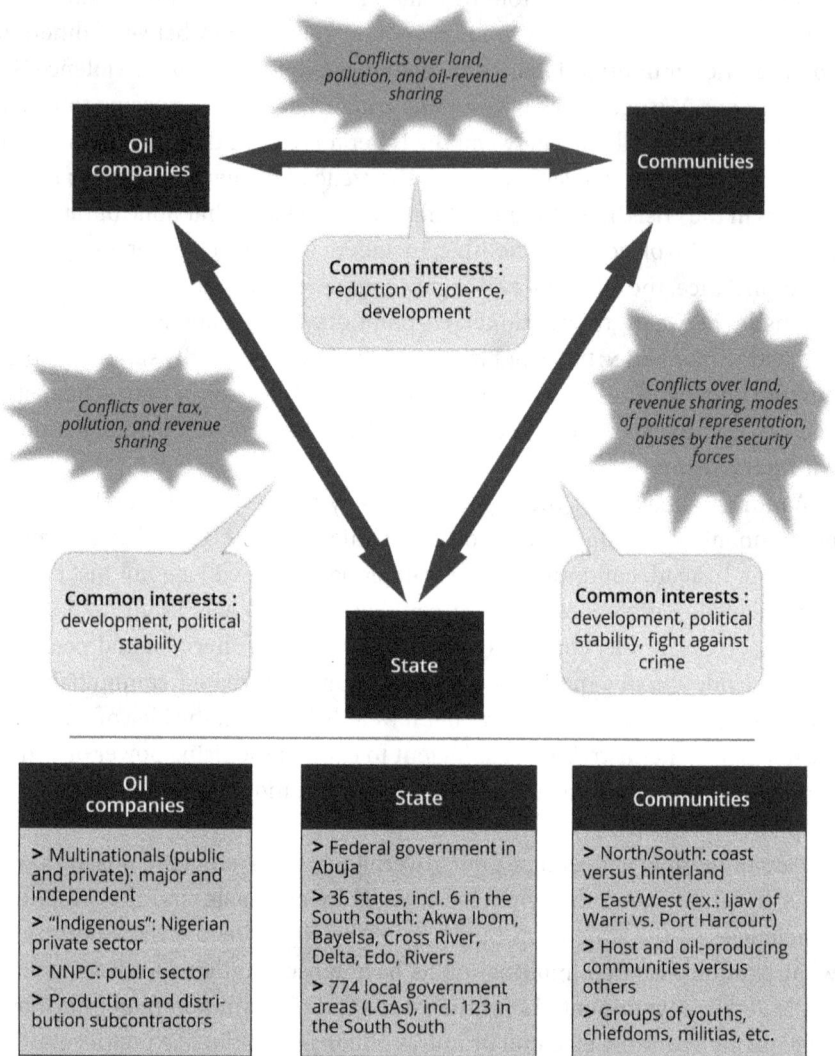

Oil companies	State	Communities
> Multinationals (public and private): major and independent	> Federal government in Abuja	> North/South: coast versus hinterland
> "Indigenous": Nigerian private sector	> 36 states, incl. 6 in the South South: Akwa Ibom, Bayelsa, Cross River, Delta, Edo, Rivers	> East/West (ex.: Ijaw of Warri vs. Port Harcourt)
> NNPC: public sector	> 774 local government areas (LGAs), incl. 123 in the South South	> Host and oil-producing communities versus others
> Production and distribution subcontractors		> Groups of youths, chiefdoms, militias, etc.

FIGURE 1   Key stakeholders and their relationships in the Niger Delta crisis

they vandalize pipelines to steal crude, refine it illegally, and sell it on the black market. Beyond the opposition between transnational corporations and a vague entity referred to as "civil society", conflicts in the Niger Delta highlight the importance of local dynamics that are often overlooked by theorists of the resource curse.

FIGURE 2   A woman in her canoe at Iko, a village in Akwa Ibom State (2009)

References

Auty, Richard. 1993. *Sustaining Development in Mineral Economies: The Resource Curse Thesis*, London, Routledge.

Migdal, Joel. 1988. *Strong Societies and Weak States. State-Society Relations and State Capabilities in the Third World*, New Jersey, Princeton University Press.

PART 1

From Ebony to Black Gold: A Turbulent History

∴

First Stirrings

Nigerian Independence and the Niger Delta Republic (1960–1966)

As my plane began its descent toward Port Harcourt on my first visit to the Niger Delta in 1989, I was immediately struck by the beauty of the sky at night-fall. Against the red glow of the setting sun, the flames from the oil-well flares projected strange shadows onto the canopy of heaven. The atmosphere soon changed as the plane's descent took us through the thick layer of clouds in which the tropical city is permanently shrouded. Landing was sometimes a perilous affair in a region known for its rainfall and humidity. Every now and then, a lone cow would slip through the fence surrounding the airport and begin chewing on weeds growing through the tarmac. Veering off course, the plane would end up landing in scrubland.

It took me nearly a year to realize that almost no one is buried in Port Harcourt. In the colonial township, there is an old cemetery near the hospital, not far from the prison where the celebrated writer Ken Saro-Wiwa was hanged by the military junta in 1995. But it is no longer in use. Port Harcourt is an artificial town, lacking a soul and a center, an urban sprawl typical of a black gold rush. It now bears little resemblance to the tranquil garden-city that the British wanted to build. People come here to work, sometimes to have fun, but seldom to live. When someone dies here, the body is usually returned to the countryside to be buried in the village.

1 From the Slave Trade

Established in 1912, Port Harcourt is a relatively recent colonial creation. By contrast, the Niger Delta has a more ancient history. With a few exceptions such as the Ogoni, the communities living along the coast were once active participants in the transatlantic slave trade. The merchants of city-states such as Bonny, Opobo, and Brass sold prisoners of war and Ibo people captured in the hinterland, in exchange for weapons and liquor. The Bight of Biafra thus became one of the favored African destinations of European ships. On the coast, only the neighboring Kingdom of Benin to the west of the delta opposed the slave trade, when one of its rulers banned the sale of men but not women (Fuglestad 2018: 13–15).

FIGURE 3   Aerial view of Port Harcourt (2011)

As a consequence, one which is still visible today, the region became infested with arms and pirates. For example, among the Ibo on the mainland, the so-called Aro mercenaries specialized in reselling serfs, insolvent debtors, and prisoners of war along the coast. They also routinely abducted in broad daylight children who had been left alone at home while their parents worked in the fields. Led by chiefs known as *Dimkpa* (a "master thief of men"), their commandos, termed *Ohafia* or *Ekumeku* in Ibo, would roam the countryside hunting for isolated targets, and thus kidnapping the youth on a grand scale (Obichere 1988: 52).

Further south along the coast, the slave trade fueled violence between rival groups who attempted to seize the goods imported by Europeans, especially weapons. Piracy was rife when the British began prohibiting slavery and promoting legal commerce. For instance, Ijaw war canoes attacked ships moored near trading posts on the coast. In 1856, the British consul thus recommended that his allies, the Itsekiri of Warri, arm themselves and set up convoys to travel on pirogues, not unlike the advice given to ships today to sail together under military escort along the Niger Delta coastline (Lloyd 1963: 221).

In other words, firearms were already present in abundance before the British resorted to their usual gunboat diplomacy to "pacify" and ultimately colonize the region under the pretext of maintaining free navigation and trade.

To assert its authority, the colonial master then tried to recover the arsenals built over several centuries of barter trade. After deporting the King of Opobo, one of the main slave trading posts in the Niger Delta, Britain first attempted in 1888 to confiscate by force the firearms in circulation within the region. This policy failed to achieve anything and, from 1892 onward, the colonial master had to offer money to buy back weapons. However, the initiative met with little success, partly because the promised compensations were never paid to the families who had agreed to hand over their firearms and war canoes.[1] In a similar vein, the authorities struggled to ensure compliance with a 1902 edict that prohibited and penalized the possession and trade of weapons (Ukeje 2006).

2   To Oil Exploration

Over time, the slave trade was progressively replaced with the legitimate commerce of agricultural products such as palm oil (Jones 1989). In 1884, the Niger Delta officially became a British protectorate with a kind of prophetic name: "Oil Rivers". In the view of some Nigerian historians from the region, there was thus a strong continuity in the competition for resources whose commercial value evolved according to demand, the nature of the products, and the types of outlets in the context of rentier economies: first the slave trade in the eighteenth century, then palm oil in the nineteenth century, and finally crude oil and gas today.

In the early days of British colonization, for example, the puncheon of palm oil was akin to a form of currency, much like the oil barrel today. Interestingly enough, this unit of measurement was also used to determine the daily fine that the chiefs of the coastal city-states had to pay when they arbitrarily seized ships that had already paid them a toll fee called *comey*.[2] Such a system is reminiscent of the penalties that the Nigerian government now intends to introduce under a 2021 law to encourage local communities to prevent attacks and pipeline sabotage by threatening to cut off their subsidies if they fail to protect oil facilities.

In the region, some researchers thus draw comparisons between oil production and the slave trade. According to Ugo Nwokeji (2008: 65), a historian

---

1   It was not until the end of a trial in 1945 that the descendants of the customary chiefs of the time were finally able to secure a small amount of money (Jaja 1991: 109ff).

2   See, for instance, articles 14 and 8 of the treaties signed in 1856 and 1879 with customary chiefs in Nembe and Brass to protect the freedom of trade and navigation within the Niger Delta (Alagoa 2018: 231, 246).

who first studied at the University of Port Harcourt, "the parallels and reso-
nances are striking". He argues that, like present-day oil multinationals, only
trading companies in the past had "the technology and capital" necessary
to trade on a global scale. To carry out their activities, both benefited from
state support while enriching dubious middlemen, exacerbating corruption,
fueling violence, and drawing opprobrium from humanitarian organizations.
Ugo Nwokeji concluded that, ultimately, neither the traders of yesteryear
nor present-day oil companies have contributed to the development of the
Niger Delta.

A native of Okrika, a suburb of Port Harcourt, the historian Tekena Tamuno
(2011: ix, 37) has also emphasized the importance of the colonial legacy. From
the vegetable oil produced in palm groves to the mineral oil extracted from
deposits, he went as far as to argue that the Niger Delta was continuously at
war since the establishment of a first British consulate in 1849 until the signing of an amnesty granted to armed militants in 2009. Seemingly unaware of
the periods of peace during the colonial era, Tamuno draws a direct parallel
between the punitive expedition led by the British in Akassa in 1895 and the
massacre perpetrated by Nigerian soldiers in Odi in 1999 to defend the interests of the Royal Niger Company a century ago or the oil majors today. In both
cases, Tamuno notes, the rebels asked for protection from the Ijaw god of war,
Egbesu, while the authorities retaliated with no regard for the collateral damage caused to civilians.

In the eyes of some Niger Delta militants, oil companies are thus viewed
as present-day slave traders. However, the comparison does not withstand
closer scrutiny. For example, the authorities responded very differently when
their economic interests were under threat. In 1895, the British did set up a
parliamentary committee to investigate the massacres of Akassa.[3] They eventually acknowledged the wrongdoing of the Royal Niger Company, whose
charter was revoked in 1899, thus paving the way for the establishment of a
"proper" colonial administration.[4] A hundred years later, by contrast, President
Olusegun Obasanjo ignored the rule of law and made no attempt to try the

---

3   The raid was actually a retaliation. The Nembe of the hinterland had indeed attacked the
    Royal Niger Company's headquarters at Akassa. They had destroyed its warehouses, looted
    its property, kidnapped some employees and cut off heads to be taken back as war trophies.
    Prisoners were eaten as part of spiritual ceremonies to combat both the British and a small-
    pox epidemic (Falola & Heaton 2008: 102).
4   At the time, the British government compensated the company with half the revenue to be
    possibly generated by the extraction of mineral resources in territories formerly under its
    control. Initially granted for a period of 99 years, this royalty was eventually revoked in 1949
    (Siollun 2021: 154).

military responsible for the Odi massacre. To stop the spiral of violence in the Niger Delta, the Nigerian government also failed to consider revoking the oil concessions granted to companies such as Shell or Chevron.

From a structural point of view, moreover, the political economy of transnational corporations today has little in common with the slave trade. Examined in Chapters 9 and 12, this economy rather shows the complexity of financial capitalism. The oil industry does not require a lot of manpower. It is hardly comparable to the colonial plantation economy, which decimated entire countries when it was based on forced labor.[5] An analysis of the oil industry instead requires a review of the conditions of its emergence in Nigeria. At the time of independence in 1960, the Niger Delta indeed played a relatively minor role in the national economy. Nigeria was then a major agricultural producer. Most of its revenue came from exports of cocoa, groundnuts, timber, and palm oil in other parts of the country, notably the Northern and Western Regions. No one could have predicted the extent to which oil production would transform the lives of Nigerians.

The first forays into the industry were, admittedly, hardly promising. Before the First World War, the British government quickly gave up its policy of funding bitumen exploration campaigns in Nigeria, preferring instead to invest in oil in Trinidad (Ofonagoro 1979, Steyn 2009). The first concession expired in 1912. Oil exploration subsequently resumed in 1937 and then again in 1946, this time under the aegis of Shell, in which the British government held shares. The prospectors' initial focus was on Ibo regions in the hinterland, because the creeks of the Niger Delta were difficult to access. In 1951, a first well was drilled in Ihuo near Owerri, followed in 1953 by a second one in Akata, a small village close by. Nothing came of it.

Three years later, it was in the Niger Delta that Shell finally found oil for the first time in commercial quantities in Oloibiri, an Ijaw village in present-day Bayelsa State. Further west, other exploration campaigns proved successful in Bomadi, Burutu, and Ughelli, where prospectors drilled wells in Erumukowharie, Afiesere, Umolo, Olomu, Uzere, Oleh, Aviara, Olomoro, and Kokori in 1957 and 1958. In the east, toward Port Harcourt, Shell then discovered oil in Bomu and Afam, two Ogoni villages, and opened a refinery in Eleme in 1965. Exports of crude began in 1958 and grew continuously until the outbreak of the Biafran War in 1967. Exploration campaigns also confirmed the presence of oil at sea. The US firm Gulf Oil, later renamed Chevron, opened

---

5   As with the Belgian Congo, the French colony of Oubangui-Chari (today's Central African Republic), for instance, lost almost half of its population between 1890 and 1940 (Saulnier 1998: 81–96, Ewans 2017).

FIGURE 4   Oloibiri, Nigeria's first commercial oil discovery by Shell in 1956 (2011)

an office in Nigeria in 1961 and discovered the country's first offshore deposit, Okan 1, in late 1963, approximately sixty kilometers west of Warri.

However, commercial prospects were still nascent. Prices were low and the industry was dominated by the cartel of the so-called Seven Sisters, all of which were British or American. Despite being West Africa's largest oil producer, Nigeria faced tough competition from the Middle East and sought to diversify its foreign partners. Allegedly the most honest petroleum minister in the country's history, Yusuf Maitama Sule (1929–2017) began negotiations with Italy and France in 1967 to grant concessions to Agip (Azienda Generale Italiana Petroli), a branch of the Eni group (Ente Nazionale Idrocarburi), and Safrap (Société Anonyme Française de Recherches et d'Exploitation Pétrolières), which would later become Elf (Bourne 2015: 105).

3   Isaac Boro and the Niger Delta Republic (1966)

In other words, the oil industry was growing rapidly when the region's first rebellion after independence broke out. Proclaimed in 1966, the Niger Delta Republic was a short-lived affair. It went unnoticed abroad and the experience lasted barely twelve days. Nonetheless, the event was significant inasmuch as its leader, Isaac Adaka Boro (1938–1968), is now seen as a revolutionary icon among young Niger Delta militants. Furthermore, his arguments in favor of

the region's independence were rooted in long-standing demands. At a constitutional conference held in London in 1957, traditional chiefs from the coast
had indeed cited treaties signed during the 1880s and 1890s to claim that their
ancestors had agreed to the establishment of British protectorates without
conceding their lands and giving up their sovereignty.

In 1960, Nigeria's independence was obtained peacefully. But it was a cause
of unease among the peoples of the Niger Delta, since it signaled the end of
protectorate treaties that prompted the British to defend their interests. At
the time, coastal minorities were under the domination of the Ibo within a
vast Eastern Region, whose capital, Enugu, was located far inland. The latter
formed a much bigger group. Known for their economic dynamism, they were
accused of "invading" cities such as Port Harcourt. In 1966, Nigeria's first coup
d'état also highlighted their thirst for power. Led by Ibo officers from the East,
it was a bloody affair and resulted in the elimination of key Muslim politicians
from the ruling Northern People's Congress, which was allied to the Niger Delta
Congress, a small regionalist party.

These events were a key factor in the decision of Isaac Boro, an obscure
young Ijaw police officer, to take up arms and declare the independence of
a bogus republic in remote creeks. His Niger Delta Volunteer Force (NDVF)
was poorly equipped and numbered just a few hundred men. The uprising
was soon crushed by the Nigerian army, but the seeds of rebellion had been
planted. The NDVF's members wanted to defend the interests of Ijaw people
who, they argued, had been abandoned by the central government in favor of
the country's largest groups, known as the "Big Three": the Hausa, the Yoruba,
and the Ibo. In retrospect, Isaac Boro's militiamen were also viewed as precur-
sors of demands related to "resource control", a claim that would later focus
on the sharing of federal oil revenues with a special bonus for so-called host
communities.

In 1966, however, Nigeria's oil industry was still nascent. Production grew
from 5,000 barrels a day in 1958 to half a million a day in 1967 and from 10% of
the country's export revenues in 1962 to 33% before the Biafran War (Pearson
1970). But Nigeria's economy had yet to be affected by the "resource curse"
when Isaac Boro proclaimed a Delta Republic. In 1966, 55% of the country's
GDP (Gross Domestic Product) came from agriculture, compared with just 10%
from oil (Adejumobi & Aderemi 2002: 195). The issue of mineral resources was
not central to Isaac Boro's claims, which rather focused on the political "balkanization" of the Ijaw in the Eastern and Mid-Western Regions. Likewise, the
Ijaw State Union, one of the Niger Delta's many ethnic lobbies, had not mentioned oil when, in 1957, it testified before a commission dedicated to the protection of minorities and chaired by a former British Member of Parliament,

FIGURE 5   A painting of Isaac Adaka
             Boro in Bayelsa State (2011)

Henry Willink. At the time, the region's leaders had instead called for the creation of a federation including a Rivers State, which, for them, would have been
sustainable through the export of timber from forests located for the most part
in the neighboring province of Benin (Vickers 2010: 146).

NDVF young fighters nonetheless understood the importance of oil production, and they sought to block production to assert their power. On 24 February
1966, one day after proclaiming their Niger Delta Republic, they attacked a
Shell and BP (British Petroleum) drilling site in Abasare near the Forcados
River. At Odi, on River Nun, they were also "happy", in Isaac Boro's own words
(1982: 144), to throw grenades onto a pipeline. Their attacks soon forced Shell to
stop its operations in Abari. Two days later, the rebels destroyed some facilities
in Oloibiri, thereby putting an end to production in the Mid-Western Region.
Within just twelve days, they were able to cut off a fifth of the country's total
oil production (Ellis 2016: 86).

However, the rebellion ultimately failed. Entrenched in isolated creeks, it
garnered little support, including and especially from the local elites. From
their camp in the village of Polaku in Sabagreia near Koroama, between
Yenagoa and Abasare, NDVF "freedom fighters" could only roam the coves and
inlets of the central and western parts of the delta. They had no contact with
populations around Port Harcourt to the east, and they fought only for the Ijaw.

They even terrorized local fishing communities, if we are to believe the post-humous account of Maman Vatsa, a general who was subsequently accused of attempting a coup and executed by the junta of Ibrahim Babangida in 1985 (Dappa-Biriye 1995: 54).

Isaac Boro's political activism was shortlived. After being captured by Nigerian soldiers, he was briefly imprisoned. Once pardoned, he enlisted in the army, thereby anticipating the amnesty granted by the federal government to Niger Delta "militants" in 2009. Major Isaac Boro died on the front in 1968 while fighting against the Biafran secessionists.[6] The fact that he eventually joined forces with the "federals" was significant; the Ijaw feared the Ibo's power in the Eastern Region even more so than the remote domination of a central government based, at the time, in Lagos. Isaac Boro's failed revolution thus foreshadowed another far more devastating secession: the Biafran War.

4   Toward the Secession of Biafra

Inspired by the precedent of 1966, the Nigerian government believed that it would easily overpower the mutineers who, in 1967, declared the independence of a republic encompassing the entire Eastern Region—including, therefore, the Niger Delta. However, the Ibo, who were leading the insurrection, put up a dogged resistance. Unlike the few dozen militiamen of the NDVF, the entire population was mobilized. The fighting dragged on, lasting nearly three years while the ruthless blockade set up by the Nigerian army caused a huge famine. As it took place in Africa's most populous country, the Biafran War was one of the deadliest conflicts seen on the continent.

The Ibo were not predestined for secession. A highly enterprising people, they had spread across the entire territory of Nigeria to leave their densely populated homeland in the Eastern Region. At independence in 1960, moreover, their leaders were committed nationalists driven by a firm belief in the merits of republican unity within the framework of a centralized state (Forsyth 1969: 99). What convinced the secessionists to opt out of Nigeria were the pogroms inflicted by Muslims on the Ibo in the North in 1966.

At the time, several hundred thousand "refugees" were forced to return in haste to their homeland in the East. The leader of the secession, Colonel Odumegwu Ojukwu, spoke repeatedly of a religious genocide committed

---

6 The causes of his death are unclear. According to one version, he was murdered by his commanding officer, Colonel Benjamin Adekunle, who was jealous of his rapid promotion to the position of Major (Obasanjo 1980: 50–2).

against Christians and, in the case of the Ibo, against a predominantly Catholic people. He thus hoped to secure the support of Western powers and to galvanize resistance among Biafrans engaged in a war of survival against an enemy vastly superior in numbers. Incidentally, he also sought to win the hearts and minds of non-Ibo coastal minorities whose migrants in the North were not spared by the 1966 pogroms, especially the Ibibio and the Efik of present-day Cross River State.

Such a community of suffering and religion might conceivably have brought together the Christian populations from the Niger Delta and the hinterland of the Eastern Region. There is no doubt that they shared many economic and political interests against Lagos, the capital in the West, and the Muslims in the North, who had been accused of rigging the 1962 census to monopolize key positions of power. In a sense, the Biafrans' claims overlapped with the Niger Deltans' concerns. For example, both Odumegwu Ojukwu and Isaac Boro complained that the Ibo and the Ijaw were not receiving a fair share of the government's budget. In 1965, so they argued, the Eastern Region had contributed 35% of the national revenue, which, at the time, exceeded 140 million pounds. Yet it had received just 14% in return, despite accounting for 22% of Nigeria's total population (Mezu 1969: 793).

Biafran propaganda, disseminated through radio, thus sought to build on the resentment of coastal communities against the military junta of Colonel Yakubu Gowon in Lagos. The secessionists argued that if northern Muslims took control of the Eastern Region, they would be first in line to pocket mineral revenues from the Niger Delta. Biafra's three provinces, so they insisted, would be far better off if they were to share the oil wealth among themselves rather than redistributing royalties among the twelve federated states recently created by the Nigerian government (Onoh 1983: 116). Odumegwu Ojukwu also sought to reassure populations living on the coast by granting them political advantages. On the advice of an Ekoi from Cross River, he created eight provinces in which non-Ibo minorities became a majority. In the same vein, the 29 colonial divisions were replaced by twenty provinces (Forsyth 1969: 112). Moreover, key posts within the Biafran Republic were given to individuals from Cross River. For example, the Chief of Army Staff and Vice-President was an Efik, General Philip Effiong, while the head of the civil service, Ntieyong Udo Akpan, was an Ibibio.

Here and there, various groups along the coast supported the Biafrans, with the aim of either settling personal scores or escaping the domination of the Niger Delta Ijaw. For example, in Yenagoa, now the capital city of Bayelsa, the Epie and the Atissa joined the secessionists, opposed as they were to the creation of a Rivers State in which they would represent a minority. Before the war, they were already voting for the NCNC (National Council of Nigeria and the Cameroons), the leading party of the Ibo, and they continued to supply Biafrans with contraband throughout the hostilities (Nwajiaku 2009). Likewise, the Ikwerre to the north of Port Harcourt supported the rebels. They were already assimilated to the Ibo by coastal peoples, and one of them, Francis Ellah, was appointed Biafra's representative in London before being elected senator during the Second Republic in 1979 (Onyegbula 2005). To the east of Port Harcourt, some Ogoni also joined the secessionists to oppose neighboring Ijaw on the coast and preserve their economic interests with Ibo traders in the hinterland.

Elsewhere in the Niger Delta, however, most people chose to side with the federals. For example, when they invaded the Mid-Western Region in June 1967, the Biafrans received no support from locals despite declaring the independence of a short-lived Republic of Benin. Besides the usual concerns about Ibo expansionism, two key factors tipped the scales: the massacres perpetrated by the rebels and the political maneuverings of the government in Lagos. Three days before the declaration of Biafran independence on 30 May 1967, Colonel Yakubu Gowon had remodeled the Nigerian federation to attract coastal minorities and satisfy demands expressed since the 1950s to escape Ibo domination in the East. With Rivers and the South-East (present-day Cross River), the Niger Delta thus acquired two of the twelve states carved out from the four regions existing in 1966.

The setbacks suffered by the Biafrans also had the effect of throwing coastal populations into the arms of the federal government. The poorly organized secessionists suffered from a hyper-centralized command structure under the control of an authoritarian, arrogant, and determined colonel, Odumegwu Ojukwu. The result was that they soon lost control of the ports of Calabar and Bonny, in July and October 1967 respectively. Rather than admit their own failings, the Biafrans accused the Niger Delta's minorities of having betrayed them by facilitating reconnaissance operations by the Nigerian army (Alabi-Isama 2013). Denounced as "saboteurs" (*sabos* in pidgin), the region's inhabitants were imprisoned in insalubrious camps where many succumbed to disease or famine. The celebrated writer Ken Saro-Wiwa (1992), who led a protest against oil companies in the 1990s, thus denounced the existence of a second genocide, this time by the Ibo against minorities in the Niger Delta.

5   Controversies Surrounding the Question of Genocide

The question has remained controversial to this day. The genocide denounced by the Ibo was directed against them, not against the Niger Delta people; nor did it fit within the traditional definitions of the term. The junta led by Yakubu Gowon undeniably committed a crime against humanity when it imposed a blockade aimed at starving and defeating the rebels. However, the idea was not to exterminate an entire people on the basis of its religion, language, and cultural identity (Bartrop 2012, Moses & Heerten 2018). The Ibo living on the federal side were left unharmed, as were the Biafrans who, once captured, agreed to fight loyally alongside the Nigerians (Alabi-Isama 2013: 658). In the same vein, the government made no move to eliminate the survivors after the war, in 1970. On the contrary, it provided them with funds (albeit not much) to help them rebuild their homes.

The discussion around famine in Biafra, the focus of the international community in 1968, masked the more genocidal nature of the purges and pogroms carried out by the Nigerian army following the first military coup d'état in 1966. At the time, the intention was not just to settle disputes but to get rid of the Ibo once and for all. After the proclamation of independence of the Eastern Region in 1967, by contrast, Yakubu Gowon used hunger as a weapon of war to force the secessionists to surrender. Once the rebels were surrounded following the loss of Port Harcourt and their last point of access to the sea in 1968, the blockade by the Nigerian army had a devastating impact on the people living within the Biafran enclave. However, the objective remained military, like the siege of the British Navy against Greece during the Nazi occupation in 1942. In 1968–1969, the aim was to overpower the secessionists rather than exterminate civilians, who were, in a sense, collateral victims of a lethal strategy.[7]

From this point of view, the Biafran tragedy differs significantly from famines associated with a deliberate strategy of elimination of an entire segment of the population—for instance, in Russia in 1932—or that reflected the indifference, or even the impotence, of the authorities, as was the case in Bangladesh in 1974 and in Sudan in 1983 (Marcus 2003). In Nigeria, the army did not intend to commit a genocide. But its blockade did amount to a crime against humanity under international humanitarian law and its provisions in respect of the delivery of food aid to civilians. As a result, at the end of the war,

---

7 Thus, many authors make no reference to the case of Biafra in their historical inventories of genocides. However, they sometimes consider that the repression of the Islamist junta in Sudan against Muslims in Darfur from 2003 was genocidal. See, for example, Kiernan 2007, Lemarchand, 2013, Jonassohn, 1997.

the federal government quickly opted to forget about the past on the grounds of reconciliation.

The issue remains unresolved to this day. Conflicting narratives about the war depend to a large extent on whether one takes the point of view of the Federal Government, the Ibo, or the Niger Delta people. However, the trauma of Biafra left a deep impression, and few lessons were learned. Despite being far more numerous, the Ibo secessionists were defeated. Therefore, today's Niger Delta militants know that they have no chance of securing a military victory to gain independence. In a sense, the Biafran failure definitively ended Isaac Boro's dreams of an Ijaw Republic.

References

Adejumobi, Said & Aderemi, Adewale. 2002. "Oil and the Political Economy of the Nigerian Civil War and Its Aftermath", In *The Nigerian Civil War and its Aftermath*, edited by Eghosa Osaghae, Ebere Onwudiwe & Rotimi Suberu: 191–206. Ibadan: John Archers.

Alabi-Isama, Godwin. 2013. *The Tragedy of Victory: On-the-Spot Account of the Nigeria-Biafra War in the Atlantic Theatre*. Ibadan: Spectrum.

Alagoa, Ebiegberie Joe. 2018. *Kaliye Opuye, Opuye Kaliye: A History of Nembe, Central Delta Niger*. Port Harcourt: Onyoma.

Bartrop, Paul. 2012. "Getting the Terminology Right", In *The Nigeria-Biafra War: Genocide and the Politics of Memory*, edited by Chima Korieh: 43–60. Amherts (NY): Cambria.

Boro, Major Isaac Jasper Adaka. 1982. *The Twelve-Day Revolution*. Benin City: Idodo Umeh Publishers.

Bourne, Richard. 2015. *Nigeria: A New History of a Turbulent Century*. London: Zed Books.

Dappa-Biriye, Harold. 1995. *Minority Politics in Pre- and Post-Independence Nigeria*. Port Harcourt: University of Port Harcourt Press.

Ellis, Stephen. 2016. *This Present Darkness. A History of Nigerian Organized Crime*. London: Hurst.

Ewans, Martin. 2017. *European Atrocity, African Catastrophe: Leopold II, the Congo Free State and its Aftermath*. London: Routledge.

Falola, Toyin & Matthew Heaton. 2008. *A History of Nigeria*. Cambridge: Cambridge University Press.

Forsyth, Frederick. 1969. *The Making of an African Legend: The Biafra Story*. Harmondsworth: Penguin.

Fuglestad, Finn. 2018. *Slave Traders by Invitation: West Africa's Slave Coast in the Precolonial Era*, Oxford: OUP.

Jaja, Solomon Odini. 1991. *Opobo since 1970*. Ibadan: University of Ibadan Press.

Jonassohn, Kurt. 1997. "Hunger as a Low Technology Weapon, with Special Reference to Genocide", In *Genocide Perspectives*, edited by Colin Tatz, vol. 1: 263–288. Sydney: Macquarie University.

Jones, Gwilym Iwan. 1989. *From Slaves to Palm Oil: Slave Slave Trade and Palm Oil Trade in the Bight of Biafra*. University of Cambridge: African Studies Centre.

Kiernan, Ben. 2007. *Blood and Soil: A World History of Genocide and Extermination from Sparta to Darfur*, New Haven: Yale University Press.

Lemarchand, René (ed.). 2013. *Forgotten Genocides: Oblivion, Denial and Memory*, Philadelphia: University of Pennsylvania Press.

Lloyd, Peter Cutt. 1963. "The Itsekiri in the Nineteenth Century: An Outline Social History", *The Journal of African History* 4 (2): 207–31.

Marcus, David. 2003. "Famine Crimes in International Law", *The American Journal of International Law* 97 (2): 245–281.

Mezu, Okechukwu. 1969. "Du Nigéria Oriental à la République du Biafra", *Esprit* 387 : 787–806.

Moses, Dirk & Lasse Heerten (eds). 2018. *Postcolonial Conflict and the Question of Genocide: The Nigeria-Biafra War, 1967–1970*. New York: Routledge.

Nwajiaku, Kathryn. 2009. "Heroes and Villains: Ijaw Nationalist Narratives of the Nigerian Civil War", *Africa Development* 34 (1): 47–67.

Nwokeji, Ugo. 2008. "Slave Ships to Oil Tankers", In *Curse of The Black Gold: 50 Years of Oil in the Niger Delta*, edited by Michael Watts & Ed Kashi: 63–5. Brooklyn (NY): Powerhouse Books.

Obasanjo, Olusegun. 1980. *My Command: An Account of the Nigerian Civil War, 1967–1970*. Nairobi: Heinemann.

Obichere, Boniface. 1988. "Slavery and Slave Trade in Niger Delta Cross River Basin", In *De la traite a l'esclavage du VXIIIe au XLVeme siècle: Actes du Colloque International sur la traite des Noirs, Nantes 1985*, edited by Serge Daget, vol. 2. Paris: L'Harmattan.

Ofonagoro, Walter Ibekwe. 1979. *Trade and Imperialism in Southern Nigeria, 1881–1929*. New York: Nok.

Onoh, James. 1983. *The Nigerian Oil Economy: From Prosperity to Glut*. London: Croom Helm.

Onyegbula, Godwin Alaoma. 2005. *The Nigerian-Biafran Bureaucrat: An Account of Life in Biafra and within Nigeria*. Ibadan: Spectrum.

Pearson, Scott. 1970. *Petroleum and the Nigerian Economy*. California: Stanford University Press.

Saro-Wiwa, Ken. 1992. *Genocide in Nigeria: The Ogoni Tragedy*. Port Harcourt: Saros.

Saulnier, Pierre. 1998. *Le Centrafrique: entre mythe et réalité*. Paris: L'Harmattan.

Siollun, Max. 2021. *What Britain Did to Nigeria: A Short History of Conquest and Rule*. London: Hurst.

Steyn, Phia. 2009. "Oil Exploration in Colonial Nigeria, c. 1903–58", *The Journal of Imperial and Commonwealth History* 37 (2): 249–274.

Tamuno, Tekena Nitonye. 2011. *Oil Wars in the Niger Delta, 1849–2009*. Ibadan: Stirling-Horden Publishers.

Ukeje, Charles. 2006. "Small Arms and Light Weapons Proliferation in the Niger Delta in Historical Perspective", In *Small Arms and Light Weapons. Proliferation and Collection in the Niger Delta, Nigeria*, edited by Amadu Sesay & Antonia Simbine: 1–38. Ibadan: College Press & Publishers.

Vickers, Michael. 2010. *A Nation Betrayed: Nigeria and the Minorities Commission of 1957*. Trenton (NJ): Africa World Press.

CHAPTER 2

Mirages in the Midst of War

The Secession of Biafra (1967–1970)

The year is 1988. As a student, I cannot afford a plane ticket all the way to Lagos. I decide instead to land in Cotonou, a cheaper destination, and to cross the Benin–Nigeria border on foot. I am the only white person at the border post and the driver sent by friends to meet me there has no trouble spotting me. An Ibo hailing from eastern Nigeria, he picks me up in a magnificent 504 built in Peugeot's Kaduna factory. He likes the French and tells me his life story as we drive.

"I was a captain in the Biafran army when I was sixteen", he says in pidgin with a sense of pride. "We were surrounded by Nigerian troops, and we had to make do with what we had. It was terrible. We were hungry and we lacked everything. We drove cars without tires. There wasn't any fuel left. My motorbike just about worked on a palm oil blend".

Stories about fuel scarcity and empty reservoirs are hardly consistent with the commonly held view that oil played a driving role in the conflict. What is the truth of the matter? Beyond the debates surrounding genocide, many observers, including Niger Delta militants, see the Biafran drama as a war for oil. If we are to believe dominant narratives, the prospects offered by the black gold galvanized both the secessionists and the federals to fight to the death. As for international oil companies, they are thought to have financed the warring parties together with foreign powers keen to lay their hands on the Niger Delta's deposits. In other words, the Ibo did not resist until they were exhausted because they feared for their lives in the event of surrender, but because they coveted the oil wealth hidden beneath their feet.

The question remains: Is it possible that people risked their lives and, in many cases, died during the hostilities simply because they hoped to take control of oil-rich resources? Rather, were they not fighting because they feared extermination in the wake of the 1966 pogroms? To answer this question, we need to delve deeper into the detail of the arguments surrounding the role played by mineral resources. For "oil was hypnotic to those who wanted an uncomplicated explanation for the Nigerian civil war" (Africa Research Group 1970: 16).

FIGURE 6   A Shell oil well abandoned in Akwa Ibom State (2009)

1   The Great Game of Alliances

This is not new: when seeking to analyze the reasons that incite them to kill each other, the warring parties in armed conflicts often overlook their own responsibilities by pointing an accusatory finger at scapegoats abroad. In Nigeria, the Biafran secession revealed a complex game of alliances that differed significantly from the usual patterns of Cold War politics, with the United States remaining neutral. On the one side, the federals were supported (for different purposes) by Britain, Nasser's Egypt, and the Soviet Union. On the other side, the Biafrans secured the backing of France, Portugal, several African countries and, to a lesser extent, Maoist China.

Britain sought to defend Nigeria's territorial unity to protect its economic interests. Its former colony's mineral reserves had taken on a new strategic importance since the nationalization of the Suez Canal in 1956 had highlighted the vulnerability of oil supply routes to Europe. When the Biafran crisis broke out, London was also losing control of the Gulf of Aden and Southern Yemen, which had gained independence, while Arab countries moved to suspend oil exports to Britain to punish allies of Israel during the Six-Day War of 1967. By this time, Nigeria was known to have become a major producer and already supplied 10% of Britain's crude oil imports (Uche, 2008). Lending support to the secessionists was therefore out of the question, since Lagos might then retaliate by blocking its oil exports to Britain. On the contrary, joining the Nigerian side had the effect of bringing the British closer to the Arab camp, which took a position against Biafra in order, according to some authors, to prevent the emergence of, and competition from, a newly independent oil-producing country (Uchendu 2012: 122).

The British government, which had shares in Shell-BP, also feared French interference and support for the secessionists against the English-speaking giant. At the time, the Paris branch of the Rothschild's bank was suspected of having negotiated with the Biafrans to secure exclusive rights to explore and extract oil for a period of ten years.[1] Likewise, British diplomats believed that Elf-Safrap, which was largely owned by the French government, had bribed the leader of the secession, Odumegwu Ojukwu, in order to terminate the concessions granted to Shell-BP in the event of victory (Uche 2002: 42). In Lagos, Colonel Yakubu Gowon went as far as to claim publicly that Biafra had granted exclusive rights to a French firm to exploit all the mineral resources of the former Eastern Region (Clarke 1987: 127).

However, it is impossible to corroborate these allegations with archival evidence. France had been on poor terms with Nigeria since Lagos had broken diplomatic relations with Paris in 1961 in protest against French nuclear testing in Algeria. With closer ties to the francophone countries surrounding the anglophone giant, the government of General Charles de Gaulle felt little affinity for the federals, despite supplying them with weapons at the start of the war. Later, it would express dismay at the desperate struggle of a Christian people claiming to be the victims of a genocide perpetrated by Muslims. It was when the famine expanded in 1968 that the French services arranged their first deliveries of weapons and food to the Biafrans, and not in 1967 when the latter still had a chance of securing control of the oil wells (Bach 1980: 265).[2]

As for the other players involved in the conflict, such as Egypt and the Soviet Union, it is difficult to see what their oil interests in this affair might have been. In Lisbon, for example, Antonio de Oliveira Salazar's ultra-conservative regime was focused first and foremost on maintaining its colonies in Africa. It helped Biafra, to punish Nigeria for supporting liberation movements in Angola and

---

1 The American ambassador in Lagos claimed that he saw this document but journalist Susan Cronje alleged it was a fake (Griffin 2015: 120; Cronje 1972: 201; Cervenka 1971: 113–114).

2 For a version according to which General de Gaulle agreed as soon as October 1967 to deliver to the Biafrans arms officially exported to Côte d'Ivoire and taken from stocks seized from the Germans and Italians during the Second World War, after deleting their serial numbers, see Griffin 2015: 122.

Guinea Bissau. Moreover, Lagos was one of the largest contributors to the budget of the Organization of African Unity (OAU), which had consistently issued motions opposing Portugal's colonial wars. Finally, as a potentially wealthy country, Nigeria was viewed as serving Salazar's propaganda strategy by demonstrating that African states were not ready for independence. It was therefore in response to Lagos's diplomatic position that Portugal allowed Biafra to open a representation in Lisbon, print their own currency, and route supplies through the ports of Bissau and São Tomé. Once the Ibo were trapped in their enclave from 1968 onwards, Salazar also provided them with their only telex link to the rest of the world (Seibert: 2018: 269).

2   The Pragmatism of Oil Companies

Given this international context, it is important not to overestimate the role played by oil in the secession. At the outbreak of hostilities, the only two companies operating in rebel-held territory, Shell-BP and Elf-Safrap, initially took a wait-and-see approach. Trapped in the middle of the fighting, they sought to maintain contact with all parties to the conflict, a position reminiscent of the travails of the agribusiness firm Lonrho during the Mozambican Civil War some twenty years later. The Biafrans threatened for a while to shut down the oil wells in an attempt to force the multinationals to pay them taxes. According to a witness, however, they did not really believe they would succeed in getting royalties (Davis 1973). Elf-Safrap's major concessions, for instance, were in the Mid-Western State, on the government's side, where they roughly doubled those in Biafra (Ekundare 1972: 53). If the company agreed in June 1967 to pay some royalties to the secessionists, it was not by order of the French government, but to safeguard its wells located in Iboland. Despite being much closer to the military junta in power in Lagos, Shell-BP also argued for a case of force majeure to satisfy the rebels' demands by paying them a token amount, a bank transfer subsequently blocked by the British.

By contrast, the US company Gulf Oil had no need for an agreement with the secessionists on account of the location of its wells, situated far from the conflict zone and less directly impacted by the fighting. Operating the country's only offshore deposit, which had been in operation in Okan since December 1963, the company suffered little from the Nigerian blockade and was able to maintain and even expand its activities throughout the hostilities (Frynas and Mellahi 2003). As for other US companies, such as Phillips and Amoseas (American Overseas Company, a consortium formed by Chevron and Texaco), they played an insignificant role. Established in Brass, Tenneco (Tennessee Gas

Transmission Company) had no active operations and Mobil began production only at the end of the war.

Meanwhile, within Biafra, the interruption of links to the coast forced Elf-Safrap to close its wells and withdraw. After the fall of Port Harcourt in May 1968, many people believed that the secessionists would be quickly defeated since their last point of access to the sea had been cut off. By this stage, the oil companies that were still in activity had no scruples about siding openly with Lagos, and they were not alone in this respect. The well-known trading firm UAC (United Africa Company), which managed the port of Burutu in the Niger Delta, was also forced to cease operations in rebel-held regions. This was less of a problem since, unlike Shell-BP and Elf-Safrap, most of its investments were located in areas under government control. Moreover, the war was an opportunity to get rid of some assets. For example, despite efforts to relaunch its activities when oil production began in the area in 1964, Burutu had no roads or railway links and could not compete with Escravos and Forcados, which had direct access to the sea. UAC was losing money and was only too happy to sell its facilities when the port was nationalized by the Nigerian government in 1970 (Fieldhouse 1994: 470ff).

Ultimately, it was the logic of profit that determined the position taken by multinationals. Pragmatism prevailed. For example, to preserve its good relations with the military junta in Lagos, the UAC urged London not to recognize the independence of Biafra or support an arms embargo against the federal government. As for Shell-BP, its backing for Nigeria was duplicitous since the Anglo-Dutch firm continued to sell oil to the Portuguese island of Sao Tomé, from where planes supplied the secessionists. Henry Alexander was perhaps one of the rare businessmen of the time to support Yakubu Gowon out of conviction: a former British general and the head of a maritime company that owed three quarters of its revenue to contracts with Shell-BP, he was part of an international observation mission accused of denying the genocide and abuses committed by the Nigerian army.

In fact, oil companies had little control over events. They played no role in the 1966 pogroms which, in the North, led to the Ibo returning to the East and opting for secession. Once the hostilities started, moreover, their facilities were destroyed or vandalized, causing oil spills on some occasions, such as in Rumuekpe, northwest of Port Harcourt. With the exception of Gulf Oil, their production either collapsed or stagnated, and they suffered severe losses. The lack of archival evidence, finally, belies the idea that some companies wanted to support Biafra to obtain concessions on more favorable fiscal terms than those granted by Nigeria. Conspiracy theories were rather fueled by the usual fantasies surrounding the role of oil in conflicts, sometimes taking the form of self-fulfilling prophecies when the mere possibility of discoveries was enough to trigger clashes (Frynas, Wood & Hinks 2017, Pérouse de Montclos 2014, Colgan 2013, Vicente 2010, Weszkalnys 2014). Even the United States, which remained neutral throughout the hostilities, were suspected of supporting Biafra to defend Mobil's interests, despite the fact that the only American oil company in activity, Gulf Oil, always worked on the federal side (Cervenka 1971: 459).

As for Yakubu Gowon, he was accused of settling scores at the end of the war. For example, in April 1971, the government forcibly acquired 35% of Elf-Safrap's shares, compared with 33% in the case of Agip seven years earlier, allegedly to punish the French for backing Biafra (Onoh 1983: 23, Olorunfemi, Adetunji & Olaiya 2014: chap. 1). However, business prevailed once again. In wanting to rebuild its war-torn economy, the Nigerian government was desperate for funds. As a result, it hastened to resume oil production, which soon picked up, rising above a million barrels per day in 1970, double the level recorded in early 1967. When new blocks were attributed, Shell-BP was not given special treatment for its alignment with Lagos over Elf or Agip, both of which were suspected of supporting Biafra. On the contrary, Nigeria sought to diversify its international partners and reduce its dependence on the Anglo-Dutch firm, whose share in the country's total production gradually fell from 100% in 1958 to 51% in 1981 (Ndimele 2018: 22). In fact, the purchase of Elf-Safrap's shares was merely a prelude to future nationalizations. The pro-Biafra position taken by General de Gaulle also had no impact on the resumption of trade at the end of the conflict. Nigeria quickly became, in 1972, the first supplier, and then client, of France in sub-Saharan Africa (Bach 1980: 265).

3 Oil: A Resource for Conflict or an Obstacle to War?

Oil was not even the main financial resource for the warring parties throughout the hostilities. As already noted, production stopped relatively quickly within Biafra and was restricted to the Mid-Western Region, outside the secessionist enclave. On the federal side, it fell to a low of 52,000 barrels per day in 1968, nearly ten times less than before the war (Onoh 1983: 45). As a result, the revenues generated by crude oil exports declined from 258 million dollars in 1966 to 199 million dollars in 1967 and 109 million dollars in 1968, before rising to 422 million in 1969, when the army took control of the last fields in rebel-held areas and the Nigerian government completed works at the Forcados terminal to replace the Bonny facility, which had been destroyed at the very beginning of the fighting in 1967 (Naanen & Tolani 2014: 29).

On the Biafran side, the secessionists stopped earning royalties in the very first months of their self-proclaimed independence. After the fall of Port Harcourt in 1968, no investors were bold enough to consider purchasing mining rights within Biafra, which by then was clearly heading for defeat. Moreover, after the introduction of a new currency in Nigeria, the secessionists had to launch their own Biafran pound, which, because it was not recognized internationally, was worth nothing. In the absence of oil companies, their last remaining option for accessing convertible foreign currency was largely limited to international aid from humanitarian organizations and, to a lesser extent, funds from the French secret services and transfers from Ibo in the diaspora and other regions of Nigeria, as well as private donations (Lindsay 1969).

From a financial point of view, oil therefore played a minor role, particularly since the parties to the conflict made every effort to deprive their enemy of royalties. While the federals blocked exports of crude from Biafra, the secessionists attacked oil wells on the government side. For example, as early as March 1967, shortly before the proclamation of independence, Odumegwu Ojukwu forbade sales to the north of products originating from the Port Harcourt refinery, which had been in operation since October 1965. By a Nigerian general's own admission, however, the secessionists did not defend the Bonny oil fields "with the seriousness they deserved" (Alabi-Isama 2013: 657). Their control was clearly not their priority and, when the real fighting started in July 1967, their loss signaled, in a sense, the defeat of the Biafrans far more than the entry of the rebels into the war.

From May 1968, the separatists were completely surrounded and their last access to the sea was cut off. They could no longer use the refinery in Port Harcourt and were forced to process crude oil extracted from the hinterland with the help of former Shell Ibo engineers using a siphoning system now known as "bunkering". In Uzuakoli, the Biafrans set up a makeshift facility capable of refining up to 100,000 liters per day until it was seized by the Nigerian army in April 1969. The rebels also attacked oil wells on the federal side. In June 1968, they formed a small air force which, under the command of the Swedish Count Gustav von Rosen, began bombing Shell facilities and forced the company to suspend its operations. In June 1969, they were even able to attack the Port Harcourt refinery and the Forcados oil terminal, interrupting deliveries of fuel to Lagos.

However, the Biafrans were reluctant to destroy facilities that they hoped to take over one day. Above all, they wanted to prove that the Nigerian government was not capable of protecting the industry. The main objective was to instill fear and dissuade oil companies from pursuing their activities; nevertheless, the Biafran attacks were not always successful and sometimes even proved counterproductive. A good example is the assault carried out on 9 May 1969 against an Agip base in Okpai near Kwale on the west bank of the Niger River, some 70 kilometers to the south of the city of Onitsha. The Biafran commandos killed one Lebanese and ten Italians working there. They also captured eighteen expatriates (fourteen Italians, three Germans, and one Jordanian) who were sentenced to death by a "special tribunal", before subsequently being pardoned by Odumegwu Ojukwu and released a month later in exchange for a ransom estimated at three million dollars. The operation was disastrous for the reputation of the rebels (Doron 2014). The Biafrans, who first benefited from the support of the Catholic Church, were now likened to gangsters. Through the mediation of Portugal, the pope pleaded with Ojukwu to free the hostages, who were eventually handed over to a delegation from the NGO Caritas in Owerri.

Rather than funding the war, mineral resources galvanized Biafrans to fight for independence. The point has been made by a number of Nigerian researchers, who argue that oil was not the primary cause of the secession, which was mostly triggered by the pogroms of 1966 (Isumonah 2002: 32). Nonetheless, mineral resources provided arguments to prove the economic viability of the Republic of Biafra before the eyes of the world.[3] In 1967, the government of the Eastern Region already hoped to earn over half of the total oil revenues forecast for the whole of Nigeria by 1970 (Pearson 1970). Such an expectation is thought to have encouraged Odumegwu Ojukwu to opt for secession rather than to rest content with a de facto separation within a vast federation (Leapman 1970).

On the Nigerian side, the possibility of losing a significant portion of oil revenues also had the effect of pushing Gowon's military junta to enter the war with the aim of quashing the rebellion through force rather than negotiating with the insurgents. In June 1967, Shell-BP's decision to pay a token amount of royalties to the rebels caused the government to extend its blockade to crude exports from Port Harcourt, resume its offensive, and take control of the Bonny terminal a month later. Some supporters of Biafra even hold that it was the oil wealth that subsequently pushed Gowon to leave the Ibo to starve and commit a "genocide" by ruling out any possibility of compromise (Ezeani 2013: 114, Forsyth 1969: 100, 109).

In all likelihood, the warring parties were probably unaware of just how bountiful the oil rent would prove to be. In 1967, Shell-BP had announced its intention to develop its activities by investing up to £52 million in 1969 alone with a view to increasing its production from 500,000 barrels per day to two

---

3 For a similar case in Somaliland, see Pegg 2018.

million by 1972 (Omaka 2016: 50). However, oil companies often underestimated their reserves to reduce their tax liabilities (Biersteker 1987: 72). Shell-BP in particular is thought to have deliberately attempted to delay production from Nigeria to ensure that international prices would continue to rise and would not affect the market capitalization of its huge concessions in the Arab-Persian Gulf (Schätzl 1969). In other words, it is unclear just how much both the Nigerian government and the Biafrans knew about the scale of the oil rent in the event of victory. For instance, diplomats from the US embassy did not divulge such explosive information and noted that the production figures officially reported by Lagos were invariably lower than those circulating within the industry (Klieman 2012: 158).

4   Disagreements over Revenue Sharing

The question of the distribution of oil revenues was nonetheless one of the main points of contention between the Nigerian government and the Biafrans. Odumegwu Ojukwu did not directly couch his claims in these terms, for the thesis of a genocide was the key element to justify his decision to secede. Furthermore, he was keen not to appear too close to foreign companies since his father, a millionaire, sat on the board of Shell. The "President" of Biafra claimed to be a progressive and was desperate to demarcate himself from the leader of the Katanga secession, Moise Tshombe, who had been vilified a few years earlier by his African peers as a stooge of Western imperialism (Klieman 2012: 162).

Of course, this does not mean that Ojukwu had no views on oil. In early 1967, while he was still governor of the Eastern Region, he quickly collected all the royalties from the extractive industry without handing anything over to Lagos (Watts 1997). The remodeling of the Nigerian federation was not, of course, to his liking. He would have lost the control of the Port Harcourt refinery and 90% of the country's oil production if he had agreed to assume leadership of the small East Central State created by Gowon three days before the declaration of Biafran independence. At the very start of the war in June 1967, Ojukwu's representatives therefore tried to negotiate a compromise with the industry. Some of the wells were not under Biafran control. So they did not demand all the proceeds from crude oil exports, but a distribution based on the previous share of the East. This revenue included half the royalties paid to the central government and a quarter of a fund made up of 30% of the remaining amount to finance the development of the country's four regions in proportion to their demographic weight. In total, Ojukwu hoped to get 57.5% of the oil windfall (Davis 1973).

The disagreements between the federals and the rebels thus highlighted an issue that has remained a key feature of conflicts in the Niger Delta ever since: the sharing of the oil rent. At the time of independence, the British had left a budgetary system that enabled the regions to retain half of the revenues generated by their natural and mining resources, with the rest going to the central government and an equalization fund. This arrangement suited the country's major agricultural areas, especially the predominantly Muslim North. But the easy money derived from the black gold in the Niger Delta destabilized the deal while stirring up tensions between the coastal Eastern and Mid-Western regions, which were now competing to discover and exploit new oil fields (Rupley 1981: 261). According to Marxist-inspired structural analyses, the increase in oil production also precipitated centralizing tendencies that played a major part in the Biafran secession (Watts 1983: 376).

It is important, however, to get the sequence of events right. It was not the Gowon junta that initiated a process of centralization to take control of the oil rent. After a first military coup d'état in January 1966, it was rather an Ibo from the East, General Johnson Aguiyi-Ironsi, who undertook to break the regional counter-powers by passing a highly controversial unification decree. His main purpose was not to monopolize the oil rent but to put an end to the ethnic and political quarrels that had undermined the First Republic since independence. The attempt to centralize Nigeria also reflected the special position of a

FIGURE 7   A Biafra postal
             stamp (1967)

people, the Ibo, who were disseminated throughout the country, who held key posts in the civil service and who had a far higher level of education than their Muslim counterparts in the north through having attended Christian mission-ary schools in the south.

After the fall of the Ironsi regime following a second coup in July 1966, Gowon veered in the opposite direction with a view to re-establishing regional autonomy. In May 1967, he federalized Nigeria and divided its four regions into twelve states to erode Ojukwu's power and win the hearts and minds of the Niger Delta people. Except for a decree which, in January 1967, granted more powers to the central government to collect royalties from the extractive indus-tries, it was primarily during the Biafran War, and not before, that the Gowon junta asserted its intention to promote national unity and take control of the oil rent by passing a law in November 1969 that challenged the prerogatives of regions in the sharing of revenues from mineral resources.

In this respect, one should not overstate the almighty power of the black gold when revisiting the events leading up to the Biafran secession. The claims of authors who view oil as a crucial factor in the origins, development, and internationalization of the conflict are often speculative, and even sometimes wrong. For example, Jean-Louis Clergerie (1994: 200, 211ff) based his arguments on production figures dating from the oil boom of the 1970s, after, and not before, the outbreak of the Biafran War. Overlooking the Niger Delta's minor-ities, he also argued that the Ibo were the first to benefit from oil revenues in Nigeria because they were a "coastal" people. However, a few pages further on, he acknowledged that there was no evidence that oil companies were involved in triggering the crisis and funding the rebels to obtain new concessions.

Anthony Kirk-Greene (1975: 6–7), a historian and former British civil serv-ant in Northern Nigeria, went further still by minimizing the role of the 1966 massacres and the fear of genocide in the secession of Biafra. According to him, "the ultimate casus belli was oil". What better proof, so he argued, than the fact that the federals took the decision to deploy the army in the Eastern Region only after they heard of rumors of partial payment of royalties to the leader of the secession, Odumegwu Ojukwu? Somewhat surprisingly, Anthony Kirk-Greene also placed on a par the mass murder of Ibo civilians and mili-tary personnel during the pogroms of July 1966 and the assassination of senior political figures from the north during the January 1966 coup. In doing so, he ignored the role played by the trauma of the huge displacement of people who lost all hope of national unity after being forced to return to their homeland in the East. His purely economic interpretation of the determinants of the Biafran crisis paid no attention to the identity-based aspirations of a popula-tion struggling for its survival.

Yet it was clearly the fear of genocide that drove the Ibo to continue fighting after the fall of Port Harcourt in 1968, despite the rebels knowing that they had lost the war from a military point of view. One should thus render unto Caesar what is Caesar's. Oil did not cause the secession of the Eastern Region. Throughout the hostilities, the warring parties fought for the control of some wells, but production collapsed. Financially speaking, oil was a minor contributor to the federal budget and the Biafrans gained almost nothing from it. In practice, it was primarily international humanitarian aid that helped prolong the hostilities by keeping the rebels' dream of independence alive (Pérouse de Montclos 2009).

References

Africa Research Group. 1970. *The Other Side of Nigeria's Civil War*. Cambridge (Mass.): ARG.

Alabi-Isama, Godwin. 2013. *The Tragedy of Victory: On-the-spot Account of the Nigeria-Biafra War in the Atlantic Theatre*. Ibadan: Spectrum.

Bach, Daniel. 1980. « Le Général de Gaulle et la guerre civile au Nigeria », *Revue Canadienne des Etudes Africaines* 14 (2) : 259–272.

Biersteker, Thomas. 1987. *Multinationals, the State, and Control of the Nigerian Economy*. New Jersey: Princeton University Press.

Cervenka, Zdenek. 1971. *The Nigerian War, 1967–1970: History of the War, Selected Bibliography and Documents*. Frankfurt am Main: Bernard & Graefe.

Clarke, John Digby. 1987. *Yakubu Gowon: Faith in a United Nigeria*. London: Cass.

Clergerie, Jean-Louis. 1994. *La crise du Biafra*. Paris: Presses universitaires de France.

Colgan, Jeff. 2013. "Fuelling the Fire. Pathways from Oil to War", *International Security* 38 (2): 187–180.

Cronje, Susan. 1972. *The World and Nigeria: The Diplomatic History of the Biafran War, 1967–1970/* London: Sidgwick & Jackson.

Davis, Morris. 1973. "Negotiating About Biafran Oil", *Issue* 3 (2): 23–32.

Doron, Roy. 2014. "Biafra and the AGIP Oil Workers: Ransoming and the Modern Nation State in Perspective", *African Economic History* 42: 137–156.

Ekundare, Olufemi. 1972. "The Political Economy of Private Investment in Nigeria", *Journal of Modern African Studies* 10 (1): 37–56.

Ezeani, Emefiena [2013], *In Biafra African Died. The Diplomatic Plot*. London: Veritas Lumen.

Fieldhouse, David Kenneth. 1994. *Merchant Capital and Economic Decolonization: The United Africa Company, 1929–1987*. Oxford: Clarendon Press.

Forsyth, Frederick. 1969. *The Making of an African Legend: The Biafra Story*. Harmondsworth: Penguin.

Frynas, Jerdrzej George and Kamel Mellahi. 2003. "Political Risks as Firm-Specific (Dis)Advantages: Evidence on Transnational Oil Firms in Nigeria", *Thunderbird International Business Review* 45: 541–565.

Frynas, Jedrzej George, Geoffrey Wood & Timothy Hinks. 2017. "The Resource Curse without Natural Resources: Expectations of Resource Booms and Their Impact", *African Affairs* 16 (463): 233–260.

Griffin, Christopher. 2015. "French Military Policy in the Nigerian Civil War, 1967–1970", *Small Wars and Insurgencies* 26 (1).

Isumonah, Adefemi. 2002. "Biafra: A Failed National Project", In *The Nigerian Civil War and Its Aftermath*, edited by Eghosa Osaghae, Ebere Onwudiwe & Rotimi Suberu: 31–40. Ibadan: John Archers.

Kirk-Greene, Anthony. 1975. *The Genesis of the Nigerian Civil War and the Theory of Fear*. Uppsala: Scandinavian Institute of African Studies.

Klieman, Kairn. 2012. "U.S. Oil Companies, the Nigerian Civil War, and the Origins of Opacity in the Nigerian Oil Industry", *Journal of American History* 99 (1): 155–165.

Leapman, Michael. 1970. "Nigerian Civil War in Retrospect", *Venture (Socialism and the Developing World)* 22 (4): 17–20.

Lindsay, Kennedy. 1969. "How Biafra Pays for the War", *Venture, Journal of the Fabian Colonial Bureau* 21 (3): 26–27.

Naanen, Ben & Patrick Tolani. 2014. *Private Gain, Public Disaster: Social Context of Illegal Oil Bunkering and Artisanal Refining in the Niger Delta*. Port Harcourt: Niger Delta Environment and Relief Foundation.

Ndimele, Prince Emeka (ed.). 2018. *The Political Ecology of Oil and Gas Activities in the Nigerian Aquatic Ecosystem*. London: Academic Press.

Olorunfemi, Michael, Akin Adetunji & Ade Olaiya. 2014. *Nigeria Oil and Gas: A Mixed Blessing? With A Chronicle of NNPC's Unfulfilled Mission*. Lagos: Kachifo Limited.

Omaka, Arua Oko. 2016. *The Biafran Humanitarian Crisis, 1967–1970: International Human Rights and Joint Church Aid*. Madison: Fairleigh Dickson University Press.

Onoh, James. 1983. *The Nigerian Oil Economy: From Prosperity to Glut*. London: Croom Helm.

Pearson, Scott. 1970. *Petroleum and the Nigerian Economy*. California: Stanford University Press.

Pegg, Scott. 2018. "Oil to Cash in Somaliland: A Debate Whose Time Has Come". *Journal of Modern African Studies* 56 (4): 619–643.

Pérouse de Montclos, Marc-Antoine. 2009. "Humanitarian Aid and the Biafra War: Lessons not Learned", *Africa Development* 34 (1): 69–82.

Pérouse de Montclos, Marc-Antoine. 2014. "Les fantasmes géopolitiques du pétrole dans les pays en guerre ... ou pas", *Hérodote* 155 : 9–21.

Rupley, Lawrence. 1981. "Revenue Sharing in the Nigerian Federation", *The Journal of Modern African Studies* 19 (2): 257–277.

Schätzl, Ludwig. 1969. *Petroleum in Nigeria*. Ibadan: Oxford University Press.

Seibert, Gerhard. 2018. "São Tomé and the Biafran War (1967–1970)", *International Journal of African Historical Studies* 51 (2): 263–292.

Uche, Chibuike. 2002. "Money Matters in a War Economy: The Biafran Experience", *Nationalism and Ethnic Politics* 8 (1): 29–54.

Uche, Chibuike. 2008. "Oil, British Interests and the Nigerian Civil War", *The Journal of African History* 49 (1): 111–135.

Uchendu, Egodi. 2012. *Dawn for Islam in Eastern Nigeria: The History of the Arrival of Islam in Igboland*. Berlin: Klaus Schwarz Publishers.

Vicente, Pedro. 2010. "Does Oil Corrupt? Evidence from a Natural Experiment in West Africa", *Journal of Development Economics* 92 (1): 28–38.

Watts, Michael. 1983. *Silent Violence: Food, Famine and Peasantry in Northern Nigeria*. Berkeley: University of California Press.

Watts, Michael. 1997. "Black Gold, White Heat", In *Geographies of Resistance*, edited by Steve Pile & Michael Keith. New York: Routledge: 33–67.

Weszkalnys, Gisa. 2014. "Anticipating Oil: The Temporal Politics of a Disaster Yet to Come", *Sociological Review* 62 (1, Supplement): 211–235.

CHAPTER 3

Boom or Doom?

From Prosperity to the Economic and Social Crisis (1971–1989)

Ibo chop people! In pidgin, these words are extremely aggressive and more or less explicitly refer to cannibalism and even human sacrifice among the most primitive peoples at the time of the transatlantic slave trade. However, the person who uttered them was definitely not a cockney. When he received me at his home in 1990, Harold Dappa-Biriye was a venerable elderly gentleman, a pioneer of Rivers State and a respected leader in Port Harcourt. Located at Moscow Road in the old administration district near the ugly offices of the present-day Federal Secretariat, his home had the appearance of a colonial bourgeois residence. We conversed quietly in a library lined with books, with a faint but pleasing smell of polish filling the air.

Ibo chop people! The brutality of the words is impossible to reconcile with Harold Dappa-Biriye's general demeanor. But it does point to the acrimony felt by coastal people against former slaves from the hinterland. Indeed, the Ibo seized the opportunities offered by missionary schools to climb the social ladder. A highly enterprising people, they became traders or civil servants and thus took their revenge over the coastal city-states, which had dominated and exploited them up until the nineteenth century. Inevitably, their success attracted the envy of the Niger Delta's notables, who were dreaming of the glory days of their ancestors at the time of the transatlantic slave trade. Sometimes seen as the Jews of Africa, the Ibo were accused of all kinds of misdeeds, from witchcraft to fraud. A number of scientists also invoked the Hamitic hypothesis of superior races to explain the Ibo's capacity to adapt to the constraints of a market economy and respond successfully to the challenges of Western-inspired modernity (Levine 1966, Ottenberg 1959).[1]

1   The Reconstruction Era

The end of the Biafran War wiped the slate clean. In 1970, both the Niger Delta and the Ibo hinterland were in disarray. Officially, the slogan of the Gowon

---

1   For a critical analysis of these views, see Dike & Ekejiuba, 1990: 324.

© MARC-ANTOINE PÉROUSE DE MONTCLOS, 2024 | DOI:10.1163/9789004697911_005

junta proclaimed that there were no winners or losers. But the reality was quite different. The Ibo had been defeated and the people of the Niger Delta had won. The former had been ousted from the coast, where they were forced to abandon properties that had been requisitioned, taken over by squatters, or given to locals who had joined the federal side.[2] By contrast, despite being minorities within the former Eastern Region, the latter had secured two states, the South East and Rivers, both of which would benefit from the easy money generated by the oil boom of the 1970s.

The so-called 3-R policy (Reconciliation, Reconstruction, Rehabilitation) thus confirmed the contrasting treatment of the Ibo in the hinterland by the Federal Government. No extermination took place, let alone any genocide. Except for eleven cases of extra-judicial killings and twenty Ibo officers being taken to court for their involvement in the coup d'état of January 1966, the Biafran fighters were disarmed and confined in camps without being formally arrested. Following their surrender, some were amnestied while others were treated as deserters on the basis that they had left the Nigerian army shortly before the declaration of Biafran independence in May 1967. Around sixty officers were reintegrated at an equivalent rank. As for the rest, they were deprived of their retirement pensions upon their release in October 1974. However, more than forty years later, they were symbolically reintegrated into the Nigerian army along with some of the putschists of January 1966, on the recommendation of a reconciliation commission established in June 1999 under the chairmanship of Judge Chukwudifu Oputa at the end of the military dictatorship (Dada, Siben & Godowoli 2011).

In some respects, civilians received less favorable treatment. Because of the lack of supplies, malnutrition continued even after the end of hostilities in 1970. Under the aegis of Anthony Ukpabi Asika, a former Ibo lecturer at the University of Ibadan turned governor of East Central State and the only civilian to hold such a position in a military regime, the authorities distributed aid that was all too often misappropriated or inadequate. The Federal Government also pledged to help people resume a normal life by paying every household a fixed sum of twenty Nigerian pounds. The measure was designed to facilitate the economic reintegration of families who held old bank notes and whose savings had been wiped out when the junta in power in Lagos decided

---

2 In principle, the government was to facilitate the restitution of vacant property to its rightful owners, which was indeed the case for the Ibo of Kano in the North. In the Niger Delta, however, the Rivers and South-East States refused to apply federal decrees, until the regime of Murtala Muhammed, which came to power in 1975, tried to speed up the resolution of disputes brought before the courts (Wolpe 1974).

to change currencies in 1968. However, government subsidies were paid very irregularly. Furthermore, no provisions had been made to compensate the Ibo for the properties that they had lost in the Niger Delta or that had been destroyed in the East Central State. Since they could not recover their savings, inhabitants of the former Biafra were thus prevented from benefiting from the "indigenization decrees" of 1972 designed to enable Nigerians to purchase shares in nationalized companies (Maiangwa 2016).

Adding to this was the revenge taken by the Niger Delta's elites, who took possession of properties abandoned during the war. Before the conflict, the Ibo were estimated to own approximately 80% of Port Harcourt's real estate (Wolpe 1974, Pérouse de Montclos 1999). Their dominant position had been the cause of significant tensions, first with the locals in the 1940s and later between the different groups in power within the Eastern Region at the time of independence in 1960. By way of backlash, the departure of the Ibo and the end of the war were, by contrast, an opportunity for the Niger Deltans to assert their rights by claiming to be the customary owners of the land.

The case of Ken Saro-Wiwa, the future leader of the Ogoni rebellion against Shell, is symptomatic in this regard. At the beginning of the Biafran War, he fled to Lagos and was appointed administrator of Bonny province while his family remained in Bane, a village in Ogoniland. Retaliation soon followed: accused of being saboteurs and traitors, his parents were attacked by Ibo soldiers, who destroyed and burned down their home. They were then deported to a camp for displaced persons in Ikot Ekpene, to the east, where Ken Saro-Wiwa eventually came to their rescue at the end of the hostilities. In return, the leader of the Ogoni protest never concealed his hatred for the Biafrans. A commissioner for education in Rivers State until 1973, he was one of the most fervent supporters of the total confiscation of properties abandoned by the Ibo.

Resentment against the secessionists was no less intense in the western part of the delta. Biafran soldiers had committed abuses in the region, notably in Koluama, an Ijaw village from where Isaac Boro had launched his rebellion in 1966 and where several dozen residents were deported, killed, tortured, or recruited by force as a form of punishment for having requested support from the federals (Oputa Panel 2002, vol. 4: 37). The difference with Port Harcourt was that the Ibo had fewer interests in the area, which was not highly urbanized. Concentrated around Asaba on the west bank of the Niger River opposite Onitsha, they suffered less from the conflicts which, in the city of Warri, mainly pitted Itsekiri urban dwellers against rural Ijaw.

2   A Relentless Race to Create New States

Throughout the region, land disputes, economic competition, and political divergences nonetheless had the effect of deepening the divisions between coastal and inland communities. Despite being targeted by the 1966 pogroms in the north, the Niger Delta minorities felt that the Biafran War was a good opportunity to end the Ibos' domination, since the Gowon junta granted them two states, Rivers and South East, to encourage them to join the federals (Forsyth 1969: 65, 85). At the time, the decision to split the Eastern Region into three separate entities was a key factor in Ojukwu's decision to secede, since it amounted to Nigeria reneging on commitments made during last-ditch negotiations conducted in Aburi, Ghana, shortly before the declaration of Biafran independence.

The problem was not new. During the colonial era, the Niger Delta minorities had already protested against a system which, in their eyes, should have conformed to the logic of the four cardinal points. British Nigeria consisted of three regions (North, West, and East) that left no space for the South. A petition dated 17 August 1955 sent to the governor in Enugu thus called for the creation of an administrative entity grouping the Benin, Delta, Rivers, Calabar, and Ogoja coastal provinces, while leaving Onitsha and Owerri to the Ibo, together with the Abakaliki and Afikpo Divisions. In a sense, the idea was to re-establish the former British protectorate of Oil Rivers with the Bini of Benin City, the Ijaw in the western part of the Delta, the Ibibio of Akwa Ibom, the Efik of Calabar, and the Ejagham-Ekoi and Mbembe further inland in present-day Cross River State near the border with Cameroon.

Yet the coastal minorities were incapable of presenting a united front against the Ibo. They formed a sort of ethnic and linguistic puzzle with, from east to west, the Efik of Calabar, the Ibibio of Uyo, small communities in and around Port Harcourt, the Ijaw from the central Niger Delta, the Urhobo around Ughelli, the Itsekiri from Warri, and the Bini, or Edo, from the kingdom of Benin (see map 3). Each sub-region also had its own interests to defend. Launched in 1953, the movement for the creation of a COR (Calabar-Ogoja-Rivers) State, for example, was initially supported by figures such as Udo Udoma, a senator and president of Ibibio Union, Harold Dappa-Biriye (né Wilcox), an Ijaw leader from Port Harcourt, and Bishop Davies Manuel, a Kalabari chief from Degema (Tamuno 1972, Pérouse de Montclos 1999).[3] In its early days, the

---

3 For detailed biographies of the main political players of this period, see Okara & Anwuri 1988: 34–35.

project benefited from a crisis within the NCNC (National Council of Nigeria and the Cameroons), the party in power, when an anti-Ibo bloc was formed in the Parliament in Enugu to oppose the eviction of an Efik, Eyo Ita, from his position as prime minister of the Eastern Region. The latter went on to establish his own National Independence Party, while Bishop Davies Manuel founded a short-lived Niger Delta People's Congress in 1951.

These various groups were united in opposing the Ibo leader of the NCNC and the future president of Nigeria at independence, Nnamdi Azikiwe, who replaced Eyo Ita as prime minister and rejected calls for a partition of the Eastern Region. However, they failed to mobilize grassroots communities, who remained indifferent to the distant disputes of politicians in Enugu. At the elections held in late 1953, the two groups calling for the creation of COR State, the National Independence Party and the United Nigeria Party, were able to maintain their majority only in Calabar province, where the project had originated. They failed to secure the support of the Ijaw and the Bini in the western parts of the Niger Delta, and the dream of a vast Southern Region died with them.

In the east, toward the border with Cameroon, the COR project was also beset by internal struggles within Calabar and Ogoja provinces, its core territories. In 1949, a representative from Uyo at the Lagos Legislative Council had proposed to launch an "Iboku National Congress" to federate the Ibibio, the Efik, the Enyong, the Eburutu, and the Qua branch of the Ekoi. However, a dispute soon arose between the Ogoja in the hinterland and the Efik on the coast. Led by one Michael Ogon and a doctor from the NCNC, Samuel Efem Imoke, the former wanted an Ogoja State that would be governed from Ikom and that would include the Ejagham-Ekoi and the Mbe near the Cameroonian border. Meanwhile, the Efik campaigned for the creation of a Cross River State with an administrative centre in Calabar. Their demands continued after the independence of Nigeria in 1960. In 1966, a group of Efik and Ibibio chiefs defied the military ban on politics and called for the creation of a Calabar State without the Ogoja minorities in the hinterland. In 1980, they renewed their demands when civilians returned to power.

Further west in the Niger Delta, there were also mounting claims to establish new regions without the Ibo in the hinterland. As early as 1956, non-Ijaw peoples had called for a separate Port Harcourt State during hearings held before a commission tasked with protecting minorities and chaired by a former British MP, Henry Willink. However, the Ijaw and Harold Dappa-Biriye preferred a larger Rivers State. As for the Bini of Benin Province, known today as the Edo, they wanted, and obtained, their own Mid-Western Region in 1964.

Demands continued unabated following the Biafran defeat and the end of the Ibo domination in the former Eastern Region. Coastal minorities now fought for local power within increasingly smaller administrative units. In the South East State created by Gowon in 1967, for example, the Efik from Calabar opposed the so-called "Ibanor" movement federating the Ibibio, the Annang, and the Oron in the west. In late 1969, as the Biafran War was still raging, the latter called for the creation of a Mainland State (Akinyele 1996: 85). The Ibibio eventually achieved their goal when the military junta established an Akwa Ibom State in 1987. During constitutional negotiations in 1995, however, they continued to call for a partition of their new administrative unit into two entities: Itai, centered around Ikot Ekpene, and Atlantic, with its capital in Oron.

Established in 1967, Rivers State was not spared by fragmentation, in this case to escape Ijaw domination. Calls for a separate Port Harcourt State resurfaced in 1973 (Elaigwu 1986: 183). For example, Ken Saro-Wiwa campaigned for the creation of an administrative unit covering Port Harcourt, Ahoada, and Ogoni Divisions—that is, the Etche, the Abua, the Ndoni, the Ekpeye, the Egbema, the Enganni, the Ikwerre, the Ogoni, and the Ogba communities who lived between the Ibo of the hinterland and the Ijaw on the coast. In the same vein, he accused the Ijaw military governor of the state, Alfred Diete-Spiff, of misappropriating public funds in favor of his homeland community in Brass. As a result, the famous writer was forced to resign from his position of regional commissioner for education. However, he did not give up: when civilian rule was reinstated in 1979, he again criticized the elected governor, Melford Okilo, an Ijaw who refused to give in to the demands of minorities calling for Rivers State to be dismantled.

As for the Ijaw, the failure of an independent Niger Delta Republic in 1966 did not stop them from pressing the government to create new administrative units. When the military junta divided the Nigerian federation into nineteen states in 1976, they complained of being scattered between Ondo, Bendel, and Rivers, where they remained a minority. Four years later, civilians returned to power and the Ijaw again called for a Niger Delta State, but to no avail. It was only in 1996 that they finally got a Bayelsa State, where they were the majority community.

3   Centralized Federalism

From the beginning of the Biafran War in 1967, the federalization of Nigeria thus opened a kind of Pandora's box with ever smaller administrative units that helped the government to divide and rule. Despite his opposition to the unification decree of Johnson Aguiyi-Ironsi in 1966, Colonel (later General) Yakubu Gowon was a centralist. He dismantled regional powers and embodied the slogan coined from his name during the Biafran War: Go On With One Nigeria (GOWON). In the Niger Delta, he laid the foundations for the structure that would gradually entrench the federal government's control over oil production. For instance, just one month before the end of the Biafran War, Decree No. 51 of 1969 gave the military junta exclusive ownership of mineral resources. Two years later, the federal government decided to keep all the revenue that was generated by offshore wells and that previously funded the former regions' budget.

Four main factors served to reinforce this process of political and economic centralization: the development of joint ventures, the nationalization (or "indigenization") of some foreign firms, the establishment of a public oil corporation, and the introduction of a highly controversial Land Act. To begin with, the 1969 decree revoked the concessions that had been granted for thirty years with an automatic renewal clause. After the Biafran War, oil companies had to obtain new exploration and production permits with licenses issued on an annual basis. The length of their mineral leases was shortened to twenty years and renewal options were limited. In addition, royalties were now designed to compensate for the versatility of the market: instead of being based on the value of stored crude oil before export, they were calculated according to a

FIGURE 8   Gas flaring at Bori in Ogoniland near the Eleme Port Harcourt Refinery (1994)

fixed price displayed up front and known in the industry as the "posted price" (Soremekun 1995: 180).

The federal government also increased its share in foreign companies producing oil, from 0% in 1963 to 35% in 1973, 55% in 1974 and, in the specific case of Shell, 80% in 1979 on account of the nationalization of BP—a percentage subsequently reduced to 60% in 1989 and 55% in 1993. Before the Biafran crisis, Agip had been the only operator in which Nigeria had purchased shares from the outset: 33% in 1964. However, the easy money earned from the post-war oil boom gave the government the means to realize its ambitions, with revenues from crude exports exceeding ten billion dollars in 1977. The Gowon junta first acquired a 35% stake in Elf in 1971, followed by Mobil, Gulf, and Shell-BP in 1973. Under a 1974 decree, the government increased its share again, this time up to 55%. From then onward, its public company, NNPC (Nigerian National Petroleum Corporation), held a 60% majority stake in all joint ventures with multinationals extracting oil in Nigeria. The only exceptions were Agip and Shell-Elf, where the government's share was limited to 55%.

The establishment of a national oil company was a key element of this policy. It complied with the regulations set by the decree of November 1969 and followed the recommendations of OPEC, which Nigeria joined in July 1971. Initially known as the NNOC (Nigerian National Oil Corporation) before its subsequent merger with the Ministry of Petroleum Resources, NNPC was officially established in 1977. As early as 1976, it launched its first offshore drilling project while finding oil onshore at Ogba 1 in Oredo near Benin City. In 1978, it then acquired a super-tanker to export crude under a Nigerian flag, naming it Oloibiri after the country's first well to start production in 1958. However, the ship was never used and was eventually converted into a storage unit known as Tuma. NNPC produced no oil either despite the discovery of another deposit on the Adofi River near Kwale in present-day Delta State in 1981. It was only in 1988 that it established an operational and commercial arm headquartered in Benin City, the NPDC (Nigerian Petroleum Development Company), which was allocated ten blocks in 1991, including the Oredo and Adolfi deposits.

The international context and compliance with OPEC regulations were among the reasons for the military takeover of the industry, which coincided with a global wave of nationalizations in the Middle East and North Africa following the oil crisis of 1973. But the main goal was to fund Nigeria's reconstruction while promoting national unity after the Biafran War. In this regard, the management of the oil wealth served political objectives that sometimes went against the logic of economic profitability. For example, after the nationalization of the Port Harcourt refinery in 1973, the government fixed and subsidized a single retail price for fuel all over Nigeria, regardless of the distance traveled by tankers supplying gas stations. Such a policy significantly benefited poor regions located to the north in the Sahel, far from the coast and the oil fields. It also helped guarantee continuity of supplies in the wake of the shortages seen at the end of the Biafran War when the demand for fuel rocketed and exceeded the storage capacity of private operators.

On the other hand, the one-price policy deterred investors in the petrochemical and distribution sectors, thereby forcing the government to step in. The military juntas funded the construction of new refineries that began operating in Warri in 1978 and Kaduna in 1980, while the Port Harcourt unit was extended in 1989. To promote national unity, the authorities also established a company named Unipetrol that took over the gas stations purchased by the government. As for BP, its distribution network was seized and renamed African Petroleum following its nationalization in 1979 to punish the company for continuing to sell oil to Rhodesia and South Africa's racist regimes, despite an international embargo. The case of BP was emblematic in this regard since it asserted Nigeria's newfound power and led to the suspension of diplomatic relations with the former colonial power between 1984 and 1986.

Finally, to complete the takeover of oil production, military rulers reformed the ownership rights of mineral resources. For Murtala Muhammed and, later, Olusegun Obasanjo, the first aim was to assert the pre-eminence of the state over land in general to put an end to long-standing local conflicts. However, the idea was also to enable foreigners to invest in the extractive industry. In practice, the 1978 Land Use Act amplified the regulations of the 1956 Oil Pipeline Act and the 1969 Petroleum Act that allowed the expropriation of legitimate residents to make way for oil facilities. The difference was that the revocation of customary land use rights was now in the hands of state governors, while the families expelled from their homes were prevented from taking the matter to court to contest the amount of compensation owed to them (Akpan 2005: 142).

Niger Delta people thus felt dispossessed, as they did not enjoy the benefits typically available to residents of other oil-producing countries. For example, in the United States, citizens maintain full ownership if oil is discovered on their property, either on an individual basis in Texas, Arkansas, and Pennsylvania, or on a collective basis in California and Indiana, where it is considered impossible to redistribute revenues according to the surface area of the deposits beneath each plot. In Canada, there are also special provisions for Indian and Inuit communities whenever oil and gas are extracted in their reservations.[4]

---

4 In 2006, for instance, three indigenous groups—the Sahtu, the Gwich'in, and the Inuvialuit—secured a 33% stake in gas and oil projects operated by a consortium set up by Shell, ExxonMobil, and Conoco in the delta of the Mackenzie River near the Arctic Ocean.

FIGURE 9   Mangrove Swamp (2004)

However, nothing of the kind exists in Nigeria, where the military in power put in place all the elements that fed the conflicts of the 1990s.

4   The Uprising of Evangelists, Naked Women and the Youth

In the Niger Delta, opposition to abuses by the government and oil companies thus turned sour. The uprising of the Ogoni youth is the most well known internationally. However, other forms of unrest also emerged. For example, in 1990, a strange, ill-prepared, and ultimately unsuccessful coup was staged by Niger Delta military officers, businessmen, and evangelical groups who blamed northern Muslims for "siphoning" resources from the south. While the leader of the putsch, Major Gideon Gwarzo Orkar, was a Tiv from Nigeria's Middle Belt, his followers came from the coastal regions of Bendel, Cross Rivers, and

---

By contrast, the industry was seriously challenged in regions that did not benefit from such arrangements, as in British Columbia in 2008 and 2009, where the gas facilities owned by EnCana were targeted by saboteurs who accused the company of endangering the lives of locals.

Rivers. The coup was allegedly financed by an Urhobo from present-day Delta State, Great Ovedje Ogboru, who had made his fortune in the fish trade.

The rebels aimed to overthrow General Ibrahim Babangida to end the domination of northern Muslims, who were seen as parasites living off the south's oil revenues. Orkar and his men had a common phobia of Islam, a view shared by the most extremist evangelists in the Niger Delta. They called for the expulsion of all northern Muslims living in the south, including those working in the civil service, who were to be suspended. They also wanted to excise the Sahelian states of Bauchi, Borno, Katsina, Kano, and Sokoto from the federation, while "repatriating" Nigerian citizens living there but originating from other regions.

The coup led by Major Orkar thus bore no resemblance to the palace revolutions that usually pitted northern officers against each other. It was a bloody affair, like all previous attempts to replace northerners with southerners, or vice versa. The repression was just as fierce. Orkar was executed along with forty accomplices, while General Babangida purged the army of Niger Delta officers suspected of supporting the coup. Ijaw soldiers especially were singled out. Some deserted and went into hiding back home, where they are thought to have trained and armed the militants of the Niger Delta rebellions of the 2000s.

Just as surprising were the protests staged by Ijaw or Urhobo women stripping off to blame, shame, and ridicule the police and oil companies. With a few exceptions, most of these demonstrations occurred in the western part of the Niger Delta.[5] The women went naked to prove their courage and the power of their curse, as undressing in public rendered men impotent, according to local customs. In exposing their vaginas, they also showed that they could both give life and take it back. Their provocation and their outrage were so shocking that they sometimes neutralized the police and oil expatriates.

For example, in 1984, in Oghafere near Ethiope, Urhobo women of the Ugharefe clan stood up against an American firm, Pan Ocean. Despite the arrival of the police, they blocked the road and besieged the company's offices to prevent employees from accessing the premises. They also began to undress to demand electricity and drinking water as rightful compensation for pollution and expropriation. Their strategy proved successful. The Pan Ocean manager made no attempt to call for the intervention of a third party and satisfied all the women's demands.

---

5 In the east in 1986, for instance, women blocked access to Bonny Island's oil terminal and heliport to complain about the brutality of Shell's security services. Yet they did not go naked.

In the same vein, in Ekpan near Ukpe in March 1986, several thousand women from another Urhobo clan, the Uvwie, gathered outside the Warri NNPC refinery and threatened to take off their clothes if they did not get financial compensation, jobs, contracts, electricity, and school grants for their children. The setting was more urban, however, and they were less fortunate than their rural sisters in Oghafere two years earlier. This was because they had targeted a state corporation and the response from the authorities was more brutal. Eventually, the protesters were marginalized by the community patriarchs, who stepped in to lead the negotiations (Turner & Oshare 1993).

Demonstrations by angry and sometimes naked women continued nonetheless, such as in Okutukutu and Etegwe in 1991 and Obunagha in 1992. For instance, in July 2002, Itsekiri women occupied the Escravos oil terminal and the Chevron-Texaco facilities in Abiteye, Makaraba, Otuana, and Olera Creek (Turner & Brownhill 2002, Ukeje 2004). In July 2003, Ijaw women then took over a flow station in Amukpe near Sapele to demand that Shell provide jobs and basic services (Turner & Brownhill 2004). In Gbaramatu, again, women attempted to prevent the installation of a Chevron gas pipeline in Chanomi Creek in May 2009 and September 2011 (Babatunde 2018). However, the economic, political, and international context was very different. The military were no longer in power and crude oil prices were on the rise. By contrast, the protests of the 1980s took place during the Cold War when Nigeria was sinking into an economic crisis and had to comply with the World Bank's Structural Adjustment Program. At the time, oil prices were low, the debt burden was enormous, and the government was forced to cut its social expenditure and reduce the number of workers in the civil service.

References

Akinyele, Rufus Taiw. 1996. "States Creation in Nigeria: The Willink Report in Retrospect", *African Studies Review* 39 (2): 71–94.

Akpan, Wilson. 2005. "Putting Oil First? Some Ethnographic Aspects of Petroleum-related Land Use Controversies in Nigeria", *African Sociological Review* 9, (2):134–52.

Babatunde, Abosede Omowumi. 2018. "From Peaceful to Non-Peaceful Protests: The Trajectories of Women's Movements in the Niger Delta", In *The Unfinished Revolution in Nigeria's Niger Delta: Prospects for Socio-Economic and Environmental Justice and Peace*, edited by Cyril Obi & Temitope Oriola: 103–119. London: Routledge.

Dada, Joel, Nfor Eric Siben & Halima Godowoli. 2011. "Reintegration of the Former Biafran Soldiers into the Nigerian Army after the Civil War", *Maiduguri Journal of Peace, Diplomatic and Development Studies* 3 (2): 95–101.

Dike, Onwuka & Ekejiuba, Felicia. 1990. *The Aro of South-Eastern Nigeria, 1650–1980.* Ibadan: Ibadan University Press.

Elaigwu, Isawa. 1986. *Gowon: The Biography of a Soldier-Statesman.* Ibadan: West Books Publishers.

Forsyth, Frederick. 1969. *The Making of an African Legend: The Biafra Story.* Harmondsworth: Penguin.

Levine, Robert. 1966. *Dreams and Deeds: Achievement Motivation in Nigeria.* Illinois: Chicago University Press.

Maiangwa, Benjamin. 2016. "Revisiting the Nigeria-Biafra War: The Intangibles of Post-War Reconstruction", *International Journal of World Peace* 33 (4): 49–50.

Okara, Gabriel & Anwuri, Christopher. 1988. *Who's Who in Rivers State of Nigeria.* Port Harcourt: Pen Group.

Oputa Panel (Human Rights Violations Investigation Commission). 2002. *Report.* Abuja: n.d.

Ottenberg, Simon. 1959. "Igbo Receptivity to Change". In *Continuity and Change in African Cultures,* edited by Bascom, William Russell & Melville Herskovits: 93–126. Chicago: University of Chicago Press.

Pérouse de Montclos, Marc-Antoine. 1999. "Port Harcourt, la 'cité-jardin' dans la marée noire", *Politique africaine* 74: 42–50.

Soremekun, Kayode. 1995. *Perspectives on the Nigerian Oil Industry.* Lagos: Amkra Books.

Tamuno, Tekena Nitonye. 1972. "Patriotism and Statism in the Rivers State, Nigeria", *African Affairs* 71 (284): 264–281.

Turner, Terisa & Brownhill, Leigh. 2002. "La guerre du pétrole des femmes au Nigeria", *Travail, capital et société* 35 (1): 132–164.

Turner, Terisa & Brownhill, Leigh. 2004. "Why Women Are at War with Chevron: Nigerian Subsistence Struggles against the International Oil Industry", *Journal of Asian and African Studies* 39 (1): 63–93.

Turner, Terisa & Mukoro, Oshare. 1993. "Women's Uprising against the Nigerian Oil Industry in the 1980's", *Canadian Journal of Development Studies* 14 (3): 329–57.

Ukeje, Charles. 2004. "From Aba to Ugborodo: Gender Identity and Alternative Discourse of Social Protest among Women in the Oil Delta of Nigeria", *Oxford Development Studies* 32 (4): 605–617.

Wolpe, Howard Eliot. 1974. *Urban Politics in Nigeria: A Study of Port Harcourt.* Berkeley: University of California Press.

Shell, the Dictator and the Writer

The Ogoni Revolt (1990–1999)

Kenule Saro-Wiwa, known as "Ken", does not look impressive at first sight. He is a rather short person, yet is widely known as an activist. He smokes his pipe when I meet him in 1994 in the small office of his bookstore on Aggrey Road, right in the middle of the old colonial town of Port Harcourt. A writer, the leader of the Movement for the Survival of the Ogoni People (MOSOP), he tells me about passive resistance and his struggle against oil companies, especially Shell, the largest in Nigeria. He invites me to a demonstration organized in Eeken, a village south of Bori, the capital of Ogoniland.

The masquerade is already going on when I arrive. Men are wearing wooden masks and women are dancing, while children hide their faces behind the leaves of local plants. I am the only white man in the crowd and I am invited to give a speech. I am embarrassed. What should I say? I take the microphone and thank the organizers for their invitation; but the worst is yet to come. The atmosphere is festive and I am now asked to sing! Completely taken by surprise, I don't know what to do. As a last resort, I improvise a chorus based on the *Marseillaise*. My voice sounds horrible but the audience seems to be delighted. Listeners politely applaud me.

Little did I know that, one year later, Ken Saro-Wiwa would be identified as a prisoner of conscience by Amnesty International and hanged by the military junta of General Sani Abacha. His extra-judicial killing caused an international scandal, so much so that Nigeria was threatened with economic sanctions and expulsion from the Commonwealth. According to a cellmate, the body of the Ogoni leader was dissolved in acid to prevent protesters from gathering around his grave. After the end of the military dictatorship, this testimony was disputed by a commission of inquiry led by Judge Chukwudifu Oputa, because the detainee was unlikely to have been able to see Ken Saro-Wiwa's execution from the room where he was jailed. Since then, however, the story has been confirmed by a common law prisoner who, pardoned in 2019, had been compelled to transport the bodies of the murdered Ogoni activists to the bush, where the military reportedly sprayed them with acid before burying them near a place called Bolokiri (Aborisade 2019).

How did this happen? A priori, there was no reason that Ogoni peasants would lead the fight against oil companies. Unlike Ijaw fishermen in the coastal

FIGURE 10   Ken Saro Wiwa in his office on Aggrey Road, the headquarters of MOSOP in Port Harcourt (1994)

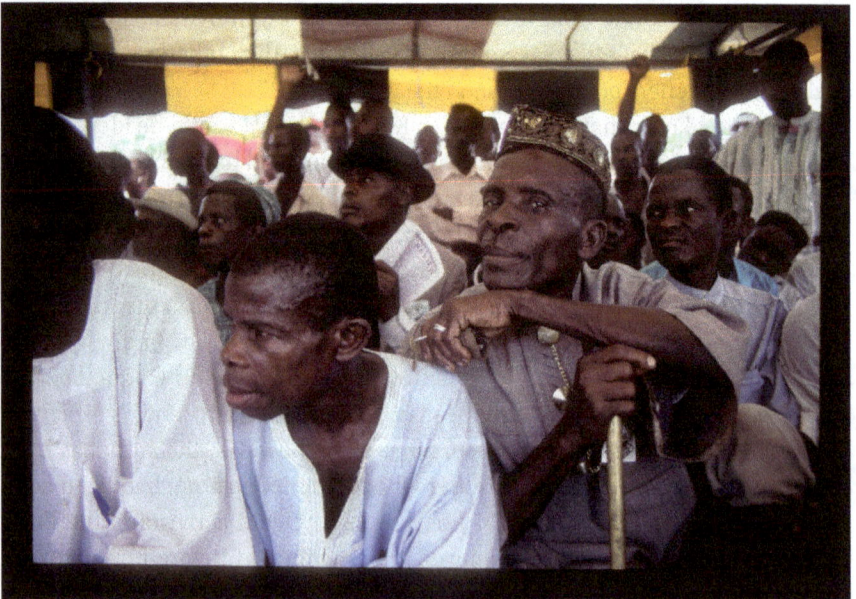

FIGURE 11   A MOSOP demonstration at Eeken in Rivers State, following clashes with the Andoni (1994)

western parts of the Niger Delta, they are rather farmers inland. They did not take part in the transatlantic trade and were mainly involved in palm oil production. More open to colonial penetration than the coastal communities who resisted the British to preserve their monopoly on the slave trade, the Ogoni quickly converted to Christianity and sent their children to mission schools. Some became palm oil traders; others entered positions in the civil service.

1 The Ogoni, an Emerging Minority

The origin of the Ogoni is disputed by local historians (Kpone-Tonwe 1997, Loolo 1981). According to some legends, they first settled on the coast, in Nama, and arrived by sea from Ghana or, possibly, from Akwa Ibom if we give credit to their linguistic affinity with the Ibibio of the region of Uyo, just east of Bori. Divided into several clans, the Ogoni did not exist as such when the British occupied the Niger Delta, and it is possible that their name came from a pejorative word, *igoni*, which refers to "foreigners" among the Ibani of Bonny Island. It was not until the translation of the New Testament into the Khana dialect in 1930 that a common Ogoni language developed and gradually replaced the Ibo lingua franca.[1] Meanwhile, the development of a state administration also helped to foster a pan-Ogoni identity among clans such as the Nyo Khana, Ken Khana, Tai, Babbe, and Gokana, to which the Eleme and the Ban Ogoi linguistic minorities are sometimes added.

At the beginning of colonization, these various groups were divided among the provinces of Calabar, Owerri, and Rivers. But their position changed with the reorganization of Native Authorities by the British. First placed under the jurisdiction of Ahoada in 1925, the Eleme began in 1932, for example, to ask to join the Opobo Division and were finally included in 1947 in a new Ogoni Division that had just been created in Rivers Province. Other clans that spoke Ogoni also tried to escape from the rule of rival neighbors such as the Ndoki in the north, the Okrika in the west and, in the south, the Andoni, with whom they clashed over fishing rights in 1922 and 1937 (Ekoriko & Olukoya 1993: 17). When the latter obtained their own administrative entity in 1931, they pressed the British to be merged into one Ogoni Division headquartered in Bori.

---

1 Languages are indeed important markers of ethnic identities: during the 1966 pogroms, southern migrants in northern Nigeria were thus identified and killed because they could not speak Hausa; during the Biafra secession war in 1967–1968, Niger Delta minorities were then seen as "traitors" and executed if they could not pronounce correctly passwords in Ibo when traveling from one village to another (Ugochukwu 2009: 35).

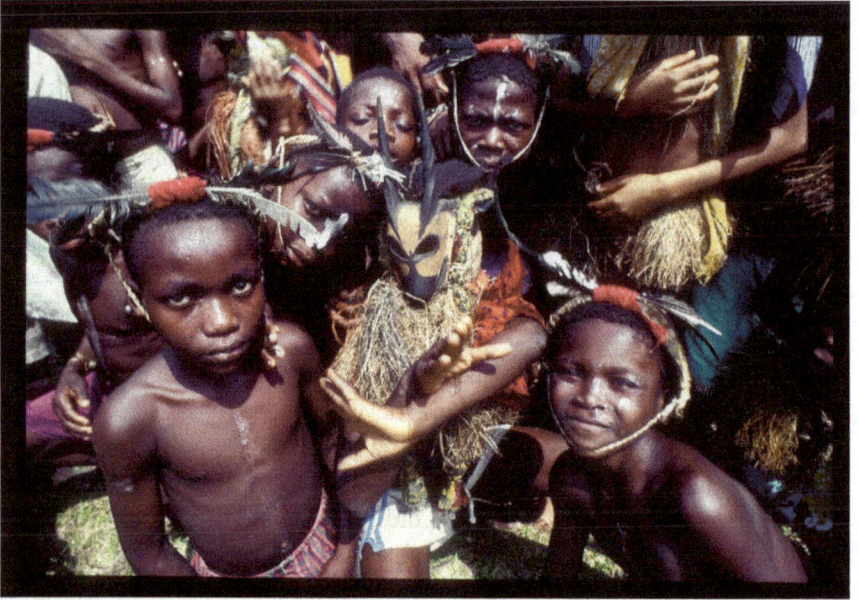

FIGURE 12   An Ogoni Masquerade (1994)

FIGURE 13   An Ogoni Masquerade (1994)

In a way, MOSOP was thus a nationalist and modern extension of the many ethnic lobbies formed during colonization and after independence: the Ogoni Central Union in 1945, the Ogoni Development Union in 1947, the Ogoni State Representative Assembly in 1950, the Ogoni Progressive Union in 1955, the Ogoni Divisional Union in 1962, the Ogoni National Congress in 1970, and the KAGOTE Association (Khana, Gokana, Tai and Eleme) in 1978. Yet it never overcame internal rivalries. As independence approached, for instance, the urban Eleme distanced themselves from the rural Ogoni, who were poorer. Closer to the coastal people, they considered themselves to be more civilized. Their opposition was also political. While the Ogoni voted for the Yoruba-dominated AG (Action Group), they approached Nnamdi Azikiwe and the Ibo of the NCNC (National Council of Nigeria and the Cameroons) to demand in 1959 that the country's first refinery be built in Alesa, one of their villages in the suburb of Port Harcourt, where the Eleme petrochemical complex was to be inaugurated in 1965.

Like elsewhere in the Niger Delta, the fight for a larger share of the oil rent was then to exacerbate and fragment communal identities. The Eleme, in particular, wanted to defend their own economic interests. Better endowed than the rural Ogoniland, their territory included the Port Harcourt refinery, oil wells in Ebubu and Ogale, a fertilizer plant, a naval base and the port of Onne, which gave access to the ocean and served the entire region (Isumonah 2004). While Ogoni farmers were more directly affected by pollution, the Eleme townspeople had other sources of income and did not want Shell to leave as long as they benefited from its revenues. As a result, their in-house historian claimed that they were not related to the Ogoni and were in fact of Ibibio origin. In the 1980s, he also began to campaign for the creation of a micro-state of Nchia, whose administrative headquarters would have been in Eleme (Ngofa 2006). When MOSOP was founded in 1990, the Eleme remained loyal to the Nigerian government, refused to sign the Ogoni Bill of Rights, and took advantage of the military repression against their rivals to renew their demand for a state of Nchia that would have included the Ogoni, Andoni, Ibani, Opobo, and Etche.

Ken Saro-Wiwa was quite ambiguous in this respect. Since the Biafran War, he knew that the Ogoni, a very small minority in Nigeria, had no chance of gaining independence and his intention was certainly not to take up arms like Isaac Boro did in 1966. Moreover, he always rejected the secessionist project of an Ijaw Delta Republic. Rather, he preferred a kind of ethnic confederation and asked for a better application of local autonomy in a genuine federal system (Bagia 2009: 80). At the constitutional conference organized by the Abacha dictatorship in August 1995, some activists thus called for the creation of an

Ogoni state headquartered in Bori and delimited by the Opobo, Andoni, Imo, and Bonny rivers to include the Khana, Gokana, Tai, Oyigbo, and Eleme clans.

A priori, MOSOP thus resembled ethnic movements that abound in the Niger Delta and, in general, throughout Nigeria. With its own national anthem and flag, the organization complained that the Ogoni were economically marginalized and politically discriminated against. It argued, for example, that they had never received the position of governor or deputy governor since the creation of Rivers State in 1967. In the same vein, it demanded a direct control of oil resources based on an Ogoni tradition according to which one fifth of the palm wine harvest should go to the owner of the trees (Kpagane 2013: 27). In 1992, MOSOP eventually gave Shell an ultimatum. Its militants blocked access to production sites and insisted that the company should leave the area if it did not agree to pay them royalties directly.

Compared with other groups in the Niger Delta, however, Ken Saro-Wiwa innovated on two main issues: environmental protection and the modernization of an ethnic nationalism based on the notion of "genocide". The Ogoni leader was a clever activist, and he built his opposition to Shell and the military dictatorship by posing as a revolutionary man, a representative of the masses, and an ecological militant—a position that gave him the support of green lobbies in the West. At the time, environmental protection was not important in Nigeria. Ken Saro-Wiwa was probably the first to introduce this issue into the political battlefield. He was connected to NGOs such as Greenpeace, Survival International, and Friends of the Earth through two British filmmakers, Kay Bishop and Glen Ellis, who came to Nigeria to shoot a documentary on the bloody repression of protesters against Shell in Umuechem in October 1990. In July 1991, Saro-Wiwa thus added an ecological addendum to the Ogoni Bill of Rights, which had been signed in August 1990 on the basis of communal and political demands only (Okonta 2008: 200). In a posthumous book, he even claimed that environmental protection was so important that it was a top priority that took "precedence" over everything else (Saro-Wiwa 1995: 169).

It would be misleading in this respect to assume that the Ogoni struggle was, from the very beginning, "a response to the violence perpetrated upon the environment by the slick alliance of state and capital", as Michael Watts (2001: 192) writes it. Other factors interfered and some authors even went as far as arguing that the Ogoni Bill of Rights was just another scam to extort money from the government and oil companies (Maja-Pearce 2005: 5). Ken Saro-Wiwa was thus suspected of raising ecological issues to promote his personal political ambitions and gain international support. Whatever the case, the integration of environmental demands into an ethnic struggle was definitely a strategic move.

In this regard, it is difficult to know if ecological issues were really popular. For example, American political scientist Clifford Bob argues that the Ogoni succeeded in gaining the support of international green lobbies because they were better connected than the Ijaw, who suffered just as much from oil pollution (Bob 2001). Historically, however, Ijaw and Itsekiri traders in the region of Warri were the first to get in touch with Europeans from the sixteenth century onward. The Ogoni, on the other hand, lived in the hinterland, apart from the city-states along the coast. In the context of the dictatorships of generals Ibrahim Babangida and Sani Abacha, moreover, they did not enjoy the favors of the ruling class, especially when an Ijaw from Okrika, Rufus Ada George, was elected governor of Rivers State in 1992. In fact, the Ogoni had no comparative advantage in promoting their cause internationally, if not for Ken Saro-Wiwa's intelligence.

The political skills of the MOSOP leader did not stop there. Abroad and in Nigeria, Ken Saro-Wiwa was good at developing narratives about the Ogoni as a minority victim of a "double genocide", first by the Ibo during the Biafran War, then by the Abacha regime after the annulment of the 1993 elections (Osha 2007: xi). The military repression was quite bloody indeed. According to some estimates, over 2,000 civilians were killed in 1993–1995 (Pegg 1999: 474). Surrounded, the Ogoni were also attacked by the Andoni in July 1993, the Okrika in December 1993, and the Ndoki in April 1994. In such a context, it was no small success for Ken Saro-Wiwa to mobilize the youth against rival groups and customary chiefs, who were challenged as "vultures" and accused of diverting oil revenues for their own profit. At the height of his glory, Ken Saro-Wiwa even gave the impression that he wanted to replace the traditional authorities when he was called *Mene Akpo Ban Ogoi*, the "All-powerful king of the Ogoni" (Kukah 2011: 128).

2   MOSOP between Contestations and Divisions

Despite his aura, however, Ken Saro-Wiwa was unable to control the anger of young militants, who from 1993 onward completely blocked Shell's roads and production in the sub-region. From its foundation in 1990, MOSOP was in fact torn apart by internal quarrels and generational conflicts. At the beginning, its president, Garrick Leton, was a moderate who used to work with the ruling class and the military. The first Ogoni to obtain a PhD in the 1950s, he had been a federal minister of education in 1978 and had already been accused of building primary schools all over Nigeria except in his homeland. Within MOSOP, Garrick Leton was soon to be challenged by young radicals led by Saro-Wiwa.

Personal disputes sometimes went back a long way. During the Biafran War, Ken Saro-Wiwa had been the only one to join the federal government. At the time, the Ogoni were rather wary of the Gowon junta. They used to trade a lot with the Ibo and had suffered from the 1966 pogroms. Therefore, most of the founders of MOSOP, including Garrick Leton, supported the secessionists: with a scholarship from the government of the Eastern region to study in Great Britain, Ignatius Kogbara was to become Biafra's ambassador in London, while Edward Kobani headed the propaganda department of the rebels. The latter, who prevented the election of Ken Saro-Wiwa to the Constituent Assembly in 1977, also joined the party of the Ibo in 1979 before being banned from political life in 1984, when a coup d'état re-established a dictatorship.

From 1991 onwards, MOSOP leaders then disagreed on how to deal with oil companies and the federal government, especially when the military cancelled the results of the 1993 elections and returned to power under the aegis of General Sani Abacha. Ken Saro-Wiwa opposed conservative elders who, like Chief Edward Kobani, were willing to accept compromises such as the creation of ten more local governments rather than an Ogoni state. Most of MOSOP's leaders were retired civil servants or businessmen living on public contracts. They were therefore more compliant to government pressure (Okonta 2008: 220). On the other hand, Ken Saro-Wiwa was more independent because he lived off his income as a writer and television producer. In 1993, he thus called for a boycott of the elections and disapproved of Garrick Leton, who ran under the banner of the Social Democratic Party (SDP).

The schism was inevitable. Within MOSOP, Ken Saro-Wiwa was accused of favoring the Bane of his home village against the Gokana clan of his arch-rival Edward Kobani, who was more eager to find an understanding with Shell because most of the oil wells in Ogoniland were located in his area. In addition, the writer was blamed for raising a kind of militia, the NYCOP (National Youth Council of Ogoni People), to challenge the power of traditional chiefs, dismiss his opponents, and intimidate the population to ensure that voters would boycott the elections. Ken Saro-Wiwa eventually succeeded in pushing Garrick Leton and Edward Kobani to resign, and in July 1993 he seized the MOSOP presidency. His coup de force was highly contested. Indeed, Ken Saro-Wiwa counted the ballots of young people who had no right to vote, and he did not wait for the renewal of the board to dissolve the movement's executive bodies and hold elections immediately after the departure of Garrick Leton and Edward Kobani.

The writer's "putsch" would in fact sign his death warrant when, the following year, NYCOP activists killed four Ogoni traditional leaders, an act for which he would be charged with murder. After his extra-judicial execution,

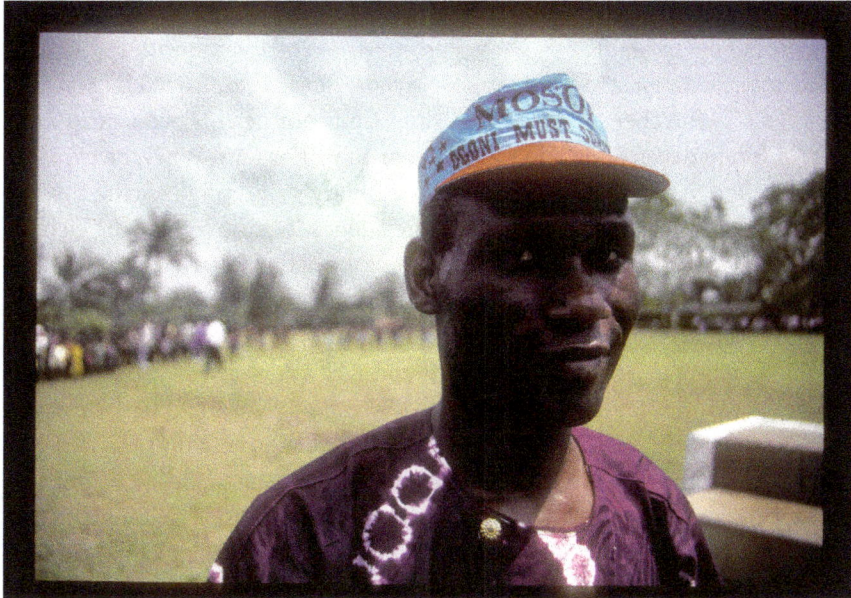

FIGURE 14   The president of NYCOP (National Youth Council of the Ogoni People), Goodluck
Diigbo, at Eeken in Rivers State (1994)

Ken Saro-Wiwa was then celebrated internationally, especially in the United
States, as a human rights activist, a brave environmental activist, and a hero
of the struggle of the Niger Delta minorities against oil giants. In Nigeria, too,
he is generally remembered as a pioneer and a martyr for democracy, ignoring
the fact that he directed the propaganda office of the military junta at the end
of the 1980s, MAMSER (Mass Mobilization for Self Reliance, Social Justice, and
Economic Recover). In the Niger Delta, however, not everyone shares this martyr view. Before his arrest and tragic death, many Ogoni villagers saw Ken Saro-
Wiwa as a city boy, a demagogue, an upstart and a troublemaker who put his
own interests first.[2] As for Ike Okonta, a researcher and an activist who clearly
had no sympathy for Abacha, he claimed that political opportunism already
pushed the Ogoni leader to join the federal side in 1967 (Okonta 2008). At the
time of the trial of Ken Saro-Wiwa in 1995, Leton Garrick even accused him of
using the misfortunes of his people for personal ends.

---

2   Interviews of the author with Ogoni farmers in Bori and Okwale in September 1990 and
February 1994.

Such an opinion obviously reflects the deep enmity of the establishment, traditional chiefs, and Gokana who preferred to collaborate with the Abacha junta after being ousted from MOSOP in 1993. But it is confirmed by Matthew Kukah, a well-respected Catholic bishop from northern Nigeria, who led a mediation between Shell and the Ogoni in 2005. Ken Saro-Wiwa, he explains, did not want to remain MOSOP's general secretary, so he mobilized the youth to overthrow his rivals and take over the presidency. To attract them, he claimed that, thanks to his international connections, he had managed to get $1 million in compensation from Wilbros, a Canadian subcontractor in the oil industry (Kukah 2011: 119–145).

The situation then deteriorated rather quickly. As a member of the Rivers State government after the Biafran War, Ken Saro-Wiwa had been in touch with a young officer named Sani Abacha. The two men actually lived for some time in the same area of Port Harcourt. Because he personally knew him, Ken Saro-Wiwa thus took the initiative in September 1993 to approach General Sani Abacha to persuade him to restrain the repression led by Major Paul Okuntimo in Ogoniland. Initially, the dictator complied because he needed people's support to remove interim president Ernest Shonekan and seize power in a coup d'état two months later. Ken Saro-Wiwa therefore refrained from criticizing Sani Abacha, as he was himself preparing a campaign to be elected at a constitutional conference due to open in Abuja in June 1994 (Okonta 2008: 245). While the meeting was eventually boycotted by the opposition, the Ogoni leader met his ultimate fate. On 21 May 1994, NYCOP militants massacred four traditional chiefs of the Gokana clan, including Edward Kobani. They did not just kill them. They cut them into pieces and ate them, which prevented the bodies from being found and the funerals from taking place (Kukah 2011: 119–145). Ken Saro-Wiwa was accused of having a hand in the killings.

3   A Bitter Victory

In spite of its impact abroad, MOSOP's struggle finally ended on a bitter note. On the one hand, Ken Saro-Wiwa effectively forced Shell to withdraw permanently from Ogoniland, a first in the history of the Niger Delta. Accused of violating human rights, polluting the region, and supporting a military dictatorship, the oil major saw its image tarnished internationally. As a result, it attempted to save face and promoted an Ogoni, Basil Omiyi, who was the first Nigerian to become its managing director and head its operations in the country, from 2004 to 2009. Shell also had to rethink its relationship with security forces in Nigeria and ended up, twenty years later, by massively disinvesting and selling its wells onshore.

As for the elect-presidents in power in Abuja after the end of the military dictatorship in 1999, they had to take into account the demands of the Niger Delta minorities and raise to 13% the share of oil revenues going to producing states. In the same vein, MOSOP became a sort of official organization and was consulted to advise the authorities. In 2008, its president after Ken Saro-Wiwa, Ledum Mitee, thus chaired a government committee to recommend technical solutions to end the Niger Delta crisis; in 2012, he later joined a federal agency, NEITI (Nigeria Extractive Industries Transparency Initiative).

In Nigeria and abroad, MOSOP's struggle was also a source of inspiration. In Ireland, for example, the villagers of Erris invoked the abuses of British colonial rule and the martyrdom of the nine Ogoni executed by the Abacha junta to oppose Shell's attempts to lay a gas pipeline through their fields, a protest that earned them a few months in prison in June–September 2005 (Onuoha 2008). In Nigeria, MOSOP inspired the name of MASSOB, the Movement for the Actualization of the Sovereign State of Biafra, which was set up after the end of the military dictatorship to defend the rights of the Ibo (Okonta 2014: 361). Under the aegis of Ralph Uwazurike, a lawyer and a graduate of political science from the University of Bombay, this organization had a priori nothing to do with oil production and pollution. But in 2001 its members blocked some filling stations, kidnapped petrol attendants, and threatened to attack tankers headed for the north, claiming they were responsible for the shortage of fuel in the south-east.

In the Niger Delta, finally, the Ijaw took over the struggle against pollution (Ukeje 2001). As soon as November 1995, a human rights activist, Robert Azibaola, set up an NGO, ND-HERO (Niger-Delta Human and Environmental Rescue Organization), to protest against the extra-judicial killing of Ken Saro-Wiwa. Two years later in August 1997 in Aleibiri, a Bayelsa village affected by a Shell oil spill six months earlier, a lawyer, Oronto Douglas, then launched a movement, Chikoko, named after the organic soil on which the mangroves grow.[3] Before the elections of February 1999 that marked the end of the military regime, the struggle of Ken Saro-Wiwa also inspired the creation of another

---

3 In January 1993 in Benin City, Oronto Douglas had first participated in the creation of another NGO, Environmental Rights Action (ERA), which published a report called *Terror in Ogoni Land* on the repression of MOSOP. With a British environmental activist, Nichols Ashton-Jones, and an Ibo lawyer, Uche Unyeagocha, he was then arrested and beaten by the military while trying to find the place where Ken Saro-Wiwa had been jailed. Oronto Douglas later became personal adviser to President Goodluck Jonathan after his election in April 2011.

group, MOSIEND (Movement for the Survival of the Ijaw Ethnic Nationalities in the Niger Delta).[4] The MOSOP's experience, finally, was clearly in the minds of the drafters of the Ijaw's Kaiama Declaration, the Ikwerre's Rescue Charter and the Oron's Bill of Rights.

On the environmental front, however, the situation has been much less rosy. In Ogoniland, oil spills continued, for instance in Bodo in 2008 (Pegg & Nenibarini 2013). According to a United Nations survey carried out in 2010, pollution became worse than it was in 1993, when Shell had to withdraw from the region. In "a volatile security context", MOSOP demonstrations and block-ades indeed forced the company to evacuate its oil fields "in an abrupt and unplanned manner". Shell left the area in such a hurry that it did not have time to decommission its facilities properly (UNEP 2011: 99). Subsequently, obstruc-tions by young activists prevented access to abandoned and poorly sealed wells, while thieves, the so-called "bunkerers", took advantage of the compa-ny's departure to loot crude oil pipelines, causing enormous environmental damage. In 2008, the mining license of Shell was finally revoked and trans-ferred to shady local firms that had no technical or financial capacity to follow basic environmental standards: first Belemaoil in 2015, then RoboMichael in 2018 and Sahara Energy in 2021.[5] Although they obtained the agreement of some traditional Ogoni leaders, none of these companies were able to resume oil production, while the government of Rivers State gave up the idea of partic-ipating in the operations. In 2021, Bodo was still the largest bunkering point in the entire region (Ebiede, Bassey & Asuni 2021: 375).

From a security point of view, the situation has not improved either. While the return to a civilian regime brought the country out of the dark years of military repression, clashes related to electoral, political, land, and criminal conflicts have continued since 1999. According to the NigeriaWatch database, Ogoniland experienced higher levels of lethal violence in 2015–2019 than those recorded before the 2009 amnesty, when the armed rebellion of the Ijaw was in full swing in the central and western Niger Delta. From a political point of view, the MOSOP struggle has also shown its limits. At the national level, the Ogoni crisis of 1995 certainly contributed to the demand for democracy, together with the large strikes of 1994 and the mobilization of the extra-parliamentary

---

4 Unlike MOSOP, however, MOSIEND did set up a sort of armed branch, the Egbesu Boys of Africa, when its founder, Timi Ogoriba, was jailed by the authorities in Yenagoa.

5 Belema Oil was founded in 2012 by Jack-Rich Tein Jr., an Ijaw from Kula in Akuku Toru Local Government Area (LGA), where it was supposed to maintain marginal fields operated by Shell. As for RoboMichael, it was a small company specializing in oil distribution, not production.

opposition in Lagos. But the return to civilian rule remained very much under the control of the military. In practice, it resulted primarily from the unexpected death of the dictator, Sani Abacha, as well as the retirement, in the longer term, of the most politicized officers who took power after their victory over Biafra in 1970 (Ehwarieme 2011). As for MOSOP, it sank into endless quarrels.

Following the execution of Ken Saro-Wiwa, the Ogoni movement was divided between the factions of his brother, Owens Wiwa, and a lawyer, Ledum Mitee. While the former had to go underground, the latter was suspected of complicity with the military because he was the sole defendant to escape execution after the 1995 trial. Moreover, he was accused of receiving $23,000 from an oil drilling company, Saipem, in 1994. Yet he was elected MOSOP president in 1995 and held on to power for seventeen years (Hunt 2005: 170). It was only in 2012 that he was replaced by an interim, Ben Naanen, a historian from the University of Port Harcourt and the very first secretary of the organization in 1990 (Kpagane 2013: 13). In 2015, the new MOSOP elect-president, Legbosi Saro Pyagbara, was then contested by a rival, Mike Lube-Nwidobie, and a dissent "third force" that emerged under the aegis of Goodluck Diigbo, a former leader of NYCOP. During internal elections conducted in 2018, the organization finally failed to decide between its two self-proclaimed presidents, Fegalo Nsuke and Prince Nuyete Biira. Today, MOSOP is just a shadow of its former self. It depends on state subsidies and is described as moribund since it has lost the support of international funders.

Certainly, Ken Saro-Wiwa did not die in vain, for his "martyrdom" continues to inspire militants in the region. But he did not succeed in uniting the various communities of the Niger Delta around a common political project. On the contrary, he promoted ethnic nationalism, defended a narrow vision of regionalism, and divided the Ogoni themselves by reviving their clan oppositions while rejecting the authority of their traditional chiefs.

In Rivers State, for instance, Gokana and Khana are now considered to be the local government areas (LGAs) with the highest frequency of inter-community conflicts (Arokoyu & Ochulor 2016). The sad end of Ken Saro-Wiwa also had important consequences in the whole region. It demonstrated the futility of passive resistance and convinced some activists that it was useless to negotiate with the federal government. After the death of Sani Abacha in 1998 and the return of civilians to power in 1999, a new and more violent phase began, with young militants who decided to take up arms.

This time the revolt came from the Ijaw of the central and western Niger Delta. In a way, it reproduced the cleavages observed within MOSOP between the elders, who were ready to negotiate compromises, and the youth, who were much more radical. As with the Ogoni, the struggle started with an ethnic lobby, the Ijaw National Council (INC), which was founded in Lagos in October 1991 and launched in November in Patani, Delta State, by traditional chiefs under the aegis of the Ijaw People's Union. Its first presidents were a reverend until 1994, Christopher Dime, and, until 2000, a businessman who turned out to be a Nigerian intelligence officer, Joshua Fumudoh. Their successors were professors of political science and pharmacology at the University of Port Harcourt, Kimse Okoko until 2008 and Atuboyedia Obianime until 2011. Deposed and replaced in 2012 by an acting president by the name of Joshua Ebiakpor Benemeseigha, the latter narrowly missed being kidnapped and murdered when he was accused of embezzling the organization's funds and trying to sell oil illegally. As for Kimse Okoko, a former consultant with Shell, he fell out with his legal counsel, Henry Seriake Dickson, who became governor of Bayelsa in 2012. Elected in 2013, the new INC president, Senator Tari Sekibo, died after a year in office. He was succeeded in 2015 by a lawyer, Boma Obuoforibo, who was impeached for gross misconduct and replaced in 2016 by one Charles Harry and, in 2021, by a professor, Benjamin Okaba. The interference of politicians who supported different candidates for president exacerbated these internal divisions.

Like MOSOP, INC also experienced a nationalist drift and developed a narrow vision of an ethnic community based exclusively on blood rights. Initially founded in 1991 by the Ijaw elite of Lagos, it was revived in 1994 in the Niger Delta, in Patani, where it officially adopted a blue, red, and green flag. Among the personalities attending the event were people as different as Harold Dappa-Biriye, the veteran of the creation of Rivers State in 1967, and Asari Dokubo, the future leader of the armed rebellion in 2003. Dissension soon erupted with the emergence of two competing organizations: FNDIC (Federation of Niger Delta Ijaw Communities) in 1997 and IYC (Ijaw Youth Council) in 1998. The first started as a militia named after Isaac Boro's NDVF (Niger Delta Volunteer Force) to fight the Itsekiri of Warri, where its founder, Bello Oboko, had been a municipal councilor at the end of the 1980s. It was rebranded as FNDIC in 2001 when Asari Dokubo set up his own armed group, the Niger Delta Volunteer People's Force (NDPVF) (Ukiwo 2007: 602).

As for IYC, it was founded in Kaiama, Isaac Boro's home village. Despite a name referring to the youth, the new organization considered all Ijaws under the age of forty to be full members and claimed to coordinate the various militant groups in the region, despite the mistrust of INC's elders. Inspired by the Ogoni Bill of Rights, drafted eight years earlier by MOSOP, IYC's militants issued a Kaiama Declaration in December 1998 that reiterated Ijaw's property rights over oil resources, called for the withdrawal of Nigerian "occupation troops" and threatened extractive companies that refused to stop their operations and that relied on the army to resume their activities. At the time, the period seemed more favorable to these demands. Indeed, General Sani Abacha had died in June 1998 and the military had promised to return power to civilians by organizing presidential elections in February 1999. But hopes for a democratization of the Nigerian federation were soon to be dashed by repression.

4   The Odi Massacre and the Beginning of the Ijaw Rebellion

The tragedy occurred in November 1999 in Odi, a small village in Bayelsa State, where the army carried out reprisals after the assassination of twelve policemen by a local gang. Several factors contributed to the crisis. First, the Ijaw had begun to form militias and acquire weapons to fight the Itsekiri during communal clashes in the town of Warri in March 1997. This conflict had shown that people could meet their objectives by resorting to violence, contrary to Ken Saro-Wiwa's strategy of passive resistance. Indeed, the Ijaw finally obtained the relocation of the administrative headquarters of Warri South LGA, a change they had initially demanded in vain through negotiations with the authorities (Oriola 2013: 86–87).

Throughout the 1990s, the communal tensions that plagued Lagos also led the Ijaw to call up the youth to resist assaults by the Oodua People's Congress (OPC). This xenophobic ethno-nationalist militia wanted to defend the identity of the Yoruba natives by expelling "foreigners" from Nigeria's largest conurbation. In 1999, some youth from Odi were thus mobilized to avenge the Ijaw killed by the OPC. On their way to Lagos, they came up against policemen who tried to arrest them and lost seven men in the fighting. The "militants" then stormed the police stations of Kaiama and Patani, while kidnapping an Indian worker who was later released (Azaiki 2009: 22).

The federal government reacted quickly. President Olusegun Obasanjo, who had just been elected, was himself a former military man who had fought against the Biafrans. He wanted to assert his authority and strike hard to avoid the Ogoni revolt spreading to the Ijaw. As he said later, he considered that oil revenue was the "blood money" that the Niger Delta people had to pay to thank the federal government for freeing them from the Ibo during the Biafran War. In Bayelsa, Olusegun Obasanjo was thus ready to proclaim a state of emergency in order to impose the federal rule and circumvent an elect-governor who supported Ijaw nationalism. Moreover, the president did not try restrain the army because he was already busy removing the officers most compromised with Abacha and did not want to confront frustrated military who had reluctantly relinquished power to civilians.

Soldiers acted accordingly and perpetrated a massacre in Odi. Some authors even go as far as claiming that this was "the largest deployment of troops since the end of the Biafran war" (Rowell *et al.* 2005: 24). Yet there were more Nigerian soldiers engaged in Liberia in 1990 or in northern Nigeria to quell the revolt of the Islamist sect Maitatsine during operations that killed more than 4,000 people in ten days in Kano in 1980. It is in fact difficult to know precisely what really happened in Odi in 1999. No commission of inquiry was set up, and the suspects arrested at the time managed to escape from the prison of Port Harcourt before recording their statements. But the graffiti left by soldiers who wanted to avenge the dead policemen left no doubt about the possibility of extra-judicial executions (Albert 2003). Also, the bombings of the Nigerian Army killed many civilians by causing a large fire, as Niger Delta fishermen generally keep fuel drums at home for their canoes.

In any case, the death toll was high. When the soldiers left, the village of Odi was nothing but smoking ruins. Between 43 and 2,483 people died, depending on the figures provided by the authorities or the militants. After the Ibo and the Ogoni, the Ijaw now had their own "genocide" to build the narratives of their rebellion in the 2000s. Ken Saro-Wiwa's strategy of passive resistance had failed, overwhelmed by young thugs within MOSOP and NYCOP. The Ogoni predicament suggested that violence was the only language that the government would understand. In 1966, it is true that Isaac Boro's uprising had been defeated in a few days (Omoyefa 2010, Oriola 2013). But in 1999, the Odi massacre legitimized a rebellion that was to develop on a much larger scale.

References

Aborisade, Sunday. 30 Aug. 2019. "Soldiers Poured Acid on Saro-Wiwa after Execution—Eyewitness". Lagos: *Punch*. https://punchng.com/soldiers-poured-acid-on-saro-wiwa-after-execution-eyewitness/ (accessed 17 March 2022).

Albert, Isaac Olawale. 2003. *The Odi Massacre of 1999 in the Context of the Graffiti Left by the Invading Nigerian Army*. Ibadan: University of Ibadan.

Arokoyu, Samuel Bankole & Ochulor, Evangeline Nkiruka. 2016. "Spatial Patterns of Community Conflicts (1990–2015) and Its Implication to Rural Development in Rivers State". *World Rural Observations* 8 (1): 27–37.

Azaiki, Steve. 2009. *The Evil of Oil*. Ibadan: Y-Books.

Bagia, Terry. 2009. *Delta in Distress: The Politics and Perils of Petroleum Patronage in Nigeria*. Bloomington (Indiana): AuthorHouse.

Bob, Clifford. 2001. "Marketing Rebellion: Insurgent Groups, International Media, and NGO Support". *International Politics* 38 (3): 311–333.

Ebiede, Tarila Marclint, Celestine Oyom Bassey & Judith Burdin Asuni (eds). 2021. *Insecurity in the Niger Delta. A Report on Emerging Threats in Akwa Ibom, Bayelsa, Cross River, Delta, Edo and Rivers States*. London: Adonis & Abbey Publishers.

Ehwarieme, William. 2011. "The Military Factor in Nigeria's Democratic Stability, 1999–2009". *Armed Forces and Society* 37 (3): 494–511.

Ekoriko, Moffat & Sam Olukoya. 16 August 1993. "Brothers at War: In Rivers and Akwa Ibom States, Various Communities Engage in Ethnic Clashes". Lagos: *Newswatch Magazine*.

Hunt, Timothy. 2005. *The Politics of Bones: Dr. Owens Wiwa and the Struggle for Nigeria's Oil*. Toronto: McClelland & Stewart.

Isumonah, Adefemi. 2004. "The Making of the Ogoni Ethnic Group". *Africa* (London) 74 (3): 433–453.

Kpagane, Mmuen. 2013. *The 3-Dimensions of the Ogoni Revolution and the Unanswered Questions*. Ibadan: Stirling-Horden Publishers.

Kpone-Tonwe, Sonpie. 1997. "Property Reckoning and Methods of Accumulating Wealth among the Ogoni of the Eastern Niger Delta". *Africa* (London) 67 (1): 130–158.

Kukah, Matthew. 2011. *Witness to Justice: An Insider's Account of Nigeria's Truth Commission*. Ibadan: BookCraft.

Loolo, Godwin. 1981. *A History of the Ogoni*. Port Harcourt: manuscript.

Maja-Pearce, Adewale. 2005. *Remembering Ken Saro-Wiwa and Other Essays*. Lagos: The New Gong.

Ngofa, Obo Osaro. 2006. *The Complete History of Eleme*. Ibadan: Freedom Press.

Okonta, Ike. 2008. *When Citizens Revolt: Nigerian Elites, Big Oil and the Ogoni Struggle for Self-Determination*. Trenton (NJ): Africa World Press.

Okonta, Ike. 2014. "'Biafra of the Mind': MASSOB and the Mobilization of History". *Journal of Genocide Research* 16 (2–3): 355–378.

Omoyefa, Paul. 2010. "The Niger Delta Conflict: Trends and Prospects". *African Security Review* 19 (2): 70–81.

Onuoha, Austin. 2008. *When Communities Confront Corporations: Comparing Shell's Presence in Ireland and Nigeria*. London: Adonis & Abbey.

Oriola, Temitope. 2013. *Criminal Resistance? The Politics of Kidnapping Oil Workers*. Farnham: Ashgate.

Osha, Sanya. 2007. *Ken Saro Wiwa's Shadow: Politics, Nationalism and the Ogoni Protest Movement*. London: Adonis & Abbey Publishers.

Pegg, Scott. 1999. "The Cost of Doing Business: Transnational Corporations and Violence in Nigeria". *Security Dialogue* 30 (4): 473–484.

Pegg, Scott & Zabbey Nenibarini. 2013. "Oil and Water: The Bodo Spills and the Destruction of Traditional Livelihood Structures in the Niger Delta". *Community Development Journal* 48 (3): 391–405.

Rowell, Andy *et al.* 2005. *The Next Gulf: London, Washington and Oil Conflict in Nigeria*. London: Constable.

Saro-Wiwa, Ken. 1995. *A Month and a Day. A Detention Diary*. London: Penguin.

Ugochukwu, Françoise. 2009. *Biafra, la déchirure: sur les traces de la guerre civile nigériane de 1967–1970*. Paris: l'Harmattan.

Ukeje, Charles. 2001. "Oil Communities and Political Violence: The Case of Ethnic Ijaws in Nigeria's Delta Region". *Terrorism and Political Violence* 13 (4): 15–36.

Ukiwo, Ukoha. 2007. "From 'Pirates' to 'Militants': A Historical Perspective on Anti-State and Anti-Oil Company Mobilization among the Ijaw of Warri, Western Niger Delta". *African Affairs* 106 (425): 587–610.

UNEP. 2011. *Environmental Assessment of Ogoniland*. Nairobi: United Nations Environment Programme.

Watts, Michael. 2001. "Petro-Violence: Community, Extraction, and Political Ecology of a Mythic Commodity". In *Violent Environments*, edited by Nancy Lee Peluso & Michael Watts: 189–212. Ithaca (NY): Cornell University Press.

CHAPTER 5

Militants or Pirates?

The Armed Struggle of the Ijaw (2000–2009)

The year is 2004. The departure of the military and the return of civilians to power herald a new era. Yet fighting in the Niger Delta continues unabated. I have been trying for nearly two weeks to meet Nigeria's public enemy number one, Asari Dokubo. The latter is an Ijaw and a former student unionist who converted to Islam before going underground to fight against oil companies and the government of President Olusegun Obasanjo. His attacks on pipelines and flow stations made him famous with his men of the Niger Delta Volunteer People's Force (NDPVF), a group named after Isaac Boro's militia in 1966.

I am eventually able to contact a relative of Dokubo, Opunabo Christian Inko-Tariah. He is the editor of *Hard Truth*, a local newspaper in Port Harcourt. An Ijaw, he knows the area well and tells me to be ready to move without notice and at any time. I stay put, waiting for his phone call. When the day finally comes, we travel along a small country road west of Port Harcourt. The further we go, the fewer cars we see. The atmosphere becomes oppressive. Eventually, the only people we see are walking or biking. Along the roadside, houses in the bush are in ruins. It seems unlikely that they were abandoned mid-construction, as the army attacked the area not long ago.

We are now the only people on the road when a car suddenly appears out of nowhere and starts following us. Behind its tainted windows, I can see Dokubo's men checking that we have no escort. The tar road ends in front of a jetty. The car behind us also comes to a stop to block us from turning around. My driver turns deathly pale. He thinks I am about to be kidnapped.

I am told to walk toward the jetty. I do not have to wait long. Three speed-boats appear carrying armed men wearing red headbands, the color of Egbesu, the Ijaw god of war.[1] They look like pirates. I board one of the speedboats with Chris and we set off immediately at great speed. However, as we approach a creek, we come across a Nigerian Navy warship. I begin to worry. Will they open fire? The Egbesu boys show no concern, waving to the crew as we pass by the ship.

---

1 Sometimes, the so-called Niger Delta militants also carry white flags that are symbols of the purity of the sky, the sea, and the forest (Courson & Odijie 2020: 9).

I am dumbfounded:

"So, you're not at war?"

"No", they reply, "we do business together".

This is the context in which Dokubo claims to be leading a political armed group, yet lives off the spoils of plunder by stealing and reselling crude oil with the complicity of Nigerian soldiers and sailors. We arrive in one of the young rebels' hideouts, consisting of a few huts in a remote creek. I struggle to get ashore: there is no pontoon and I have to climb the roots of mangrove trees to get out of the water and pull myself up onto dry land. We discuss the conflict. Dokubo voices arguments heard many times elsewhere. He has just a dozen men with him. The weapons are concealed and must be somewhere else, to ensure I will not disclose the real location of the group's base.

By the time we return, the Nigerian Navy ship has gone, but there are many more Egbesu boys waiting for us when we get back to the car. So far, my safe conduct has worked and I have not been asked for any money. However, the boys want a tip and become more and more pressing. We struggle to get into the car, which by now is surrounded by angry "militants". The boys start pounding the windows and shaking the vehicle, as if wanting to flip us over. Fortunately for us, Chris knows how to handle this kind of situation. He half-opens a window

FIGURE 15   Asari Dokubo and his guerrillas of the Niger Delta People's Volunteer Force (NDPVF) at Ogbakiri, Rivers State (2004)

and throws out a wad of naira. The notes scatter everywhere and the Egbesu boys rush to grab them, leaving the path clear for us to speed off.

1   Greed or Grievance?

Are we really talking about freedom fighters? Or about young criminals who extort funds from the government and oil companies? There is no consensus on this issue. The renowned economist Paul Collier insisted that greed was the main driver of the rebellion, while overlooking the political dimension of the conflict (Collier 2000, Collier & Vicente 2009, Oyefusi 2007). However, NDPVF and its successors also needed money to fund their struggle. Dokubo himself claimed to be a sort of Robin Hood, a social bandit who plundered local resources to give oil back to the Niger Delta people (Hazen 2010: 94). If we are to believe available figures, the number of pipeline sabotages reached a peak with NDPVF in 2005 but declined thereafter when another armed group, the Movement for the Emancipation of the Niger Delta (MEND), took over in 2006 and the government eventually granted an amnesty to the "militants" in 2009 (Anifowose, Lawler, Horst & Chapman 2012: 644).

Undoubtedly, money does not explain everything, and it would be misleading to assume that personal enrichment is the only driving factor behind the rebellion. Unlike Paul Collier, Michael Watts (2007) and Nigerian researchers such as Ukoha Ukiwo (2007) have emphasized the historical depth and complexity of the multiple causes of the crisis. The political economy of the rebellion relied on pipeline sabotage, oil theft, and the financial support of corrupt politicians. Kidnappings, maritime piracy, and extortion would not have provided enough revenue to maintain a permanent group of fighters capable of being mobilized at any time (Pérouse de Montclos 2012).[2] As for the quantity of barrels stolen, accurate figures were not easy to come by and did not always provide reliable information on the funding capacity of rebels, because of the variations in oil prices. Thus, the volume of crude bunkered by criminals or militants allegedly fell from a high of 724,000 barrels per day in 2001 to 100,000 in 2006 and 2007, before rising again to 150,000 in 2008. However, this downward trend was offset by the increase in oil prices. The value of thefts of crude was estimated at \$6.3 billion in 2008, as against \$1.5 billion in 2000 (Asuni 2009a: 6).

---

2 For a comparison with Somalia, confirming the low yield of acts of piracy, see Bahadur 2012: 227.

FIGURE 16   An illegal refinery at Isaba, near Warri (2011)

In general, it is difficult to establish whether extortion is driven by greed or by the need to fund a political cause. Is violence simply an act of despair by young thugs with nothing to lose? Or is it a means of climbing the social ladder? A combination of the two is not impossible either. The rebels undoubtedly took up arms to secure a greater share of oil revenues. However, many of them also served the interests of mafia-like politicians who used them to get rid of rivals and win elections. As Akin Iwilade (2014: 592) argues, Niger Delta militants are not outcasts from a social and economic point of view; on the contrary, they are integrated into power networks designed for the misappropriation of oil revenues. Their position is not incompatible with occasional rebellion against their sponsors.

Militants or criminals? Academic opinions differ. For example, American scholar Jennifer Hazen (2010: 82) views NDPVF as a "particular type of social movement organisation", a sort of ethnic militia that bears no resemblance to a gang or a terrorist group. According to her, Asari Dokubo is a charismatic leader and a hero for the youth, yet she acknowledges that he has little popular support. As evidence of this, his militia disappeared along with him after he was imprisoned by the government. Ultimately, NDPVF was nothing but a minor dissident faction of the IYC (Ijaw Youth Council), a kind of radical armed wing without a real social base.

Asari Dokubo was clearly no match for Ken Saro-Wiwa's intellectual stature. The Nigerian ruling class generally viewed him as just another bandit. For instance, President Olusegun Obasanjo (2014: 305) recalled his encounter with Niger Delta rebels invited to Abuja for negotiations in October 2004.

> They came, almost forty of them including leaders like Asari Dokubo and Ateke Tom, and I received them in my Executive Council Chamber. I made them relax and we went into close discussion. Some of them were antagonistic to one other. Some acrimony developed and I started to hear such words as 'I killed your father because you killed my brother'. My Chief of Staff was horrified and at one time he called my attention to the fact that I was sitting among murderers. I acknowledged that to him.

Asari Dokubo was not, however, a mere gang leader. The son of a retired judge from one of the royal families of Buguma, he was well-born, coming from an Ijaw Kalabari clan, the Tariah, which also produced figures such as Henry Odein Ajumogobia, Nigeria's Minister for Foreign Affairs in 2010–2011, and Opunabo Christian Inko-Tariah, the editor of *Hard Truth*. Dokubo, whose real name was Melford Goodhead, initially studied law—although he never graduated—before dabbling in journalism. Like Isaac Boro on the Nsukka campus, he began his career as a militant by becoming involved in student unionism, in his case at the University of Calabar. In 1992 and 1998, he entered politics by standing as a candidate for a seat in the Rivers State House of Assembly and as the Chairman of the Asari-Toru LGA, initially for the SDP (Social Democratic Party). Though never elected, he then contributed to the foundation of IYC, becoming vice-president in 1998 and president in 2001, while forming a small group called Kirimani that would form the embryo of NDPVF and seek to federate the Ijaw clans in Rivers under the acronym Okonbia (Okrika, Kalabari, Opobo, Nkoro, Bille, Ibani, and Andoni).

Dokubo, who was soon banned from IYC, actually emerged on the political scene during the 2003 elections, when he began supporting the party in power, the PDP, and the outgoing governor of Rivers, Peter Odili. At the time, he had nothing but praise for his mentor, who had tasked him with eliminating the local opposition. As Dokubo proclaimed: "I want to state it clearly and put it on record that I am a supporter of Dr. Peter Odili, the Rivers State governor. I love him as an individual. I appreciate his qualities".[3] In practice, Dokubo mobilized unemployed youth to beat up opposition candidates and disrupt

---

3 Asari-Dokubo in an interview cited by Eberlein 2005.

elections in their constituencies. He particularly targeted the eastern and southern suburbs of Port Harcourt in the Okrika LGA, where Rufus Ada George was at loggerheads with Peter Odili, his former deputy when he was governor of Rivers in 1992–1993. At the end of the military dictatorship in 1999, Rufus Ada George had failed to secure the PDP nomination to stand as state governor and had joined the ranks of the ANPP, not without a sense of betrayal.

However, the elimination of Rufus Ada George was not enough to defuse the situation in Rivers. Peter Odili was unable to maintain control of the gangs that had helped him to be re-elected in April 2003. Things turned sour. Dokubo, who hailed from the eastern part of the Niger Delta, broke with Odili and opted for armed struggle through the connections that he had forged with western Ijaw during his time as president of IYC. In October 2003, he set up NDPVF in Olugberebu, right in the heart of Delta State and the kingdom of Gbaramatu, before launching a political branch known as the Niger Delta People's Salvation Front in July 2004. Among the Ijaw, he also benefited from support through matrimonial alliances. Though a convert to Islam, he was married in church to a Christian from Warri, Caroline, who had lived in Germany and who headed up the women's branch of IYC, earning her the nickname "Mama Luta".

When I met him again in February 2011, this time at his home in Warri, Dokubo was a free man. He had been released from jail in June 2007, just after the election of President Umaru Yar'Adua. A month later, however, he had to escape a raid by the security forces and went into exile in London, from where he invested money in the creation of a Cotonou-based foundation that was to teach Arabic in French-speaking Africa and that was named KARH (King Amachree Royal Highness) in reference to an Ijaw king. Dokubo later returned to Nigeria in April 2009 when an Ijaw from Bayelsa, Vice-President Goodluck Jonathan, replaced at short notice Umaru Yar'Adua, who had just died from illness before the end of his term.

In the meantime, the former guerrilla had put on weight and become a "big man". When I saw him again, he wanted to pose as a respectable leader and denied any involvement in acts of banditry or fraud to help Governor Peter Odili be elected in April 2003. As he told me: "Our struggle was political, it had nothing to do with money. NDPVF militants have never been mercenaries or gangsters. They were occasional fighters, volunteers who devoted part of their time to the Ijaw cause". In Dokubo's view, it made no sense to grant them an amnesty since they were not outlaws or ordinary criminals. The founder of NDPVF clearly wanted to distinguish himself from his rivals and successors who benefited from his time in prison to take his place as leaders of the armed struggle. He described them as "a bunch of criminals", although MEND was set up specifically to call for his release.

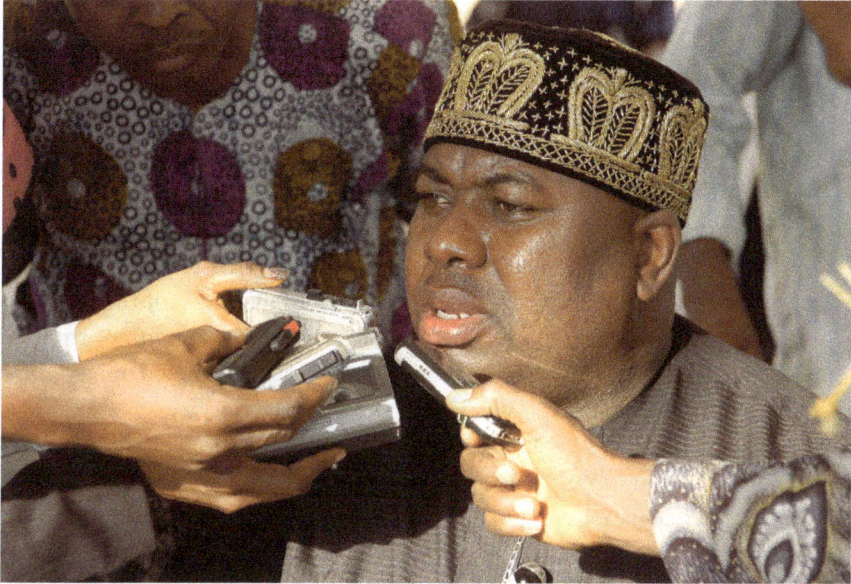

FIGURE 17   Asari Dokubo at a press conference in Edo State (2011)

Accused of sedition, Dokubo was detained in secret in Abuja between September 2005 and June 2007 before being released—officially for medical reasons on account of his high blood pressure and diabetes, unofficially to show the government's good faith in seeking to reach an agreement with the rebels. In the meantime, other fighters founded MEND. In Bayelsa State, Ebikabowei 'Boyloaf' Victor-Ben mounted his own camps in Ezetu, Azuzuama, and Agge in Ekeremor and Southern Ijaw LGAs. As for African Owei, he established a base in Osiaperemo Creek to take over a dissident NDPVF faction, the Reformed Niger Delta Peoples Volunteer Force. After fighting alongside MEND's leaders such as Commander Amadabo, Prince Odolo, and Tom Polo, finally Henry Bindodogha went to Edo State to set up the NDFF (Niger Delta Freedom Fighters) (Oriola 2013: 39, 95).

2   The Emergence of MEND (2006–2008)

A new generation of young rebels thus emerged as the sense of persecution felt by Ijaw nationalists was exacerbated by the simultaneous arrests, in September 2005, of the founder of NDPVF, Asari Dokubo, the Governor of Bayelsa, Diepreye Alamieyeseigha, and a well-known banker in Rivers, Ebimiti Banigo

(Watts 2007: 645). The PDP men who used to control Niger Delta "militants" were also removed from the political scene while President Obasanjo sought to tighten his grip on the ruling party. Such was the case, for example, of the governors of Delta and Bayelsa, respectively James Ibori, who eventually had to run away to Dubai, and Diepreye Alamieyeseigha, who supported IYC and was arrested in London on suspicion of money laundering. At the same time, the military repression in Rivers pushed some NDPVF commanders to seek refuge in Delta State and to put their personal differences aside to combine forces under the aegis of MEND (Asuni 2009b: 17). Finally, the arrest of the leader of the Klansmen Konfraternity, one of the many gangs in the region, contributed to a rapprochement with the insurgents, briefly uniting various armed groups against a common enemy (Oriola, Haggerty & Knight 2013: 74).

Like Dokubo's NDPVF, MEND was polymorphic and ambivalent in its relation to crime. Around the village of Korokorose in Bayelsa State, for example, journalist Michael Peel (2009: 192) reported how its "militants" pushed the residents of a hamlet, Ikebiri I, to sabotage and loot a pipeline in order to sell stolen crude and fund the rebellion. As a result, MEND and its accomplices turned down Agip's offer of money to repair the damage and to put an end to oil spills that polluted the environment and impoverished fishing communities living nearby. The young "militants" argued that they redistributed to villagers part of the revenue they earned from trafficking. Combined with kidnappings and maritime piracy, their predatory behavior nonetheless raised questions about financial motivations. A former MEND "fighter" thus publicly acknowledged the opposition within the movement between economic "entrepreneurs" such as Tom Polo, a traditionalist who believed in the protection of Egbesu to enrich himself, and modern political "militants" who, like Henry Okah, were generally more educated and resorted to extortion, kidnappings, and bank robberies to fund their struggle.[4]

Compared with NDPVF, however, the Niger Delta rebellion took a new turn. In January 2006, the MEND's first public action was to attack Agip's offices in Port Harcourt, killing eight police operatives and a passer-by during a raid designed to kidnap oil expatriate workers. The movement sought to be exclusively clandestine and militarily more professional than Dokubo's group, which had developed out of an official organization, IYC. Initially, MEND had no known faces, just a mysterious spokesman allegedly based in London and going by the name of Joe Gbomo. However, it soon gained power and expanded its reach beyond the western and central parts of the Niger Delta, where it was

---

4 Akpos Nabena, cited *in* Etim 2007.

led by "militants" such as Henry Okah, Government Ekpemupolo (aka 'Tom Polo' or 'General Tammo'), and Ebikabowei Victor-Ben, also known as 'General Boyloaf'. In June 2008, it surprised observers by mounting an audacious attack against an offshore Shell platform called Bonga, far from the coast. In July 2009, it then targeted oil facilities in Lagos, its first onshore operation outside the Niger Delta.

Finally, in October 2010 on Eagle Square, at the very heart of the federal capital Abuja, MEND set off two car bombs, killing sixteen people during official ceremonies commemorating the fiftieth anniversary of Nigeria's independence. The drift into terrorism was not consistent with the agenda of a militant organization that claimed to be willing to spare civilians. Himself an Ijaw, President Goodluck Jonathan maintained that the October 2010 attack had actually been carried out by Islamists from the north. One of his collaborators even went as far as to try to persuade Henry Okah, the group's spokesman, who at the time was in exile in South Africa, to use his influence to get MEND to retract its claim and deny its involvement in the Eagle Square bombing in Abuja (Adeniyi 2017: 30).

As a general rule, the movement tended to spare civilians. There were several reasons for this. First, unlike Isaac Boro in 1966, it did not need to engage in racketeering among the population since it funded itself by stealing and reselling crude oil. It also adhered to cultural norms that required its men to follow initiation rituals and abstain from sexual activity before going off to fight. Unlike many other guerrillas in Africa, MEND "militants" were not known for raping women; rather, it was the members of the security forces who were responsible for sexual violence in the Niger Delta (Oriola 2012, Omotola 2009, Lenning & Brightman 2009, Ukeje 2004). Third, MEND sought to limit the use of force because its primary goal was to secure politico-financial advantages rather than destroy and reform the entire system ex nihilo. Its position was thus reminiscent of the ambivalence of IYC, which in its 1998 Kaiama Declaration left room for ambiguity and requested for the withdrawal of either all oil companies or only those that had called on the army to protect their facilities and refused to pay royalties to Ijaw communities.

In practice, MEND avoided causing damage that might have had a long-term impact on the industry and deprived the region of revenue. For example, its combatants never used their rockets to shoot down helicopters carrying supplies to offshore platforms at sea or oil facilities in the bush, an attack that would have immediately resulted in a general interruption of production. Similarly, they avoided executing expatriates held captive. The only known case of a hostage being killed during one of their kidnappings came as a result of friendly fire by the Nigerian army during a failed rescue mission.[5]

In addition, MEND resorted to ambushes rather than terrorist attacks. It carefully avoided direct confrontation with the security and defense forces, grouped under a Joint Task Force (JTF) since 2003.[6] In power until 2007, President Obasanjo himself restrained the army from fighting after the Odi massacre that tarnished his image in 1999. It was his successor, Umaru Yar'Adua, who resumed the offensive under the aegis of a new Chief of Army Staff from the north, Abdul-Rahman Dambazau. A month before Abuja decided to grant an amnesty to the rebels, the only real battle between the army and MEND thus took place in May 2009 in Delta State around "Camp No. 5", a stronghold of Tom Polo. By contrast, the NDPVF bases were never taken by the Nigerian army, as Dokubo gleefully reminded me in expressing his frustration at having been sidelined.

3   The 2009 Amnesty

The June 2009 presidential amnesty was a game-changer, though it did not put an end to the violence. The main objective was to demobilize the rebels to ensure resumption of oil production, a process that the authorities proudly claimed to be driving without UN intervention. The initiative nonetheless highlighted the government's weakness. Unlike the Boko Haram group in the remote savannah of northeastern Nigeria, the Niger Delta rebellion had economic leverage to force Abuja to engage in dialogue by blocking oil production, the main source of government revenue. The amnesty amounted to recognizing the legitimacy and power of a movement whose negotiators, known as the "Aaron Team", included retired generals and celebrities such as Wole Soyinka, the Yoruba recipient of the Nobel Prize for Literature, alongside Henry Okah, who, at the time, was in prison.

---

5   https://www.petroleumafrica.com/hostage-killed-in-firefight/.
6   Initially set up with the army, the air force, the navy, the police, and the secret services, the JTF was first created in 1994 to secure northern Nigerian borders, where it became operational in 1998. In the Niger Delta, it was joined in 2012 by civilian defense forces, the departments of immigration, customs, and prisons, as well as the Nigeria Maritime Administration and Safety Agency (NIMASA) and the National Intelligence Agency (NAI). It took different names under Operations Restore Hope in 2009, Pulo Shield in 2012 and Delta Safe in 2016. Given the government's lack of transparency, however, it is difficult to establish the exact number of operatives involved in the area, with estimates in the region of 9,000 men in the mid-2010s.

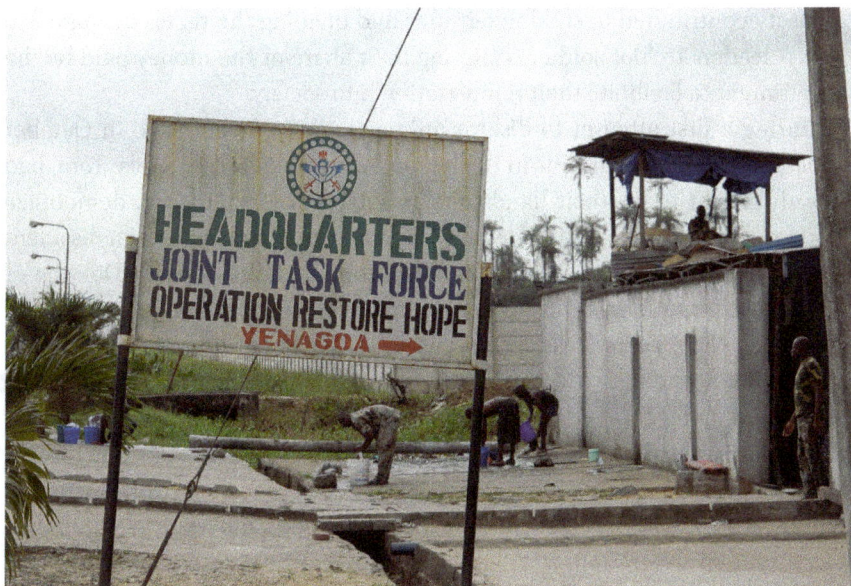

FIGURE 18   The headquarters of the JTF (Joint Task Force) in Yenagoa, Bayelsa State (2011)

However, MEND was not representative of the Niger Delta's peoples. Shortly before the April 2007 general elections, it briefly gave the impression of wanting to turn itself into a political party by seeking to win several seats in the National Assembly at Abuja and the regional parliaments of oil-producing states. But it lacked supporters and a social base. IYC, which had closer ties to NDPVF, thus criticized a movement that thwarted its hopes of securing a monopoly to speak with one voice. For instance, its president, Chris Ekiyor, described MEND as a "faceless organization that was created as a child of necessity" but that could not claim to "talk for us".[7]

The June 2009 amnesty was not without drawbacks in this respect. First, like other African demobilization programs, it rewarded violence. Civilian victims of the conflict were ignored and, except for a few cases, received no compensation to help them pay for their medical costs and rebuild their homes. Moreover, the Nigerian government appeared to exclude some of the region's armed groups, especially in the Bakassi peninsula of Cross River State, where fighters had attacked Cameroonian gendarmes to continue their trafficking and contest an international agreement along a disputed border. Lastly, the

---

7   Interview in *Sunday Vanguard* 22 Nov. 2009, Lagos: 43.

amnesty contributed to stoking tensions and dividing the rebels by opposing MEND leaders to foot soldiers claiming their share of the money paid by the government to facilitate their reintegration into society.

During a first attempt to disarm militants across Rivers State in October 2004, the two main warlords in the region, Asari Dokubo and Ateke Tom, had already fought to lay their hands on the subsidies earmarked to demobilize 4,000 men, a grossly over-inflated figure. At the time, the leader of a dissident faction based in Tombia, Prince Ipallibo Farah, had also accused Dokubo of failing to distribute the funds received from the government of Peter Odili. His group, the Niger Delta Strike Force, gathered all sorts of hoodlums to oppose NDPVF before siding with an opposition candidate, Prince Tonye Princewill, who stood under the Action Congress at the Rivers regional elections in May 2007 (Hazen & Horner 2008: 131).

Likewise, the implementation of the June 2009 amnesty provoked tensions within MEND. The pay gap between commanders and their "lieutenants" caused much frustration. In August 2010, for example, Soboma George was assassinated in Port Harcourt by his own men, who accused him of monopolizing government subsidies. Others opted to make war again, such as John Togo, who eventually died following a bombing by the Nigerian air force near Warri in July 2011. In the creeks, fighters also opposed "political militants" who were better educated and who conducted the negotiations with the government. In a petition signed by John Togo, Ezekiel Akpasibe-Owei, "General" Pastor Reuben, John Isiaye, Alex Preye, Frank Ibigone, and Pius Wareyai, the "military" leaders thus contested Henry Okah's legitimacy to defend their interests in Abuja. They described him as an arrogant "paper general without a battalion": he did not live in the creeks, did not command men, and was definitely not in a position to negotiate a surrender.[8]

In retrospect, the failures of the amnesty seemed predictable. No official texts had been drafted to stipulate the terms of the demobilization, disarmament, and reintegration of the rebels. The lack of transparency of the process paved the way for manipulation and disputes. From a legal perspective, moreover, the amnesty pardoned individuals who had never been the subject of legal proceedings. Unilaterally decreed by the federal government, it was not voted in parliament and did not result from an agreement negotiated with the rebels. Nor were the Niger Delta communities consulted or involved in identifying the "militants" and locating their bases (Aghedo 2013: 276, Okorie 2018: 62). The generous compensation paid to the rebels also left much room

---

8 *Sunday Vanguard* 22 Nov. 2009. Lagos: 7.

for embezzlement. Over time, the amnesty budget went out of control. The government had initially announced funding of $145 million in 2009. Thanks to increasing revenues derived from the resumption of oil production, however, the program ended up costing $1.68 billion in five years. In 2017, its budget tripled again and exceeded $180 million, a quarter of the police payroll and three times the capital expenditure of the Nigeria Rural Electrification Agency (SDN 2021: 4). In total, the rehabilitation of Niger Delta militants ranked among the most expensive demobilization operations in the world (Nextier 2020: 4, Aghedo 2013: 274, Nwajiaku-Dahou 2014, Ebiede, Langer & Tosun 2020).

The interference of corrupt and mafia-like politicians did little to help in this regard. The Minister of Interior Godwin Abbe, a man from Edo State and a retired general, was the first to put in place the presidential amnesty program from July 2009 onward. But most of his successors were Ijaw politicians who were accused of mismanagement and taken to court. For example, Timi Alaibe attempted to use the resources of the presidential amnesty program to support his electoral campaign against the Bayelsa governor Timipre Sylva, until he had to resign from his position in December 2010. Originally from Ondo and a former spokesman of IYC, Kingsley Kuku, who succeeded him in January 2011, was then accused of embezzling funds and forced to go into exile to escape the charges brought by the federal body tasked with fighting corruption. Heading up the amnesty program between March 2015 and March 2018, General Paul Boroh was subsequently dismissed and arrested by the EFCC (Economic and Financial Crimes Commission) following the discovery of $9 million in cash at his home in Abuja. Appointed in April 2018, Charles Dokubo, a professor from Rivers, was also suspended for misappropriation in February 2020 and replaced by an interim committee.

The presidential amnesty program thus gave the impression of being just another institution designed for the misappropriation of oil revenues. In an interview, Charles Dokubo admitted it himself as he described the various mechanisms used to divert government subsidies (*Amnesty News* 2019: 25–29). For instance, employees of the amnesty program secured funds for their own children rather than for former MEND fighters. Local subcontractors were also awarded contracts that they failed to perform despite pocketing the 15% advance provided in invitations to tender. As for the allowances earmarked for demobilized fighters, they did not always reach their intended recipients because of delays in payment and misappropriations. Initially, the federal government drew up lists with MEND and directly managed the subsidies. However, the procedures changed, and the task was soon entrusted to rebel leaders who had no scruples about taking commissions.

The list of beneficiaries was thus riddled with many names of fake and "ghost" fighters added in 2010 and 2013. The number of individuals supposedly eligible for the program was grossly inflated. In late 2007, a confidential note from the JTF estimated that MEND and its various franchises were barely capable of mobilizing more than 1,800 youth in Bayelsa and Delta states (Sayne 2013: 6). Most of them had no military training and nobody cared to define precisely "militant" according to a capacity to handle a weapon.[9] But in 2009, figures were rounded up and the rebels registered a total of 30,000 beneficiaries: 20,192 in 2009, 6,166 in 2010, and 3,642 in 2013. In Port Harcourt alone, for example, a warlord such as Ateke Tom was hardly able to mobilize 1,000 men to fight; yet he collated some 10,000 names (Eke 2014: 757). As for Ebikabowei Victor-Ben "Boyloaf" in Bayelsa, he understood the amnesty as a kind of compensation and included in the list of beneficiaries people who were not combatants but who had been directly affected by the struggle by being driven out of their villages.[10]

The disarmament procedures were just as dubious. In July 2004, the governor of Rivers, Peter Odili, had already undertaken to buy back the rebels' weapons at higher prices than on the black market, with old rifles reaching ₦250,000 (₦ is the symbol for Nigerian currency, the naira) instead of ₦125,000 when purchased new from traffickers (Aghedo 2013: 27). His policy thus served to increase the resellers' profit margins. In December 2007, his counterpart in Bayelsa, Timipre Sylva, also launched his own disarmament program in return for the payment of subsidies to the rebels. However, both initiatives failed to put an end to the violence and arms trafficking. For example, just 3,000 weapons were recovered in Rivers. In June 2009, the federal government therefore decided to proceed differently: instead of trying to buy illegal weapons, it set about funding social aid to fighters who agreed to lay down their arms and undergo professional training. As a first step, the rebels were registered in Obubra Camp in Cross River State. Yet they were not to receive any financial compensation when they handed over firearms that were officially destroyed in May 2011 in the barracks of the Nigerian army's 82nd Division in Enugu.

In the absence of independent verification, it is difficult to establish how many weapons were really recovered. Different sources reported figures ranging between 2,700 and 214,000 units, most of them coming from Bayelsa and Rivers (Nwokolo & Aghedo 2018, Oluduro 2012). What we do know, however,

---

9   In late 2009, independent sources mentioned 26,361 "militants", nearly double the number of applicants (15,260) officially recorded by the authorities for demobilization (Etekpe 2012: 100).

10   Interview with the author in Abuja in November 2021.

is that heavy weapons continued to circulate in the Niger Delta. The young "militants" still had the means to purchase them as they got richer and closer to corrupt military officers involved in arms trafficking. It is thus likely that the amnesty program actually served to facilitate the procurement of weapons, especially through the Nigerian army and President Goodluck Jonathan's national security adviser, General Owoye Andrew Azazi, an Ijaw (Nwajiaku 2010: 21, Sahara Reporters 2010).

The results were no better on the social front. According to various sources, between 11,000 and 27,000 of the 30,000 demobilized fighters benefited from professional training courses during the period 2010–2020 (Nwokolo & Aghedo 2018, *Amnesty News* 2019: 25–29). Once again, however, reliable figures have been hard to come by. Despite the fees paid to a wide range of consultants, the matter long remained shrouded in secrecy. It was only in 2019 that the heads of the amnesty program put in place an evaluation committee tasked with assessing their work. In the meantime, some "militants" traveled abroad to study while others attended training centers dedicated to maritime professions in Oboama (Rivers), basic skills in Kaiama (Bayelsa), electricity in Bomadi (Delta), the oil industry in Agadagba-Obon (Ondo), and agriculture in Gelegele (Edo).

However, these training courses were no guarantee that former fighters would find work. Furthermore, the allowances paid to them, amounting to ₦65,000 per month, were nearly four times higher than the minimum wage, thus discouraging young "militants" from seeking employment. The amnesty remuneration system acted instead as an incentive for former fighters to resort to threats to continue receiving subsidies. Some organized street demonstrations and blocked roads, while others went back to sabotaging pipelines when the government considered suspending or reducing their allowances. For instance, the attack in Abuja on 1 October 2010 was reportedly carried out to "punish" President Goodluck Jonathan for considering an end date to the amnesty program. In the same vein, a new armed group, the Niger Delta Avengers, emerged in February 2016 to call for an extension of the payments granted to rebels. Their first act was to attack a Shell pipeline to interrupt crude oil exports from the Forcados terminal. The sabotage was very professional, because some of the militants had received underwater welding training under the amnesty program![11]

---

11   In the same vein, some beneficiaries of the program who got a job as sailors helped pirates attacking their boat at sea (Ebiede, Langer & Tosun 2020: 13, Jacobsen 2022: 24).

In short, the amnesty did not solve the underlying security problems. Thefts of crude oil and kidnappings continued after 2009. Incidents of pipeline sabotage even rose again from 2015 onward. Also, the beneficiaries of the amnesty still settled their scores with Kalashnikovs.[12] In practice, they continued to exercise a kind of military right of veto over the pursuit of oil and gas extraction. The boundaries between militancy and crime thus became more blurred. Unlike "social bandits" such as Asari Dokubo, who first plundered the Niger Delta to fund his struggle, before enriching himself, "traffickers" such as Henry Okah, Tom Polo, and Ateke Tom combined business and politics from the outset, while "pirates" used the crisis to justify their predatory activities.

References

Adeniyi, Olusegun. 2017. *Against the Run of Play*. Lagos: Kachifo Ltd.

Aghedo, Iro. 2013. "Winning the War, Losing the Peace: Amnesty and the Challenges of Post-Conflict Peace-Building in the Niger Delta, Nigeria". *Journal of Asian and African Studies* 48 (3): 265–278.

Amnesty News 1 (3), December 2019. Abuja.

Anifowose, Babatunde, Damian Lawler, Dan van der Horst & Lee Chapman. 2012. "Attacks on Oil Transport Pipelines in Nigeria: A Quantitative Exploration and Possible Explanation of Observed Patterns". *Applied Geography* 32 (2): 636–651.

Asuni, Judith Burdin. 2009a. *Blood Oil in the Niger Delta*. Washington DC: United States Institute of Peace.

Asuni, Judith Burdin. 2009b. *Understanding the Armed Groups of the Niger Delta*. New York: Council on Foreign Relations.

Bahadur, Jay. 2012. *The Pirates of Somalia: Inside their Hidden World*. London: Profile Books.

Collier, Paul. 2000. "Rebellion as a Quasi-Criminal Activity". *Journal of Conflict Resolution* 44: 839–853.

Collier, Paul & Pedro Vicente. 2009. *Votes and Violence: Evidence from a Field Experiment in Nigeria*. Oxford: Oxford University.

Courson, Elias & Michael Odijie. 2020. "Egbesu: An African Just War Philosophy and Practice". *Journal of African Cultural Studies* 32 (4): 493–508.

Eberlein, Ruben. 2005. *On the Road to the State's Perdition? Authority and Sovereignty in the Nigerian Niger Delta*. Leipzig University: Institute of African Studies.

---

12   For example, in Bayelsa State in December 2020 and January 2021, the home of one of the former MEND commanders, Eris Paul "Ogunboss", was bombed by militants who accused him of misappropriating federal government funds.

Ebiede, Tarila Marclint, Arnim Langer & Jale Tosun. 2020. "Disarmament, Demobilisation, and Reintegration: Analysing the Outcomes of Nigeria's Post-Amnesty Programme". *Stability: International Journal of Security & Development* 9 (1): 1–17.

Eke, Surulola James. 2014. "No Pay, No Peace: Political Settlement and Post-Amnesty Violence in the Niger Delta, Nigeria". *Journal of Asian and African Studies* 50 (6): 750–764.

Etekpe, Ambily. 2012. "Peace and Development in Nigeria: The Amnesty Experience in the Niger Delta of Nigeria". *Journal of Law and Conflict Resolution* 4 (6): 94–102.

Etim, Tony Ita. 11 May 2007. "Niger Delta—Militants Disagree, Expose Kidnappers". Lagos: *Daily Champion*.

Hazen, Jennifer. 2010. "From Social Movement to Armed Group: A Case Study from Nigeria". In *Armed Groups and Contemporary Conflicts: Challenging the Weberian State*, edited by Keith Krause: 80–99. London: Routledge.

Hazen, Jennifer & Jonas Horner. 2008. *Small Arms, Armed Violence, and Insecurity in Nigeria: The Niger Delta in Perspective*. Geneva: Graduate Institute of International Studies.

Iwilade, Akin. 2014. "Networks of Violence and Becoming: Youth and the Politics of Patronage in Nigeria's Oil-Rich Delta". *The Journal of Modern African Studies* 52 (4): 571–595.

Jacobsen, Katja Lindskov. 2022. *Pirates of the Niger Delta: Between Brown and Blue Waters*. Vienna: UNODC (United Nations Office on Drugs and Crime).

Lenning, Emily & Sara Brightman. 2009. "Oil, Rape and State Crime in Nigeria", *Critical Criminology* 17 (1): 35–48.

Nextier. 2020. *Report on the Assessment of the Presidential Amnesty Programme*. Abuja: Nextier SPD (Security, Peace and Development).

Nwajiaku, Kathryn. 2010. *The Politics of Amnesty in the Delta Niger: Challenges Ahead*. Paris, IFRI.

Nwajiaku-Dahou, Kathryn. 2014. *The Niger Delta Amnesty: Lessons Four Years on*. Abuja: NSRP.

Nwokolo, Ndubuisi & Iro Aghedo. 2018. "Consolidating or Corrupting the Peace? The Power Elite and Amnesty Policy in the Niger Delta Region of Nigeria". *Chinese Political Science Review* 3: 322–344.

Obasanjo, Olusegun. 2014. *My Watch, vol. 2: Political and Public Affairs*. Lagos: Kachifo.

Okorie, Mitterand. 2018. "Presidential Amnesty and Resource Control Militancy in a Petro-State". In *The Unfinished Revolution in Nigeria's Niger Delta: Prospects for Socio-Economic and Environmental Justice and Peace*, edited by Cyril Obi & Temitope Oriola: 60–75. London: Routledge.

Oluduro, Olubayo & Olubisi. 2012. "Nigeria: In Search of Sustainable Peace in the Niger Delta through the Amnesty Programme". *Journal of Sustainable Development* 5 (7): 48–61.

Omotola, Shola. 2009. "Dissent and State Excesses in the Niger Delta, Nigeria". *Studies in Conflict and Terrorism* 32 (2): 129–145.

Oriola, Temitope. 2012. "The Delta Creeks, Women's Engagement, and Nigeria's Oil Insurgency". *British Journal of Criminology* 52 (3): 534–555.

Oriola, Temitope. 2013. *Criminal Resistance? The Politics of Kidnapping Oil Workers.* Farnham: Ashgate.

Oriola, Temitope, Kelvin Haggerty & Andy Knight. 2013. "Car Bombing 'with Due Respect': The Niger Delta Insurgency and the Idea Called MEND". *African Security* 6 (1): 67–96.

Oyefusi, Aderoju. 2007. *Oil and Propensity to Armed Struggle in the Niger Delta Region of Nigeria.* New York: World Bank, Policy Research Working Paper no. 4194.

Peel, Michael. 2009. *A Swamp Full of Dollars: Pipelines and Paramilitaries at Nigeria's Oil Frontier.* London: IB Tauris.

Pérouse de Montclos, Marc-Antoine. 2012. "Piracy in Nigeria: Old Wine in New Bottles?". *Studies in Conflict and Terrorism* 35 (7): 531–541.

Sahara Reporters. 2010. "Secret Army Report Implicates NSA Azazi, Ibori, Alamieyeseigha, Henry and Sunny Okah in Sale of Military Weapons to Niger Delta Militants". https://saharareporters.com/2010/10/30/secret-army-report-imp licates-nsa-azazi-ibori-alamieyeseigha-henry-and-sunny-okah-sale (accessed 18 January 2018).

Sayne, Aaron. 2013. *What Next for Security in the Niger Delta?* Washington DC: United States Institute of Peace.

SDN. 2021. *Nigeria's Presidential Amnesty Programme:Untangling the Dependencies That Prevent It Ending.* Port Harcourt: Stakeholder Democracy Network.

Ukeje, Charles. 2004. "From Aba to Ugborodo: Gender Identity and Alternative Discourse of Social Protest among Women in the Oil Delta of Nigeria", *Oxford Development Studies* 32 (4): 605–617.

Ukiwo, Ukoha. 2007. "From 'Pirates' to 'Militants': A Historical Perspective on Anti-State and Anti-Oil Company Mobilization among the Ijaw of Warri, Western Niger Delta". *African Affairs* 106 (425): 587–610.

Watts, Michael. 2007. "Petro-Insurgency or Criminal Syndicate?" *Review of African Political Economy* 34 (114): 637–660.

The Gangster and the Godfather

Ordinary Crime and Amnesty in a "Democracy" (2010–2020)

I am traveling with a French television crew shooting a documentary film about oil conflicts in the Niger Delta. We have retreated to the anonymity of a hotel room in Warri to speak over the phone to John Togo, one of the last rebels who refused to join the amnesty process. The line is bad, the conversation is broken, and I am struggling to understand pidgin. Togo is threatening to attack oil companies yet again. After many twists and turns, our television crew can eventually film him in his Gbaramatu hideout in Delta State. With a huge scar across his cheek, John Togo has the right face for the job. He was to be killed a few months later by the army.

It is early 2011. In Abuja, Goodluck Jonathan has succeeded President Umaru Yar'Adua, who died of ill health, and he is about to be elected under the banner of the PDP (People's Democratic Party), the party in power since the end of the military dictatorship in 1999. It is the first time that a Niger Delta Ijaw is to head up Africa's most populous country. Some are hopeful that his election will help reduce tensions in oil-producing areas. Even the last rebels who rejected the amnesty claim to like him. As John Togo said in pidgin during an interview granted to our TV crew: "I will support my blood and I will cast my vote on Goodluck Jonathan".[1]

1 An Ijaw President: Goodluck Jonathan (2010–2015)

However, the conflicting expectations of the insurgents and oil companies were not to be met. The son of a modest family of fishermen from Bayelsa State, as he liked to portray himself, Goodluck Jonathan came to power by accident, as befits his name.[2] In practice, he benefited from a fortunate chain of circumstances to climb the political ladder. He started out with the honorific position of Deputy Governor of Bayelsa before succeeding the incumbent,

---

1 Entitled *Delta du Niger: la guerre du brut*, this 52-minute documentary was first broadcast on the French TV channel France 5 on 11 October 2011.

2 Before him, another Ijaw from Bayelsa State, Christopher "Pere" Ajuwa (1941–2017), had already stood unsuccessfully in the 1993, 2003, and 2007 presidential elections.

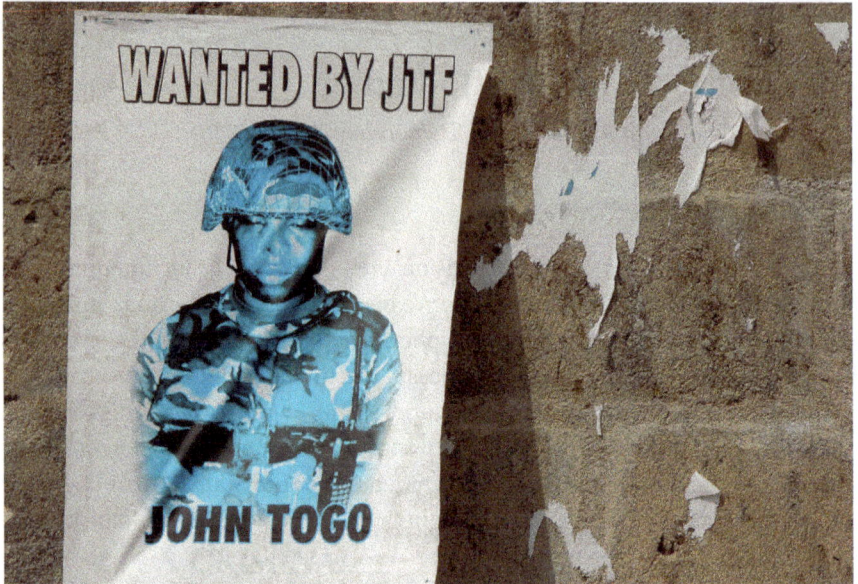

FIGURE 19   The red notice of John Togo in Yenagoa, Bayelsa State (2011)

Diepreye Alamieyeseigha, when the latter was arrested in London and jailed in Nigeria for money laundering in 2005. At the time, the sitting president since 1999, Olusegun Obasanjo, was maneuvering to amend the constitution and earn the right to stand for a third term. But he failed to get his way and was forced to hold an election in 2007. To be able to continue playing a leading role in politics, he therefore supported Umaru Yar'Adua and Goodluck Jonathan, respectively governors of Katsina and Bayelsa states, to be elected as president and vice-president under the banner of the PDP.

Obasanjo assumed that the two men would be easy to manipulate given their lack of support and network at the national level. Both were of rural origins and had governed vassal states carved out on the territory of more powerful regions—namely, Kaduna and Rivers (Bolaji 2017: 59). Goodluck Jonathan in particular was not a leading figure in the Niger Delta. A professor of zoology at the University of Port Harcourt, he came from an Ijaw minority in the Bayelsa hinterland, the Ogbia, who spoke a dialect that the Kalabari from the coast did not understand. Moreover, he was widely seen as a stooge who had entered politics in 1999 at the instigation of his mentor Albert Horsfall, a former senior official in the intelligence services of Ibrahim Babangida and subsequently the director of a federal agency, OMPADEC (Oil Mineral Producing

Area Development Commission), under the dictatorship of General Sani Abacha.

In the Niger Delta, the outgoing governor of Rivers State, Peter Odili, was far more influential, powerful, and ambitious than Goodluck Jonathan. He posed a greater threat to Obasanjo because he had the money and the connections to fund the PDP's campaign in the hope of being nominated to stand in the 2007 presidential elections. However, his rising power was a cause for concern to many people. Odili was involved in various shady affairs and, within the PDP, rivals took this opportunity to get rid of him on allegations of corruption. The outgoing governor of Rivers State acknowledged in his autobiography that he chose to abandon his presidential ambitions in return for his opponents dropping their case against him (Odili 2012). In both Abuja and Port Harcourt, Odili was also seen as unreliable since he was thought to have been first elected in 1999 after betraying his mentor, Rufus Ada George. In 2007, Obasanjo therefore transferred his support to Goodluck Jonathan. His aim in doing so was to make the task easier for Yar'Adua and to avoid the agonies that had marred his second term when his own vice-president, Atiku Abubakar, had moved over to the opposition.

Goodluck Jonathan initially held up his end of the bargain. At the 2007 elections, he brought the Niger Delta votes to the PDP. With the 2009 amnesty, his Ijaw background also appeared to be an asset in helping to maintain a fragile peace in the oil-producing areas. Although contested even in his homeland in Bayelsa, Jonathan benefited from a state of grace and maneuvered to co-opt the local elite. At the beginning, his strategy proved fruitful and was reminiscent of the tactics used by Obasanjo, a Yoruba who had successfully contained the secessionist threat posed by the OPC (Oodua Peoples Congress), an ethnic militia, despite the lack of support in the southwestern Yoruba strongholds during his first election in 1999 (Nwajiaku 2010: 28).

Over time, however, Goodluck Jonathan came to be seen as a puppet under the control of Yar'Adua and northern Muslims in Abuja. Criticisms from Niger Delta militants quickly surfaced. Henry Okah, one of MEND's leaders, found him "timid, cowardly [...] and unintelligible, revealing a lack of intellectual depth". Chief Edwin Clark, a mediator and a Niger Delta veteran, also held Goodluck Jonathan in low regard. "He is a decrepit man, one of those people who parade themselves in oil companies pretending to have control over militants" (Abidde 2017: 94–95). A former NDPVF commander who joined MEND, Ebikabowei Victor-Ben, a.k.a. "General Boyloaf", did not mince his words either, describing Goodluck Jonathan as:

FIGURE 20   Goodluck Jonathan during his electoral campaign (2011)

a glorified federal house-boy. He is not somebody who is part of this struggle. He is just opportuned (sic) to be here. They know that the man will betray us, that is why they kept him there […] in Aso Villa, just as an observer, a flower to decorate the place, a yes member, he doesn't have any say. So that guy is one of the biggest problems we have, in fact, he is the biggest problem we have in Niger Delta now, that is the truth.[3]

Yar'Adua's death in 2010 and Jonathan's election in 2011 made little difference. The new president in Abuja continued to be castigated as a clumsy and incompetent onlooker, a second-rate operator who was not up to the task of developing Africa's most populous country and containing Boko Haram's jihadist rebellion in the northeast. Even Oronto Douglas, one of his closest advisers, privately admitted that Jonathan was already incompetent when he governed Bayelsa State after succeeding Diepreye Alamieyeseigha in 2005.[4] His wife did not help in this matter. She was reputed to be highly corrupt and contributed to the downfall of her husband by confronting key figures in the Niger Delta,

---

3   Amai 2008. See also Sunday Vanguard 1 June 2008. Lagos: 9, 18.

4   https://wikileaks.org/plusd/cables/07LAGOS3_a.html.

for instance in Okrika, her home community, where she publicly humiliated the governor of Rivers, Rotimi Amaechi, during an official visit in the outskirts of Port Harcourt.

During his term as president, Goodluck Jonathan thus saw his political base fade away. Confirming the adage that your best friends are often your worst enemies, much of the revolt came from the Niger Delta. Faced with a threat of impeachment, Rotimi Amaechi drove the rebellion. Aside from his personal dislike of Goodluck Jonathan's wife, he resented the fact that Abuja had deprived Rivers of wealthy territories. Following arbitrations by the federal government, 46 oil wells were transferred to neighboring Abia State, while Bayelsa State recovered five major deposits, including the Soku field operated by Shell (Adeniyi 2017). According to Amaechi, this redrawing of administrative boundaries was designed to restrain his political ambitions and weaken him by depriving him of revenue. As evidence of this, Abuja also sought to dismiss him from the Governors' Forum, a highly influential cross-party group that he had chaired since 2011 (Lalude 2014).

Now publicly opposed to a second term for Jonathan in the lead-up to the 2015 elections, Amaechi left the PDP to join northern Muslim dissenters who, under Muhammadu Buhari, formed a coalition in 2013, the APC (All Progressives Congress), with the Yoruba in the southwest. This platform helped build alliances on a broader basis at the national level. Even if local supporters were still influenced by cronyism, the APC's strategy was more inclusive than the PDP's ethno-regionalist's approach (LeVan 2019: 2). Goodluck Jonathan was now isolated. He had lost the support of Olusegun Obasanjo and was unable to contain the hemorrhage from the PDP to the APC, despite forcing Amaechi to stand down out as chairman of the Governors' Forum. Jonathan was also suffering from his poor image as a corrupt and increasingly impotent politician, while the Boko Haram insurgency expanded and carried out attacks in Abuja. To his credit, however, he stands as one of the few African presidents to have publicly acknowledged his electoral defeat and to have agreed to stand down without objection, losing to Muhammadu Buhari. Even militants in the Niger Delta made no effort to contest the results and oppose the departure of a president viewed by many as a kind of traitor.

2   Muhammadu Buhari, or the Dashed Hopes of a Democratic Transition (2015–2020)

In 2011, Goodluck Jonathan had been the first Ijaw to be elected to lead the most populous country in Africa. Under the banner of the APC, the election of Muhammadu Buhari in 2015 was another first, albeit of a different kind. Never before had the opposition secured a win at the ballot box at the national level. It was also the first time that Nigeria experienced a change of government other than through a political assassination or a coup. As in 2011, there was every reason to be hopeful. Although the Niger Delta remained under the control of PDP governors, President Muhammadu Buhari was elected to fight corruption and work toward Nigeria's economic development, giving the impression that, at last, he would be the right person to reform the governance of a country ravaged by nepotism, cronyism, and the misappropriation of oil revenues.

The illusion was short-lived. A northern Muslim and a former military dictator in power in 1984–1985, Muhammadu Buhari initially attempted to put an end to the financial aberrations associated with the 2009 amnesty. However, he was soon challenged by a new wave of pipeline sabotage that forced him to heed the rebels' demands and consider extending their allowances. Nigeria's new strongman needed oil revenues just as much as his predecessors had done, and he eventually yielded by agreeing to engage in negotiations that had virtually no chance of leading to a lasting solution without a deep reform of political governance. Abuja therefore continued to provide subsidies or contracts to activists who, in the case of many of them, existed only on paper, not

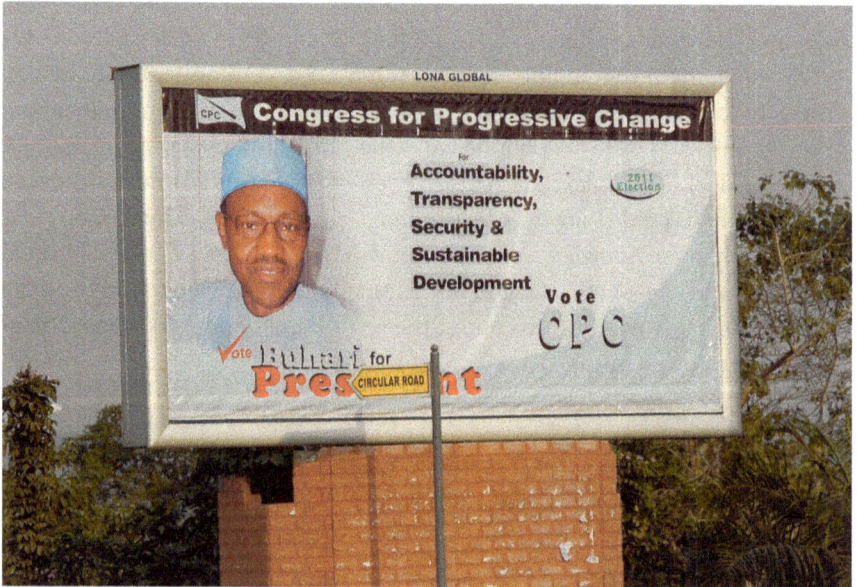

FIGURE 21   Muhammadu Buhari during his electoral campaign (2011)

to mention those who refused amnesty, such as Asari Dokubo, or who were killed by the army, such as John Togo (SDN 2021: 5).

Peace in the Niger Delta remained fragile and precarious, although the situation was by no means comparable to the chaos experienced between 2005 and 2007. The armed groups that emerged after MEND were often small and short-lived, and they contributed to further fragmenting the insurgency. No single faction was able to form a regional coalition and there was a sense of fatigue among the rebels. Following the collapse of crude prices in 2015, Muhammadu Buhari's re-election in 2019, and the coronavirus crisis in 2020, many militants seemed to be waiting for the next president to resume the hostilities and negotiate a greater proportion of revenues from oil and gas production.

Meanwhile, crime and bunkering continued unabated. The former MEND leaders got rich through fraudulent business schemes, and their success encouraged a new generation of pseudo-militants to threaten to resort to violence and, sometimes, take up arms to secure their share of the oil wealth and indefinitely extend negotiations over the payment of reintegration allowances. The military also appeared to be satisfied with this fragile status quo and did not want a long-lasting peace that would have forced them to withdraw and lose significant revenue. The JTF (Joint Task Force), which essentially combined the army and the police, benefited from a dedicated budget and was granted regular subsidies from the secret funds held by the region's governors, an "official slush fund" known as the "security vote". In addition, corrupt officers received kickbacks from bunkering activities in exchange for protecting the extraction and the transportation of stolen oil shipments. Some went as far as to provide weapons to their "partners" or to directly oversee their own tapping points along pipelines, while others resold the fuel they seized or escorted the thieves to avoid consignments being stopped by other security operatives (Bish *et al.* 2022: 36, Pérouse de Montclos 2021).

3   The Business of Amnesty

In short, the 2009 amnesty solved nothing. Like the international oil companies, the federal government was under the illusion that money could buy anything, including social peace. In 2009, its disarmament program was designed to meet short-term objectives and achieve some form of respite to facilitate a rapid resumption of oil and gas production (Molly 2011). The authorities focused on the security of the extractive industry rather than on the region's human development. The presidential amnesty program was not conceived to drive long-term political solutions. Instead, the federal government opted to broaden the JTF's mandate to include the fight against kidnapping, bunkering, and organized crime, thereby justifying the continued deployment of the armed forces. No plans were made for reforming the region's governance and facilitating the resolution of communal micro-conflicts that continued to fuel the rebellion.

Even if they were designed to support peace, development efforts had little impact given the scale of embezzlement. Initiatives on the ground seldom achieved anything and were not integrated into the public policies of government institutions at a regional or federal level, such as through the Ministry of Niger Delta or the Niger Delta Development Commission (NDDC). Programs that aimed at reintegrating MEND fighters were also developed in isolation from the oil multinationals and their corporate social responsibility, although their initial goal was not to reduce unemployment so much as to satisfy the rebels to ensure that they would not be tempted to take up arms and interrupt production again.

In practice, the amnesty process consisted in awarding official positions and lucrative contracts to the insurgents. After placing his war booty in an Islamic foundation that he set up in the neighboring Republic of Benin, for example, Asari Dokubo got a job in the Nigerian pilgrimage agency and developed its private security business with companies such as Boro Security & Telecommunications, Sylvia Security, and Riverbend Security (ICG 2006: 10). Meanwhile, his rival, Ateke Tom, became a traditional chief in Okrika Island and invested in Nollywood, the Nigerian film industry—a bit like Ganiyu Adams, the leader of the OPC militia who, in return for surrendering in Lagos in 2001, was granted an honorific title and organized beauty contests to promote Yoruba culture. As for Ebikabowei Victor-Ben, the federal government gave him a villa in Abuja, while the company he set up in 2010, Bensam Maritime Oil & Gas Ltd, secured contracts with Shell and Chevron. His nickname, "Boyloaf" ("the boy who loves bread"), speaks volumes about his greed and was given by his schoolmates because of his reputation for gluttony.

In Delta State, the MEND's leader, Government Ekpemupolo, a.k.a. "Tom Polo", also benefited from the generosity of the 2009 amnesty. He managed a small logistics company before becoming a guerrilla fighter. He then fought in the creeks while his father continued to do business with oil companies between 2005 and 2008. In 2009, the amnesty provided him with an opportunity to move up market. The company that he established took a 6% stake in a pool of Polish investors keen to finance a consortium, Neconde, to purchase the OML (Oil Mining Lease) 42 sold by Shell in Gbaramatu for $700 million in 2011.

With the amnesty, former rebellion leaders were also able to diversify their economic interests. For example, Soboma George was awarded the management of one of Port Harcourt's most frequently used gas stations. Others founded private security companies to protect pipelines. Tom Polo secured the highest bid with a contract worth $22.9 million, against $9 for Asari Dokubo and $3.8 each for Ebikabowei Victor-Ben and Ateke Tom (Eke 2014, Oriola, Haggerty & Knight 2013, Adibe, Nwagwu & Albert 2018). In addition, his company, Global West Vessel Specialists Nigeria Limited (GWVSNL), was awarded ₦16 billion in 2011 from the Nigeria Maritime Administration and Safety Agency (NIMASA) to patrol the coastal waters from Calabar to Lagos. In some cases, the commercial prospects were so attractive that they helped reconcile former enemies. For instance, to secure a contract worth ₦5 billion from NNPC in 2012, rival warlords from Rivers launched a private security company named ADEF, the letters standing for Ateke Tom, Dokubo Asari, "Egberipapa" (the nom de guerre of Sobomabo Jackrich), and Farah Dagogo (The Hard Truth 2012).

By entrusting pirates with the task of protecting the pipelines that they used to plunder, the amnesty process thus contributed to institutionalizing crime. Warlords and gang leaders became businessmen. In Port Harcourt, Ateke Tom built his own "private pipeline" to steal refined oil from the neighboring Eleme refinery. In Brass (Bayelsa State), Agip was forced to install a loading point 25 kilometers from the coast to provide militants with unfettered access to their "share" to ensure that they would not blow up the company's pipelines onshore.[5] The system consolidated the impunity of bandits to such an extent that, in Delta State, car thieves were surprised to find themselves arrested by the police despite having benefited from the demobilization programs (Okocha 2010).

Activists opposed to armed struggle were quite ambiguous in this respect. As the head of a "technical" committee tasked by Abuja with finding solutions to the crisis, the president of MOSOP, Ledum Mitee (2008), recommended in 2008 that Henry Okah be released on bail and that an amnesty be granted to all militants willing to lay down their arms. However, he did not specify how the federal government should deal with criminals engaged in both fighting and oil or arms trafficking. As for the authorities, they ignored the rule of law and chose to close their eyes to the dubious activities of demobilized militants. They assumed that such a system would help to avert a resumption of hostilities and another drop in oil production. They knew that the crisis could not be solved by use of force and so did not reckon on an unlikely return to war. On the

---

5 Anonymous interviews with oil subcontractors conducted in Lagos in February 2014.

contrary, both the federal government and oil companies seemed prepared to tolerate an "acceptable level" of bunkering, which according to experts should not exceed 10% of production to avoid an excessive loss of revenue that might compel the authorities and the industry to request a major military intervention (Nyheim, Zandvliet & Morrissey 2003: 63).

4 The Institutionalization of Crime

Throughout the terms of presidents Goodluck Jonathan and Muhammadu Buhari, the co-optation of the rebels by means of public contracts and promotions within government agencies thus revealed the deep collusion between insurgents and officials. From 2009 onward, the amnesty had the effect of entrenching the corrupt political system that Nigerians ironically call "godfatherism", a neologism derived from Francis Ford Coppola's film *The Godfather* (Albert 2005). The integration of protestors in government institutions, however, was not a new phenomenon. As soon as 1974 in present-day Delta State, called Bendel at the time, an Isoko, Francis Okpozio, had, for example, begun to organize demonstrations against Shell. His group blocked access roads to the wells, seized seismographic equipment, and detained several oil workers for a few hours. Francis Okpozio then stopped disrupting public order when he was elected to the Bendel State Assembly in 1979. Later on, he even lent his full support to the authorities and took part in the semblance of constitutional conference held by Sani Abacha's dictatorship in 1994 (Omoweh 2007: 234–235).

The difference in the 2009 amnesty had more to do with the number of young "militants" integrated into official bodies as they continued to attend to their criminal activities. For example, despite kidnapping four US citizens working for a Chevron subcontractor (Global Services) in 2007, the leader of the Niger Delta Freedom Fighters (NDFF), Henry Bindodogha, was appointed special adviser to the governor of Edo, with the task of restoring security in the creeks, while one of his lieutenants, Ezekiel Apesibiri, continued the struggle (Oriola 2013: 39, 95). As for Tom Polo's associate, Patrick Ziakede Akpobolokemi, he became director of NIMASA (Nigerian Maritime Administration and Safety Agency). In Delta State, Kelvin Ibruvwe was in fact one of the few gang leaders to be excluded from the amnesty. Specialized in kidnapping, he founded in 2013 a short-lived LIMUP (Liberation Movement of the Urhobo People) in Kokori, a village to the northeast of Warri, but he was arrested shortly afterward (Oyewole 2018: 35).

Delta State is a textbook case of the system of co-optation of young "militants" getting older and wealthy. For example, George Timinimi was a spokesman for the FNDIC (Federated Niger Delta Ijaw Communities) ... and a former vice-chairman of the Warri South-West Local Government Council. In 2003, he granted asylum to Asari Dokubo, who fled attacks by his rival Ateke Tom in Port Harcourt (Dokubo 2018). George Timinimi subsequently fell out with Tom Polo and MEND. In 2008, a year before the amnesty, he joined the Delta State government as special adviser for Ijaw affairs and, later, commissioner for water resources. In 2015, he was number two on the PDP list that saw Ifeanyi Okowa elected governor. To secure a better position, he subsequently transferred his allegiance to the APC after President Muhammadu Buhari came to power in Abuja.

In fact, Goodluck Jonathan's departure in 2015 did nothing to change the system. Initially, President Muhammadu Buhari and his party, the APC, briefly considered putting an end to the amnesty program. Tom Polo again went on the run after refusing to turn himself in to answer numerous allegations of fraud. As for his deputy Patrick Ziakede Akpobolokemi, he was accused of embezzlement and dismissed from his position at the NIMASA. The government also terminated security contracts entered into by NNPC with ADEF, the consortium of warlords led by Asari Dokubo and Bajeros, a small company (Akinadewo 2015). Operational problems played a role too. In late 2012, the blatant amateurism of local private security companies and their inability to combat piracy resulted in the authorities ending their partnership with Tom Polo and abandoning a program, the so-called OFSL (Oil Facilities Surveillance Limited), that aimed at employing demobilized militants to supervise pipelines (Uguru 2013).

Nonetheless, Niger Delta governors remained loyal to the PDP and continued to protect the rebels. In Rivers, for example, four militants from MEND and Ateke Tom's militia—Victor Dabotorudima Adams, Abiye Abaku Farah Dagogo, Adoki Tonye Smart, and Chisom Promise Dike—were elected to the State Assembly in 2015. Ezenwo Nyesom Wike, a former commissioner for education under Rotimi Amaechi, also became PDP governor in Port Harcourt thanks to the support of former fighters such as Ateke Tom, Sobomabo Jackrich "Egberipapa", and Solomon Ndigbara, a.k.a. "Osama bin Laden" (Akasike 2014, Ibanga 2015). In the same vein, Asari Dokubo's sister, Boma Goodhead, was elected twice to the National Assembly, in 2015 and 2019, where she represented Akuku-Toru. After being elected to the Rivers State Assembly in 2015, Farah Dagogo also made it to Abuja in 2019, representing the Degema and Bonny constituency.

Delta State followed a similar trajectory. After the 2009 amnesty, the region was dominated by figures close to Tom Polo, whose half-brother, George Ekpemupolo, chaired the Warri South-West Local Government Council in

2008–2011 and again in 2014–2017. His nephew, Julius Gbabojor Pondi, was, for example, elected twice as a member of the House of Representatives for Burutu in 2015 and 2019. Having co-founded the FNDIC, which served as a legal front for MEND, Tom Polo's cousin, Kingsley Burutu Otuaro, also enjoyed a successful career in politics. Appointed special adviser to Governor James Ibori in 2005–2007, he joined his successor Emmanuel Uduaghan on the board of the local development commission (DESOPADEC) in 2011–2014 and was finally elected as the state's deputy governor of Ifeanyi Okowa in 2015 and again in 2019 (SDN 2018). Many other examples could be given. Thomas Ereyitomi, an Itsekiri from Ugborodo on the Escravos River, was a businessman who, like Tom Polo, had initially made his fortune as a Chevron subcontractor between 1986 and 1993. In 1998, he was suspected of involvement in the assassination of Samuel Metseaghanrun, his predecessor at the head of the Ugborodo Community Trust. Nonetheless, between 2004 and 2010, he took the reins of the foundation, which was funded by Chevron and reformed in 2008 (Faleti 2009). Under Governor Emmanuel Uduaghan after 2007, he was appointed as the head of the Delta State Waterways Security Committee and, eventually, elected PDP representative for Warri in 2019.

The dividing line between politics and crime thus became ever more blurred. According to some activists, more than 5% of governors' cabinet positions in Niger Delta states were held by former militants who, in many cases, had a criminal record—or did not, yet should have been tried (Oriola 2013: 28). Members of parliament were also involved in illegal and violent activities, such as Nimi Barigha-Amage, a former Elf engineer from Nembe who founded the Iseinasawo militia in 2000 and was elected senator in Abuja in 2007. As for the "traditional" ruling class, it was seen as unscrupulous, venal, and corrupt, ready to stir up violence and manipulate the rebels to remain in power and negotiate a larger share of oil revenues with Abuja. On the pretext of fighting unemployment, state governors and chairmen of local councils recruited young militiamen and used the so-called security vote on a discretionary basis to eliminate the opposition, rig elections, and circumvent constitutional provisions that prohibited them from creating their own police forces.

The population was not duped. Low voter turnout rates and polling results spoke volumes about the general distrust of the ruling class. For example, in Rivers State, 41% of respondents said that politicians were the first responsible for the proliferation of weapons. In Delta State, 53% laid the blame on local officials, their security personnel, warlords, traditional chiefs, the police, and bunkerers. In Bayelsa, one third of those surveyed also identified politicians as the main suppliers of firearms to gangs operating in the region.[6] This rural state is actually a textbook case of bad governance, as its creeks concealed all kinds of underground activities.

5   Bayelsa and Rivers in Troubled Waters

Bayelsa was ravaged by political violence as soon as Sani Abacha's dictatorship ended (Alapiki 2013). Diepreye Alamieyeseigha, a former military, wanted to become the PDP governor in Yenagoa at any cost. To ensure his victory in the February 1999 elections, he had to secure the eastern constituency, an area which accounted for around 40% of the state's voters. He therefore made a deal with some of the local gangs fighting over oil revenues. In Bayelsa East, he supported the men of one George Fente against a militia known as the "Small Fish" (*Isongu Furo*), which backed the APP (All People's Party) candidate, Jonathan Lionel-Omo. Once elected, Alamieyeseigha then tried to defuse the situation by appointing his rival as commissioner for environment. However, the Bayelsa East constituency was not spared from the fighting. It suffered a dozen casualties when the governor was re-elected in April 2003 and established a virtual one-party regime by buying the support of the nine remaining opposition members in the state assembly in Yenagoa.

After Alamieyeseigha's arrest in London in September 2005, the April 2007 elections were less violent despite the assassination of four PDP leaders. The opposition was wiped out, and the ruling party won all the constituencies. As the election results were contested, the Court of Appeal in Port Harcourt ordered fresh elections, which confirmed Timipre Sylva's victory in May 2008. Like Rotimi Amaechi, his counterpart in Rivers, the latter had been a student at the University of Port Harcourt and was allegedly a member of the Vikings, a gang of cultists. He therefore had little trouble forging links with criminal and rebel groups to negotiate deals in the wake of the June 2009 amnesty. Commanders such as Ebikabowei Victor-Ben ("Boyloaf"), Africanus Ukparasia ("General Africa"), Paul Eris ("General Ogunboss"), Joshua MacIver ("Izon Tukpa"), and Selky Kiley ("General Young Shall Grow") all lived for a while in the governor's residence.

At the same time, Timipre Sylva continued to maintain his predecessors' good relations with Ijaw nationalists. Thanks to him, the first president of IYC

---

6   The surveys were conducted in 2005 among 100 people in Rivers State, 67 in Bayelsa State, and 127 in Asaba, Uvwie, and Warri in Delta State (Nsirimovu 2005: 17, Abayomi *et al.* 2005: 116, Isumonah, Tantua & James 2005: 76).

FIGURE 22   Timipre Sylva, Bayelsa State Governor (2011)

between 1998 and 2001, Felix Tuodola, joined the NDDC before being appointed
state commissioner for culture in 2011.[7] Nengi Ikiba, a former aspirant for the
Bayelsa House of Assembly in the 2011 general elections, was among the few
not to secure a post. A founding member of IYC and, later, the Icelanders—an
armed group set up with Ateke Tom and Soboma George—he had established
his own gang, the Greenlanders, and was eventually arrested for murder in
2013 (Gbemudu 2013). As for Timipre Sylva, he was again challenged, taken to
court, and forced to stand down. He subsequently left the PDP and joined the
party of President Muhammadu Buhari, who appointed him Minister of State
for Petroleum Resources in Abuja in August 2019. Meanwhile, his successor
in Yenagoa from February 2012 onward, Henry Seriake Dickson, continued to
co-opt rebels. In August 2016, he named Joshua MacIver as caretaker chair-
person of Southern Ijaw LGA, the state's largest local government (Oyadongha
2016). In August 2016, he also appointed Africanus Ukparasia to head the
Bayelsa Waterway Security Taskforce, then the Southern Ijaw's Local Council
in February 2019.

---

7   His name is sometimes spelt Tuodolo or Tuodolor.

Rivers, a more populous and urbanized state, was not spared from godfatherism either. Since the end of General Sani Abacha's dictatorship, its political life was marked by violence and collusion between elected representatives, criminal groups, and militants. As in Bayelsa, Governor Peter Odili first sought to secure the support of Ijaw nationalists when he was elected for a first term in 1999. At the IYC elections in 2001, he "sponsored" the candidacy of Asari Dokubo, a Rivers man, against Felix Tuodola, who was backed by Diepreye Alamieyeseigha in Bayelsa. In return, the founder of NDPVF had no scruples in helping the PDP and Odili to win the 2003 election. Despite his opposition to the government, Dokubo thus aimed to consolidate his leadership and finance his armed struggle, as he openly told me when I met him in his hideout in 2004.

In 2003, however, the founder of NDPVF failed in his bid to be re-elected president of IYC. The vote was even called off after descending into a pitched gun battle. The Ijaw leader felt abandoned by his mentor and fell out with Odili, whom he publicly accused of electoral fraud. Now determined to silence his former ally, the governor of Rivers State responded by financing Dokubo's great rival in the outskirts of Port Harcourt, Ateke Tom and his Niger Delta Vigilantes (NDV). The conflict between the two warlords focused on Okrika and the Cawthorne Channel to the south, near the Bonny terminal on the coast. However, the whole of Rivers State was engulfed in political violence at the time. For example, north of Port Harcourt, the chairman of the Etche Local Government, Ephraim Nwuzi, recruited thugs to eliminate his opponents and allegedly killed one of them in June 2006 (Albin-Lackey 2007: 64– 66). Following a brief police investigation, he emerged unscathed, an impunity that characterized the two terms served by Peter Odili until May 2007.

The outgoing governor of Rivers State was himself accused of embezzlement, electoral fraud, and collusion with gangsters. For example, a *New York Times* journalist reported how his collaborators distributed weapons and subsidies to thugs to steal ballots in the April 2003 election with the complicity of the Nigerian police (Schmidle 2009). In March 2009, the Rivers State Truth and Reconciliation Commission, chaired by Judge Samuel Obakayode "Kayode" Eso, also recognized the governor's responsibility in political violence during his two terms (Onoyume 2009). However, the matter went no further. Unlike his counterparts in Delta and Bayelsa states—that is, James Ibori and Diepreye Alamieyeseigha—Peter Odili was never jailed for his misdeeds. Indeed, the former Rivers governor was able to avert numerous attempts to take him to court, thanks to his acquaintances in Abuja and within the PDP, which he largely funded.

Of course, such impunity did little to encourage his successors to reform the governance of the state. Elected under the banner of the PDP in October 2007,

Rotimi Amaechi came from Diobu, a poor neighborhood of Port Harcourt, and was allegedly a member of the Vikings cult society when he was a university student. His connections with organized crime helped him to negotiate directly with armed gangs to secure a fragile peace in Rivers State before the end of his second term in May 2015. Thereafter, his commissioner for education, Ezenwo Nyesom Wike, carried on with the same style of governance when Rotimi Amaechi, now a personal enemy, left the PDP and joined the party of President Muhammadu Buhari, who appointed him Minister for Transports in Abuja. Elected in April 2015, the new governor continued to appoint insurgents to positions within official bodies. In November 2016, he also declared another amnesty, which led to the return of just a thousand firearms, an insignificant figure compared with the 22,430 "militants" who had officially claimed their "pensions" as former fighters (Ebiri & Akenzuwa 2016).

References

Abayomi, Francis *et al.* 2005. "The Proliferation of Small Arms and Light Weapons Survey in Delta State", In *Oiling Violence: The Proliferation of Small Arms and Light Weapons in the Niger Delta*, edited by Okechukwu Ibeanu & Fatima Kyari Mohammed: 101–156. Lagos: Friedrich-Ebert-Stiftung.

Abidde, Sabella Ogbobode. 2017. *Nigeria's Niger Delta: Militancy, Amnesty, and the Post-amnesty Environment*. Lanham (MD): Lexington Books.

Adeniyi, Olusegun. 2017. *Against the Run of Play*. Lagos: Kachifo Ltd.

Adibe, Raymond, Ejikeme Nwagwu & Okorie Albert. 2018. "Rentierism and Security Privatisation in the Nigerian Petroleum Industry: Assessment of Oil Pipeline Surveillance and Protection Contracts". *Review of African Political Economy* 45 (156): 345–353.

Akasike, Chukwudi. 28 May 2014. "Rivers: Knocks, Kudos Greet Wike's Romance with Ex-Militants". Lagos: *The Punch*.

Akinadewo, Gabriel. 18 Aug. 2015. "Pipeline Security: Asari Dokubo, Fasehun, Adams Threaten NNPC". Lagos: *Vanguard*.

Alapiki, Henry. 2013. "Politics, Friends and Foes in Bayelsa State". In *Nigeria's Critical Election, 2011*, edited by John Ayoade & Adeoye Akinsanya: 157–173. Lanham (Md.): Lexington Books.

Albert, Isaac Olawale. 2005. "Explaining 'Godfatherism' in Nigerian Politics". *African Sociological Review* 9 (2): 79–105.

Albin-Lackey, Chris. 2007. *Chop Fine. The Human Rights Impact of Local Government Corruption and Mismanagement in Rivers State, Nigeria*. New York: Human Rights Watch.

Amai, Emma. 31 May 2008. "Inside N-Delta Militants Hideout! I Don't Think There'll Be Peace". Lagos: *Vanguard*.

Bish, Alexandre *et al.* 2022. *The Crime Paradox: Illicit Markets, Violence and Instability in Nigeria*. Geneva: Global Initiative against Transnational Organized Crime.

Bolaji, Mohammed. 2017. *On a Platter of Gold: How Jonathan Won and Lost Nigeria*. Lagos: Kachifo.

Dokubo, Asari. 31 Dec. 2018. "Me, Henry Okah, 'Jomo Gbomo', Judith Asuni and the Niger Delta Insurgency". *Sahara Reporters*.

Ebiri, Kelvin & Owen Akenzuwa. 16 Nov. 2016. "22,430 Militants, Cultists Embrace Amnesty, Surrender Arms in Rivers". Lagos: The Guardian.

Eke, Surulola James. 2014. "No Pay, No Peace: Political Settlement and Post-Amnesty Violence in the Niger Delta, Nigeria". *Journal of Asian and African Studies* 50 (6): 750–764.

Faleti, Stephen. 2009. *Challenges of Chevron's GMOU Implementation in Itsekiri Communities of Western Niger Delta*. Zaria: IFRA.

Gbemudu, Emma. 6 July 2013. "Who is Nengi Ikiba?": 17–18. Lagos: *Saturday Mirror*.

Hard Truth (The). 29 March 2012. Port Harcourt: 2.

Ibanga, Inyene. 15 April 2015. "Ex-Militants among Newly Elected Lawmakers in Rivers Assembly". Abuja: *Premium Times*.

ICG. 2006. *The Swamps of Insurgency: Nigeria's Delta Unrest*. Brussels: International Crisis Group.

Isumonah, Adefemi, Ben Tantua & Nengi James. 2005. "The Proliferation of Small Arms and Light Weapons in Bayelsa State", In *Oiling Violence: The Proliferation of Small Arms and Light Weapons in the Niger Delta*, edited by Okechukwu Ibeanu & Fatima Kyari Mohammed: 57–100. Lagos: Friedrich-Ebert-Stiftung.

Lalude, Goke. 2014. "Nigerian Governors Forum", In *The Jonathan Presidency: The Sophomore Year*, edited by John Ayoade, Adeoye Akinsanya & Olatunde Ojo: 216–235. Ibadan: John Archers.

LeVan, Carl. 2019. *Contemporary Nigerian Politics: Competition in a Time of Transition and Terror*. New York: Cambridge University Press.

Mitee, Ledum. 2008. *Report of the Technical Committee on the Niger Delta*. Port Harcourt, PDF File.

Molly, Desmond. 2011. "DDR: Niger Delta and Sri Lanka: Smoke and Mirrors?" *Journal of Conflict Transformation & Security* 1 (1): 111–132.

Nsirimovu, Anyakwee. 2005. "Report of a Study on Small Arms and Light Weapon Proliferation in Rivers State". In *Oiling Violence: The Proliferation of Small Arms and Light Weapons in the Niger Delta*, edited by Okechukwu Ibeanu & Fatima Kyari Mohammed: 157–195. Lagos: Friedrich-Ebert-Stiftung.

Nwajiaku, Kathryn. 2010. *The Politics of Amnesty in the Delta Niger: Challenges Ahead*. Paris: IFRI.

Nyheim, David, Luc Zandvliet & Lockton Morrissey (eds). 2003. *Peace and Security in the Niger Delta: Conflict Expert Group Baseline Report for Shell*. London: WAC Services.

Odili, Peter. 2012. *Conscience and History: My Story*. Lagos: Vanguard Media.

Okocha, Chuks. 8 Sept. 2010. "Post Amnesty Blues". Lagos: *This Day*: 23.

Omoweh, Daniel. 2007. *Shell Petroleum Development Company, the State, and Underdevelopment of Nigeria's Niger Delta: A Study in Environmental Degradation*. Trenton (NJ): Africa World Press.

Onoyume, Jimitota. 11 March 2009. "Nigeria: Truth Commission Blames Rivers Crises on Odili, Obasanjo Govts". Lagos: Vanguard.

Oriola, Temitope. 2013. *Criminal Resistance? The Politics of Kidnapping Oil Workers*. Farnham: Ashgate.

Oriola, Temitope, Kelvin Haggerty & Andy Knight. 2013. "Car Bombing 'with Due Respect': The Niger Delta Insurgency and the Idea Called MEND". *African Security* 6 (1): 67–96.

Oyadongha, Samuel. 2 April 2016. "Ex-Militant Leader, 7 Others Make Local Govt Caretaker List in Bayelsa": 6. Lagos: Vanguard.

Oyewole, Samuel. 2018. "The Urhobo Militant Movements and the Contentious Ijaw Domination of the Niger Delta Struggle". In *The Unfinished Revolution in Nigeria's Niger Delta: Prospects for Socio-Economic and Environmental Justice and Peace*, edited by Cyril Obi & Temitope Oriola: 28–40. London: Routledge.

Pérouse de Montclos, Marc-Antoine. 2021. "Nigeria: la fin de l'Eldorado". *Futuribles* 441 : 5–19.

Schmidle, Nicholas. 4 Dec. 2009. "The Hostage Business". New York: *The New York Times*.

SDN. 2018. *Agitators to Legislators: The Migration of Ex-Militants into Niger Delta Politics*. Port Harcourt: Stakeholder Democracy Network.

SDN. 2021. *Nigeria's Presidential Amnesty Programme: Untangling the Dependencies That Prevent It Ending*. Port Harcourt: Stakeholder Democracy Network.

Uguru, Hilary. 4 June 2013. "Rising Niger Delta Oil Theft Threatens Security". Dakar: *IRIN*.

PART 2

And What about Oil?

∵

In Search of Lost Oil

Dutch Disease under the Tropics

Between Brass and Okpoama, a beautiful beach of fine sand seems to stretch out forever along the Atlantic coast of Bayelsa State. Whale skeletons can sometimes be found there, for no apparent reason. The area is remote and difficult to access. Travelers have to cross the entire Niger Delta to reach it, a journey that takes two hours on a speedboat. There are no tourists here. While the beach itself is pristine, the sea is not suitable for swimming because of the strong current. The waters are also known to be dangerous as the crews of passing boats are often attacked by pirates.

Nothing suggests that the situation will improve since demolition work began in 2010 to build a natural gas liquefaction plant in the area. Here and there, fishermen can be found along the beach. The prospect of their peaceful villages being devastated and polluted by a giant factory is a cause for concern. I am accompanied by Celestine Akpobari, an Ogoni environmental activist. He asks a fisherman how he feels about the LNG (liquefied natural gas) project.

"We are afraid", he replies.

"But what exactly are you afraid of?" asks Celestine.

"Well, we're worried that oil companies won't come here!"

Celestine is surprised. He expected a different answer, one about the damage that the project would cause to the environment.

The fisherman continues:

"Well, we want money, jobs, schools, and free clinics. We want oil companies to come and work here. We're afraid the project won't go ahead."

1 Biased Analyses

These hopes are hardly consistent with the conventional view of the oil industry and its harmful impact. Many journalists and researchers have echoed the dominant narratives of the resource curse.[1] For them, the root cause of the Niger Delta crisis is oil production. In some cases, the biases are extremely

---

[1] For an attempt at an overview of the literature on this subject, see Pérouse de Montclos 2014.

FIGURE 23   Okpoama Beach in Bayelsa State (2011)

FIGURE 24   A ghost factory: Brass-LNG (2011)

pronounced, and it is not uncommon to come across books that seem to be written by scholars but are in fact authored by Greenpeace consultants or "academic militants" who put the blame only on transnational corporations, starting with Shell (Okonta & Douglas 2001, Rowell *et al.* 2005). There is often no critical distance from the subject of investigation. Some authors have even sympathized with the cause of Niger Delta militants, such as Rebecca Golden Timsar (2015), a former American collaborator of Médecins Sans Frontières who once attended the initiation ceremonies of Egbesu fighters.

For example, Michael Watts, a prolific Marxist geographer at Berkeley University, has aptly analyzed the criminal tendencies of the ruling class and armed rebels. However, he has steered clear of criticizing political activists such as Ken Saro-Wiva, who was the head of the military propaganda of General Ibrahim Babangida, or Oronto Douglas, the spokesman for Diepreye Alamieyeseigha in Bayelsa and, later, a special adviser to Goodluck Jonathan in Abuja, two individuals who rank among Nigeria's most corrupt governors and presidents ever.[2] On the other hand, Watts has consistently denounced the misdeeds of international oil companies. He has even accused them of stirring up violence to divide and rule, despite the fact that they would benefit more from avoiding confrontations that are detrimental to their operations. Shell in particular has been suspected of pouring oil on the fire, to preserve its preeminent position and dissuade competitors from exploring the Niger Delta (Frynas 1998: 458).

Some Nigerian researchers have also argued that "oil majors seem to prefer a more violent approach [...] in sharp contradiction" to the softer diplomatic moves of the Nigerian government (Omotola 2009). According to Shola Omotola, for example, they have often requested Abuja to send additional troops and lobbied Western governments for a possible military intervention in the Niger Delta. However, Omotola failed to mention that Nigeria is the majority stakeholder in the industry. Moreover, its security forces need no instruction from foreign companies to commit massacres. By law, the private security firms hired by oil majors are not permitted to carry firearms, an exclusive state privilege. In the Niger Delta, violence in the industry has in fact more to do with the brutality of a predatory government seeking to secure its interests in a rentier economy. As for Western powers, they are unwilling to consider a military intervention in Africa's most populous country.

Yet many social scientists from the Niger Delta have continued to develop partial analyses, and their articles have sometimes been published by academic

---

2   See, among many others, Watts 2015, 2007.

journals that failed to make any mention of their militant position.[3] Biases have taken different forms, from celebrating the rebels to putting all the blame on international oil companies only. Some authors thus considered MOSOP and IYC as NGOs and mediators, despite the fact that they were direct parties to the conflict (Ibeanu 2006: 47). Others have downplayed the financial and criminal dimension of the crisis. For instance, Paul Ugor (2013: 288), a native of Cross River, viewed the theft of crude oil as an act of resistance and argued that illegal refineries were "creative alternative strategies [...] for claiming the social and economic rights" of the poor. In a similar vein, authors from the region have generally described Niger Delta armed rebels as "militants" while labeling Boko Haram insurgents as "terrorists".

Sabella Ogbobode Abidde (2017: xxi) even portrayed Henry Okah as his "brother" in the preface to his book. The son of a former navy officer from Delta State, the latter was a spokesman for MEND and a trafficker who sold weapons to all sides, including those fighting each other (Dokubo 2018). After being extradited from Angola in February 2008, he was detained for a while by the Nigerian government. In July 2009, however, he was released to encourage the Niger Delta rebels to come out of the creeks following the amnesty granted a month earlier. Having gone back into exile, Henry Okah was then sentenced in January 2013 by a South African court to 24 years in prison for arms trafficking and his role in the terrorist attack that resulted in the death of sixteen people in Abuja in October 2010.

Fortunately, some Nigerian activists-turned-researchers have also produced critical analyses of the protests. A case in point is Omolade Adunbi (2015), an academic who, before moving to the United States, first worked in Lagos for a human rights organization, the CLO (Civil Liberties Organisation), where he collaborated with Niger Delta campaigners such as Oronto Douglas, Ken Saro-Wiwa, Ledum Mitee, and Felix Tuodola, the first president of IYC. As for Akin Iwilade (2014), a Nigerian based in Britain, he has steered clear of the dominant narratives about popular resistance to international oil companies and a state working hand-in-hand with multinationals. Uncovering the reality of the patronage networks that fuelled violence in the region, he has rather shown that armed militants from the Niger Delta were driven primarily by their integration into a predatory and corrupt system.

Some researchers from the region have also acknowledged how difficult it was not to be manipulated by informants and empathize with suffering populations (Ukiwo 2011). Their capacity to maintain analytical objectivity is

---

3   See, for example, Von Kemedi 2003.

particularly commendable given that the extractive industry seldom draws sympathy. Enclosed in their bunkers, oil workers appear cut off from their social environment and driven only by the quest for profit, displaying no interest in local communities, with the exception of sexual encounters. Moreover, Nigeria is a textbook case of the "Dutch disease", the name given to the collateral damage caused by oil and gas production, especially in the context of rentier economies.

The easy money of the 1970s boom indeed exacerbated corruption and consolidated authoritarian military and civilian regimes that dipped into state coffers to finance clientelistic networks and remain in power. At the time, the embezzlement of public funds was so widespread that Nigeria became heavily indebted while at the same time failing to use the oil wealth to build a solid industrial base and develop basic services over the long term. Capital flight probably exceeded $86.5 billion between 1970 and 1996, rising to $129.5 billion if we include the revenues that could have been generated by these funds. As Nigeria sank into economic crises during the dictatorships of General Ibrahim Babangida and General Sani Abacha, misappropriated funds invested abroad could have financed the country's economic take-off and paid back its debt. Depending on how interest rates are calculated, they have been estimated to represent between 2.8 and 4.1 times the debt's value (Boyce & Ndikumana 2001).

The Niger Delta was not spared from the "Dutch disease". The easy money earned from oil disrupted the plantation economy of the colonial era, which was a major source of employment. For example, in Delta State, agro-forestry and the production of palm oil collapsed, as shown by the case of a company such as African Timber & Plywood. Meanwhile, the commercial ports of Burutu and Sapele (which became a Nigerian navy base) declined. The prevailing insecurity, institutionalized corruption, and the difficulty of obtaining land certificates also deterred local investors, while the rural exodus pushed the elites to Nigeria's major urban centers, chief among them Lagos. Finally, as noted by an Urhobo researcher from the region, oil revenues generated a state of social anomie (Onokerhoraye 2011: 548–549):

> The spirit of self-reliance in Urhoboland has gradually given way to the spirit of laziness, idleness, and unpardonable dependency on government and oil companies. In a sense, government and oil companies seem to have crowded out the development efforts of local communities and social organizations.

At the national level, the effects of the 1970s boom can still be felt today. Nigeria remains highly vulnerable to changes in world commodity prices, whether upwards or downwards. The financial structure of its extractive industry means that it is not protected from international market fluctuations. Hydrocarbon resources still represent 95% of its exports, a proportion that has remained largely unchanged since Nigeria became a natural gas exporter in 1999. As for the diversification of its GDP during the 2010s, it was mainly driven by the collapse of crude oil prices and large-scale disinvestment by extractive companies. However, oil and gas production has continued to account for 65% of all government revenue, compared with 80% in the mid-1970s (Ross 2003: 17, Thurber, Emelife & Heller 2010: 5, 10). Gas in particular offers huge potential. Nigeria has the largest reserves in Africa and exploits only a quarter of them.

In short, given its financial and structural impact on the economy, oil is an ideal suspect for the troubles facing the country as a whole and not just those of the Niger Delta. The international visibility of transnational corporations also explains why the majors are so exposed to attacks from human rights organizations and environmental lobbies. It would be far more difficult to campaign against national oil companies or domestic firms that are opaque and do not care much about their public image. From a marketing perspective, advocacy NGOs find it easier to target and denounce well-known listed majors (Pérouse de Montclos 2019).

2 Toward a Pluralistic Interpretation of Nigeria's Problems

Undoubtedly, the role of the resource curse should not be overestimated. First, corruption, prevarication, and predatory violence already existed before independence and the beginnings of oil production. The development of a market and monetary economy during the colonial period does not explain everything either. Based on barter, the slave trade also played an important role in fuelling deadly competition, particularly on the coast. Thus the logic of capital accumulation did not spare the Ijaw chiefs of Nembe in the nineteenth century. One of them, for instance, became so rich that he was nicknamed *Din akpa ina akpa lagha* ('No purse is equal to mine'), a title reminiscent of a satirical novel that mocked the ostentation of the Nigerian bourgeoisie during the 1970s oil boom: *My Mercedes is Bigger Than Yours* (Alagoa 2018: 135, Nwankwo 1975).

Today, many other factors, including demographic pressure and generational gaps, explain the political conflicts, social tensions, and community clashes in Africa's most populous country. Indeed, resource competition relates more generally to access to land and the sharing of state revenues, thus extending well beyond oil exploitation. For example, in central Nigeria, rural Benue State has seen many conflicts opposing Fulani cattle breeders to Jukun and Tiv farmers. As in the oil industry, government projects have also affected indigenous communities. In the late 1970s, again in Benue, the construction of a bridge over the Katsina-Ala River deprived the Etulo of their main livelihood, which involved transporting passengers from one bank to the other. This small fishing community was eventually forced to convert to agriculture, a move that pitted them against the Mbagan, a Tiv clan (Jibo, Simbine & Galadima 2001: 18, 34).

Resource conflicts are clearly not limited to developing countries and extend to raw materials other than oil, as with the Native Americans of Wisconsin who resisted plans to establish an open-pit copper mine in the early 1990s (Gedicks 1993). For example, to the north of Nigeria, in the Republic of Niger, indigenous communities and environmental lobbies have focused their protests on uranium exploitation by the French company Areva. As if mirroring Ken Saro-Wiwa's fight against Shell in the Niger Delta, the Tuareg writer Issouf Ag Maha denounced the radioactive contamination of groundwater in the region of Arlit. He also adapted his approach to the expectations of a Western audience, to secure the support of international anti-nuclear organizations such as Greenpeace. Meanwhile, the rebels of the MNJ (Mouvement des Nigériens pour la Justice, or Niger Movement for Justice) took up arms in 2007 to demand, among other things, that native populations be given priority for jobs in their area, together with an increase from 15% to 50% of the share of mining revenues allocated to the region's municipalities (Grégoire 2011: 214). However, aside from a small number of isolated kidnappings and car thefts, Niger's uranium exports remained unaffected by the conflict.

Like other raw materials, oil raises many issues around political governance. Studies comparing Nigeria with Siberia, Alaska, Venezuela, Ecuador, Peru, Colombia, and Papua New Guinea have shown that populations living in producing regions are more likely to remain peaceful and see their demands met if the state is rich, has alternative sources of revenue, does not dominate the extractive industry, promotes economic diversification, and does not seek to restrict private investment initiatives (Haller *et al.* 2007: 584, Luong & Weinthal 2010). The coordination of protest movements and the support of local populations or the international community are not enough to reform oil and gas governance. Even if they have the right to form associations and unions, communities living in producing areas face almost insurmountable obstacles when the authorities divide them to monopolize the most profitable sectors of the economy. Ultimately, the stability of these regions is determined primarily by the quality of conflict-regulation institutions, the rule of law, an independent judiciary, courts that work properly, a government that promotes environmental protection, and a democratic constitution that protects minorities and effectively guarantees human rights.

In practice, Nigeria fulfils almost none of these conditions. Many causes account for its poor "state of the state". Oil can hardly be isolated from other factors when examining corruption, the mismanagement of public services, and the violence of the ruling class. Historically, for example, the legacy of the colonial state and the introduction of a market economy played an important role. Moreover, the cultural obligations of solidarity and reciprocity, associated with traditional extended families, have fed nepotism (Chabal & Daloz 1999, Smith 2001). Some Nigerians even view corruption as a kind of African heritage.

For example, according to Ifeanyi Onwuzuruigbo (2011), cronyism reflects ancient traditions found in barter economies that relied on slavery, the payment of tribute, and various forms of pawnship and apprenticeship that involved entrusting poor children to the wealthy.[4] According to him, today's caciques are the heirs of the Ibo big man (*ogaranya*), the Yoruba warlord (*baba ogun*), and the Hausa master (*maigida*). Now considered godfathers in the mafia sense of the term, they are reminiscent of customary chiefs, since their role is to protect vassals and subalterns who support them during and between elections. We find echoes of this relationship between masters (*nnam-ukwu*) and servants (*odibo*) at the time of the slave trade in Iboland, or in the nineteenth-century Yoruba refugees who settled in Ibadan under the protection of leaders called "small father" (*baba kekere*), "boss" (*baba isale*), or "savior" (*baba nigbejo*).

Significantly, Muslim-dominated northern Nigeria, where no oil is produced, has also experienced various forms of cronyism that are reminiscent of today's forms of political patronage.[5] Thus, among the Hausa in the northwest, the "household head" (*maigida*) was both a landlord and a middleman earning toll fees and receiving kola nuts by way of payment for facilitating sales of livestock and permitting herds to cross his territory. As for the Kanuri in the northeast, an area now ravaged by the Boko Haram conflict, their chiefs of districts (*aja*), cantons (*lawan*), and villages (*bullama*) would typically take 10% of peasants' harvest on behalf of the sultan of Borno, the *Shehu*. The payment of this tribute, known as *ngaji*, was later banned by the British, who wanted to employ salaried workers to centralize tax collections and contain the power of landlords in a feudal society. To avoid funds being misappropriated, the

---

4   See also Albert 2005.
5   For examples drawn from Borno and Kano, see Cohen 1970: 259, Smith 1964, Pierce 2016.

colonial authorities also forced the *lawan* and the *bullama* to limit the number of vassals in their debt.[6] However, Kanuri peasants still wanted to pay homage to the sultan of Borno, and they secretly continued to give a tribute to the district chiefs, whom they viewed as vassals of the *Shehu* rather than civil servants working for a public service. As a result, the illegal payment of *ngaji* became synonymous with bribery (Cohen 1964: 505, Krings 2004: 277).

All over Nigeria, extended family structures and population pressure also played a part in the redistribution of wealth to distant relatives who had no qualms about asking for money, a job, or a contract in the name of ethnic solidarity. However, it would be wrong to put present-day corruption and nepotism solely down to the legacy of African tribalism. For many Nigerians, it is primarily colonization that "corrupted" and "destroyed" the moral values of traditional societies (Arinze 2008). For example, the widespread culture of *dash* (a "baksheesh" in pidgin) has its origins in the transatlantic slave trade. The term comes from the Dutch *dasje*, a word referring to a small piece of material used by European navigators to barter captives for firearms and trinkets (Ellis 2016: 70). As in the case of *ngaji* in Borno, the British colonization of the Niger Delta had the effect of establishing a fiscal monopoly for the state, while criminalizing the toll fees and custom duties, known as *comey*, once paid to communities when crossing their creeks.

3   Godfatherism by Way of Democracy

At the time of independence in 1960, the political class continued to rely on regional structures rooted in cronyism. But military dictatorships and the easy money of the 1970s' oil boom undoubtedly exacerbated the misappropriation of public funds. Designed to thwart ethnic secession and marginalization, the federal system put in place at the end of the Biafran War encouraged nepotism through the recruitment of civil servants based on their regional origins rather than on merit. In principle, the introduction of quotas aimed to consolidate national unity and help the north catch up with the south, where people tended to be better educated and more developed. In practice, however, these positive discrimination policies prevented the administration from recruiting

---

6   Not without contradiction, this policy contributed to reducing the government's tax base, as fewer people were available to collect the so-called *jangali* tax among pastoral communities. It also contradicted attempts to rationalize the levy of taxes during seeding time, when farmers were at home, and the rainy season, when cattle breeders remained in Borno before moving their herds south to look for greener pastures.

competent workers when no suitable indigenous candidates could be found. Since then, attempts to reform the civil service at the local government level have failed, as in Sokoto State in 2015.

Another damaging legacy from the military dictatorships of the 1970s and 1980s was the culture of conspiracy and secrecy fostered by the Nigerian army. The prevailing opaqueness facilitated the embezzlement of public funds. It also contributed to disseminating a negative image of opportunistic and unscrupulous civilian politicians, seen as voracious conmen and vampires backed by invisible forces, black magic, and the human sacrifices of initiation societies. For example, the clique of northern Muslims in power in the 1980s was referred to as the "Kaduna Mafia". During the following decade under Sani Abacha's kleptocracy, the image of the ruling class deteriorated even further compared with the idealized view that many Nigerians had of the time of independence, when leaders bought votes and maintained cronies to help develop the country rather than for their own personal gain.

Oil or no oil, the notion of "godfatherism" thus encompassed practices of corruption and patronage which, far from being "aberrant", were constituent elements of the formation of the state in sub-Saharan Africa (Diamond 1987: 581, Pierce 2006: 900). The expression was specifically used to describe the Fourth Republic from 1999 onward. It referred to godfathers who funded stooges and from the shadows called the shots in the political game. Indeed, newly created parties received neither subsidies nor member fees at the end of the Sani Abacha dictatorship. As a result, many candidates who did not have the means to fund political campaigns asked dubious "investors" to support and protect them. Once elected, they were then expected to pay back their debt in the form of public contracts, tax breaks, and loan facilities. But things often turned nasty when they disagreed about the sharing of the state's prebends.

After several decades of dictatorship, the establishment of a Fourth Republic also failed to lay the foundation for a new social contract. In 1999, there was initially widespread public distrust of a democratic transition overseen by the army, a process previously halted in 1993 when two generals, Ibrahim Babangida and Sani Abacha, challenged the election results, leading to yet another period of military rule. Civilian politicians were not trusted either since the disastrous experience of the Second Republic during the 1979 oil crisis. For example, someone such as Bola Ige, a Yoruba, personified shameless opportunism as he allegedly funded the three main parties competing for the 1999 elections: the PDP, the AD, and the APP. After his defeat at the AD primaries, he joined the PDP and entered government as Minister of Mines and Power before being appointed Attorney General, a position he held until his assassination in 2001. Meanwhile, the AD was assumed to be the main opposition party, yet its candidate, Olu Falae, was a former finance minister under Ibrahim Banbangida's junta and the key figure behind the Structural Adjustment Program that had crushed the Nigerian middle class and caused large numbers of civil servants to lose their jobs in the mid-1990s.

When considering the role of oil, the catastrophic legacy of military dictatorships therefore needs to be placed in perspective. Many African countries have experienced coups and high levels of corruption, yet did not produce either oil or gas. In Nigeria, the easy money of the 1970s boom undoubtedly contributed to exacerbating the weakness of an already fragile state. Moreover, it challenged the social contract that existed at the time of independence. Indeed, it funded authoritarian governments whose economic power was based on royalties rather than on the collection of head taxes that would have compelled them to be more accountable to citizens. However, to view oil as the root of all the evils affecting Nigeria is a step too far.

The black gold has also had positive consequences. A factor of both secession and unity, it enabled the Nigerian state to rebuild the regions ruined by the Biafran War. In the same vein, the 1970s boom financed the "green revolution", the development of public schools and the fight against drought, desertification, and soil erosion in the northern part of the country (Falola 1997: 9). Moreover, the new wealth of Nigeria helped to reduce the tax burden on peasants, even if it deprived the rural masses of their political leverage when their agricultural production constituted the bulk of the state's income (Berry 1984). In addition, the misappropriation of oil revenues not only served to fund the cronies of successive military juntas, but also to buy social peace and bond the political class to secure a share of the so-called national cake (Fjelde 2009). Ben Naanen (1995: 135), an Ogoni from the Niger Delta, thus remarked that "the threat of structural collapse of Nigeria as a corporate entity [seemed] undermined by the country's overwhelming dependence on oil, which [acted] as a unifying force".

4   Oil and Violence: A Complex Relationship

Many factors actually underline the need for nuance when considering the role of oil. First, the production of crude is by no means the primary cause of lethal violence in Nigeria. Structurally, the oil industry employs a small workforce. In 1975, at the peak of its very rapid expansion, it provided work for only 4,500 employees and 15,000 subcontractors (Madujibeya 1976: 285). By definition, it is therefore less deadly than, say, gold mining in South Africa or plantation agriculture in Belgian Congo in the early twentieth century. Furthermore, some of the features of the Niger Delta crisis can be found elsewhere in Nigeria in areas that produce no crude. Finally, a closer analysis within the region highlights the diversity of conflicts that are unrelated to extractive activities.

The information available in the NigeriaWatch database thus shows that most violent deaths reported in Nigeria have nothing to do with the production of crude oil and are associated instead with ordinary crime, politics, and accidents (Pérouse de Montclos 2018).[7] The Boko Haram insurrection in the northeast and land disputes in the Middle Belt have been far more deadly in this respect. Likewise, the perpetrators of lethal violence are seldom oil companies, and the conflicts of the Niger Delta have not caused major forced migrations. Figures available over a twenty-year period confirm this. In 1997, just 50,000 of the 1,270,000 internally displaced persons registered nationally came from areas affected by, among other things, oil conflicts (Hampton 1998: 51). As for the 248,000 displaced people recorded in 2019, none came from the Niger Delta, the main regions affected being the north and the Middle Belt.[8]

Oil-related violence therefore needs to be placed in perspective. First, the media are usually more interested in incidents where international oil companies are involved, while farmers' conflicts in remote rural areas tend to receive less attention. It is also important to distinguish between production and distribution. The upstream and downstream sectors of the industry face different risk factors. For example, depending on their footprint, companies investing in both sectors are more likely to be associated with violence than those operating only in exploration and production, especially offshore.

There are several reasons for this. First, geographically, oil production is concentrated in four of Nigeria's 36 states; hence its limited impact on violent incidents reported across the country. From a chemical point of view, crude is also less flammable than petrol and, therefore, less likely to cause deadly explosions. Finally, in social terms, exploration and production require a smaller workforce than distribution. Extraction activities are often located in sparsely populated rural areas, meaning that there are fewer victims when they cause conflicts.

By contrast, flammable refined products are distributed across all 36 states of the Nigerian federation. The data from the NigeriaWatch project show that gas

---

7   Based at the University of Ibadan, the NigeriaWatch project archives its sources to ensure that each incident can be verified on a case-by-case basis. The database is continuously updated by Nigerian researchers and represents the country's most comprehensive and long-running source of information on violence in Nigeria. Its methodology and its records are available at: http://www.nigeriawatch.org/index.php?html=4.

8   https://www.internal-displacement.org/countries/nigeria.

FIGURE 25   Akpo oil field, off the coast of Rivers State (2009)

stations and fuel trucks present significant risks, the former because they keep cash and are the target of holdups, the latter because they tend to be poorly maintained and often cause devastating road accidents when they explode in the middle of a traffic jam. At a national level, petrol price increases are also a cause of social tension, because they have a direct impact on transport costs and, ultimately, inflation and the availability of staple goods.[9] On a number of occasions, they have led to demonstrations, riots, and brutal repression. Since 2020, moreover, attempts to deregulate petrol prices have revived a structural problem. Indeed, the consumption of refined products is growing faster than the population, partly due to smuggling to neighboring countries. As a result, the Nigerian government is less and less able to pay the subsidies intended to keep prices low, while it has to import petrol at the real market price because of the collapse of its refining capacity.

---

9   The price of petrol increased by 74% in October 1978, 31% in April 1982, 97% in March 1986, 6% in April 1988, 43% in January 1989, 4% in December 1989, 17% in March 1991, 614% in November 1993, 300% in October 1994, 67% in December 1998, 20% in June 2000, 33% in June 2003, 25% in May 2004, and 50% in January 2012 (Azaiki 2009: 224). In June 2023, again, it increased by 416% when the government eventually stopped subsidizing the import of refined products.

The Niger Delta is no exception in this respect. The region is also impacted by increases in petrol prices and accidents related to refined products. However, explosions of paraffin stoves or NNPC pipelines of fuel tend to receive little coverage in the media. Indeed, journalists are usually more interested in crude production. Moreover, the victims rarely go to hospital because they fear being accused of complicity in acts of sabotage or bunkering. As a result, such incidents often remain out of sight, as shown by a study conducted among approximately fifty burn victims between 2009 and 2013 in Kegbara-Dere and Bodo, two Ogoni communities in the Gokana LGA of Rivers State (Naanen & Tolani 2014: 69).

As for conflicts in the region, many of them are not related to oil and gas production. According to some estimates, up to 85% of the population living in the Niger Delta have no contact at all with the petroleum industry (Ahonsi 2011: 29). By contrast, other industrial sites in the region have been a cause of tension, as in Delta State between the Oghareki and Oghafere Urhobo clans of Oghara over a rubber plant in Sapele in 1963, or between the Ijaw Ogbe, the Urhobo, and the Itsekiri over the Aladja steelworks in 1996. At the border between Rivers and Bayelsa states, again, the control of construction sand quarries caused clashes in 1992 between two Ijaw communities, the Kalabari from Soku and Elem-Sangama, on the one hand, and the Nembe of Oluasiri, on the other.

Fishing and farming rights are also a cause of disputes. In present-day Bayelsa State alone, approximately sixty such incidents reportedly occurred between 1809 and 1959, just one year before independence (Ebiye 2008). Today, conflicts often oppose indigenous farmers and cattle breeders who come from the north and who destroy harvests while moving their herds to slaughterhouses in the major urban centers of southern Nigeria. For example, in Ohoror-Uwheru, a town in the Ughelli North LGA of Delta State, clashes resulted in the death of around twenty people after the army stepped in and fired into the crowd in early 2004 (Azaiki 2009: 37–38). In 2006, pastoralists disguised as soldiers also settled scores by killing half a dozen villagers in Eleke Afara in the Etche LGA in northern Rivers State.

In the same vein, indigenous communities have fought over land rights and engaged in border disputes without oil being a factor. For example, at the border of Akwa Ibom and Cross River states, the Ibibio of Itu and the Efik of Odukpani have clashed over a territory inhabited by the Ikorofiong in Ikot Offiong. Thought to be descendants of the Mbiabo, one of the seven royal families of the Efik of Calabar, this minority was keen to fall under the authority of Cross River to escape the control of the Ibibio from Akwa Ibom. Following a court ruling in their favor, however, the Ikorofiong were attacked by their neighbors from Oku Iboku in March and May 2000. Their village was burned down, forcing them to seek refuge in Usung Esuk in the Odukpani LGA of Cross River State, where they were again subject to violence in December 2001. However, there was no oil in the area, only unfounded rumors that contributed to inflaming the situation, about the possibility of a seismic drilling project (Effanga 2000).

Many residents actually believe that community conflicts are far more deadly than clashes involving the security forces or oil companies. This is the story that emerged from surveys carried out in thirty villages throughout the Niger Delta in 2006 (Ibaba 2009: 569). Of course, such perceptions depend on how incidents are understood, reported, and coded when moving to a more granular individual level. Over the period 2006–2021, the NigeriaWatch database showed that, in a state such as Rivers, around 60% of all violent deaths resulted from ordinary crime, the other main causes of fatalities being political conflicts and road accidents.

Local perceptions also point to a hierarchy that downplays the role played by the oil industry. Surveys conducted in 2005 speak volumes in this regard. In Rivers State, 41% of respondents accused politicians of being responsible for the permanent state of violence, while oil companies were cited by just 18%. In Delta State, the figures stood at 53% and 6% respectively. Finally, in Bayelsa State, 55% of those surveyed reported that armed violence was linked to chieftaincies, party primaries, elections, civil service appointments, and the competition for community development funds. By contrast, far fewer respondents cited bunkering activities, the distribution of oil subsidies, and access to jobs in extractive companies as a cause of fatal incidents (Nsirimovu 2005: 17, Abayomi 2005: 116; Isumonah, Tantua & James 2005: 76). The authorities also confirmed that the Niger Delta's problems related first and foremost to bad governance. For example, an adviser to the governor of Cross River once reported that nearly half of the state's politicians were members of armed gangs (Ebiede, Bassey & Asuni 2021: 190). Established in 2007 and chaired by Judge Kayode Eso, the Rivers State Truth and Reconciliation Commission reached broadly similar conclusions. At the end of the hearings, it publicly acknowledged that the region's conflicts were essentially caused by underdevelopment, gangsterism, and interference by corrupt politicians funding insurgents to eliminate their opponents (Aghedo 2013: 272). By contrast, the extractive industry played a role in violence only when companies tried to repel attacks by bandits by calling for the security forces to intervene. Ultimately, oil was mainly seen as a major cause of frustration and disappointment, because its revenues were misappropriated and the associated profits primarily served to reimburse the huge costs incurred by exploration and production. Moreover, its exploitation required significant amounts of capital but provided few jobs.

References

Abayomi, Francis *et al.* 2005. "The Proliferation of Small Arms and Light Weapons Survey in Delta State", In *Oiling Violence: The Proliferation of Small Arms and Light Weapons in the Niger Delta*, edited by Okechukwu Ibeanu & Fatima Kyari Mohammed: 101–156. Lagos: Friedrich-Ebert-Stiftung.

Abidde, Sabella Ogbobode. 2017. *Nigeria's Niger Delta: Militancy, Amnesty, and the Post-amnesty Environment*. Lanham (MD): Lexington Books.

Adunbi, Omolade. 2015. *Oil Wealth and Insurgency in Nigeria*. Bloomington: Indiana University Press.

Aghedo, Iro. 2013. "Winning the War, Losing the Peace: Amnesty and the Challenges of Post-Conflict Peace-Building in the Niger Delta, Nigeria". *Journal of Asian and African Studies* 48 (3): 265–278.

Ahonsi, Babatunde. 2011. "Capacity and Governance Deficits in Response to the Niger Delta Crisis". In *Oil and Insurgency in the Niger Delta: Managing the Complex Politics of Petro-Violence*, edited by Cyril Obi & Siri Aas Rustad: 28–41. London: Zed Books.

Alagoa, Ebiegberie Joe. 2018. *Kalĩye Opuye, Opuye Kalĩye: A History of Nembe, Central Delta Niger*. Port Harcourt, Onyoma.

Albert, Isaac Olawale. 2005. "Explaining 'Godfatherism' in Nigerian Politics". *African Sociological Review* 9 (2): 79–105.

Arinze, Peter Emeka. 2008. "An Examination of Corruption in Nigerian Economy". *Hemispheres: Studies on Cultures and Societies* 23: 61–75.

Azaiki, Steve. 2009. *The Evil of Oil*. Ibadan: Y-Books.

Berry, Sara. 1984. "Oil and Disappearing Peasantry: Accumulation, and Underdevelopment". *African Economic History* 13: 1–22.

Boyce, James & Ndikumana, Léonce. 2001. "Is Africa a Net Creditor? New Estimates of Capital Flight from Severely Indebted Sub-Saharan African Countries, 1970–96". *Journal of Development Studies* 38 (2): 27–56.

Chabal, Patrick & Jean-Pascal Daloz. 1999. *Africa Works: Disorder as Political Instrument*. Oxford: Currey.

Cohen, Ronald. 1964. "Conflict and Change in a Northern Nigerian Emirate". In *Explorations in Social Change*, edited by Zollschan, George & Walter Hirsch: 495–521. London: Routledge & Kegan Paul.

Cohen, Ronald. 1970. "Social Stratification in Bornu". In *Social Stratification in Africa*, edited by Arthur Tuden & Leonard Plotnicov: 225–267. New York: The Free Press.

Diamond, Larry. 1987. "Class Formation in the Swollen African State". *Journal of Modern African Studies* 25 (4): 567–596.

Dokubo, Asari. 31 Dec. 2018. "Me, Henry Okah, 'Jomo Gbomo', Judith Asuni and the Niger Delta Insurgency". *Sahara Reporters.*

Ebiede, Tarila Marclint, Celestine Oyom Bassey & Judith Burdin Asuni (eds). 2021. *Insecurity in the Niger Delta. A Report on Emerging Threats in Akwa Ibom, Bayelsa, Cross River, Delta, Edo and Rivers States.* London: Adonis & Abbey Publishers.

Ebiye, Sam. 2008. "The Niger Delta and the Izon (Ijaw) Nation in Politics, War and 2007 Peace Building". In *Oil, Democracy, and the Promise of True Federalism in Nigeria,* edited by Augustine Ikein, Diepreye Alamieyeseigha & Steve Azaiki: 211–214. Lanham (Md.): University Press of America.

Effanga, Obo. 2000. "The Violence in Odukpani LGA of Cross River State". In *Hope Betrayed? A Report on Impunity and State-Sponsored Violence in Nigeria,* edited by Innocent Chukwuma *et al.:* 169–184. Lagos: Centre for Law Enforcement Education.

Ellis, Stephen. 2016. *This Present Darkness. A History of Nigerian Organized Crime.* London: Hurst.

Falola, Toyin. 1997. "Nigeria in the Global Context of Refugees: Historical and Comparative Perspectives". *Journal of Asian and African Studies* 32: 5–21.

Fjelde, Hanne. 2009. "Buying Peace? Oil Wealth, Corruption and Civil War, 1985–99". *Journal of Peace Research* 46 (2): 199–218.

Frynas, Jedrzej Georg. 1998. "Political Instability and Business: Focus on Shell in Nigeria". *Third World Quarterly* 19 (3): 457–478.

Gedicks, Al. 1993. *The New Resource Wars: Native and Environmental Struggles against Multinational Corporations.* Boston: South End Press.

Grégoire, Emmanuel. 2011. "Niger: un État à forte teneur en uranium". *Hérodote* 142: 206–225.

Haller, Tobias *et al.* (eds). 2007. *Fossil Fuels, Oil Companies and Indigenous Peoples: Strategies of Multinational Oil Companies, States, and Ethnic Minorities—Impact on Environment, Livelihoods, and Cultural Change.* Berlin: Lit Verlag.

Hampton, Janie (ed.). 1998. *Internally Displaced People: A Global Survey.* London: Norwegian Refugee Council.

Ibaba, Ibaba. 2009. "Violent Conflicts and Sustainable Development in Bayelsa State". *Review of African Political Economy* 36 (122): 555–573.

Ibeanu, Okechukwu. 2006. *Civil Society and Conflict Management in the Niger Delta: Scoping Gaps for Policy and Advocacy.* Lagos: Cleen Foundation.

Isumonah, Adefemi, Ben Tantua & Nengi James. 2005. "The Proliferation of Small Arms and Light Weapons in Bayelsa State", In *Oiling Violence: The Proliferation of Small Arms and Light Weapons in the Niger Delta,* edited by Okechukwu Ibeanu & Fatima Kyari Mohammed: 57–100. Lagos: Friedrich-Ebert-Stiftung.

Iwilade, Akin. 2014. "Networks of Violence and Becoming: Youth and the Politics of Patronage in Nigeria's Oil-Rich Delta". *The Journal of Modern African Studies* 52 (4): 571–595.

Jibo, Mvendaga, Antonia Simbine & Habu Galadima. 2001. *Ethnic Groups and Conflicts: The North Central Zone of Nigeria*. University of Ibadan, Programme on Ethnic and Federal Studies: vol. 4.

Krings, Matthias. 2004. "Farming the Frontier—Hausa Migrants and the Politics of Belonging on the Former Lake Floor of Lake Chad (Nigeria)". In *Living with the Lake. Perspectives on History, Culture and Economy of Lake Chad*, edited by Matthias Krings & Editha Platte: 268–90. Köln: Rüdiger Köppe.

Luong, Pauline Jones & Erika Weinthal. 2010. *Oil Is Not a Curse: Ownership Structure and Institutions in Soviet Successor States*. Cambridge: Cambridge University Press.

Madujibeya, Sylvanus Azuwueze. 1976. "Oil and Nigeria's Economic Development". *African Affairs* 75 (300): 284–316.

Naanen, Ben. 1995. "Oil Producing Minorities and the Restructuring of Nigerian Federalism: The Case of the Ogoni People". *Journal of Commonwealth and Comparative Politics* 33 (1): 46–78.

Naanen, Ben & Patrick Tolani. 2014. *Private Gain, Public Disaster: Social Context of Illegal Oil Bunkering and Artisanal Refining in the Niger Delta*. Port Harcourt: Niger Delta Environment and Relief Foundation.

Nsirimovu, Anyakwee. 2005. "Report of a Study on Small Arms and Light Weapon Proliferation in Rivers State". In *Oiling Violence: The Proliferation of Small Arms and Light Weapons in the Niger Delta*, edited by Okechukwu Ibeanu & Fatima Kyari Mohammed: 157–195. Lagos: Friedrich-Ebert-Stiftung.

Nwankwo, Nkem. 1975. *My Mercedes Is Bigger than Yours*. London: Heinemann.

Okonta, Ike & Oronto Douglas. 2001. *Where Vultures Feast: Shell, Human Rights, and Oil in the Niger Delta*. San Francisco: Sierra Club Books.

Omotola, Shola. 2009. "'Liberation Movements' and Rising Violence in the Niger Delta: The New Contentious Site of Oil and Environmental Politics". *Studies in Conflict & Terrorism* 33 (1): 36–54.

Onokerhoraye, Andrew Godwin. 2011. "Urhobo Unity in Contemporary Times", In *The Urhobo People*, edited by Onigu Otite: 531–88. Ibadan: Gold Press Ltd.

Onwuzuruigbo, Ifeanyi. 2011. "Re-Contextualisation of the Concept of *Godfatherism*: Reflections on Nigeria". In *Democratic Elections and Nigeria's National Security*, edited by Isaac Olawale Albert, Nathaniel Danjibo, Olusola Isola & Stephen Faleti: 292–318. University of Ibadan: Peace and Conflict Studies Programme.

Pérouse de Montclos, Marc-Antoine. 2014. "Oil Curse, State Instability, and Violence in Developing Countries: Theoretical Lessons for Nigeria". Ibadan: IFRA-Nigeria.

Pérouse de Montclos, Marc-Antoine. 2019. *Au-delà des stéréotypes: la culture politique du pétrole et l'État en Afrique*. Bordeaux : LAM (Les Afriques dans le Monde).

Pérouse de Montclos, Marc-Antoine (ed.). 2018. *Ten Myths about Violence in Nigeria.* Ibadan, IFRA.

Pierce, Steven. 2006. "Looking Like a State: Colonialism and the Discourse of Corruption in Northern Nigeria". *Comparative Studies in Society and History* 48: 887–914.

Pierce, Steven. 2016. *Moral Economies of Corruption: State Formation and Political Culture in Nigeria.* Durham: Duke University Press.

Ross, Michael. 2003. *Nigeria's Oil Sector and the Poor.* London: UK Department for International Development.

Rowell, Andy *et al.* 2005. *The Next Gulf: London, Washington and Oil Conflict in Nigeria.* London: Constable.

Smith, Daniel Jordan. 2001. "Kinship and Corruption in Contemporary Nigeria". *Ethnos* 66 (3): 344–364.

Smith, Michael Garfield. 1964. "Historical and Cultural Conditions of Political Corruption among the Hausa". *Comparative Studies in Society and History* 6 (2): 164–194.

Timsar, Rebecca Golden. 2015. "Oil, Masculinity, and Violence: Egbesu Worship in the Niger Delta of Nigeria". In *Subterranean Estates: Life Worlds of Oil and Gas,* edited by Hannah Appel, Arthur Mason & Michael Watts: 72–89. Ithaca: Cornell University Press.

Thurber, Mark, Ifeyinwa Emelife & Patrick Heller. 2010. *NNPC and Nigeria's Oil Patronage Ecosystem.* Stanford University: Freeman Spogli Institute For International Studies.

Ugor, Paul. 2013. "Survival Strategies and Citizenship Claims: Youth and the Underground Oil Economy in Post-Amnesty Niger Delta". *Africa* 83 (2): 270–292.

Ukiwo, Ukoha. 2011. "Hidden Agendas in Conflict Research: Informants' Interests and Research Objectivity in the Niger Delta". In *Researching Violence in Africa: Ethical and Methodological Challenges,* edited by Christopher Cramer, Laura Hammond & Johan Pottier: 137–153. Leiden: Brill.

Von Kemedi, Dimieari. 2003. "The Changing Predatory Styles of International Oil Companies in Nigeria". *Review of African Political Economy* 30 (95): 134–139.

Watts, Michael. 2007. "Petro-Insurgency or Criminal Syndicate?". *Review of African Political Economy* 34 (114): 637–660.

Watts, Michael. 2015. "Chronicle of a Future Foretold: The Complex Legacies of Ken Saro-Wiwa". *The Extractive Industries and Society* 2: 635–644.

CHAPTER 8

The End of the Trinity

The State, Oil Companies, and "Civil Society"

Choba is a rough suburban neighborhood near the University of Port Harcourt. When I used to go to teach, I would sometimes see burning tires on the roadside next to the charred remains of people suspected of theft and lynched by an angry mob. The Alliance Française, where I also worked, was situated in a richer area of the city, near the old colonial township, and seemed to be spared from violence. This was no doubt an illusion. On one occasion, our secretary, a frail lady, turned up at the office in a particularly cheerful mood and told us that her neighbors had finally managed to rid the area of burglars. They had killed one of them with a hammer after giving him a thorough beating.

It is difficult to imagine the daily challenges experienced by many people living in the Niger Delta. The security forces play their part in the violence. As soon as I arrived in Port Harcourt, I was threatened by a police officer pointing a gun at me in a bid to earn a *dash* while I was driving my Nigerian-made Volkswagen Beetle. Not long after that, I had to go to the police station to rescue my watchman, who was facing unfounded charges of complicity in a burglary. When I arrived, I found him exhausted and locked up in chains in a grimy cell. He was thirsty and had not eaten for three days. I had to pay a bribe to free him on bail before carrying him all the way to my car, giving him some food, and releasing him.

1 Cult Societies

The University of Port Harcourt was also violent. Its campus was infested with gangs known as "cult societies" because of the initiation rituals that new members were required to undergo. Historically, these groups emerged out of the student unions that had been banned by the military juntas in the 1980s. As they moved underground, they gradually slid into crime by engaging in racketeering, prostitution, and drug trafficking on campuses. Most federal universities, however, were located on the outskirts of urban centers when they were built during the 1970s' oil boom. The military in power at the time were careful to keep them at a distance, to limit the impact of student protests. As a result,

FIGURE 26   A Nigerian policeman (2011)

cult societies were initially restricted to universities, although they were later able to gradually establish branches on campuses all over the country.

The situation in Rivers State was somewhat different in this respect, not least because of the early conjunction with urban street gangs (Pérouse de Montclos 2012). From 1993, the emergence of self-defense militias on the University of Port Harcourt campus forced cult societies to retreat into town, where they began to spread in high schools (Ebiede, Bassey & Asuni 2021: 363). Despite their student base, the rapprochement was made easier by the fact that, like street gangs, they drew inspiration from maritime piracy for their initiation rituals, adopting names such as the Seadogs, the Buccaneers, the Corsairs, or the Vikings, a secret society with a branch at the University of Port Harcourt known as "Alpha Marine".

The phenomenon thus began to spread and proliferate beyond campuses. In 2004, a local law identified and listed as many as 130 cult societies in Rivers State alone, some with memberships of just twenty people, others with over a thousand members, such as the Greenlanders, a youth gang led by one Chukwudi Osah in Marine Base along the creeks of Port Harcourt (see Appendix 1). Rural areas and smaller urban centers were not spared either. From Bonny Island, for instance, a secret society created under the aegis of the Ibani goddess of rivers, Agaba, established lodges such as the Millenium Boys, the 007, and the Diobu

United in Port Harcourt, or the Bayside Boys and School Boys in Calabar. In rural areas, the group also expanded beyond its ethnic homeland and included Ibibio, Ogoni, Ibo, and Annang members (Pratten 2007: 89).

In town, however, these criminal organizations bore little resemblance to the secret societies that used to dispense justice and maintain order in small villages before colonization. Inspired by a modern global culture that magnifies violence on social media, their initiation rituals mostly ensured that their young members adhered to *omerta*, a mafia-like code of silence. In other words, their aim was certainly not to promote respect for customary chiefs, who tended to be viewed with deep suspicion because of their close ties to the government and oil companies. The so-called Egbesu boys, for example, could hardly claim to be upholding an Ijaw tradition of worshipping the god of war. Rather, locals viewed them as outcasts (Timsar 2015). According to two-thirds of the respondents of a poll conducted among fifty residents of Yenagoa in Bayelsa State, the Egbesu boys were quite isolated and had to be distinguished from ethnic militias, with whom they maintained tense relations (Sesay, Ukeje, Olabisi & Odebiyi 2003: 130).

Far from seeking to defend old traditions, cultists served instead as henchmen for local politicians and formed a breeding ground for fighters involved in all sorts of conflicts. They often played a central role in battles with oil companies. For example, in Bukuma, a community in Degema LGA to the southwest of Port Harcourt, one Onengiye-Ofori Terika, a.k.a. "Occasion Boy", established in 1999 a gang based in the small town of Tombia to extort money from Shell and contest the dominance of its liaison officer, a lawyer called Somina Elekima, who had been accused of embezzling the company's social funds since 1995, when he imposed himself as a key intermediary in relations with local residents. The group, named Okomera, eventually gave birth to a secret cult society, Deybam, and led to the emergence of a rival organization, the Agun Youths Association of Bukuma, as part of an attempt to put an end to its abuses (Von Kemedi 2006). Similarly, in Rumuekpe to the north of Port Harcourt, Emeka Woke, the Chairman of Emuoha LGA's council and an ally of Rivers State Governor Peter Odili, supported the emergence of a gang led by one Otamini Agala in 2005 to oppose the Shell liaison officer, Friday Edu "Pele", who was supposed to redistribute funds earmarked to finance development projects in the community. The ensuing clashes resulted in dozens of casualties, and, in a bid to secure weapons, the various competing factions turned to MEND "commanders"—respectively Farah Dagogo and Soboma George (Amunwa 2011: 32–35, Burgis 2015: 199).

In many cases, oil thus exacerbated tensions because of the financial stakes involved. For example, in present-day Bayelsa State, one Clever Oseiferekuma, a.k.a. "Osei", mobilized the youth of the Odioma clan into a militia to fight the Kalabari of Rivers State and claim ownership of the Soku deposits in 1992. From 1996 onward, the conflict pitted the Odioma of Brass against the Bassambari of Nembe, who were vying for control of the Obioku oil wells. Renowned for his magical powers, Clever Oseiferekuma finally became a local leader of the PDP and, in 2000, began to support a cult society organized under the aegis of a spirit called Teme. His group, Iseinasawo, initially fought against a rival organization, Isongufuro, before targeting Shell and Agip in 2005. Clever Oseiferekuma ultimately required oil companies to stop production in order to settle scores within his own community (Courson 2006).

2   On the "Irresponsibility" of Oil Companies in the Violence

In such a context, the role played by transnational corporations when attacked by armed gangs needs to be reconsidered. Their share of responsibility in the fighting operates at several levels when they call on security forces or fund criminal groups in an attempt to buy social peace. Their presence, as we have seen, is sufficient to stir unrest. As a result, oil companies seek, understandably, to protect their facilities by turning to security and defense forces. However, the NigeriaWatch database shows that the police and the army shoot and kill in more than half of all the cases of lethal incidents in which they are involved—a trend that can hardly be put down to error or collateral damage, pointing instead to a system of institutionalized impunity (Pérouse de Montclos 2016).

In other words, oil companies rely on security and defense forces with little power to control their excesses. They are aware of the risk of misconduct and so bear a degree of responsibility for violence. However, the primary culprits are the trigger-happy operatives who kill civilians on behalf of a predatory sovereign state. As noted by Scott Pegg, the responsibility of oil companies is far more direct when they supply, finance, and transport troops called to the rescue (Pegg 1999: 479). Examples include Chevron in Delta State and Shell in Rivers State in the 1990s. Chinese oil companies, which arrived in Nigeria at a later stage, have also been accused of using similar tactics by pushing for a rapprochement with Beijing to help Abuja procure weapons that Washington had refused to sell in order to avoid a bloodbath (Obi 2008: 422).

Turning to security operatives well known for using excessive force obviously exposes transnational corporations to media and judicial sanctions. The suppression of the Umuechem protest in October and November 1990 is a typical case in point. To restore order, Shell requested the intervention of anti-riot units, the Mopol (Mobile Police), which killed eighty people in neighboring villages of Etche LGA, to the north of Port Harcourt. Set up at the initiative of the then military governor of Rivers State, Colonel Godwin Osagie Abbe, an inquiry commission subsequently found that the protestors had demonstrated peacefully, that they were unarmed, and that there was no imminent risk of attack against oil facilities and expatriates (Frynas 2003: 105). Shell was thus heavily criticized for overstating the scale of the threat.

Due to the international impact of the Ogoni crisis in 1995, the oil majors subsequently had to revise their security policies. For instance, they gradually ceased to hire and pay special police forces who were specifically assigned to them and who, in theory, were unarmed. Known as Spy ("Supernumerary"), these agents had often proved unreliable. From 2004, moreover, they took Shell and ExxonMobil to court in a vain attempt to be transferred from the public to the private sector as full-time "in-house" employees. Their protests had the effect of accelerating the withdrawal of oil companies. By 2006, Chevron had only 100 Spy agents on its books, as against 215 in 2002, while ExxonMobil had just 460, compared with 700 before 2004 (ICG 2006, Pérouse de Montclos 2003).

3   The Use of Militias and Security Contracts: Corporate Contributions to Crime

The alternative was to hire private security guards. In 2002, Chevron contracted the local subsidiary of Group4Securicor, Outsourcing Services Ltd, one of Nigeria's largest operators in the sector, with some 3,000 staff distributed throughout the country. Often managed by foreign advisers (typically former army or special forces officers), such firms sometimes sought to restrain the abuses of Nigerian policemen or soldiers to avoid exacerbating tensions. However, oil companies and their subcontractors have also maintained dangerous links with gangs paid to avert attacks. Driven by a logic of profit, they made the same mistake as the federal government during the 2009 amnesty, believing that money would be enough to buy social peace. Worse still, they went as far as to grant pipeline security contracts to "militants", thereby putting the wolf to guard the sheep and perpetuating a vicious circle in which oil money and criminality feed into each other.

In fact, even before the 2009 amnesty, the majors already used to pay racketeering groups that threatened to attack them. For example, from 2003 in Jones Creek in Delta State, Shell contracted two local firms, IPSS (Integrate

Production System Surveillance) and Shad-Ro Services, with close ties to the rebels and headed, respectively, by Messio German and Shadrack Otuaro, the half-brother of the secretary general of the FNDIC (Federation of the Niger Delta Ijaw Communities), Kingsley Otuaro (Peel 2009: 162). The situation was also murky in neighboring Bayelsa State. As early as 2001, Governor Diepreye Alamieyeseigha mobilized the members of a secret society known as Iseinasawo to combat piracy and form a militia, the Bayelsa Volunteers Anti-Sea Piracy Squad. Two Shell subcontractors, Geomatics and Octopus Holdings, then paid them to root out a rival organization, the Isongufuro, and ensure safe passage for oil workers in the territories of Nembe, Odioma, and Obioku (Courson 2006: 21, Amunwa 2011: 43). Similarly, near Yenagoa and the Gbarantoru oil wells, a gang called Uwou Pele Ogbo was entrusted in 2002 with the task of repelling youths who had threatened to disrupt Shell's operations (Pendleton 2004: 31).

The same logic prevailed in Rivers State, where it was less expensive to pay militants than to repair damaged pipelines. In 2005, for instance, Shell allegedly contracted Dukoaye Security Services, a firm controlled by Alali Horsefall, Asari Dokubo's deputy and a leader of the Niger Delta Volunteer People's Force (ICG 2006: 10). At the time, Shell also employed some 9,000 youths to guard its abandoned facilities in Ogoniland. The fiefdom of Ken-Saro-Wiwa's MOSOP was a showcase in this regard. In Tai LGA, Shell paid the security services of a PDP stalwart, Monday Ngbor, who had instigated political violence during contested elections in 2003. And in K-Dere, Gokana LGA, the oil giant entered into surveillance agreements with vigilantes serving the interests of local politicians during the 2007 elections (Amunwa 2011: 27).

The amnesty granted by the federal government in June 2009 had the effect of institutionalizing these practices. Demobilized militants established their own security firms, thereby exacerbating competition to obtain contracts from the oil industry. For example, in January 2010, a MEND leader in Bayelsa State, Eris Paul, a.k.a. "Commander Ogunboss", began operating his own business, Eristex Pipeline Patrol, to eliminate a local company, Fanus Koki & Sons Ltd, and protect Shell wells in Diebu Creek in Southern Ijaw LGA (Okhomina 2010). Gangs of youths also played a part, albeit more informally. To secure its Adibawa field in Rivers State, Shell entered into deals with the most violent groups of the Edagberi of Joinkrama 4, an Ijaw community of Ahoada West, where a demonstration against the company had already caused six deaths in March 2005. In April 2010, the oil major entered into an agreement with an "interim committee" that had just killed rivals and deposed traditional chiefs to take control of the local council. Six months later, however, members of this faction sabotaged pipelines to obtain more financial compensation and secure

FIGURE 27   The bodyguards of a politician in Edo State (2011)

cleaning contracts in collusion with some of the company's staff. In Bayelsa State too, Ijaw youths from Ikarama attacked the Okordia-Rumuekpe trunk line in August 2011 because Shell had decided to stop paying them incentives designed ... to prevent acts of sabotage (Amunwa 2011: 42).

Since then, the "militianization" of oil-producing areas has continued unabated. For example, in Obagi, an Egi community in Rivers State, Total has been accused of financing a "youth forum" that acted as a vigilante group, monopolized security contracts, and cracked down on protestors with the support of the police (Ovadia 2016: 186). Rather than helping to pacify the situation, development efforts have also contributed to fueling conflicts. As they have grown in scale, corporate social responsibility programs have provoked resentment because they have failed to lead to tangible results, while compensation paid by the oil industry has often been diverted by traditional chiefs, liaison officers, and oligarchs collaborating with gangs (Faleti 2009: 24, Frynas 2005: 589).

The focus on so-called host communities in particular has caused tensions with villagers living outside extractive areas. In the Ogba-Egbema-Ndoni and Eastern Obolo LGAs of Rivers State and Akwa Ibom State, respectively, surveys thus showed that grievances against oil companies have tended to increase in direct proportion to the distance from wells and pipelines, no doubt because remote communities felt a greater sense of neglect (Renouard *et al.* 2008: 8).

In addition, development and welfare projects on the territory of host communities have seldom been inclusive, because they have generally been implemented by engineers and managers prioritizing technical solutions without considering social issues (Frynas 2005). In the absence of standards and guidelines, finally, villages and individuals of equivalent status have not received the same levels of compensation, which depend on the approaches taken by different companies and subcontractors.

In fact, the industry's main goal was to buy social peace and certainly not to satisfy a wide range of competing demands. To be accepted by locals, oil companies have sometimes rewarded the communities most willing to cooperate.[1] In other cases, however, they have focused on troublemakers to try to put an end to sabotage. As a result, their development projects have often targeted the most restive communities and youth. Oil companies have thus been accused of favoring criminals while seeking to divide and rule. Some have publicly admitted the limitations of their social policy in this regard. For example, Shell has acknowledged that the payment of cash compensation has occasionally fueled conflicts within communities and between rival groups (Idemudia & Ite 2006: 199). In one of its official magazines, Total also once published an interview with an Egi chief of Obagi who complained that the group's development programs had brought insecurity by attracting migrants.[2]

4   Three Divided "Blocs"

Undoubtedly, the situation is quite complex. The Niger Delta's various problems highlight the need to move beyond any simplistic opposition between, on the one hand, oil companies and their allies in government and, on the other, a vague, brave "civil society". In reality, none of these "blocs" are homogeneous and monolithic. For example, civil society, a catch-all concept, conceals many internal contradictions: ethnic antagonisms, class struggles, personal rivalries, age-group conflicts, etc.[3] Since the end of the Biafran War, in particular, the coastal communities of the Niger Delta have fought against each other to secure their share of the so-called national cake, in contrast to the period just

---

1 During Ken Saro-Wiwa's trial in 1995, the prosecution witnesses thus included many beneficiaries of Shell's water conveyance programs in Bodo, the "capital-city" of Ogoniland (Aaron & Patrick 2013: 348).
2 Chief Oris Uchendu Onyiri, quoted in *Total itinéraire(s)* 2, 2013: 25.
3 For critiques of the notion of civil society, see Ikelegbe 2001, Pérouse de Montclos 2018: 67–71.

before and after independence when they briefly tried to unite to resist interference by both the central government and the Eastern Region.

As for the ruling class, it has remained notoriously divided by personal rivalries, political parties, cronyism, and tribalism—not to mention the disputes
opposing the federal government, the 36 states, and the 774 LGAs of Nigeria in
the distribution of oil revenues. For example, from the end of the military dictatorship in 1999, Abuja and the coastal states fought over controlling the proceeds from offshore production until 2006, when the Supreme Court settled
the conflict by ruling in favor of the central government. In 2000, Imo and Abia
states also took legal action to recover oil wells located on a disputed border
with Rivers State, where operations had been suspended by a commission led
by Justice Mamman Nasir in 1976 (*Newswatch* 2000).

At the federal level, the political class is not unified either when it comes
to the development of the industry. For example, the main opposition candidates at the 2007 presidential elections recommended either privatizing joint
ventures, with Atiku Abubakar, or returning to the nationalization programs
of the 1970s, with Mohammed Buhari. Over time, the ruling class has admittedly been relatively consistent in its policy of promoting Nigerians in the oil
industry, first through "indigenization" decrees, and later through laws on the
"local content" of transnational corporations. In other areas, however, the government has lacked coherence and vision. Every president since the end of
the military dictatorships in 1999 has thus been infatuated with projects that
never materialized and that were subsequently abandoned, as with Umaru
Yar'Adua's plans for a trans-Saharan pipeline or Goodluck Jonathan's project
for a gas liquefaction plant in Brass.

The international oil companies themselves can hardly be said to form a
homogeneous capitalist and industrial bloc. They are driven by the search
for profit and, despite some degree of cross-shareholding between subsidiaries (such as Total's and Shell's) in Nigeria, they compete to obtain OPLs (Oil
Prospecting Licenses) and, if they find deposits in sufficient commercial quantities, OMLs (Oil Mining Leases). Moreover, their interests diverge according
to their size, their experience in the industry, their technology, their degree of
social integration in the local context, their contractual regimes, their char-
ters, their international dimension, the origin of their capital, and the location of their wells. The sector also includes a public company, NNPC (Nigerian
National Petroleum Corporation), and a myriad of "independent" operators,
"subcontractors", and "indigenous" firms.

As further evidence of this heterogeneity, oil workers are typically at loggerheads with management. The industry has some of the country's most active
unions, whether in the public or private sectors. Lockouts in oil company

offices and mining sites are a relatively common occurrence. On occasion, protests can even turn violent, although not as a result of union directives. The occupation of pumping stations often involves oil engineers, contractors, and youths tasked with ensuring security. Many instances of pipeline sabotage are, in fact, insider jobs. Sometimes, dismissed or retired staff have also expressed their discontent by attacking oil companies, which have generally done little to monitor former employees. For example, in Bayelsa State in 1991, an engineer who used to work for Elf, Nimi Barigha-Amage, mobilized Nembe youths and formed a militia which, by 2000, had morphed into a secret society called Iseinasawo (Watts 2004: 63). In Delta State, Tom Polo was first a contractor for Shell and Chevron before participating to the foundation of militant platforms such as FNDIC and MEND. His engineering and organizational skills helped him to command fighters and develop crude oil theft on an industrial scale. Likewise, Ebikabowei Victor-Ben, a.k.a. "General Boyloaf", used his knowledge of the Bayelsa coast and the maritime industry to plan the MEND's spectacular 2008 attack on Bonga, a Shell rig in deep offshore waters.

FIGURE 28   Ebikabowei Victor-Ben "Boyloaf", one of the founders of MEND, in
             Abuja (2021)

5   The Trade Unions

By contrast, oil workers live in a world apart. They earn significantly more than their counterparts in the civil service and enjoy better social protection compared with other companies in the formal private sector. In Nigeria, they form a sort of "labor aristocracy" that has come to replace the coal miners who had led the famous strikes repressed by the British in Enugu in 1949 (Falola 2009). Their organizations—namely, NUPENG (Nigeria Union of Petroleum and Natural Gas Workers) and PENGASSAN (Petroleum and Natural Gas Senior Staff Association of Nigeria)—were initially founded in 1978 when the military signed a Trade Union Decree with the aim, among other things, of unifying company-based unions to strengthen state control over a sector due to be nationalized. During the economic crisis of the 1980s, blue-collar and white-collar workers then rose up against the Structural Adjustment Plan introduced by the World Bank, which led to numerous job losses. They also took part in the major strikes held in 1994 against the dictatorship of Sani Abacha (Nwokeji 2007: 65).

To this day, the oil industry remains Nigeria's most heavily unionized sector. According to estimates, 100% of production workers and around 50% of contractors belong to a union. However, labor organizations have lost members since the collapse of oil prices in the mid-2010s. The recession made large numbers of staff redundant, a phenomenon reminiscent of the 1983–1986 economic crisis, when the industry employed some 10,000 people in the public sector, with a further 10,000 working for international oil companies and another 10,000 employed by domestic and foreign contractors (Turner 1986: 41). Growing job insecurity has also weakened a workforce increasingly hired on a short-term basis. Since 2005, finally, salaried workers are no longer required to join a union.

Just as the industry includes majors and domestic firms operating alongside a public company, oil engineers, accountants, tanker drivers, mechanics and welders thus do not form a monolithic bloc. The point can be illustrated by the establishment of two unions: NUPENG and PENGASSAN. The first defends the interests of manual workers. Despite a drop in its membership from 14,000 in 1988 to 8,000 in 2005, it retains significant influence inasmuch as it is capable of blocking refineries and fuel distribution across the entire country (Kraus 2018: 400, Houeland 2015: 29). As for PENGASSAN, it represents white-collar workers and, if we are to believe its own figures, its membership increased from 14,000 at the end of the military dictatorship in 1999 to 21,000 in 2019.

Both unions have sometimes cooperated when negotiating collective bargaining agreements with oil companies. However, their social bases differ widely and the diversification of professional statuses has not been conducive to mobilization. Moreover, NUPENG and PENGASSAN no longer hold a monopoly since the introduction in 2005 of a law (the Trade Union Act) aimed at deregulating labor organizations and promoting freedom of choice. With growing job insecurity, moreover, unionized workers are increasingly challenged by contractors recruited on an ad hoc basis and who sometimes play the role of "yellows" to break strikes. They also face conflicts with indigenous day laborers hired in host communities to meet the requirements of "local content" regulations and corporate social responsibility programs.

Such opposition reveals a wide gap with the Niger Delta rebels who kidnap oil workers, whether Nigerians or expatriates. In the past, Marxist authors highlighted the possibility of an alliance between the "labor aristocracy" and the militants during the large strike of July 1994, when half of the PENGASSAN demands coincided with the claims of host communities in oil-producing areas (Turner 1997: 81). However, no evidence has ever emerged of any real attempt at coordinating unionists and MOSOP activists. Likewise, in June 2003, the national strike against rising fuel prices took place independently of the women's protests that were ongoing at the same time against Shell and Chevron in the Niger Delta (Turner & Brownhill 2004). Since then, union activists in the industry have remained relatively disconnected from militants of all sorts, especially from the jobless youth in the creeks.

References

Aaron, Kiikpoye & John Patrick. 2013. "Corporate Social Responsibility Patterns and Conflicts in Nigeria's Oil-Rich Region". *International Area Studies Review* 16 (4): 341–356.

Amunwa, Ben. 2011. *Counting the Cost: Corporations and Human Rights Abuses in the Niger Delta*. London: Platform.

Burgis, Tom. 2015. *The Looting Machine: Warlords, Tycoons, Smugglers and the Systematic Theft of Africa's Wealth*. London: William Collins.

Courson, Elias. 2006. *Odi Revisited? Oil and State Violence in Odioma, Brass LGA, Bayelsa State*. Berkeley: University of California, Institute of International Studies.

Ebiede, Tarila Marclint, Celestine Oyom Bassey & Judith Burdin Asuni (eds). 2021. *Insecurity in the Niger Delta. A Report on Emerging Threats in Akwa Ibom, Bayelsa, Cross River, Delta, Edo and Rivers States*. London: Adonis & Abbey Publishers.

Faleti, Stephen. 2009. *Challenges of Chevron's GMOU Implementation in Itsekiri Communities of Western Niger Delta*. Zaria: IFRA.

Falola, Toyin. 2009. *Colonialism and Violence in Nigeria*. Indianapolis: Indiana University Press.

Frynas, Jedrzej Georg. 2003. "The Oil Industry in Nigeria: Conflict between Oil Companies and Local People". In *Transnational Corporations and Human Rights*, edited by Jedrzej Georg Frynas & Scott Pegg: 99–114. London: Palgrave Macmillan.

Frynas, Jedrzej George. 2005. "The False Development Promise of Corporate Social Responsibility: Evidence from Multinational Oil Companies". *International Affairs* 81 (3): 581–98.

Houeland, Camilla. 2015. "Casualisation and Conflict in the Niger Delta: Nigerian Oil Workers' Unions between Companies and Communities". *Revue Tiers Monde* 224: 25–46.

ICG. 2006. *The Swamps of Insurgency: Nigeria's Delta Unrest*. Brussels: International Crisis Group.

Idemudia, Uwafiokun & Ite, Uwem. 2006. "Corporate-Community Relations in Nigeria's Oil Industry: Challenges and Imperatives". *Corporate Social Responsibility and Environmental Management* 13 (4): 194–206.

Ikelegbe, Augustine. 2001. "The Perverse Manifestation of Civil Society: Evidence from Nigeria". *Journal of Modern African Studies* 39 (1): 1–24.

Kraus, Jon. 2018. "The Political Struggles of Nigerian Labor". In *The Oxford Handbook of Nigerian Politics*, edited by Carl LeVan & Patrick Ukata: 387–405. Oxford: OUP.

Newswatch. 16 October 2000. Lagos: 18–23.

Nwokeji, Ugo. 2007. *The Nigerian National Petroleum Corporation and the Development of the Nigerian Oil and Gas Industry: History, Strategies and Current Directions*. Houston (TX): Rice University, James A. Baker III Institute for Public Policy.

Obi, Cyril. 2008. "Enter the Dragon? Chinese Oil Companies & Resistance in the Niger Delta". *Review of African Political Economy* 117: 417–434.

Okhomina, Osa. 12 Jan. 2010. "SPDC Backs Out of Pipeline Security Contract with Ex-Militant in Bayelsa". Abuja: *Leadership*.

Ovadia, Jesse Salah. 2016. *The Petro-Developmental State in Africa: Making Oil Work in Angola, Nigeria and the Gulf of Guinea*. London: Hurst.

Peel, Michael. 2009. *A Swamp Full of Dollars: Pipelines and Paramilitaries at Nigeria's Oil Frontier*. London: IB Tauris.

Pegg, Scott. 1999. "The Cost of Doing Business: Transnational Corporations and Violence in Nigeria". *Security Dialogue* 30 (4): 473–484.

Pendleton, Andrew. 2004. *Behind the Mask: The Real Face of Corporate Social Responsibility*. London: Christian Aid.

Pérouse de Montclos, Marc-Antoine. 2003. "Pétrole et sécurité privée au Nigeria: un complexe multiforme à l'épreuve du 'syndrome de Monaco'". *Cultures et conflits* 52 : 117–138.

Pérouse de Montclos, Marc-Antoine. 2012. "Rebelles, gangsters et cadets sociaux dans le delta du Niger: les jeunes au défi de la politique". In *L'Afrique des générations. Entre tensions et négociations*, edited by Muriel Gomez-Perez & Marie Nathalie Leblanc : 617–644. Paris: Karthala.

Pérouse de Montclos, Marc-Antoine. 2018. *Déconstruire la guerre. Acteurs, discours, controverses*. Paris: Éditions Fondation de la Maison des Sciences de l'Homme.

Pérouse de Montclos, Marc-Antoine (ed.). 2016. *Violence in Nigeria: A Qualitative and Quantitative Analysis*. Ibadan: IFRA-Nigeria, Leiden: African Studies Centre.

Pratten, David. 2007. "The 'Rugged Life'. Youth and Violence in Southern Nigeria", In *Violence and Non-Violence in Africa*, edited by Pal Ahluwalia, Louise Bethlehem & Ruth Ginio: 84–104. New York: Routledge.

Renouard, Cécile *et al.* 2008. *L'impact de l'activité pétrolière sur le développement local au Nigeria: enquêtes dans les zones d'Onelga (Rivers State) et d'Eastern Obolo (Akwa Ibom State)*. Paris: Manuscript.

Sesay, Amadu, Charles Ukeje, Aina Olabisi & Adetanwa Odebiyi (eds). 2003. *Ethnic Militias and the Future of Democracy in Nigeria*. Ile-Ife: Obafemi Awolowo University Press.

Timsar, Rebecca Golden. 2015. "Oil, Masculinity, and Violence: Egbesu Worship in the Niger Delta of Nigeria". In *Subterranean Estates: Life Worlds of Oil and Gas*, edited by Hannah Appel, Arthur Mason & Michael Watts: 72–89. Ithaca: Cornell University Press.

Turner, Terisa. 1986. "Oil Workers and the Oil Bust in Nigeria". *Africa Today* 33 (4): 33–50.

Turner, Terisa. 1997. "Oil Workers and Oil Communities in Africa: Nigerian Women and Grassroots Environmentalism". *Labour, Capital and Society* 30 (1): 67–89.

Turner, Terisa & Leigh Brownhill. 2004. "Why Women Are at War with Chevron: Nigerian Subsistence Struggles against the International Oil Industry". *Journal of Asian and African Studies* 39 (1): 63–93.

Von Kemedi, Dimieari. 2006. *Fuelling the Violence: Non-State Armed Actors (Militia, Cults, and Gangs) in the Niger Delta*. Berkeley: University of California.

Watts, Michael. 2004. "Resource Curse? Governmentality, Oil and Power in the Niger Delta, Nigeria". *Geopolitics* 9 (1): 50–80.

CHAPTER 9

Majors, Domestic Firms, and the National Company

A Multifaceted Industry

The offices of so-called indigenous oil companies are generally modest. They bear little resemblance to the huge compounds of Shell or Total in Port Harcourt, which are so vast that they look like cities. Heavily guarded behind high walls mounted with barbed wire, the enclaves of the majors are indeed modeled on base camps patrolled by police and private security operatives. Supplied by electricity from generators, they are designed to be self-contained. They have their own supermarkets, swimming pools, tennis courts, and water and fuel reserves. Their residents, both expatriates and Nigerians, live behind closed doors and move in convoys with armed escorts whenever they go to their offices or to production sites.

Domestic firms have nothing in common with these fortresses. In Lagos, their offices are concentrated along two potholed streets, Lugard Avenue and Bishop Aboyade Cole Street, in Victoria Island, a smart neighborhood. It is here that I meet Layi Fatona, a geologist who in 2012 built the first private refinery in Nigeria, in Ogbele, near Ahoada in Rivers State.[1] His unit processes only 1,000 barrels a day and is much smaller than the Dangote group's gigantic petrochemical complex, which was scheduled for completion in Lagos in 2023, after considerable delays. The Ogbele refinery is, nonetheless, an oddity. It is run by a firm founded and managed by Fatona, NDEP (Niger Delta Exploration & Production), that has neither expatriate employees nor foreign capital. Most of its staff first worked for international oil companies and so have prior experience in the downstream sector. According to Fatona, their direct vested interests in NDEP's results explain their dynamism and their loyalty, despite the risk of losing employees to the majors and their higher wages.

---

1 Technically speaking, Nigeria's first refinery, which started operating at Port Harcourt in 1965, was semi-private, half-owned by Shell-BP. In 1971, the federal government then took over a 60% stake. Built by ENI and inaugurated in Warri in 1978, Nigeria's second refinery was 100% state-owned from the outset. From the very beginning, it operated at a loss, since the petrol it produced was more expensive than imported (Turner 1977).

FIGURE 29   Apapa port in Lagos (2010)

1   Oil Production: A Wide Range of Actors

The wide range of actors operating in the industry points to the dangers of simplification. Insofar as it is entirely controlled by the Nigerian state, the national oil company is completely different from listed majors. It pays taxes to the Finance Ministry and it has generally been treated by civilian and military regimes as a "cash cow" to maintain their grip on power. The junta led by General Ibrahim Babangida, for example, plundered NNPC in such a way that the company's accounting department, located on the top floors of a Lagos skyscraper, had to be gutted by arsonists to destroy compromising documents when two separate audits began, in April 1986, to uncover the scale of embezzlement. From August 1990 onward, the first Gulf crisis then led to a sharp increase in oil prices, yet without any impact on the government's revenue. In the meantime, the Group Managing Director of the company had been "reduced to a glorified chief clerk, completely at the beck and call of the Petroleum Minister who also [doubled] as the Chairman of the Board of the NNPC" (Olorunfemi, Adetunji & Olaiya 2014: ch. 6).

The result was that Nigeria's largest public enterprise was no longer able to maintain its operations. Successive governments were so keen to keep their main slush fund that, except for a few assets in petrochemicals, they never gave serious consideration to the idea of privatizing the national oil company to ensure its financial independence and improve its performance. As early as 1988, a study by Arthur Andersen had recommended commercializing NNPC on the basis of a holding similar to that of the United Africa Company (UAC). From 2007, the Petroleum Industry Bill (PIB) also planned to privatize the national oil company to cope with the challenges of a rising competition from "independents" and the Dangote refinery, respectively in the upstream and downstream sectors. However, the government steadfastly refused to relinquish control of a bureaucratic giant that remained immune to the logic of profitability of transnational corporations—even at the risk of compromising its economic viability. Privatization was eventually the order of the day when a new law, the PIA, was passed in 2021. Yet it seemed too late: NNPC was heavily indebted and had become reminiscent of NITEL (Nigerian Telecommunications), another public entity that the government was never able to sell because of a lack of interest from potential buyers.

The national oil company is powerful only because it is a gatekeeper: a *passage obligé* for private partners in joint ventures. On paper, for instance, its operational branch, the NPDC (Nigerian Petroleum Development Company), is the largest Nigerian operator in the sector. Created in 1988, it saw its production increase from 50,000 to 130,000 barrels a day between 2010 and 2014, when President Goodluck Jonathan granted it large parts of OMLS 4, 30, 34, 38, and 41 purchased from Shell in 2008. In an interview published in *The News* on 24 February 2014, an NPDC manager even suggested targeting a daily output of a quarter of a million barrels by 2020. Yet the NNPC's operational branch failed to grow because it was not independent from the government, an issue that also affected the bogus companies that some producing states tried in vain to develop, such as Midwestern in Delta State or Bayelsa Oil in OML 56.

From a budgetary perspective, the NPDC indeed cannot reinvest profits into production without the consent of Abuja. As a government arm, moreover, it is generally viewed with distrust by Niger Delta militants and it has just as many problems with local communities as its private sector counterparts. After obtaining OML 30, for instance, the NPDC had to suspend its work in Oroni for nearly two months and wait until late 2013 before resuming operations at Uzere, which had remained closed by Shell for two years. Its track record is no better on the environmental front. Instead of leading by example for the government, the NPDC was the last company to still flare gas on a significant scale, as in Oredo in 2014. Because of insufficient capital, it was also unable to develop its deep offshore activities. Being tied to government, finally, the NPDC was not free from political interference. Thus, it could easily have secured loans guaranteed by its current operations in OMLS 4, 30, 34, 38, and 41, but it was forced by the government to contract a "strategic alliance" with two firms linked to President Goodluck Jonathan's oil minister and chief of staff. These companies, Atlantic and Septa, were not operational. Yet they received a share of the NPDC's production to raise funds abroad.

2   Transnational Corporations

Although they operate differently, transnational corporations do not form a homogeneous block either. They have never been able to come together to resist nationalization or tax rises. The early days of oil production in Nigeria are significant in this respect. When the government set out to revise its fiscal policy to meet the requirements of OPEC, Gulf, Tenneco, Phillips, Amoseas, and Safrap initially attempted to form a cartel to prevent the adoption of a Petroleum Profits Tax Ordinance which provided for a change mirroring taxation increases elsewhere on the continent. However, their lobbying failed to stop Lagos from achieving its goal. Passed in December 1966, the ordinance instead shed light on the deep divisions within the industry. While Shell had already begun secret negotiations with the Nigerian government, Gulf terminated in February 1967 its alliance with the other foreign companies. The latter eventually agreed to tax rises equivalent to 50% of their royalties to penalize their competitors among the "independents", which were smaller and less able to raise capital to make up for the shortfall (Klieman 2012: 159, Pearson 1970: 24–27).

In January 1970, the end of the Biafran War did not spell the end of these rivalries. On the contrary, the ensuing oil boom had the effect of increasing competition. Just after the war, the first tender for offshore blocks was awarded to an American firm, the Occidental Petroleum Corporation, because its director, Armand Hammer, had bypassed the others and negotiated in person with the head of the military junta in Lagos, Yakubu Gowon, to let the government take a 51% stake (Klieman 2012: 164). His initiative broke the unity of the international companies opposed to the establishment of joint ventures that were to replace the former system of concessions in which they alone bore the risks and costs associated with prospecting and producing oil.

Throughout the 1970s, the pressure exerted by the government to increase its stake in the industry thus highlighted tensions among the majors. Most international companies eventually agreed to partner with NNPC to establish joint ventures in which each party retained its legal personality while sharing the risks and costs. At the same time, they sought to resist the development of PSCs (Production Sharing Contracts), which were even more advantageous to the Nigerian state and which became increasingly common with "independent" firms such as Ashland in 1973 and Sunlink in 1987. In this system, operators were left alone to bear all the risk. In other words, the government was discharged of any financial obligations but remained the owner of concessions. In exchange, oil companies retained a portion of production once they had recovered their initial stake and paid their operating costs and tax liabilities.

The PSCs were used extensively in the development of offshore fields from 1991 onward, at a time when the junta led by General Ibrahim Babangida also sought to renew the contractual framework of joint ventures—by adding so-called JOA (Joint Operating Agreement) clauses with a view to enabling NNPC to gradually take control of all exploration and production operations (Lukman 1994). By contrast, service agreements proved unpopular because they reduced oil companies to a mere subcontracting role and required them to bear all the costs with no rights over the volumes extracted. At the end of the military dictatorship in 1999, oil production in Nigeria therefore continued to be run for the most part through joint ventures with NNPC, accounting for around 70% of the total, compared with 25% in the case of PSCs.

Contractual frameworks and foreign or national ownerships, however, are not the only criteria that distinguish different sets of operators within the industry. Companies' profiles also depend on their footprint, their size, and their type of activities. Some transnational corporations, for instance, invested at a very early stage in natural gas: the first large-scale project was developed by Chevron in Escravos in 1997. Others positioned themselves in offshore production to escape security challenges on the main land. ExxonMobil, which had little activity onshore, thus extended its assets at sea, together with Total, which rose from the fifth to the fourth oil major in Nigeria in the 2000s. Shell, Chevron, and Agip, by contrast, suffered more from unrest in the creeks of the Niger Delta between 2005 and 2009.

Regarding their footprint, most oil majors have their own maritime terminal. While Texaco used to work from the mouth of Pennington River, Shell still exports its production via Forcados and Bonny; ExxonMobil, via Qua Iboe; Chevron, via Escravos; and Agip, via Brass. Yet the exposure of international oil companies to violence depends not only on their location, but also on their production volume, their operating model, and, of course, the quality of their relations with host communities (Pérouse de Montclos 2003, Omeje 2006, Omoweh 2007). The way they implement corporate social responsibility testifies to these differences. In the absence of standards, oil companies have funded community programs without common processes and procedures. According to Kiikpoye Aaron, for example, Shell was penalized by its heavy bureaucracy, while Chevron, by contrast, was seen as more dynamic in Delta State and Agip

FIGURE 30   The Brass oil terminal (2011)

as more effective among the Ogbia of Bayelsa State, where Claude Ake, a well-known economics professor, set up a development association in his region of origin (Aaron 2012, Aaron & Patrick 2013: 353).

In other words, a whole range of factors explain why some companies fare better than others. According to data collected by the NigeriaWatch project between 2006 and 2021, for example, NNPC was the operator most frequently

FIGURE 31   Onne port in Rivers State (2011)

targeted by Niger Delta militants, well ahead of Shell, Agip, and Chevron.[2] By contrast, ExxonMobil was the least affected by lethal attacks during this period. If we are to believe its executives, this is because the company was an early promoter of "local content" among its staff. In the mid-2000s, 45% of its managers and 60% of its workers thus came from Akwa Ibom State, compared with 20% in the early 1990s. ExxonMobil also claimed it was a pioneer in reducing the proportion of its flared gas volumes in Nigeria, lowering it to around 30% of its production in the mid-2000s, compared with 70% in other companies.

Yet other reasons played a role. Unlike other companies, first, ExxonMobil did not extract oil on the mainland. As a result, it was less likely to pollute and disrupt rural communities. Thanks to its position offshore, moreover, ExxonMobil could continue exporting its production in supertankers at sea whenever access routes to its heliports and its Qua Iboe terminal were blocked by angry youths. Unlike Shell and Chevron, whose wells were far more dispersed, the company also benefited from the fact that its assets were concentrated in Akwa Ibom State and, more precisely, in four LGAs that accommodated some 300,000 inhabitants and which, for a variety of reasons, offered more potential for developing infrastructure projects.

---

2   http://www.nigeriawatch.org/.

3   "Independent" and "Indigenous" Operators

As we can see, oil majors present a wide range of profiles. In addition, they operate alongside a myriad of smaller "independent" firms. The latter include an increasing number of so-called indigenous companies that contribute a lot to the heterogeneity of the industry. "Independent" operators are Nigerian to varying degrees: Addax, Afren, and Waltersmith, for instance, are under Chinese, British, and Canadian control, respectively. However, they work with local companies and some of them are full members of a lobby, the OPTS (Oil Producers Trade Section), that groups Nigerian and foreign private firms together with transnational corporations.

Afren is a good example of this complexity. From 2007, it financed the development of an offshore field on OML 46, Eremor, with Excel Exploration and Production, a company managed by Allison Amaechina Madueke, a retired admiral and the husband of President Goodluck Jonathan's oil minister—a useful connection since the minister in question had previously worked for Shell, from which the block was purchased. As for Heritage Oil, another British company, it partnered with Shoreline Natural Resources Limited, a Nigerian firm holding a 45% stake in a block, OML 30, purchased in 2012 from Shell, Total, and Agip following the withdrawal of Conoil, a direct competitor. Such a joint venture proved relatively successful. Within two years, it increased its output from 20,000 to 44,000 barrels a day. Established in 2010 by Orikolade Karim, a businessman from Lagos, Shoreline was forced nonetheless to entrust the operational side to Heritage Oil, a controversial company registered in Jersey and led by a former British mercenary, Tony Buckingham, who had been involved in shady dealings in Uganda and in an attempted coup in Equatorial Guinea in 2004.

"Indigenous" companies are just as diverse (see Appendix 2). The pioneers emerged in the wake of the 1973 oil crisis and the nationalizations that led to the creation of NNPC in 1977. For example, Delta Oil, a local subsidiary of the US firm Pan Ocean, was founded in 1973 by an Ijaw Kalabari chief from Rivers State, Godfrey Kio Jaja Amachree (1917–1999), and it began producing three years later in Ogharefe in OML 98. At the time, the allocation of concessions was by mutual agreement, without a tender process. Nigerian entrepreneurs lacked technical resources and had no choice but to partner with Western companies to produce oil whenever they found some, as shown by the joint venture between the US firm Monsanto Oil and Niger Oil Resources, a company founded by a Yoruba politician from Abeokuta, Chief Babatunde Akin-Olugbade (1913–1987). Among these pioneers, only Henry Oloyede

Fajemirokun (1926–1978), a Yoruba from Ondo, attempted to develop a block by himself—but to no avail.[3]

During the oil boom of the 1970s, the military juntas in power did not overtly support the Nigerian private sector. They preferred to rely on a public corporation, NNPC. Nonetheless, they did let small Nigerian firms take control of fuel distribution networks, which had just been nationalized in the downstream sector, and operate marginal fields that were no longer of interest to oil majors in the upstream sector. A company such as Conoil, for instance, was incorporated in August 1984, followed by Dubri in August 1987, Solgas in September 1990, Atlas Petroleum International in December 1991, Moni Pulo in March 1992, Allied Energy Resources in June 1992, Amni International Petroleum Development in June 1993, and Express Petroleum & Gas Limited in November 1995.

In power from August 1985 to June 1993, General Ibrahim Babangida was the first to open the upstream sector to indigenous private companies, with a tender in November 1990. In the context of discretionary regimes, the attribution of oil concessions enabled northern military officers to reward their friends, including allies in the south. Political connections were more important than technical performance, and most successful bidders never produced a single drop of oil. Of the 187 licenses awarded to Nigerian firms in 1990, only two were developed, by Yoruba businessmen in Ondo and Edo states, respectively with Mike Adenuga of Conoil and Moshood Abiola of Summit Oil. It was General Sani Abacha who, after taking power in 1993, organized in 1996 another bid, which led domestic companies to venture into offshore production.

While Chevron became the first major to sell some of its mining rights to a Nigerian firm, the allocation of concessions, however, mainly concerned minor fields on the mainland. The objective of the Petroleum Marginal Fields Decree no. 23 of 1996 was indeed to develop deposits that did not interest international oil companies, because these deposits produced fewer than 50,000 barrels a day. Yet the project did not go far. Foreign companies resisted it because the new regulation compelled them to relinquish to Nigerian firms at least 60% of their stakes in joint ventures (JV) or production sharing agreements (PSA) if they failed to develop marginal fields. Moreover, the controversial decree was applied retroactively and violated previous contracts signed with the government. The allocation of concessions, finally, tended to be arbitrary because it aimed to reward businessmen loyal to the regime—including oil minister Dan Etete, an Ijaw (see Box 1).

---

3   On this period, see Forrest 1994.

BOX 1 The Allocation of Oil Concessions under Sani Abacha

Indigenous companies that received concessions were often owned by Muslims from the north with close ties to the heads of the military juntas in power in the 1990s. Notable examples include:

- Alhaji Sani Bello, a colonel from Kontagora in Niger State, whose company Amni secured OMLS 112 and 117 in August 1993 and August 1999 respectively. His son, Abu, was married to the oldest daughter of a close collaborator of Sani Abacha, General Abdulsalami Abubakar, briefly in power from June 1998 to May 1999. Amni survived the end of the dictatorship and, in March 2006, resumed operations with the British firm Afren on OML 112.
- Alhaji Ahmed Mai Deribe, from Borno, a former treasurer of the NPN (National Party of Nigeria), in power during the Second Republic and the founder of Cavendish Petroleum, which secured OML 110 in August 1996.
- Alhaji Aminu Dantata, a Hausa businessman from Kano, one of the founders of the NPN and the managing director of Express Petroleum and Gas Limited, which secured OML 108 in November 1995. To develop the block, the company partnered with a Houston-based firm called CAMAC (Cameroon-American), led by a Nigerian-American called Kase Lawal.
- Alhaji Saleh Mohammed Jambo, an *éminence grise* of the NPN and the husband of the daughter of a former governor of Kano State, in power from May 1967 to July 1975. In October 1991, his firm, NorthEast Petroleum Nigerian Limited (NEPNL), known as NorEast, was granted operating licenses for OPLS 215, 276, and 283 by General Ibrahim Babangida. However, his subsidiary, Rayflosh Petroleum, was unable to develop these fields under the Sani Abacha dictatorship.
- Alhaji Mohammed Indimi, a Muslim from Borno with ties to Sudan. A Kanuri, like Sani Abacha, he married his daughter Rahama to Ibrahim Babangida's eldest son, Mohammed. His company, Oriental Energy Resources Limited, was founded in September 1990, just two months before the opening of the first tender open to indigenous firms. Like NorEast, it produced no oil.

4 A Highly Political Nigerianization of the Industry since 1999

In 1999, the return of civilians to power obviously changed the rules of the game. Initially, there was hope that the process of allocating blocks would become more competitive and transparent. As soon as 2000, president-elect Olusegun Obasanjo, who was also oil minister, launched a tender that resulted in 31 independent companies being allocated concessions in 2003. Unlike Ibrahim Babangida and Sani Abacha, who had tried to motivate Nigerian entrepreneurs to invest in offshore production, however, Obasanjo restricted domestic firms to exploiting marginal fields on the mainland. According to some experts in the industry, he went as far as to impede the expansion of businessmen who could have threatened his control over the sector. He thus maintained the division of labor that tasked majors with the technical challenges of developing offshore production.

Indeed, the exploitation of marginal fields requires only rudimentary equipment. Under the civilian regime, Conoil (off Akassa in Bayelsa since 1999), Moni Pulo (along the coast of Cross River since 2002), and Sapetro (in the Republic of Benin since 2013) were the only Nigerian operators to venture into offshore production. To extract nearly 10,000 barrels a day in Abana on OML 114, Moni Pulo thus acquired its own oil and gas separation unit, in Agbani, as well as a submarine pipeline to store its production on an FPSO (Floating Production Storage and Offloading) vessel located 42 kilometers off the coast of Calabar, albeit still in shallow waters. By contrast, Brittania-U was unable to go beyond the mouth of the Forcados River to exploit the Ajapa deposit on OML 90 from 2010 onward.

Nigerian oil companies face many challenges. First, they lack capital and know-how. To extract oil, they consequently have to contract foreign firms and cut costs by using second-hand equipment and machinery. As a result, their rigs often break down and many of them are not operational at all. Out of 24 licenses granted to Nigerian firms in 2003, for instance, only ten were developed, while the others were revoked. Ten years later, only a dozen companies could truly be said to be operational, among them Seplat, Energia, Midwestern, Pillar, Platform, NPDC, Afren, Conoil, Moni Pulo, Amni, Brittania-U, Pan Ocean, Sapetro, and Dubri.

Others simply manage their exploitation rights on the basis of their stake in joint ventures. Oando thus purchased wells operated by Agip in Delta State from ConocoPhilips in 2014, while Waltersmith bought in 2004 a block also operated by Agip in Imo State.[4] Many domestic firms actually lack the technical capacity to develop oil fields themselves. They have therefore to rely on foreign partners. As a result, they are sometimes seen as "Trojan horses" in that

---

4   Oando (Ocean and Oil) is a group with interests in distribution that was originally a Nigerian subsidiary of Esso before acquiring a stake in Unipetrol in 2000 and in Agip in 2002.

FIGURE 32   A gas flare in Nembe, Bayelsa State (2011)

they allow oil majors to circumvent indigenization requirements and escape the pressures exerted by environmental international NGOs (Olorunfemi, Adetunji & Olaiya 2014: ch. 1). Trade unionists, in particular, suspect multinationals of working through domestic companies in order to dismiss their own staff. Consequently and quite paradoxically, some of them oppose the withdrawal of majors and favor the privatization of the industry, to increase the wages of efficient operators (Pérouse de Montclos 2014).

These perceptions capture, albeit imperfectly, the complexity of the relationships between independent companies and multinationals. Many Nigerian firms actually use political connections to preempt rights of access and resell them for a profit to foreign partners tasked with developing production. A distinction should thus be made between Sapetro, Conoil, and Moni Pulo, which were able to secure concessions for a token fee, and companies that genuinely purchased their blocks, such as Seplat, NDEP, Neconde, and Shoreline. The end of military rule did little to prevent shady deals in this regard. In 2006, for example, Starcrest Energy, the small company of a key sponsor of the ruling party, Emeka Offor, was able to extract $35 million from Addax by reselling a license initially purchased for next to nothing following a deal on OPL 291. In the same vein, President Olusegun Obasanjo was suspected of hampering the development of businesses owned by rivals such as Mike Adenuga, the founder of Conoil, who was arrested in 2006 by EFCC's operatives after searching his offices and accusing him of embezzlement in two other firms of his group, Globacom and Equatorial Trust Bank (Adetona 2010).

After the election of President Goodluck Jonathan in 2011, the process of granting blocks to domestic and international companies continued to be arbitrary and discretionary. During the sale of onshore concessions in late 2013, for instance, the government turned a blind eye to the winners of tenders. The jewel of Shell in Bayelsa State, OML 29, was thus sold to Talveras and Aiteo, two trading companies controlled, respectively, by Igho Sanomi and Benedict Peters, both of whom had been involved in fraudulent and unaudited importations of refined products with subsidies. The government also threatened to revoke licenses of businessmen who refused to finance the party of Goodluck Jonathan. The transfer of ConocoPhilips' rights to Oando was consequently delayed because the latter was associated, via the Intels group, with Bola Tinubu and Atiku Abubakar, two important figures of the opposition.[5]

The case of Atlantic Energy speaks volume about such shady deals. With close ties to the oil minister Diezani Alison-Madueke and President Goodluck Jonathan's Chief of Staff, Mike Oghiadomhe, this firm was at the heart of a

---

5   This information, together with the subsequent paragraphs, is based for the most part on the Nigerian daily press. Aside from Atiku Abubakar, Intels was also controlled by northern Muslims such as Ado Bayero, the Emir of Kano, and Umaru Yar'Adua, Goodluck Jonathan's predecessor.

scandal in 2014 that resulted in suspending the governor of the Central Bank of Nigeria, Sanusi Lamido Sanusi, after he had denounced the company's fraudulent contracts with the NPDC. As part of a scheme to embezzle oil subsidies, Mike Oghiadomhe had indeed made a deal with Seven Energy, the parent company of Septa, and Jide Omokore, a man from Kogi State and the controversial owner of Atlantic. In 2011, the government granted them privileged access to blocks purchased by the NPDC from Shell in 2008. The two companies secured rights for next to nothing, against competitors such as Heritage and Eland Oil. Septa received OMLS 4, 38, and 41; Atlantic, OMLS 30 and 34. At the time, the shortfall was estimated at $1.5 billion at current market prices. In addition, both Septa and Atlantic artificially increased their operating costs to reduce their tax bill, as noted by Sanusi Lamido Sanusi prior to his suspension in 2014. Their contracts with the NPDC were finally rescinded after the election of President Muhammadu Buhari in 2015.

The story of Atlantic Energy shows that the political protections of Nigerian businesses are a double-edged sword indeed. On the one hand, they provide unique privileges and allow operators to purchase blocks below market value. On the other hand, they make domestic companies highly vulnerable to changes in government. Their survival depends on the capacity of their executive to negotiate with shady politicians. Mocked as "AGIP", the most skilled Nigerian entrepreneurs in the oil industry are ultimately those who are prepared to fund "Any Government In Power", regardless of their political, religious, or ethnic affiliations. For people such as Mike Adenuga (Conoil), Austin Avuru (Seplat), and Kola Aluko (Seven Energy), the challenge is invariably to diversify their alliances with a view to developing their business without being exclusively tied to any particular "godfather".

Despite reversals of fortune, some companies have been quite resilient in this regard. One example is Malabu Oil & Gas, which was established in April 1998 by three highly controversial individuals: Dan Etete, the then oil minister; Mohammed Sani Abacha, the dictator's son; and Hassan Hindu, the wife of a former Nigerian ambassador to the United Kingdom. Just five days after its (unusually speedy) incorporation, the company secured two significant blocks: OPL 245 and OPL 214. The conflict of interest was so blatant that Dan Etete chose to disguise himself under a fake name (Kweku Amafagha) to conceal his stake in Malabu. After the fall of the military dictatorship, he went to live in exile in France, where he was sentenced in absentia for fraud in November 2007. In Nigeria, Malabu's license was revoked by the government of Olusegun Obasanjo after April 2003. However, Dan Etete returned to favor in the wake of the April 2007 presidential elections. He was allowed to return to Nigeria to lay charges of corruption against Vice-President Atiku Abubakar, who was eyeing OPL 245 and who had emerged in the meantime as Olusegun Obasanjo's biggest rival. In April 2011, Etete even received over a billion dollars as a result of selling blocks to Shell and Agip that he had obtained for next to nothing. In return, Malabu discretely funded President Goodluck Jonathan and his oil minister, Diezani Alison-Madueke, who ranked as one of Nigeria's most corrupt women ever.

5   Reforms in Progress

Of course, such scandals worry investors who doubt the capacity of local businesses and independent operators to take over from the majors. As a token of their commitment, some domestic companies are listed on stock exchanges, such as Afren and Seplat in London or Oando in Johannesburg, Lagos, and Toronto. In the same vein, they look for cross shareholding opportunities with foreign partners to expand their activities beyond Nigeria. In the early 2010s, this was the case of Oando and Seplat, respectively with Bourbon and Maurel & Prom, two French companies. However, most local firms tend to be far more opaque than oil majors. For example, Septa and Neconde are among the few that completely refused to cooperate with NEITI audit requirements (Sada 2013). In addition, many domestic companies are financially vulnerable. In Nigeria, they generally struggle to raise funding because of high interest rates, while internationally they do not have sufficient production to put forward as collateral for loans. This lack of capital either encourages corruption or leads to excessive over-indebtedness, as with Oando. An alternative solution adopted by some domestic firms has been to merge with larger Nigerian groups. Owned by Mike Adenuga, Conoil, for example, has tried to cover itself and secure funding by relying on the revenue generated by Globacom, the telecommunications firm of its founder. Because of flagrant conflicts of interest, however, it could not get loans from Equatorial Trust Bank, which also belonged to Mike Adenuga and which was under-capitalized before being taken over by the government in 2009–2011.

In general, domestic companies therefore have no choice but to turn to foreign investors to secure the capital required to develop their blocks. One consequence of this is that, however diverse they may be, they experience recurrent challenges associated with their highly personalized operating model, their limited cash flow, their political connections, their ethnic composition, and their technical deficiencies. Domestic companies often depend on one man and do not seem to be able to survive after the death of their founder.[6] Moreover, the few that operate wells in the Niger Delta are suspected of pumping water which is then reinjected into pipelines shared with Shell. As for the others, many of them are designed to levy tolls for access to blocks as yet another means of misappropriating oil revenue.

In other words, domestic companies are currently not a viable alternative to multinationals, especially in offshore production. Many are content to hold shares in onshore joint ventures or in shallow waters near the coast. Few are willing, as part of production sharing agreements, to take sole responsibility for the risks involved in operating wells. Conoil, Moni Pulo, Amni, and Dubri are exceptions in this regard. Most local companies are actually gatekeepers that work in a rentier economy, as foreign investors are now compelled to form consortia in which Nigerians hold a majority stake. Combined with the government's indigenization policy, these developments largely explain why the share of independent operators in production has increased while international oil companies have stagnated, reduced their activities, or disinvested. For example, in late 2012, domestic firms accounted for 11% of Nigeria's oil output, amounting to 272,000 barrels per day, compared with less than 3% in the 1990s. Some even hoped that their share would rise to 20% in the following decade and eventually reach the symbolic threshold of half a million barrels a day.

Passed in 2021, the Petroleum Industry Act (PIA) supported this policy by providing for lower taxation of marginal fields, a key focus of domestic companies. However, as a result of the COVID-19 crisis, the collapse in demand and falling oil prices, combined with persistent insecurity in the Niger Delta, have hampered efforts to reinvigorate the sector. Despite their resilience, domestic companies have seen their rate of growth slow down. In addition, their advantages compared with majors have waned as they lost their agility, became more bureaucratic, and were in turn affected by crude oil theft. For investors, their novelty became no longer attractive. Quite on the contrary, the proliferation of operators has fragmented the industry and created a more complex legal landscape. Local firms that are not operational have also penalized Nigeria by levying commission and access charges which have increased production costs. Finally, the proliferation of domestic companies and gatekeepers has enabled Niger Delta communities to trade one off against the other. In their own way, the decline of the majors and the fragmentation of the oil industry have thus reflected the divisions of an elusive civil society.

---

6 There are exceptions, of course. Being younger, the wives of Olu Benson Lulu-Briggs and Theophilus Danjuma took the reins of, respectively, Moni Pulo and Sapetro after the death of their husbands. However, it is too early to say whether the transition to the next generation has been a success. In 2018, for instance, Managing Director Rahama "Yakolo" was sacked from Oriental Energy, the oil company of her father Mohammed Indimi.

References

Aaron, Kiikpoye. 2012. "New Corporate Social Responsibility Models for Oil Companies in Nigeria's Delta Region: What Challenges for Sustainability?" *Progress in Development Studies* 12 (4): 259–273.

Aaron, Kiikpoye & John Patrick. 2013. "Corporate Social Responsibility Patterns and Conflicts in Nigeria's Oil-Rich Region". *International Area Studies Review* 16 (4): 341–356.

Adetona, Sikiru. 2010. *Awujale: The Autobiography of Oba Sikiru Kayode Adetona Ogbagba II*. Ibadan: Mosuro.

Forrest, Thomas. 1994. *The Advance of African Capital. The Growth of Nigerian Private Enterprise*. Edinburgh: Edinburgh University Press.

Klieman, Kairn. 2012. "U.S. Oil Companies, the Nigerian Civil War, and the Origins of Opacity in the Nigerian Oil Industry", *Journal of American History* 99 (1): 155–165.

Lukman, Rilwanu. 1994. "Petroleum Resources: Boom or Doom?". In *Nigeria: The State of the Nation and the Way Forward*, edited by Abdullahi Mahadi, George Amale Kwanashie & Mahmood Yakubu: 191–208. Kaduna: Arewa House.

Olorunfemi, Michael, Akin Adetunji & Ade Olaiya. 2014. *Nigeria Oil and Gas: A Mixed Blessing? With A Chronicle of NNPC's Unfulfilled Mission*. Lagos: Kachifo Limited.

Omeje, Kenneth. 2006. *High Stakes and Stakeholders: Oil Conflict and Security in Nigeria*. Aldershot: Ashgate.

Omoweh, Daniel. 2007. *Shell Petroleum Development Company, the State, and Underdevelopment of Nigeria's Niger Delta: A Study in Environmental Degradation*. Trenton (NJ): Africa World Press.

Pearson, Scott [1970], *Petroleum and the Nigerian Economy*, California: Stanford University Press, pp. 24–27.

Pérouse de Montclos, Marc-Antoine. 2003. "Pétrole et sécurité privée au Nigeria: un complexe multiforme à l'épreuve du 'syndrome de Monaco'". *Cultures et conflits* 52 : 117–138.

Pérouse de Montclos, Marc-Antoine. 2014. "The Politics and Crisis of the Petroleum Industry Bill in Nigeria". *Journal of Modern African Studies* 52 (3): 403–424.

Sada, Idris & Co Chartered Accountants. 2013. *Financial Audit: An Independent Report Assessing and Reconciling Flows within Nigeria's Oil and Gas Industry, 2009 to 2011*. Abuja: Nigerian Extractive Industries Transparency Initiative.

Turner, Terisa. 1977. "Two Refineries: A Comparative Study of Technology Transfer to the Nigerian Refining Industry". *World Development* 5 (3): 235–256.

Ruling without Governing

The Challenges of Acephalous Societies

The tar road I am traveling along was built in 2003. Five years on, it is still in good condition, but it comes to an end in Iko, a village in Akwa Ibom State. From here, travelers who want to see the ocean have to continue their journey on speedboats toward the homeland of the Obolo people.

I have come to visit the chief of a small community near Iko. The elderly gentleman lives in a concrete house. Yet his "palace" can hardly be described as luxurious. The decor is minimal, consisting of the typical sofas, honorific portraits, and wooden furniture found in many homes across the region. It is ten o'clock in the morning and a distinct smell of alcohol emanates from the chief. I assume that it is either adulterated moonshine or a hair lotion. Things soon become clear when the chief offers me a low-quality brandy, which he hastens to down in large gulps.

I am faced with one of the challenges encountered by field researchers who, in the course of their interviews, are invited to taste unusual alcoholic beverages. I can just about manage palm wine, provided it is fresh and has just been tapped. But I struggle with *ogogoro* or *kai-kai*, a kind of raffia calvados that blows a hole in your stomach as surely as an oil drill. My thoughts begin to wander: what is this old drunk a chief *of*?

"Nothing"! That would probably have been the answer from an Ibo friend of mine who was prone to mocking Nigeria's pseudo-kings. Historically, most societies in the region were acephalous. In the hinterland, some of them were alledgedly organized as "village republics". When they arrived in the Niger Delta, the British did not find rulers capable of acting as middlemen to help maintain law and order on behalf of the colonial master. As a result, they had to create "kings" from scratch, the so-called warrant chiefs, who were appointed by decree.

My Ibo friend viewed this with a degree of cynicism. As he put it, the region had already experienced the slave trade and traditional rituals that included human sacrifice. Before the colonial era, many people were captured, never to be seen again. When the British ventured further inland into the bush, local communities viewed them with terror. Picture it: white monsters

© MARC-ANTOINE PÉROUSE DE MONTCLOS, 2024 | DOI:10.1163/9789004697911_012

FIGURE 33   A traditional chief from Eastern Obolo in Akwa Ibom State (2009)

accompanied by translators from the coastal city-states where slaves used to be taken away on a journey of no return. Unsurprisingly, villagers were scared. The white man kept asking who their chief was, yet they had no chief and they distrusted outsiders. What could they say? Bewildered, they would point to an idiot, the one individual they could spare and whose disappearance would cause no harm to the village. Today, their descendants claim to be customary chiefs. But their ancestors often had little standing within their community, or they were usurpers appointed by the British to replace leaders who had resisted colonial rule and ended up being deported within or outside of Nigeria.

Given this, it is difficult to disentangle the complexity of so-called civil society as opposed to oil companies and authoritarian governments. With exceptions, many communities in the Niger Delta appear to be relatively disorganized. That is not to say that they are devoid of social structures and hierarchies. Their members include rich and poor people, descendants of slaves and free men, godfathers and subalterns. But they traditionally tended to favor reaching a consensus before taking collective decisions. Even if they had powers, their patriarchs, spiritual leaders, or warlords could not act as rulers who would be obeyed without their authority being challenged at any time.

1   An Ethnic Puzzle

This configuration was a key factor in the dispersal of the various rebel groups and the different forms of protest seen throughout the Niger Delta. So-called civil society is no more homogeneous than the oil industry in this regard. The region is usually described as an "ethnic puzzle", characterized by extreme cultural and linguistic diversity (see Map 3). Neighboring villages often speak different languages, and collective identities are highly fluid, even within groups most steadfastly opposed to oil companies, such as the Ijaw and the Ogoni.

Roughly speaking, the main people inhabiting the huge delta of the Niger River, in the geographical sense of the term, include, from west to east, the Edo in Benin City, the Itsekiri in Warri, the Urhobo and the Isoko around Ughelli, the Ijaw in Forcados all the way to Port Harcourt, the Ibani in Bonny, the Ogoni in Bori, the Ibibio around Uyo, and the Efik in Calabar. Given the mixing of multilingual populations, however, it is difficult to identify communities on the basis of clearly demarcated borders and territories. In the absence of ethnic censuses, it is also impossible to estimate their numbers. While we know that the Edo, the Urhobo, the Ijaw, and the Ibibio represent relatively large populations, estimates of their demographic weight remain highly unreliable.

In seeking to advance their political agenda, some Niger Delta militants claim that the Ijaw represent the fourth-largest ethnic group in Nigeria (Adangor 2018). However, the available data paint a completely different picture in linguistic terms. According to a demographic health survey conducted in 2013, the Ijaw account for only 2% of the national population (National Population Commission 2013: 9). This is confirmed by other sources. Carried out between 2017 and 2020 among 1,600 adults across Nigeria's 36 states, Afrobarometer surveys (2020: 6–7, 2017: 5, 59) show that the Ijaw language is spoken at home by just 1.2% of those surveyed, if we include the Kalabari and the Nembe, who are sometimes treated as separate categories. Other languages of the Niger Delta, such as the Anang, the Edo, the Efik, the Isoko, the Ibibio, the Itsekiri, the Ikwere, the Ogoni, and the Urhobo, account for 5.2% of Nigeria's total population. The percentages are only slightly higher if we refer to ethnic identification instead of vernacular languages spoken at home: between 2.5% and 3% in the case of the Ijaw in 2020 and 2017, compared with 5.2% and 10% for the other groups during the same period.

There are other difficulties. The peoples of the Niger Delta have had different names at different times in history, with the Europeans often using pejorative exonyms that were not correctly translated or pronounced. For example, the Ijaw were initially referred to as "Jos" by the Portuguese, spelt "Ijos" by the British and "Idjos" (or even "Idios") by the French (Lenfant 1905: 44). Today,

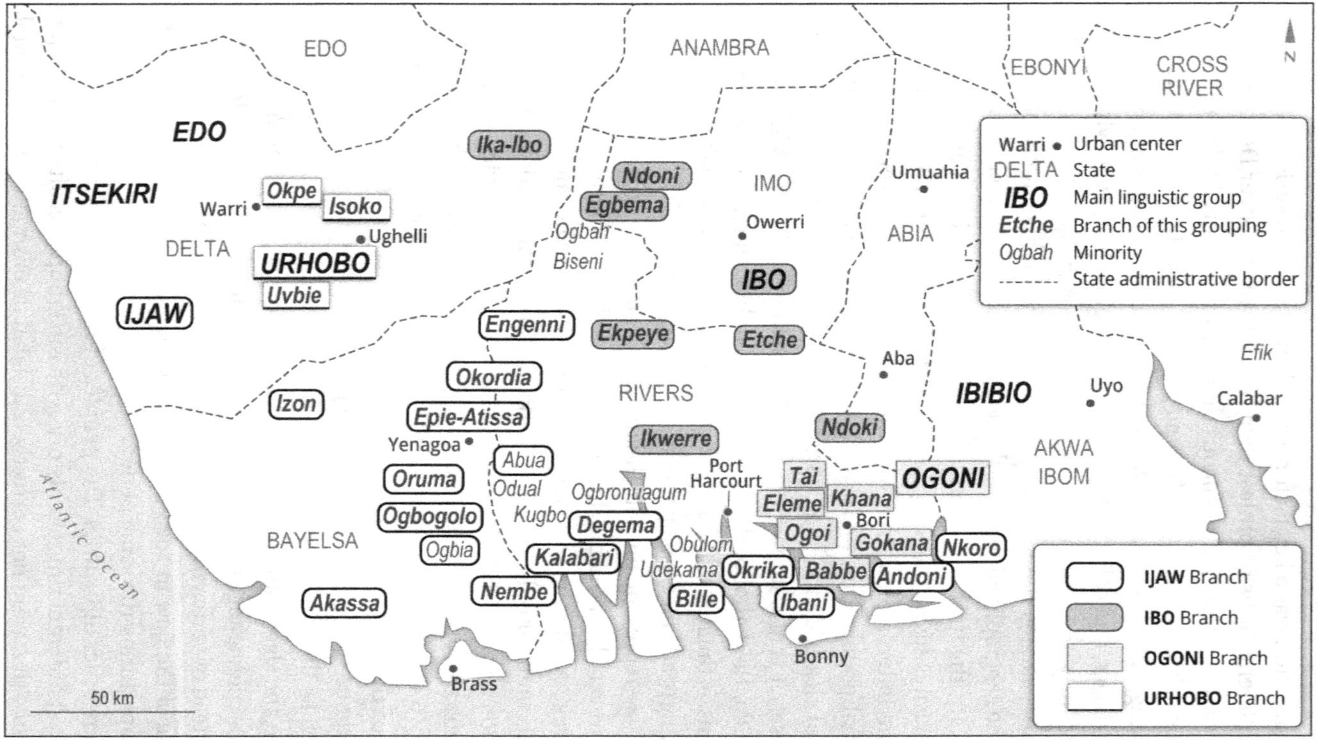

Source: M.-A. de Montclos, IRD-Ceped

Map conception: E. Opigez, IRD-Ceped

MAP 3   Some communities of the Niger Delta

they describe themselves as the Izon people, while one of their clans, the Okrika, now want to be known as the Wakirike. In the meantime, the Bini of the Kingdom of Benin became the Edo. Their neighbors in Warri, the "Iwere", were initially called "Jekri" by Portuguese seafarers, or "Irhobo" and "Selemo", as they were known among the Urhobo and the Ijaw respectively, before eventually agreeing on a vernacular name: the Itsekiri. As for the "Sobo" in the hinterland, in 1938 they were granted the right to be known officially as the Urhobo.

Other groups, by contrast, chose to retain the names used by the colonial master. Such is the case of the Ogoni. Once known as the Kana among the Ijaw, they were viewed as "foreigners" or "outsiders" (*Igoni*) by the coastal people of Bonny who accompanied the British in the hinterland; hence their name. As for the Eleme, they were very close to the Ogoni and were initially known as Mboli—meaning, "those who are different" (*mboli iche*) in the Ibo language of the Arochukwu clan, who routinely enslaved people in the hinterland. Naming processes have sometimes been somewhat arbitrary. For example, communities to the southeast of Port Harcourt were called "Andoni" after one of their many chiefs who happened to be the first to come across the British arriving from the coast. However, their equivalents in present-day Akwa Ibom State have come to be known as the Obolo, who are sometimes lumped together with the Ijaw, although the Izon of Bayelsa rarely understand their dialect.[1]

Indeed, reference to vernacular languages alone is not enough to capture ethnic boundaries. To that extent, the notion of "community" is difficult to define, and its malleability reflects the fluidity of a related concept: "civil society". Parallels are often made with clans, lineages, villages, human groupings, kingdoms, and even LGAs, depending on territorial, biological, historical, cultural, or political perspectives (Egere 2021). By contrast, others take an economic approach in referring to canoe houses, corporations, coalitions of interest, or trading leagues (Jones 1963, Wariboko 1998). In all cases, however, the notion of "community" remains fluid. Undoubtedly, the people's melting pot in the green labyrinth of the Niger Delta complicates the identification of groups defined by the vague oral legends of their ancestral founders.

For example, eastern Ijaw clans around Port Harcourt are thought to be more diverse than their counterparts in the west as a result of having absorbed minorities such as the Udekama among the Kalabari and the Abuloma among

---

1　If we are to believe their oral history, the Obolo left the Kingdom of Benin and moved to Ramby, Cameroon, before settling at the mouth of the Imo River in around 1700. Today, they claim to have some affinities with the Irombi of Cameroon, the Itsekiri of Warri, and the Ibeno of Akwa Ibom. According to some versions, the latter were Andoni who fled the raids carried out by the slave traders of King Jaja of Opobo in the 1870s.

the Okrika. As for the Ijaw fishermen in the creeks of present-day Delta State, they have been split historically between the Gbaramatu and the Egbema. In the absence of a central authority, they were scattered across various canoe houses, or clans, under traditional chiefs and priests known as *pere* ("protectors") in Warri, or *amanyananbo* ("masters of the land") around Port Harcourt. At the other end of the Niger Delta, between the ocean and the Imo River, the Obolo of Akwa Ibom also subsisted on fishing. During the era of the slave trade, they did not develop into a kingdom or a city-state, enduring instead the domination of the Opobo, a dissident group led by King Jaja, a former Ibo slave who, in 1867, established a base in Andoni territory after fleeing Bonny.

In most cases, precolonial Niger Delta was not ruled, let alone governed, by chiefs. Its leaders were endowed with a moral rather than political authority. Their position was not hereditary, and they drew their spiritual strength from secret societies in which young boys underwent an initiation process to

FIGURE 34   The spiritual leader (*pere*) of the Isaba
             community in Warri South-West in Delta
             State (2011)

become warriors (Jones 1970: 312, Northrup 1978). In general, the Niger Delta chiefs were chosen from the most powerful families, depending on their personal merits, their social skills, their fortune, and genealogical antecedents that followed rules of patrilineal succession—although there have also been a small number of matrilineal communities among the Obolo of Akwa Ibom and the Ijaw of Brass and Nembe. The coastal city-states were somewhat different in this respect since they were controlled by wealthy slave traders. However, most of these "kings" were warlords or pirates rather than chiefs in the strict sense. Power tended not to be concentrated in the hands of a single individual and was above all a matter of negotiation between the main local families.

Approached by Portuguese seafarers and missionaries as early as the fifteenth century, the Itsekiri of Warri were probably the only people in the region to have "a highly centralized government" (Lloyd 1963). Their first monarch, *olu* Ginuwa I, was a prince who had been ousted in the 1480s by the nobility of the neighboring Benin Empire. The Portuguese, who wanted to expand their trading activities in the Niger Delta, had failed to get along with the Bini of Edo and convert them to Christianity. They therefore helped Ginuwa I to consolidate his new fiefdom around Warri, a town whose name is said to derive from a sailor called Alfonso d'Aveiro. However, the Itsekiri were opposed by the Urhobo in the hinterland. The latter also claimed to hail from Benin and, according to their own historians, they had settled in Warri a century earlier, around 1370, thereby giving them more rights to the land (Ekeh 2004).

Elsewhere in the Niger Delta, chiefs had no real executive, legislative, or judicial powers. Described by the British as an "amphibian people", Ijaw fishermen, for example, had no rulers per se, being led instead by big men called *agadagba*, i.e. "fat fish" (Burns 1929: 54). Capable of mobilizing crews and arming canoes to wage wars, some of them were able to establish themselves as key middlemen in the slave trade between Europeans on the coast and the Ibo in the hinterland. However, their economic success was primarily down to their military prowess, their capacity to raise troops, and their magical powers. As a result, many of them were likened by the colonial authorities to warlords, human traffickers, pirates, and sorcerers primarily intent on extorting duties from foreign traders who tried to venture into the interior of the Niger Delta.

In a letter sent to the prime minister and the Foreign Office in 1890, the British consul in the Oil Rivers protectorate thus wrote that "native chiefs, even the best of them, are abominably unfair, biased, and corrupt in their judgments. They give their decision in favour of the highest bidder, and invariably decide in favour of the strongest against the weak" (Etekpe *et al.* 2003: 41). Moreover, chiefs were constantly embroiled in never-ending quarrels, making the Niger Delta especially difficult to govern. As early as 1865, a British parliamentary committee had recommended abandoning the outposts established on the coast to avoid becoming involved in community clashes and civils wars (Reno 2004: 610). At the time, the British had no illusions about their capacity to rule peoples described as being "idle and vindictive drunkards, thieves, liars".[2]

When London finally resorted to gunboat diplomacy to expand into the Niger Delta, its first concern was to depose and deport the warlords who are now glorified as heroes resisting the colonial conquest. Notable examples include William Dappa Pepple in Bonny in 1854, Jubo Jubogha (aka "Jaja") in Opobo in 1887, Nana Olumu in Warri in 1894, Frederick William Koko in Nembe in 1895, and Ibani Chuka in Okrika in 1896. However, to entrench their authority in the hinterland, the British needed local middlemen. Keen to limit the costs of colonization, their strategy was to govern Nigeria based on a model known as Indirect Rule, which entrusted traditional authorities with the task of levying taxes and maintaining order.

2   Warrant Chiefs and Indirect Rule

The problem was that acephalous societies within the region were not suited to such a system. In being appointed and deposed by decree in virtue of a colonial ordinance of 1910, the warrant chiefs were rulers in name only, being subject to the goodwill of the colonial master. Many locals viewed them as "non-entities", "mere upstarts", and even "rascals" (Afigbo 1972: 76, Falola 2009: 80). By granting them the right to levy taxes and deliver justice, the British promoted opportunists who often abused their newly acquired powers in societies whose traditional authorities were collegial and rarely hereditary. These developments soon met with resistance. For example, the extension of the powers of warrant chiefs to income tax collection among women triggered major riots in 1928–1929 (Matera, Bastian & Kent 2011, Gailey 1970). In the Niger Delta, the system of Indirect Rule was actually so fragile that, in some cases, the "thrones" remained vacant. For instance, in 1929, the British had to abandon their attempts to find a successor to the *pere* of the Ijaw Gbaramatu, Tanga Ukpoluko I, in power from 1913 to 1924. It was not until 1976 that a new chief, called Zai Tiemo, was finally crowned, becoming Gbaraun II.

By contrast, the system of Indirect Rule proved to be rather effective in the emirates of northern Nigeria, where traditional societies were more

---

2   See, for example, the story of a French explorer tasked with sailing up the River Niger through Forcados, where, in early 1901, France controlled a small territorial enclave by virtue of a treaty signed in 1898 to guarantee freedom of navigation (Lenfant 1905: 44).

hierarchized. But in the Niger Delta, it failed to put an end to community conflicts and quarrels over succession. For example, following the 1928 anti-tax
riots, the Urhobo continued to contest the pre-eminence of the Itsekiri by
demanding that the Warri Division be renamed Delta, a more neutral name,
while the Ijaw began to call for the creation of their own administrative entity.
Both were keen to evade the authority of a powerful Itsekiri, Dore Numa (1861–
1932), who, in 1917, had been appointed chief of Warri by the British as a reward
for the active role he had played in the eviction of Nana Olumu in 1894 (Ikime
1965). The crisis reached a peak with the restoration of the monarchy and the
coronation in 1936 of an *olu* of the Itsekiri, Ginuwa II, thereby ending the long
interregnum experienced by the people of Warri since the last incumbent's
death in 1848 (Ikime 1977).

Slowly but surely, the colonial system nonetheless consolidated "customary"
chiefdoms while fixing ethnic identities that were shaped, delimited, or clari-
fied within the Native Authorities of the British administration. For example,
in 1935, the creation of a council of chiefs in Yeghe, near Bori, contributed to
unifying the five main Ogoni clans under the aegis first of a common financial structure, then a customary court established in 1938 for the entire group.
Chosen among village heads (*menebuen*) who held a hereditary position, local
chiefs (*gbenemene barasin*) thus extended their powers as they came to be
entrusted with levying taxes and delivering justice. Further south, the creation
in 1930 of a native court also served to blend the Andoni clans around a common institution covering their former masters, the Opobo.[3] Meanwhile, on the
opposite side of the Imo River, their Obolo neighbors united around a king
more or less invented by the British and known as *Ubong Ile*.

Over time, the institutionalization of these chiefdoms gradually trans-
formed the Niger Delta. Together with missionary schools, the system of Native
Authorities enabled a select group of "big men" to climb the social hierarchy,
obtain qualifications, and, in some cases, enter politics. For example, the
"king" (*obong*) of the Efik of Calabar, James Eyo Ita, traveled to London in 1912
to defend the rights of coastal minorities during an international conference
on land ownership in Africa. In 1934, he was involved in the foundation of the
Nigerian Youth Movement in Lagos, a breeding ground for nationalist leaders
during decolonization. As independence neared, many warrant chiefs in the
Niger Delta also set about negotiating with the British over the creation of new

---

3 Established in Ngo, the previous court of the Andoni fell, by contrast, under the jurisdiction
of Opobo. It did not function well and was closed in 1923 because the British were unable to
exert proper control and supervision due to the difficulty of access.

administrative constituencies that were to give birth to states such as Cross River, Rivers, and Akwa Ibom.

At the time, coastal minorities wanted to escape from the political control of the Ibo and the NCNC (National Council of Nigeria and the Cameroons) in the hinterland. Admittedly, five of the eight paramount rulers of the Eastern Region recognized by virtue of a 1958 law originated from the Niger Delta, in Bonny, Kalabari, Nembe, Opobo, and Calabar. The other three were Ibos from Aro, Onitsha, and Oguta. However, their counterparts in the Niger Delta argued that they had a specific status because the British still paid them token fees to compensate for the loss of revenue earned from duties (*comey*) before the colonial era. In 1955, their Rivers State Congress protested when the government of the Eastern Region tried in vain to terminate subsidies that represented a proof of sovereignty. Protectorate agreements signed by the leaders of coastal city-states at the end of the nineteenth century differed from the colonization process of the Ibo in the hinterland. In the view of Niger Delta's paramount rulers, such legal technicalities justified their claim to regain their independence and become separate from the rest of Nigeria.

Insofar as they were voiced by small minorities, these demands had actually little chance of success at the national level, regardless of any prospect of future oil exploitation. After independence in 1960 and Nigeria's first coup in 1966, Niger Delta chiefs lost many prerogatives, especially in respect of land allocation, when, in 1968, the military junta abolished the British Native Authorities. However, the LGAs that replaced the old colonial system still allocated part of their budget to the payment of customary authorities (Nolte 2002). As a result, Niger Delta chiefs were able to preserve a degree of influence. In being both honorific and lucrative, their positions were highly coveted, since they provided a means of access to the compensation paid by oil companies to "host communities".

3 Political Careers and Crowns

Niger Delta's customary chiefs thus continued to play the role of mediators. During elections, the government tasked them with mobilizing voters. Keen to consolidate their reputation and publicly demonstrate their success, the most prominent politicians also sought the endorsement of customary authorities with a view to being honored during costly ceremonies. A Catholic from a small Igbo-speaking minority at the border with Imo State, the governor of Rivers between 1999 and 2007, Peter Odili, acquired, for example, a long list of honorific titles. Over the course of his two terms, he was crowned Ogbuagu I

("Warrior Who Kills Tigers") among the Egi of Orashi River, Eze Udo I ("King of Peace") among the Ikwere, Ochizuru ("King of Kingmakers") among the Ndoni, Menekorodoo ("King Who Fulfils His Promises") among the Ogoni, Ibiyekoribo ("He Who Does Good Works") among the Ijaw of Kalabari, Dein Peribo ("Peacemaker") among the Ijaw of Okrika, Enyioha I ("Great Friend of the People") among the Oyigbo in the suburbs of Port Harcourt, Eze Ugo ("King of Glory") among the Ibo Etche, Setelimabo ("Restorer") among the Ogu and the Bolo, Eze Yawe-Ugo ("Messenger Who Brings Glory") among the Ekpeye, Obom-Ekein Osotun ("Builder") among the Ijaw of Degema, Eze Okaa Omee ("King Who Fulfils His Promises") among the Omuma, Ophelegbe Arunphelegbe ("Champion of Champions") among the Ijaw of Abua, and Uja Obolo ("Beauty of Andoni") among the Andoni (Chinwe 2017).

For many politicians, such titles provide an ultimate form of recognition that transcends the ephemeral nature of their careers and electoral victories. While traditions may be fluid and are often manipulated, the authority of customary chiefs is seen as permanent, continuing beyond civilian or military regime changes. However, the proliferation of honorific titles sold to the highest bidder has adulterated their function. In addition, many chiefs today live in cities and maintain relatively loose ties with their "subjects" in the countryside. They are also often contested by youths on account of their shady deals with oil companies and corrupt politicians. In short, there is no guarantee that customary authorities are still able to assume in the Niger Delta the kind of mediating role that the British once sought to assign to warrant chiefs.

Since independence, the fragmentation of Nigeria's territorial administration has disrupted long-established power relations while rekindling ethnic fabrication processes. Federalism encouraged localism as much as Indirect Rule had fostered the community-based structures of Native Authorities. After the Biafran War, the military juntas in power divided Nigeria into increasingly small states and LGAs. In doing so, the idea was to break regional counterpowers that had exacerbated secession attempts. However, on the pretext of defending the rights of minorities and natives, the military also weakened national unity by introducing community quotas that regulated the formation of governments, the recruitment of civil servants, and access to public universities, to the point of prioritizing ethnic origin over merit.

For their part, competing political parties under parliamentary regimes sought to apply a system of power rotation known as "zoning", which favored communitarianism and cronyism at national and local levels. During the Fourth Republic, at the end of the military dictatorship in 1999, many politicians were elected after passing the test of primaries during which candidates without the right ethnic profile were eliminated. For example, in Delta

State, the Urhobo, the Itsekiri, and the Ibo shared power, with, respectively, governors James Onanefe Ibori from 1999, Emmanuel Eweta Uduaghan from 2007, and Ifeanyi Arthur Okowa from 2015. By contrast, in Rivers State, adherence to the zoning rule was more limited. The Igbo-speaking minorities tended to monopolize the governorship, first with Peter Odili, a Ndoni in power from 1999, followed by Rotimi Amaechi from 2007 and Nyesom Wike from 2015, two Ikwerre who became rivals despite their common ethnic background.

Nigeria's federal structure thus complicated the regulation of community conflicts. The proliferation of administrative entities displaced problems to an ever more granular level. For example, in 1996, the creation of Bayelsa State promoted the Ijaw of the central Niger Delta while marginalizing the Kalabari and Okrika clans of Rivers State, who had long dominated the political scene (Nwajiaku 2006: 113). Within Bayelsa itself, the redrawing of administrative borders also failed to provide lasting solutions to community conflicts.

FIGURE 35   The "king" (*eze*) of the Ikwerre in Port
Harcourt (2004)

In 1996, the division of existing LGAs deprived the Bassambari of Nembe of control over the Obioku oil wells, which now fell under the jurisdiction of the Odioma of Brass, whereas the council of traditional chiefs from the two communities had previously covered the entire territory (Courson 2006). In the same vein, Nembe LGA experienced significant tensions between two Ijaw clans, the Bassambari and the Ogboloma, who had once joined forces to take part in the notorious raid of Akassa against the Royal Niger Company in 1895. In 1997, the dispute centered around the location of the new entity's administrative seat. According to the Bassambiri, the government had initially planned to place the Ogboloma within the jurisdiction of Okoroma LGA, until a military decree arbitrarily grouped the two clans under Nembe in 1996 (Evans 2012).

The return to a civilian regime did not put an end to administrative disputes over borders and the creation of new LGAs. To take the example of Bayelsa again, the tensions between the Bassambiri and the Ogboloma of Nembe resulted instead in further violence during the PDP primaries in 2002. Even the suburbs of the state capital, Yenagoa, were affected. In 1999, Governor Diepreye Alamieyeseigha bowed to the demands of the Okordia and Zarama clans, who had been calling for their own LGA since 1987. However, the new entity was never formally recognized by the National Assembly in Abuja and therefore had no proper legal existence from a constitutional standpoint. In addition, the Biseni clan complained that their own headquarters, Agbobiri, was located in Okordia territory and demanded that it be transferred to the village of Ayakoama. The dispute degenerated into physical violence, resulting in several deaths in late 2001 (Etekpe 2012).

The proliferation of administrative entities also led to border conflicts between states. The Ijaw communities of Tsekelewu and Opuama community, in Delta and Ondo states respectively, clashed over land rights to the Egbeoma oil fields. Repeated attempts to redraw administrative boundaries did not prevent violence, especially when residents took matters into their own hands. For example, clashes caused ninety deaths in May 2000 after the villages of Itu in Akwa Ibom and Odukpani in Cross River failed to reach an amicable solution to a dispute over the boundaries between the two states. Likewise, the Ijaw of Arogbo and the Ilaje Yoruba of Okitipupa in Edo and Ondo states both claimed ownership of the Apata and Edugugba oil fields during clashes that resulted in around 500 casualties in September–December 1998, with a further fifty victims in late 1999.

4   The Case of Warri

In Delta State, Warri is a textbook case in this regard, for the community conflicts that ravaged the area throughout the 1990s lie at the root of Ijaw nationalism and the armed insurrections that followed. The largest city in the sub-region is also symptomatic because it has a reputation for being ungovernable. In 1991, the military thus opted to establish the capital of the newly created Delta State elsewhere in the Ibo hinterland, in Asaba, a smaller urban center and, incidentally, the hometown of the wife of General Ibrahim Babangida, who was in power at the time. It was not until the return to a parliamentary regime in 1999 that a civilian governor, James Ibori, decided to leave Asaba and move to Warri to mobilize residents ahead of his re-election in 2003.

Delta State is populated for the most part by Ibo in the north, Urhobo in the center, Itsekiri in Warri, and Ijaw in the south and along the coast. Historically, Warri was a trading post dominated by the Itsekiri minority and surrounded by rural communities. From this point of view, it is reminiscent of the case of Calabar where the Efik, as they became increasingly urbanized, distanced themselves from the Ibibio in the hinterland, a far larger community in numerical terms. In the case of Warri, the Itsekiri often married into the Urhobo, who supplied them with agricultural products. However, they remained a distinct people as they monopolized the slave trade with Europeans, to the detriment of Urhobo peasants and Ijaw fishermen (Ikime 1969: 41–68).

In being more open to Western modernity, the Itsekiri were able to gain the trust of the colonial master. The British found it easier to deal with their kingdom than with the acephalous communities of the Urhobo and the Ijaw. As a result, better access to education and power networks helped Itsekiri urban dwellers to win most of the trials opposing them to their rural neighbors. Community tensions were no less intense in the hinterland. For example, the Ijaw Isaba of Ogbe-Ijoh clashed over land disputes with the Urhobo Alaja of Ogbe-Sobo before the courts eventually ruled in their favor in 1934. In the meantime, the Urhobo of Ughelli had to organize themselves to defend their rights. In 1931, they launched an Urhobo Progress Union under the aegis of a wealthy trader, Mukoro Mowoe, who chaired their ethnic lobby until his death in 1948, while acting as a local councilor in Warri and being elected as a representative of the province to the assembly of the Western Region in 1947 (Otite 2011, 1973).

However, because of its economic dynamism, the port of Warri remained the main focus of political competition during the colonial era. A first crisis erupted in 1951 when King Erejuwa II succeeded Ginuwa II, who died in 1949. Once known as the *olu* of the Itsekiri, the new monarch adopted the title of *olu* of Warri, thus giving him the appearance of ruling over the entire province of the same name. Some of his vassals and allies were also promoted in the city's council of traditional chiefs. The change was made official by the Yoruba-dominated government of the Western Region, which, at the time, covered the territory of present-day Delta State (Lloyd 1974). Independence subsequently confirmed the pre-eminence of Warri city dwellers. For example, the federal finance minister in 1960, Festus Okotie-Eboh, was the son of an Itsekiri chief.

This fragile balance was then put to the test by the political convulsions of the First Republic, when the Mid-Western Region was created in 1963 and removed from the influence of the Yoruba, who had moved to the opposition at a national level. Deposed in 1964, Erejuwa II was succeeded in 1965 by Akengbuwa II, before being reinstated following the 1966 coup that placed Warri under the administration of an Urhobo officer, David Ejoor. During the military dictatorships, locals could no longer vote for parties opposed to the Yoruba and their Itsekiri allies. After the Biafran War in 1970, they continued nonetheless to protest in various ways. The Ijaw claimed that the Itsekiri could not be the rightful owners of Warri on the grounds that their *olu* had to purchase the land for his palace when he moved to the Ekurede neighborhood in 1971. Meanwhile, the Urhobo of Okere continued their legal action through the courts, as illustrated by a 1973 ruling in their favor against the Itsekiri.

The major administrative reform of 1976 revived tensions by creating a Warri LGA under the control of the Itsekiri. Ijaw and Urhobo residents complained that the mayor refused to issue them with "certificates of indigenes" and had renamed the city's streets to erase its composite make-up. They also opposed the imposition of mandatory Itsekiri teaching in all Warri schools. In a similar vein, they boycotted the traditional council set up in 1977, where Itsekiri was the only official language. In 1979, the return to civilian rule had little effect in this regard. The federal government attempted to solve the issue by placing the Ijaw of Warri under the control of two rural LGAs: Owan and Burutu. However, the Ijaw insisted that they remain within the city. In 1983, they secured the right to be reintegrated in the metropolis but failed to secure their own urban district based in Oporoza and called Nein-Ibe, a name referring to "four clans"— that is, the Gbaramatu, the Egbema, the Ogbe-Ijoh, and the Isaba. When the military returned to power in 1984, the Ijaw protested again because the junta, which was dominated by Muslim northerners, had rejected their demand for a new local government despite the fact that a state such as Kano was granted 34 LGAs in 1991, compared with twenty in 1976 and eight in 1967.

As for the Itsekiri of Warri, they still considered themselves to be a sort of urban elite surrounded by illiterate peasants and fishermen. Their obsidional complex was so extreme that they were sometimes compared to the white

Afrikaner minority in South Africa (Akiri 2006: 172). The difference is that the Itsekiri saw themselves as natives, not colonizers. To them, Ijaw and Urhobo city dwellers were rural immigrants and usurpers. As further evidence of how genuine their claim was, the Itsekiri argued that they never pretended to be the landlords of surrounding LGAs.[4] They only demanded the application of previous courts decisions, together with impartial mediations, adherence to constitutional means of conflict resolution, and a reconciliation process that would condemn violence instead of rewarding troublemakers. As a demographic minority, some even called for the federalization of their territory under the direct control of Abuja, with its own assembly of representatives and a traditional council consisting of fifteen Itsekiri, three Ijaw, and two Urhobo overseen by the *olu* of Warri.

The proliferation of administrative entities was hardly a solution in this regard, instead multiplying the points of contention when the federal government created a Delta State with twelve LGAs in August 1991, nineteen the following September, and 25 in January 1997. The Itsekiri objected to new boundaries that left them with only three LGAs, compared with two for the Isoko, three for the Ijaw, eight for the Urhobo, and the rest for other ethnic groups. As for the Urhobo, they felt under-represented in Warri, 85% of which was owned, so they claimed, by their Agbarha and Okere clans (Imobighe, Bassey & Asuni 2003: 80). In a similar vein, the Ijaw complained that the new electoral constituencies were unfair. According to them, the Itsekiri of Warri secured thirteen wards, compared with just twelve for the Ijaw, who accounted for a larger proportion of the population. For example, the three electoral wards of Ubeji, Obodo, and Ode-Itsekiri numbered only 11,000 residents, compared with 268,000 in the Ijaw-dominated wards of Bowen, Pessu, Avenue, Esisi, Ekurede, Igbudu, and Okoro.

By virtue of its economic dynamism, the largest urban area in Delta State thus continued to serve as a catalyst for existing tensions. In August 1991, the creation of two LGAs, Warri North and Warri South, once again opposed the Ijaw and the Itsekiri. The former refused to be dominated by the latter in southern suburbs, and they protested against a re-division which, in the north, forced their Ogbe-Ijoh, Isaba, and Gbaramatu clans to travel through the territory of five LGAs to get to Koko, the administrative seat of the new entity. At the constitutional conference organized by General Sani Abacha in April 1995, the Ijaw claimed that they should have their own local government, called Tarabe.

---

4 Out of Warri, the Itsekiri count small communities in Edo State. In Delta State, their main clans are the Okorodudu of Burutu in Ijawland, as well as the Oguanja-Ugbege, the Aja-Emele, and the Ugboeyiyi of Sapele and the Ugarefe and the Ugharegin of Ethiope in Urhoboland.

The authorities therefore looked for a compromise. In December 1996, the Delta State military governor, Colonel Jonah Dungs, announced the creation of two new LGAs, Warri Center for the Itsekiri and Warri South for the Ijaw.

In Abuja, however, the junta of General Sani Abacha decided otherwise. In January 1997, it established Warri South West LGA with its seat in Ogidigben, in Itsekiri territory, instead of in Ogbe-Ijoh, an Ijaw area. Soon afterwards, in March, the government held local elections that led to riots because of fraud. Many Ijaw were not permitted to vote because they had not been registered. In their view, the reason for this was simple: three-quarters of the agents put in place by the Electoral Commission were allegedly Itsekiri. Moreover, the Ijaw complained that the administrative seats of Warri North and Warri South West LGAs still favored their rivals. According to them, they should have been transferred to Oporama and Ogbe-Ijoh respectively. In the same vein, they continued to call for a change to the title of *olu* of the Itsekiri, while the Urhobo demanded a rotating presidency system for the traditional council of Warri, with a status of equivalent rank for the chiefs of their Agbarha and Okere clans.

In June 1998, the death of General Sani Abacha did not put an end to the conflict, which also impacted Chevron in January 1999. On the contrary, violent clashes developed as they now involved new Ijaw and Urhobo militias, called the Young Lions and the Okumagba Boys respectively. Moreover, some Ijaw felt threatened by the return to a parliamentary regime and the growing political influence of the Itsekiri's traditional allies, the Yoruba, who had led the opposition to military dictatorship. Many conflicts opposed the two groups—for instance, during clashes in Ilaje in Ondo State in September–December 1998. In Lagos, the OPC (Oodua People's Congress), a xenophobic Yoruba militia, even attempted to expel the Ijaw from Ajegunle, a suburb, in September–October 1999.

Interestingly, mineral resources were not a key factor in these clashes with both the Itsekiri and the Yoruba. Community conflicts within Warri predated the beginnings of oil production in Nigeria (Okoh 2016). However, the industry inevitably attracted demands for jobs and compensation. For example, in August 1976, a dispute erupted between the Ijaw Gbaramatu of Okerenkoko and the Itsekiri of Ugborodo over the ownership of a flow station operated by Chevron since October 1972 in Abiteye, along the Escravos River. In August 1977, clashes also broke out between the Urhobo of Ekpan and the Itsekiri of Ubeji over compensation during the construction of the NNPC refinery. Finally, around the Escravos oil terminal, the Ijaw accused Chevron of favoring their rivals with scholarships and jobs. Although they occupied relatively junior positions, the Itsekiri were recruited through an agency owned by the *olu* of

Warri, and they allegedly accounted for up to a third of the US company's employees in Nigeria (Amnesty International 2005: 9).

References

Adangor, Zacchaeus. 2018. "The Ijaws (IZONS) of the Niger Delta Region and Political Agitations in Nigeria: Past and Present". *Advances in Social Sciences Research Journal* 5 (3): 361–376.

Afigbo, Adiele Eberechukwu. 1972. *The Warrant Chiefs. Indirect Rule in Southeastern Nigeria, 1891–1929*. London: Longman.

Afrobarometer. 2017. *Round 7 Survey in Nigeria*. East Lansing: Michigan State University.

Afrobarometer. 2020. *Round 8 Survey in Nigeria*. East Lansing: Michigan State University.

Akiri, Chris. 2006. *The Way It Is*. Lagos: Bertie-John.

Amnesty International. 2005. *Nigeria. Ten Years On: Injustice and Violence Haunt the Oil Delta*. London: Amnesty International.

Burns, Alan. 1929. *History of Nigeria*. London: George Allen & Unwin.

Chinwe, Otunuya. 2017. "Peter Odili". In *Who's Who in Nigeria*, edited by Osso, Nyaknno. Abuja: Biographical Legacy and Research Foundation. https://blerf.org/index.php /biography/odili-dr-chief-peter-otunuya-chinwe/ (accessed 8 March 2019).

Courson, Elias. 2006. *Odi Revisited? Oil and State Violence in Odioma, Brass LGA, Bayelsa State*. Berkeley: University of California, Institute of International Studies.

Egere, Hudson Dafe. 2021. "A Contemporary Geopolitical Delineation of Niger Delta Communities: Identity in Coastal Nigeria". *Africa Today* 68 (1): 125–144.

Ekeh, Peter. 2004. *Warri City and British Colonial Rule in Western Niger Delta*. Buffalo (NY): Urhobo Historical Society.

Etekpe, Ambily. 2012. "Alternative Strategies in Conflict Resolution and Peacebuilding in the Niger Delta: A Case Study of Traditional Councils in Bayelsa State". In *Peace, Security and Development in Nigeria*, edited by Isaac Olawale Albert, Willie Aziegbe Eselebor & Nathaniel Danjibo: 319–331. University of Ibadan, Peace and Conflict Studies Programme.

Etekpe, Ambily *et al.* 2003. *Harold Dappa-Biriye. His Contributions to Politics in Nigeria*. Port Harcourt: Onyoma Research Publications.

Evans, Doibi & Opu-Nembe Improvement Union. 1 Oct. 2012. "Nembe LGA: At Last the Chicken Has Come to Roost". Lagos: *The Nation*: 46.

Falola, Toyin. 2009. *Colonialism and Violence in Nigeria*. Indianapolis: Indiana University Press.

Gailey, Harry. 1970. *The Road to Aba: A Study of British Administrative Policy in Eastern Nigeria*. New York: New York University Press.

Ikime, Obaro. 1965. "Chief Dogho: The Lugardian System in Warri 1917–1932", *Journal of the Historical Society of Nigeria*. 3 (2): 313–333.

Ikime, Obaro. 1969. *Niger Delta Rivalry: Itsekiri-Urhobo Relations and the European Presence, 1884–1936*. London: Longmans.

Ikime, Obaro. 1977. *The Member for Warri Province: The Life and Times of Chief Mukoro Mowoe of Warri, 1890–1948*. Ibadan: Institute of African Studies.

Imobighe, Thomas, Celestine Bassey & Judith Burdin Asuni. 2003. *Conflict and Instability in the Niger Delta: The Warri Case*. Ibadan: Spectrum Books.

Jones, Gwilym Iwan. 1970. "Chieftaincy in the Former Eastern Region of Nigeria". In *West African Chiefs: Their Changing Status Under Colonial Rule and Independence*, edited by Michael Crowder and Ikime Obaro. New York: Africana Pub. Corp.: 312–324

Jones, Gwilliam Iwan. 1963. *The Trading States of the Oil Rivers: A Study of Political Development in Eastern Nigeria*. London: Oxford University Press.

Lenfant, Capitaine Eugène. 1905. *Le Niger, voie ouverte à notre empire africain*. Paris: Hachette.

Lloyd, Peter Cutt. 1963. "The Itsekiri in the Nineteenth Century: An Outline Social History". *The Journal of African History* 4 (2): 207–231.

Lloyd, Peter Cutt. 1974. "Ethnicity and the Structure of Inequality in a Nigerian Town in the Mid-1950's". In *Urban Ethnicity*, edited by Abner Cohen: 223–250. London: Tavistock.

Matera, Marc, Misty Bastian & Susan Kent. 2011. *The Women's War of 1929: Gender and Violence in Colonial Nigeria*. London: Palgrave.

National Population Commission. 2013. *Nigeria Demographic and Health Survey 2013*. Abuja: Federal Republic of Nigeria.

Nolte, Insa. 2002. "Federalism and Communal Conflict in Nigeria", *Regional and Federal Studies* 12 (1): 171–192.

Northrup, David. 1978. *Trade Without Rulers: Pre-Colonial Economic Development in South-Eastern Nigeria*. Oxford: Clarendon Press.

Nwajiaku, Kathryn. 2006. "La mémoire et l'oubli: Isaac Boro et les tendances du nationalisme ijaw contemporain". *Politique africaine* 103: 106–126.

Okoh, Oghenetoja. 2016. "Who Controls Warri? How Ethnicity Became Volatile in the Western Niger Delta (1928–1952)". *Journal of African History* 57 (2): 209–230.

Otite, Onigu. 1973. *Autonomy and Dependence. The Urhobo kingdom of Okpe in Modern Nigeria*. London: Hurst.

Otite, Onigu. 2011. "The Urhobo Progress Union". In *The Urhobo People*, edited by Onigu Otite: 482–505. Ibadan, Gold Press Ltd.

Reno, William. 2004. "Order and Commerce in Turbulent Areas: 19th Century Lessons, 21st Century Practice". *Third World Quarterly* 25 (4): 607–625.

Wariboko, Nimi. 1998. "A Theory of the Canoe House Corporation". *African Economic History* 26: 141–172.

CHAPTER 11

Dividing without Ruling

Beyond Ethnicity

Yenagoa is a far cry from the noise and clamor of Port Harcourt. A new town, it is primarily an administrative center, serving as capital of Bayelsa State. To get a sense of the Niger Delta, one needs to go to the city's waterfront and board a speedboat taxi. Passengers buy their tickets at a booth on the pontoon, just as one might at a bus station. The price includes insurance in the event of an accident.

I am proud of myself; my life is estimated to be worth just over €200. The fees are shown on the ticket and range from ₦5,000 for the reimbursement of medical expenses to ₦50,000 in the event of death or a permanent disability. The ticket also stipulates that if you survive, you should submit your claim at the nearest insurance office. If not, I hope someone will inform my family in France. However, there is no telephone network and the amount paid in such cases would not even cover the cost of a flight home.

It takes nearly two hours to reach Akassa at the southernmost end of the Niger Delta. As we travel away from the creeks and approach the sea on the Nun River, waves begin to hit the boat's hull with ever greater force. It starts to rain. Passengers spread out a tarpaulin that we hold above our heads to shelter from the downpour. We are squeezed onto small wooden benches and the ride is getting markedly rougher. We all start to feel seasick as we must bend our head between our knees, plunging us into darkness beneath the tarp.

I am relieved to arrive at the end of my journey in one piece. Akassa is located at the crossroads of the Bights of Bonny and Benin. Rusted hangars testify to the once flourishing trade of the Niger Royal Company in a famous outpost that was attacked by the Ijaw of Nembe in 1895. Nature has reclaimed the colonial cemetery of Akassa. On the other side of the Nun River, a lighthouse built in 1910 seems to be in the final stages of decay. Erosion has badly damaged its metal superstructure, and its iron staircase has so many missing steps that it is impossible to access the first floor where the battery room is located. At the top, the light has stopped working altogether since being struck by lightning.

Everything points to neglect and calm, a far cry from the troubles of the Niger Delta and the oil extraction areas. If not for the lack of beaches, one

FIGURE 36   The jetty for Brass in Ogbia (2011)

might be tempted to spend holidays in Akassa. However, foreign tourists would no doubt take exception to the mosquitoes, the humidity, and the lack of comfort. Access is another challenge. My return trip to Yenagoa is as grueling as the outbound journey. This time, sixteen of us are crammed into a speedboat designed to carry just eight people. At the front, passengers must lie down on the bow to act as a counterweight when the canoe rides the crest of a wave. Capsizing is not uncommon, and I have taken care to wrap my photo camera in a plastic bag to protect it in the event that the boat overturns (the insurance does not cover a refund). The co-pilot has so little space that he must literally walk on the passengers when moving from one end of the boat to the other. My shoulders serve as a door mat and my shirt is stained with mud when I finally arrive in Yenagoa.

Akassa now feels a world away. Explorers must continue further north to experience the tumult of large Ibo cities such as Onitsha and Aba. The urban chaos, the permanent traffic jams, the fumes, and the agonizing screams of the crowds in dire straits—the contrast between the creeks on the coast and the large urban trading centers in the hinterland could hardly be greater. This is an age-old story that also highlights the lasting tensions between the Ibo and the Ijaw.

FIGURE 37   Yenagoa, the capital city of Bayelsa State (2011)

1   The Ibo and the Ijaw: Two Different Agendas

Historically, coastal city-states made their fortune by selling slaves from the hinterland to Europeans. For example, the Ibani of Bonny and the Itsekiri of Warri traded people of Ibo and Urhobo stocks respectively. As a result, coastal city-states were by far the wealthiest and most developed communities in the region. Their leaders lived in prefabricated chalets imported from Manchester, a symbol of their success and their modernity in a global world. However, with the end of the slave trade and the arrival of the British, the Ibo from the hinterland began to capitalize on the educational opportunities offered by colonization and Christian missionary schools. They invested in the market economy, climbed the social ladder, and secured high positions in the civil service. By the time of independence, things had swung the other way. The Ibo were now in control of the Eastern Region and the national government, with the head of the NCNC, Nnamdi Azikiwe, as the first president of Nigeria.

The people of the Niger Delta were bitter. They had lost their dominant position, while Ibo businessman had quite literally bought Port Harcourt. As independence neared, some tried to take action. To bypass the NCNC's political and economic hegemony, they launched a Niger Delta Congress (NDC) allied to the major Muslim party in power in the north. However, it was primarily

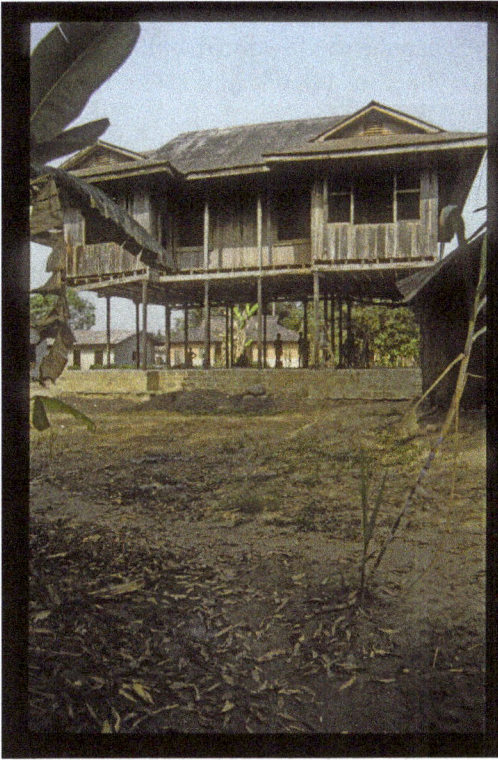

FIGURE 38   A Creek Town chalet in Cross River
             State (1990)

the military victory of the federals against the Biafran separatists that enabled them to remove their rivals, who had retreated to the hinterland. Niger Delta communities were thus able to give free rein to their resentment against the Ibo. Ken Saro-Wiwa even turned this into a key component of Ogoni martyrology, and it is significant that two of the chiefs killed by MOSOP youths in 1995, Albert Badey and Edward Kobani, had been Biafran collaborators.

The alliance with northerners lasted well beyond the First Republic and continued during the period of military rule. The leader of the short-lived Niger Delta secession in 1966, Isaac Boro, was thus pardoned by the junta of Yakubu Gowon and allowed to join the army and fight alongside federal troops against the Ibo of Biafra before dying on the battlefield in 1968. While suppressing the Ogoni revolt in 1995, General Sani Abacha, another northerner, also created a Bayelsa State for the Ijaw in 1996. The latter would not forget this. On Independence Day in 2012, the Governor of Bayelsa, Seriake Dickson, inaugurated a housing project named after General Sani Abacha. Despite being wanted on various embezzlement charges, the dictator's son, Mohammed, was even invited to the ceremony, where he was presented with a traditional title: Izon Ebidouwei—meaning, "The One Who Wants Good Things for the Ijaw".

However, with the election in 1999 of a Yoruba president from the south-west, the return to a civilian regime meant that Niger Delta minorities had to rethink their political alliances. At the national level, the Ijaw voted en masse for the ruling PDP while overlooking the parties representing the interests of Muslims from the north. This new position did not entail a rapprochement with politicians from the southwest. The Yoruba, who had led the democratic opposition to Abacha, had many conflicts with Niger Delta minorities. Their militia, the Oodua People's Congress (OPC), had for instance attempted to chase the Ijaw out of Lagos. Moreover, the Yoruba were suspected of under-mining the Niger Delta's claims for autonomy on the grounds that they had already "betrayed" the Ibo during the Biafran War.[1] As a result, Ijaw militants recommended ignoring the calls by Afenifere, a Yoruba lobby, for a national conference to renegotiate the distribution of oil revenues at a federal level (Ado-Kurawa 2008: 408).

Meanwhile, seemingly bizarre rapprochements were taking place between the Ibo and the Ijaw, who shared a common sense of having been cheated by the central government. The Niger Delta rebellion of the 2000s was largely the result of the gradual dissolution of the alliance formed with the federals during the Biafran War to counter the Ibo hegemony in the Eastern Region (Omotola 2009). Once defeated, the separatists no longer posed a threat to the Ijaw or the Ogoni. On the contrary, the oil boom of the 1970s helped to fill the develop-ment gaps that had existed at independence. The rifts with the hinterland less-ened and, over time, Ibo secessionism became a symbolic reference point for Ijaw nationalists (Nwajiaku 2009). Surveys conducted in late 2017 in Bayelsa, Delta, and Rivers states thus showed that populations on the coast were more concerned about the violence of their own politicians than demonstrations by Biafran militants (SDN 2017).

---

1   Indeed, the famous Yoruba leader and opponent Obafemi Awolowo joined the military junta of Yakubu Gowon. In 1963, he had been convicted of treason and jailed by a government led by the Igbo of Nnamdi Azikiwe and the Hausa-Fulani of Ahmadu Bello. But he was released in 1966 by Yakubu Gowon, who needed the support of some civilian politicians. It is also possible that, in 1967, Awolowo chose to remain in the Nigerian Federation so that the Yoruba could take over the government jobs vacated by the secessionists. In any case, the Igbo never forgot this "betrayal" of a Southerner and did not support the Yoruba opponents to the mili-tary dictatorship of General Sani Abacha in the 1990s. See, amongst others, Lloyd 1970: 11.

The Ibo themselves felt more resentment toward the northern military than against the Niger Delta minorities who had sided with the federals during the civil war. In 2011 and 2015, they voted en masse for an Ijaw who hailed from Bayelsa and who duly returned the favor. For the first time since the end of the civil war, President Goodluck Jonathan thus appointed an Ibo as Chief of Army Staff. In a similar vein, he showed greater clemency than his predecessors had toward Biafran militants. For example, in 2011, Jonathan pardoned the leader of MASSOB (Movement for the Actualisation of the Sovereign State of Biafra) and a thousand of his supporters. This was in marked contrast to his successor in 2015, a Muslim and a northerner who was more eager to confront and ban IPOB (Indigenous People of Biafra) militants.

In such a context, both Ibo and Niger Delta activists seemed to have a common enemy: Abuja. Like the Ijaw, Biafran militants felt dispossessed of their rights to oil revenue, especially since the secessionists' defeat in 1970 (Heerten & Moses 2014: 189). Their goal was to secure autonomy for a territory that would have included the Niger Delta and its oil fields. For example, the head of MASSOB, Ralph Uwazurike, declared that he was not fighting for the independence of the former Eastern Region but rather for the creation of the United States of the Bight of Biafra. In May 2004, he signed an agreement with Ijaw militants to form a Grand Commonwealth of the Niger Delta. In January 2009, he also expressed a desire to join forces with MEND on the grounds that armed struggle was the only language that the Nigerian government understood (Okonta 2014: 373). As for the leader of the Niger Delta Volunteer People's Force (NDPVF), Asari Dokubo, he did not hide his admiration for IPOB, and he proclaimed himself head of a provisional Biafran "customary" government in March 2021 (Abiodun 2021).

2   Discord among the Rebels

However, Niger Deltans did not want a return to Ibo hegemony. Their political elite preferred to keep the powers acquired in the wake of the Biafran War. Thus, there was little prospect of a strategic alliance between Niger Delta rebels and Ibo activists; instead, each side sought to promote its own agenda, a fact that highlighted the fragmentation of the protest movement. Within the Niger Delta, for example, MOSOP fought only for the Ogoni, not for the Ijaw, and failed to build alliances with trade unions or political parties at the national level. Ken Saro-Wiwa himself was not able to unify the different Ogoni clans, despite speaking their dialects; instead, his activism caused hard feelings that sometimes took a very personal turn.

As for the Ijaw, they did not support the Ogoni revolt when Abacha granted them Bayelsa State. Following the return to a civilian regime in 1999, their protests continued to reflect community-based dynamics. Meanwhile, other minorities in the Niger Delta felt neglected. At the time, the focus of the authorities was on Ogoni and Ijaw troublemakers who also happened to live near the largest onshore oil deposits. Activists themselves confirmed this sense of exclusion when, in 2008, they were heard by a federal committee tasked with making technical recommendations to resolve the crisis. For example, a short-lived platform of militant groups known as the Joint Revolutionary Council made reference only to the Ogoni and the Ijaw in calling for the application of the recommendations of the Willinks Commission established by the British to protect Niger Delta minorities in 1958 (Mitee 2008).

The leader of NDPVF, Asari Dokubo, was unequivocal on this issue. He once openly stated in an interview that he was only fighting for the Ijaw and complained about other communities who were seeking to take advantage of his struggle to promote their own interests (Oyewole 2018: 33). Similarly, the Ijaw National Congress did not seek to broaden its ethnic base to claim autonomy in the context of a Nigerian sovereign national conference. Proclaimed in Kaiama on 15 May 1993, the anniversary of the death of Isaac Boro, its constitution offered a purely biological definition of membership of the "Izon nation". For example, against the backdrop of a patrilineal society, Article 7 provided only for the "naturalization" of women married to an Ijaw.

Furthermore, Niger Delta ethnic lobbies were not immune to factional disputes despite their attempts to transcend clan identities to forge nations. The eastern and western Ijaw never succeeded in presenting a united front, and their divisions even extended overseas. In Britain, people from Warri joined the Ijaw People's Association founded in 1948 and based in London, while those from Port Harcourt were represented by the Rivers State Union. Likewise, the diaspora in the United States split into different bodies. Established in 1995, the Ijaw National Alliance of the Americas mainly attracted migrants living in the northeast, while the southwest was the territory of the Ijaw National Congress (Alagoa, Tamuno & Clark 2009: 676).

In Nigeria, the Ijaw Youth Council (IYC) admittedly sought to balance its membership by implementing a "zoning" system.[2] However, its general

---

2   From 1998 until 2001, its first president was a Western Ijaw (Felix Tuodola). His successors included a Kalabari from the east until 2003 (Asari Dokubo), an activist from the Central Niger Delta in 2005–2006 (Oyeinfie Jonjon), a dentist from Patani in the west in 2007–2010 (Chris Ekiyor), an Okrika from the east in 2010–2013 (Abiye Kuromiema) and, following an internal crisis in 2013–2019, another militant from the east since 2020 (Peter Igbifa).

elections often resulted in trials, brawls, and even violent clashes that required police intervention and provided an opportunity for state governors to meddle in the proceedings with a view to imposing their own candidates. For example, from 2013 to 2016, a crisis pitted two Bayelsa rivals against each other, Udenz Eradiri and Elvis Donkemezuo, who both claimed to head IYC simultaneously. In the same vein, IYC held two concomitant conventions in 2017, one in Burutu in Delta State and another in Okrika in Rivers, each electing different presidents, Eric Omare and Pereotubo Roland Oweilaemi respectively.

As for the armed militants, they also failed to avoid factional and regional disputes. NDPVF recruited in Rivers, while most of the FNDIC and, subsequently, MEND militants came from Delta State and, to a lesser extent, from Bayelsa. From 2016, the Niger Delta Avengers (NDA) sought to broaden their social base by attracting Ibo from the hinterland, Ogoni from Rivers, and Ibibio from Akwa Ibom. But to no avail: their calls for a trans-ethnic uprising were not heard, not least because they wanted to demarcate themselves from their predecessors, causing them to lose Ijaw support for MEND.

Beyond community divisions, oppositions between and within rebel groups also took the form of personal quarrels. For example, the armed struggle of NDPVF suffered badly from the rivalry between Asari Dokubo and Ateke Tom over control of Port Harcourt's southern suburbs in 2003. Meanwhile in Warri, Tom Polo took advantage of Asari Dokubo's imprisonment to assume leadership of MEND in 2005. However, his own position was then challenged following the 2009 amnesty. The Niger Delta Avengers gave him a three-day ultimatum to withdraw his men from Delta State and renounce his security contracts with oil companies. Putting their threats into action, they proceeded to bomb NNPC and Chevron pipelines in May 2016. In a similar vein, they criticized Ateke Tom, portraying him as a bandit, and denounced the criminalization of MEND. By contrast, so they claimed, they were a highly professional group and did not perpetrate terrorist attacks. The Niger Delta Avengers only sabotaged oil facilities without killing civilians or military personnel (Oriola & Ibikunle 2018).

3   Tribalism and Politics

In this context, it is clear that resource competition and violent conflicts are not limited to community issues, particularly if we consider the role of personal disputes, mafia-like politics, youth rebellions against the Elders, or simply daily crime. As for the political game, it has not always followed an ethnic logic. For example, at the end of the military regime in 1999, the Yoruba of the southwest shunned Olusegun Obasanjo, who won the elections in regions beyond his homeland. Four years later, the incumbent president was then re-elected thanks to the internal divisions of the major Yoruba party, the AD, which failed to nominate a candidate (Oshun 2005: 172). At the time, Olusegun Obasanjo also benefited from the support of Niger Delta voters, as did his successor Umaru Yar Adua, a Hausa from the north. Conversely, the defeat of President Goodluck Jonathan at the 2015 elections did not spark war in his Ijaw homeland; on the contrary, violence remained at a far lower level than it had been in the 2003–2009 period, with a few localized exceptions.

Generally speaking, ethnic identities are fluid and do not form homogenous blocks. While they play an important role when they are manipulated by politicians to mobilize people, they are fundamentally a political construct. As with the Ogoni and MOSOP, Ijaw nationalists thus dreamt of an Izon conglomerate that included culturally distinct communities. For instance, the Ogbia of Bayelsa speak a different dialect and some linguists class them as Edo. However, they have produced Ijaw champions such as President Goodluck Jonathan, environmental activist Oronto Douglas (1966–2015), or Melford Okilo (1933–2008), the first civilian governor of Rivers in 1979–1983 and a senator for Brass between 1999 and 2003.

Historically, several factors have contributed to dissolving the ethnic identities that the British sought to fix. Urbanization, first, played a crucial role. Before the colonial era, the development of city-states such as Brass and Bonny had already led to the formation of communities that defined themselves by their place of residence and their trading activities rather than by their blood ties (Dike 1956, Jones 1963, Horton 1969). Population mixing was widespread because urban dwellers expanded and incorporated newcomers. In the second half of the nineteenth century, for example, former Ibo slaves from the hinterland even seized power in Opobo on the coast. Throughout the Niger Delta, the British subsequently attempted to structure and control acephalous societies by appointing warrant chiefs and establishing Native Authorities. Following independence in 1960 and the end of the Biafran War in 1970, however, the military juntas in power until 1999 opted to phase out a colonial system that they viewed as favoring tribalism and separatism at the expense of national unity.

In the same vein, the government banned the "tribal unions" that had contributed to dividing the political class along ethnic lines during the First Republic. In the hinterland, the military mainly targeted the powerful Ibo State Union because of its close ties to the NCNC, the former ruling party. In the Niger Delta, they also sought to dismantle ethnic lobbies such as the Ibibio State Union in Akwa Ibom. In Warri Province, however, the Urhobo Progress Union was spared because, unlike the Ibo State Union, it did not lend its

FIGURE 39   Port Harcourt, the largest urban center in the Niger Delta (2011)

support to any particular political party before the 1966 coup. On the contrary, it benefited from the protection of David Akpode Ejoor, the Urhobo military governor of the Mid-Western Region at the time. It was instead the Biafran War that dealt a fatal blow to the organization, which fell into a state of lethargy under the presidency of Thomas Edogbeji Aitkins Salubi between 1961 and 1983 and Federick Esiri from 1983 to 1998. Despite the return to a more democratic regime in 1999, the Urhobo Progress Union was never able to recover its past influence. Instead, the end of military rule led throughout the Niger Delta to a proliferation of communitarian and cultural organizations which, combined with the ever increasing number of "traditional" chieftaincies, contributed to further dividing acephalous societies.[3]

In the past, tribal unions were typically funded by membership fees. Urban migrants would form a traditional cooperative to support development projects in their rural homeland. But those days are long gone. The Urhobo Progress Union now looks more like a lobby that occasionally calls for the creation of administrative entities on an ethnic basis. Despite its slogan ("Unity is Strength"), the organization has also been weakened by internal divisions. Its

---

3   For detailed lists of these groups, see Ikelegbe 2001, Ukeje 2001, Welch 1995.

new president at the end of the military dictatorship, James Ogboko Edewor, was contested immediately after his election in 1998 and briefly replaced by David Akpode Ejoor. Since then, factionalism has continuously affected the Urhobo Progress Union under the aegis of Benjamin Okumagba (a Warri chief) from 1999, Felix Ovuodoroye Ibru (a senator and the first elected governor of Delta State in 1992) from 2007, Patrick Aziza (a retired general) from 2010, Joe Omene (an engineer) from 2014, and Olorogun Moses Oghenerume Taiga (a businessman) from 2016.

Throughout the Niger Delta, the fluidity of collective identities and the fragility of grassroots organizations, which reflect the acephalous nature of traditional societies, thus challenge the dominant narratives around the role played by government and oil companies in efforts to divide and rule. The argument could just as easily be applied the other way. The peoples of the Niger Delta were already very fragmented before the arrival of the colonial master. It is important in this respect to keep in mind the chronology of events. According to historians, it is rather internal conflicts that incited the British to colonize the Niger Delta in order to secure their trading activities with the hinterland (Lynn 1995: 169). In doing so, they in turn generated clashes to put a hand on new resources. In a sense, the two processes fed into each other.

The same observation applies just as much to the oil companies that exacerbated or ignited tensions—for example, around the Mobil terminal on the Qua-Iboe River in Akwa Ibom (Leton 2006: 18). So-called host communities were already divided and fragile. The Itsekiri of the Escravos River in Delta State testify to this. To improve its social corporate performance, Chevron struggled to find reliable and representative leaders through a homemade foundation, the Ugborodo Community Trust, whose president, Samuel Metseaghanrun, was assassinated in September 1998, probably by members of the previous board, which had been dissolved for embezzlement. As a result, never-ending disputes thwarted local development efforts. Because they were unable to reach a consensus, the Itsekiri of Ugborodo felt dispossessed of their "sovereignty" when, on its own initiative, Chevron finally resorted to drafting a memorandum of understanding signed in April 2006. Residents then complained that they had been sidelined as the agreement made no provision for compensation in the event of oil spills or maintenance work on the Escravos River (Faleti 2009).

The question remains: are the Niger Delta conflicts best explained by the fragmented nature of acephalous societies or by the destabilizing impact of foreign corporations? The answer is probably a combination of both. However, the debate rages on. Nigerian scholars have generally argued that Western powers deliberately sought to divide and rule to exploit the natives. Concerning the

Niger Delta, Ambily Etekpe (2012: 320) invokes, for example, the golden age of kingdoms which, in his view, were "very strong and actively responsible for the resolution of major conflicts". According to him, it is the British who weakened them by breaking their traditional bonds and relegating customary rulers to "mere spectators". The colonial master deported "monarchs" who put up resistance in Okrika, Opobo, and Warri in the late nineteenth century, while a 1910 ordinance confirmed the right of residents and district officers to depose any chiefs they disliked.

Post-independence governments were also accused of implementing a strategy of divide and rule in the Niger Delta. For example, in 1992–1993, the Abacha regime was suspected of seeking to weaken the Ogoni by fueling intercommunity conflicts with their Andoni neighbors. Rumor has it that soldiers disguised as civilians were sent to attack the protestors. However, the Ogoni already had long-standing bones of contention with the Andoni. Twenty years earlier, in 1972, relations between the two communities had degenerated over disputed fishing rights (Ekoriko & Olukoya 1993: 17). The conflict was also of a cultural nature. Traditionally, the Ogoni preferred to marry into the Ibibio rather than into the Andoni or the Obolo, who were seen as impure because they did not kill their twins at birth.

4   Quotas, or the Illusions of Indigeneity

Undoubtedly, the role played by the government and the oil industry does not explain all the travails of the Niger Delta. As for ethnic politics, they are not the sole cause of violent conflicts either. It is therefore important to question the strategy of decision-makers and investors who believe that they can buy social peace by introducing community quotas in government institutions and corporate boards. Militants themselves sometimes seem to condone such an understanding of the crisis. Borrowing arguments already used by MOSOP and MEND, for example, the Niger Delta Avengers complained that, in their opinion, 80% of oil blocks had been granted to northerners, with just 20% remaining for the Ibo and the Yoruba (Oriola & Adeakin 2018: 140). In the same vein, some militants demanded that indigenous companies be the first in line to purchase operating rights from multinationals, while key financial players have often sought to co-opt and partner with natives to secure their investments.[4]

---

4   Such was the case of Edmund Daukoru Mingi XII, an Ogboloma Ijaw. A former oil minister under President Olusegun Obasanjo, he was the king (*amanyanabo*) of Nembe and a relative of the governor of Bayelsa State, Timipre Sylva. His name was to be found in several consortia

Nonetheless, it is not clear if this approach really helps. Playing an ethnic or a regional card does not appear to be the ultimate solution, and it certainly does not solve problems facing the youth. The Ogoni crisis thus reached its height despite the fact that Sani Abacha's oil minister, Dan Etete, hailed from the Niger Delta. Similarly, the presence of natives on the board of international oil companies did little to prevent armed attacks. The same applies to Nigerian firms that claimed to be more "acceptable", yet were also involved in local conflicts. For example, Shoreline saw its pipelines sabotaged despite (or perhaps because of) its close ties to the Ijaw husband of the daughter of a well-connected activist. Moni Pulo was not spared either. Established by a Kalabari chief from Rivers, Olu Benson Lulu-Briggs, it operated an oil field off the coast of Calabar, in Cross River State. However, in February 2007, the founder's wife, Seinye Lulu-Briggs, was kidnapped in her own community and released in exchange for a ransom.

Known to be close to Tom Polo and MEND, Neconde Energy Limited also illustrates the limitations of local content policies. Consisting of two Nigerian firms, Nestoil and Yinka Folawiyo, it purchased in 2011 the rights held by Shell, Total, and Agip in block OML 42. In partnership with Polish investors from Kulczyk Oil Ventures, Neconde was then able to drill a well in Odidi, Delta State. However, it was forced to work with the NPDC, which operated the block and had itself signed an ineffective service agreement with Atlantic Energy Drilling. As a result, its business model was hardly viable since the calculation of its production costs took no account of bunkering and racketeering by Tom Polo's friends. Kulczyk was eventually forced to pay $800 million to increase its stake in Neconde to 45%, although production plateaued at 20,000 barrels a day instead of the anticipated 40,000.

Domestic companies were something of a disappointment in this respect. Indeed, their capacity to improve interactions with host communities has little to do with the ethnic make-up of their boards or senior management. Their main assets lie in their flexibility, their ability to innovate, their small size, their proximity to key politicians, and their better integration in local corruption networks, as they escape international rules prohibiting foreign companies from paying for services in cash. Given their low profile, Nigerian operators also have the advantage of facing more reasonable demands from militants. On the other hand, they have more limited resources to implement corporate

that sought to buy Shell blocks in the mid-2010s, especially with Sapetro (Focus Energy) and Transcorp (Transnational Corporation of Nigeria).

social responsibility programs, the value of which remains to be demonstrated from a security point of view.

The weaknesses of international oil companies have undeniably been the strengths of small domestic firms. In their relations with host communities, independent operators often benefit from being new entrants to the market. As a result, they are able to circumvent long-standing issues, unlike Shell or Chevron. In addition, their managers tend to be more accessible. They are not burdened by the bureaucratic weight of multinationals and their headquarters overseas. Since they mostly employ Nigerian staff (thereby reducing their administrative costs), decision chains are also shorter, enabling them to be more responsive. The size effect is another significant factor. Nigerian firms have a limited footprint, meaning that their community relations are easier to manage when compared with the "empire" of a company such as Shell, which operates throughout scattered creeks.

However, domestic companies have failed to prevent bunkering. There is no evidence to suggest that oil thieves are concerned about whether they are stealing crude from a pipeline belonging to a local or an international company. Their financial motivations mean that they are happy to target domestic firms and multinationals alike. The difference is that Nigerian companies are more vulnerable to bunkering if they operate only one pipeline and have less money to spend on security, repair, and maintenance.

The complexity of the oil industry and the Niger Delta thus highlights the limitations of policies that prioritize ethnic issues to solve local problems. Development gaps between different communities have undeniably contributed to tensions. However, a purely ethnic interpretation of the Niger Delta's crisis is overly reductive if it fails to consider the role of personal rivalries, generational conflicts, youth protests, and the impact of political competition at the national level. A clear understanding of the multiple dimensions of internal disputes within government, the oil industry, and so-called civil society is vital in this regard. A more refined analysis of the relations between the three pillars of the resource curse trilogy is also required.

References

Abiodun, Alao. 15 March 2021. "Asari Dokubo Forms Biafra Customary Government". Lagos: *The Nation*. https://thenationonlineng.net/asari-dokubo-forms-biafra-customary-government/ (accessed 20 march 2021).

Ado-Kurawa, Ibrahim. 2008. "The Role of Resource Control and Restructuring in the Political Economy of Nigeria". In *Oil, Democracy, and the Promise of True Federalism in Nigeria*, edited by Augustine Ikein, Diepreye Alamieyeseigha & Steve Azaiki: 401–415. Lanham (Md.): University Press of America.

Alagoa, Ebiegberie Joe, Tekena Tamuno & John Pepper Clark (eds). 2009. *The Izon of the Niger Delta*. Port Harcourt: Onyoma.

Dike, Kenneth Onwuka. 1956. *Trade and Politics in the Niger Delta, 1830–1885*. Oxford: Clarendon Press.

Ekoriko, Moffat & Sam Olukoya. 16 August 1993. "Brothers at War: In Rivers and Akwa Ibom States, Various Communities Engage in Ethnic Clashes". Lagos: *Newswatch Magazine*.

Etekpe, Ambily. 2012. "Alternative Strategies in Conflict Resolution and Peacebuilding in the Niger Delta: A Case Study of Traditional Councils in Bayelsa State". In *Peace, Security and Development in Nigeria*, edited by Isaac Olawale Albert, Willie Aziegbe Eselebor & Nathaniel Danjibo: 319–331. University of Ibadan, Peace and Conflict Studies Programme.

Faleti, Stephen. 2009. *Challenges of Chevron's GMOU Implementation in Itsekiri Communities of Western Niger Delta*. Zaria: IFRA.

Heerten, Lasse & Dirk Moses. 2014. "The Nigeria–Biafra War: Postcolonial Conflict and the Question of Genocide". *Journal of Genocide Research* 16 (2–3): 169–203.

Horton, Robin William Gray. 1969. "From Fishing Village to City-State: A Social History of New Calabar". In *Man in Africa*, edited by Mary Douglas & Phyllis Mary Kaberry: 37–58. London: Tavistock.

Ikelegbe, Augustine. 2001. "The Perverse Manifestation of Civil Society: Evidence from Nigeria". *Journal of Modern African Studies* 39 (1): 1–24.

Jones, Gwilliam Iwan. 1963. *The Trading States of the Oil Rivers: A Study of Political Development in Eastern Nigeria*. London: Oxford University Press.

Leton, Marcus. 2006. *The Politics of a Company Town: A Case Study of Eket and Ibeno, Akwa Ibom State*. Berkeley: University of California, Institute of International Studies.

Lloyd, Peter Cutt. 1970. "The Ethnic Background to the Nigerian Crisis". In *Nigerian Politics and Military Rule. Prelude to Civil War*, edited by Keith Panter-Brick: 1–13. London, Athlone Press.

Lynn, Martin. 1995. "Factionalism, Imperialism and the Making and Breaking of Bonny Kingship c. 1830–1885". *Revue française d'histoire d'outre-mer* 82 (307): 169–192.

Mitee, Ledum. 2008. *Report of the Technical Committee on the Niger Delta*. Port Harcourt, PDF File.

Nwajiaku, Kathryn. 2009. "Heroes and Villains: Ijaw Nationalist Narratives of the Nigerian Civil War", *Africa Development* 34 (1): 47–67.

Okonta, Ike. 2014. "'Biafra of the Mind': MASSOB and the Mobilization of History". *Journal of Genocide Research* 16 (2–3): 355–378.

Omotola, Shola. 2009. "Dissent and State Excesses in the Niger Delta, Nigeria". *Studies in Conflict and Terrorism* 32 (2): 129–145.

Oriola, Temitope & Ibikunle Adeakin. 2018. "The Framing Strategies of the Niger Delta Avengers". In *The Unfinished Revolution in Nigeria's Niger Delta: Prospects for Socio-Economic and Environmental Justice and Peace*, edited by Cyril Obi & Temitope Oriola: 138–158. London: Routledge.

Oshun, Olawale. 2005. *The Kiss of Death: Afenifere and the Infidels*. London: Josel.

Oyewole, Samuel. 2018. "The Urhobo Militant Movements and the Contentious Ijaw Domination of the Niger Delta Struggle". In *The Unfinished Revolution in Nigeria's Niger Delta: Prospects for Socio-Economic and Environmental Justice and Peace*, edited by Cyril Obi & Temitope Oriola: 28–40. London: Routledge.

SDN. 2017. *Public Perceptions of Security Dynamics and Stabilisation Interventions in the Niger Delta*. Port Harcourt: Stakeholder Democracy Network.

Ukeje, Charles. 2001. "Youths, Violence and the Collapse of Public Order in the Niger Delta of Nigeria". *Africa Development* 26 (1–2): 337–366.

Welch, Claude Emerson. 1995. "The Ogoni and Self-Determination: Increasing Violence in Nigeria". *Journal of Modern African Studies* 33 (4): 635–649.

PART 3

The Heart of the Matter: The State

∴

Big Business and Political Power

An Uneasy Alliance

Total's latest major field onshore is in Obagi, northwest of Port Harcourt. We arrive at the site under police escort. Visitors are required to identify themselves to gain access. The concession is home to the first well operated by Elf in Nigeria, a relic dating back to 1961. Since then, modern facilities have been built to develop Obite, a nearby gas field. There, the focus is squarely on technical matters and production is overseen by engineers from Total, the firm that gave its name to the group after merging with Elf and Fina in 1999. Accordingly, the company's understanding of community affairs is rooted in a more normative approach to corporate social responsibility.

My guides are proud to show me a gas power plant that is almost ready to supply the surrounding villages with electricity. The problem is that distribution would probably rely on a notoriously ineffective public company. In addition, electricity is to be supplied free of charge because residents see Total's efforts as a form of compensation. The gas power plant is not viewed as an initiative designed to support local development but as a means of buying social peace.

Total is no exception in this respect. International oil companies in the Niger Delta use similar methods to buy peace while discharging the Nigerian government of its social responsibility in rural areas. In other words, the private sector is entrusted with the provision of basic public services, a system that does little to help reinforce the capabilities of an already weak state. As a result, development projects are centered on production areas and are not integrated into national or regional policies. Government bureaucrats do not help either. Corrupt civil servants often seek to earn extra money by delaying or even blocking the implementation of corporate social responsibility programs. For example, it takes the NNPC's Department of Petroleum Resources (DPR) an average of twelve months to authorize a simple drinking water drilling project (Onuoha 2005: 124).

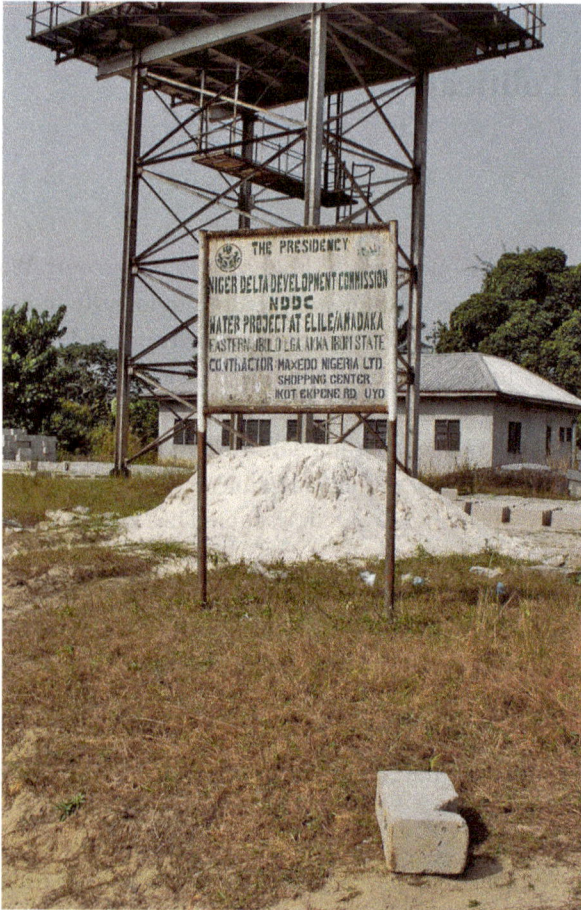

FIGURE 40   An NDDC (Niger Delta Development Commission)
             project never completed in an Akwa Ibom State
             village (2009)

1   Conflicts between Oil Companies and the State

Conflicts between foreign corporations and the federal government are a
common occurrence, yet many analysts believe that there is an objective alliance between "the Nigerian state and transnational oil companies", to quote
the Kaiama Declaration issued by IYC on 11 December 1998. Some Ijaw activists even claim that Nigeria is merely a shell of a state, while Shell holds the
power of a state. At the national and regional level, so they argue, a number
of political leaders worked for oil companies before moving into government
(Okonta & Douglas 2001). For example, Rufus Ada George, the governor of

Rivers in 1992–1993, Ernest Shonekan, the interim Head of State of Nigeria in 1993, Godwin Omene, the first director of the NDDC (Niger Delta Development Commission) in 2000, and two oil ministers under Olusegun Obasanjo in 2005 and Goodluck Jonathan in 2011, Edmund Daukoru and Diezani Alison-Madueke, all began their careers at Shell. As for Chibuzor Ogwuoha, the director of the NDDC from 2009 until his dismissal for embezzlement in 2011, he was a former Total employee at Obagi.

The financial structure of the oil industry is also indicative of common interests with government. Indeed, joint ventures and production sharing agreements involve close ties between foreign firms and the NNPC. Domestic companies play a role too, especially in the upstream sector through the development of public–private partnerships. For example, in 2013, Aliko Dangote, Africa's wealthiest businessman, announced the construction of a gigantic petrochemical complex designed to make up for the deficiencies of Nigeria's four public refineries, which were operating at a quarter of their capacity and were unable to meet local demand. The federal government supported the project by guaranteeing its access to foreign exchange and granting it tax concessions in a free zone initially planned in Ondo and eventually located in Ibeju Lekki east of Lagos, on the border with Ogun State. At one point, it was even suggested that the Dangote group would secure a monopoly on the importation of refined products and that NNPC would provide it with crude oil at cost price, as was the case with public refineries.[1]

Nevertheless, it would be wrong to assume that the Nigerian state has been "bought" by private investors. During the Cold War, "dependency" theorists depicted African governments as mere puppets controlled by the global forces of capitalism. But times have changed (Pérouse de Montclos 2019). Since the nationalizations of the 1970s, the Nigerian state has become the largest player in the industry by taking over the bulk of oil revenues. For example, when the price per barrel was $30 in the early 1980s, its share was $24.79 (86.2%), compared with just $1.21 (4.1%) going to the operators, with the remainder being absorbed in production costs, which used to be very low onshore. Today,

---

1   This last option was then abandoned following the collapse of oil prices and Aliko Dangote's determination to purchase crude on the international market to avoid the constraints associated with a company known for the irregularity of its supplies. However, the refinery's spiraling construction costs, which quadrupled to reach $19 billion, caused the site's inauguration to be postponed to 2023 and forced investors to review their position. In 2021, the federal government considered taking a 20% stake in the Lekki complex by providing a loan of $1 billion and paying the rest through crude supplies.

the oil extracted offshore is the most heavily taxed in Africa (OPTS 2018: 19). Consequently, many investors left Nigeria as production costs also rose.

After the end of the old concession regime of the 1960s, the development of joint ventures (JVS) and production sharing agreements (PSAS) was a crucial factor in this regard, together with the industry's move toward offshore fields in the 1990s. In joint ventures, the risks and investments are shared between NNPC and international oil companies. By contrast, under production sharing agreements, liability for exploration is borne solely by private operators, who recoup their costs only in the event of discovery and extraction. In addition, offshore projects tend to be more complex from a technical point of view. As a result, the risk of failure during prospection is also greater. Finally, the state has revised mining leases offshore since 2005. Current rules stipulate that investors may recoup their costs by taking only a maximum of 80% of production, while no limit was set under the 1993 tax regime.

Despite being weak and heavily indebted, the Nigerian government thus continues to play a major role in a context in which 70% of its oil and gas are now produced under PSAS, compared with just 30% under JVS (OPTS 2018: 15). There are numerous bones of contention with the majors. Unsurprisingly, these have to do first and foremost with taxation. Other points of dispute include government corruption, the proliferation of administrative hurdles, the NNPC's tendency to default on payments, and the distribution of quotas set by OPEC targets. For example, in 2017, the average amount of time required to sign a contract in Nigeria was estimated to be 38 months, compared with six in Ghana and nine in Angola (OPTS 2018: 17). All sorts of obstacles hinder the operations of transnational corporations: an official who blocks an authorization with a view to securing a bribe, a reduction in production quotas that favors "indigenous" companies and penalizes foreign firms, and so on.

Conflicts between the state and the majors also have to do with the requirements to employ nationals, to limit the number of expatriates, to finance welfare programs, to restrict imports, and to source supplies primarily from local markets. As soon as 1969, for example, the military imposed quotas on international oil companies. Local subsidiaries had to prove that at least three quarters of their managers and up to 100% of their manual workers were Nigerian.[2] The nationalisation and indigenisation decrees of the 1970s' oil boom confirmed the trend. Even if some majors were criticised for retaining control of their operations and relegating Nigerian executives to honorary positions,

---

2 The proportion of Nigerians thus rose from 7% of Shell-BP staff in 1957 to 45% in 1970. Meanwhile, the increase was from 20% to 46% for Gulf Oil between 1964 and 1970 and from 5% to 12% for Mobil between 1957 and 1970 (Madujibeya 1976: 300).

legislation passed in the 2000s and 2010s subsequently forced the industry to invest more in development projects and job creation (Ovadia 2016: 74). The laws' objectives were sometimes extremely ambitious. For example, the first drafts of the PIB (Petroleum Industry Bill) in 2007 aimed to extend the social responsibility of transnational corporations to all residents living near pipelines—including, therefore, near the Kaduna refinery in northern Nigeria. Likewise, coastal communities benefited from special provisions until 2002, when the Supreme Court ruled in favor of oil producers and recognized that using vernacular toponymy to name offshore fields or rigs conferred no ownership rights to villagers in the Niger Delta (Azaiki 2007: 224).

The laws promoting local content were another thorn in the side of the industry. While they increased operating costs, they did little to support knowledge transfer and develop the capabilities of domestic companies. For example, in 2011, a Dutch firm, Heerema, invested in Lagos's shipyards to service the Bonga FPSO, one of the world's largest platforms at sea. However, corruption and embezzlement ruined the project. As a result, Heerema was forced to transport the Bonga FPSO all the way to the Netherlands for maintenance, an additional cost that was transferred to oil operators and that reduced their corporate tax liabilities. Meanwhile, Nigeria lost out on job creation opportunities, supply contracts, tax revenue, and the rent expected from the use of the Lagos shipyards (Ovadia 2016: 87).

Since the 1990s, growing calls for a stricter application of corporate social responsibility (CSR) have also contributed to increasing production costs. From an ethical point of view, the main objective was to mitigate the collateral damage caused by the industry. This means that oil companies were to pay more attention to local needs, human rights, the environment, and a fair redistribution of their revenues (Frederick 1991). In practice, however, the implementation of CSR has been criticized by conservatives and progressives alike: the former have blamed it for reducing profit margins, while the latter see it as having put the wolf to guard the sheep by entrusting big business with promoting democratic and civic values (Ottoway 2001).

2   Corporate Social Responsibility (CSR)

In Nigeria, welfare programs funded by the private sector are not new, but they were usually restricted to the workforce of foreign firms. After independence, the extractive industry thus followed the philanthropic and paternalistic model pioneered by one of the earliest oil magnates, Ludvig Nobel (1831–1881), who established cooperatives and built an entire estate, Villa Petrolea,

FIGURE 41   Lagos Port (2010)

to accommodate his employees in Azerbaijan (LeVine 2007: 15). As for the Nigerian government, it encouraged transnational corporations to invest in the development of infrastructures across the country. Examples include Shell's refinery in Port Harcourt, Texaco's Eko Hotel in Lagos, and a solar energy research center built in Zaria by SAFRAP, the ancestor of Elf and Total.

In the Niger Delta, oil companies also funded scholarships, clinics, and small projects. In 1971, Shell opened a fish farm in Igbide near Warri and an industrial cassava plantation in Ellu near Agbarho and Ughelli in present-day Delta State. However, these initiatives were of limited scope and were not reflective of a genuine development strategy. In Irhoike near Ethiope in Delta State, the clinic built by Shell remained empty, without doctors or drugs. The Ellu plantation stopped producing cassava flour (*garri*) in 1982 and was abandoned in 1994. In rural areas, access to education did not improve either. For example, out of fifty scholarships granted by Shell to Isoko residents in Delta State between 1982 and 2002, thirty were handed out to parents or children of the company's employees, while the remaining twenty were given to traditional chiefs. In addition, none of the beneficiaries were ultimately recruited by Shell (Omoweh 2007: 245). Likewise, Chevron failed to implement projects earmarked to compensate the Itsekiri of Ugborodo for the construction of a fuel depot on the Escravos River. The scale of embezzlement was such that the development foundation it established in 1985 soon collapsed.

It was the Ogoni crisis of the 1990s that really pushed oil companies to invest in CSR in order to improve their public image and appease their relations with host communities. From welfare to development, the approach changed and became increasingly professionalized. Projects were now to be implemented by NGOs and designed to reinforce local capacities, while the majors established their own community affairs departments, starting with Shell in 1998. This was a worldwide phenomenon. For example, in 2006, the Brazilian company Petrobras spent $255 million globally on CSR programs, compared with $156 million in the case of the French group Total and $140 million for the Anglo-Dutch giant Shell (Frynas 2009: 107).

In Nigeria, the use of NGOs was a novelty and helped to implement development projects without the stigmas usually associated with oil companies. The majors sometimes attempted to partner with governmental organizations such as the UNDP (United Nations Development Programme) and Germany's GTZ (Gesellschaft für Internationale Zusammenarbeit), both of which were approached by Shell to reduce social tensions around the Soku gas project in 2003. But the most common practice has been to contract Western NGOs. Such was the case of Pro-Natura with Norway's Statoil in Akassa (Bayelsa), the Living Earth Foundation with Shell in rural communities of Cross River, and the International Foundation for Education and Self-Help with Chevron in Warri (Delta State). This new market also gave rise to a proliferation of local NGOs. For example, NNPC's operational branch, NPDC, funded Pro-Health to implement some of its CSR programs, while Shell contracted with the NDCDO (Niger Delta Communities Development Organisation) to manage fish farms in the Southern Ijaw LGA of Bayelsa State.

However, international and domestic NGOs did not meet expectations. First, they were dependent on corporate support and seemed artificial by comparison with the tribal unions that ran development projects funded by their members' fees in the 1930s, 1940s, and 1950s. Moreover, the NGOs' programs were designed primarily to buy social peace and improve the public relations of oil companies; hence, they focused almost exclusively on host communities. For example, the Nigerian branch of the British Living Earth Foundation did not generate funds locally and was established in February 1998 at the request of Shell. Subsidized from abroad, its main role was to act as a proxy to provide social services. Of the fourteen villages where it worked, only four were not located near oil fields operated by Shell (Heap 2000: ch. 8).

Accordingly, the impact of CSR programs on development has been widely contested. For example, data leaked to journalists from *The Economist* revealed

that, from 2000 to 2003, between a quarter and a third of the projects supported by Shell and evaluated after a year either did not exist or were ineffective
(Pendleton 2004). The results were no better over the longer term. According
to an internal audit, over 22% of the 581 projects initiated by the company
between 1992 and 2006 either failed or were never completed (Naanen
2012: 174). Moreover, they maintained a culture of dependence insofar as they
were seen as an obligation designed to compensate host communities who
would block production if their demands were not met (Ite 2004). In short,
CSR programs followed the logics of negotiation rather than development.

Oil companies themselves have seen their social policy as a means of continuing production and maximizing profits. Their primary goal was not to
combat poverty, a "wishful thinking, arising from either naivety, ignorance, or a
combination of both" (Aaron 2012: 271). Many companies assessed the success
of their social projects according to production levels rather than development
indicators. Also, they often entrusted the supervision of CSR programs to engineers tasked with managing extraction operations on a day-to-day basis, rather
than to experts from community affairs departments, whose trips to oil fields
were far more limited in scope because of security concerns (Zalik 2004: 413).
Finally, some companies still distributed funds without going through NGOs.
For example, Chevron gave $50,000 to victims of violence in Warri in 2003,
while Elf continued to pay subsidies directly to Obagi communities during this
period (Ngomba-Roth 2007: 167).

CSR programs disappointed many people in this regard. First, instead of
buying peace, they caused tensions because they focused on host communities and neglected groups who lived further away from oil fields. For example,
in Delta State, Ogulagha villagers complained that they did not have access to
the electricity and drinking water facilities available to residents of Forcados
near the Shell export terminal. Similarly, in Bayelsa State, only the host communities of the Soku gas project benefited from the water conveyance systems
and waste disposal services provided by Shell, causing protests in the surrounding areas. From 2003, conflicts also centered on a thermal power plant
operated by the company. Shell knew that the electrification of some areas at
the expense of others would create tensions. Under the pressure of two British
and American NGOs, Christian Aid and Catholic Relief Services, it nonetheless
accepted to supply electricity to the Kalabari of Soku and Elem-Sangama free
of charge, rather than to the Nembe of Oluasiri, who were too scattered and
who lived further away (Zalik 2011: 195).

In the 2010s, these problems took a new turn when the notion of local content was added to the mantra of CSR. One of the objectives was to enable host
communities to own development projects and, possibly, to give them a direct

stake in oil production by paying them royalties or granting them shares in joint ventures. In practice, however, these provisions never came to fruition, or even had undesirable effects. Designed to promote local supply chains, the 2010 Nigerian Oil and Gas Industry Content Development Act, for example, encouraged corruption and cronyism because it freed oil companies from having to conduct tenders if host communities were able to meet their needs. As a result, many operators ended up with a single bid despite the efforts of majors such as Total to encourage competition between different subcontractors (Ovadia 2016: 182).

In this regard, the discussions leading up to the PIB (which was eventually passed in 2021) speak volumes about failed reforms in the industry. At one stage, lawmakers considered setting up community trusts that seemed to replicate all the disadvantages of bad governance in the Niger Delta (Pérouse de Montclos 2014, 2020). In their view, these new entities were to be funded by oil companies and headed by "settlors" who were likely to be the stooges of ruling parties and corrupt state governors. Self-appointed for a period of four years, their boards could also include "outsiders" provided they were deemed to be qualified. Like CSR programs or local content policies, the main concern was not, at any rate, to consult people with a view to developing their homeland. The real aim of community trusts was to encourage "natives" to protect oil facilities and ensure the smooth running of production, or risk losing income and being forced to fund repairs in the event of attacks or acts of sabotage.

The contradictions of CSR were only made clearer. On the one hand, international oil companies were asked to act as a substitute for a weak state by developing welfare programs and basic public services in education, health, road infrastructure, housing, and electricity supply. On the other hand, they were blamed for re-colonizing the Niger Delta to secure their own enclaves.[3] Their approach to development was perceived as being disconnected from any national or regional strategy, both at the federal and local levels, and they were criticized for failing to coordinate with a government whose contribution to CSR was limited to paying part of the operating expenses of the joint ventures in which it held a majority stake.

---

3   According to some authors, their gated communities actually appeared just after the Biafran war, when oil companies re-employed Ibo technicians and had to protect them from the hostility they now faced in towns such as Port Harcourt (Daly 2022: 162).

3   From Collusion to Separation

This context points to the need to review the hypothesis of an unwavering alliance based on common interests between multinationals and the state. To make their work possible at the local level, international companies actually try to bypass a corrupt and weak government by performing political and social functions that they are not keen to take on. Such a relationship involves a form of institutionalized and mutual cheating—an open secret fully accepted by all industry stakeholders so long as they benefit from the wealth generated by oil.

American professor Kairn Klieman (2012: 164) thus reports that since the early days of the oil boom in the 1970s, the majors systematically underestimated their production to pay less tax. Meanwhile, the federal government typically sought to minimize its crude exports to comply with OPEC targets, to avoid a financial crisis, and to base its policy on realistic budget projections. As a result, official statistics tended to significantly revise real production levels downwards. The rise of NNPC as a key player in the industry then gave another dimension to this culture of mutual cheating. Looted by the military, NNPC often struggled to honor its financial commitments under JVs. To continue to produce, the majors therefore had to lend it funds repaid through tax credits. They also inflated their budgets to ensure that the Nigerian government would bear its share of operational expenses under JVs (Thurber, Emelife & Heller 2012: 723).

Inevitably, these relations of complicity and interdependence were hardly conducive to forming the basis of a genuine alliance between international oil companies and the state, especially during periods of economic crisis and collapsing oil prices. On the contrary, the industry's uneasy relations with military or civilian corrupt governments eventually had the effect of laying the groundwork for a near complete divide. First, from a geographical point of view, multinationals sought to invest at sea to escape the conflicts in the Niger Delta in the 1990s.[4] Twenty years later, offshore wells accounted for more than half of all production: 55% in 2015 compared with just 3% in 2004 (*Financial Mail* 2016). By contrast, oil fields located within the Niger Delta became increasingly less attractive. They were smaller, difficult to secure and, for geological reasons, more scattered. In addition, the army and the police were ineffective. In routinely killing civilians with impunity, they often contributed to exacerbating tensions. As a result, international oil companies funded youth militias

---

4   Such a move was not without precedent. To protect themselves against the instability affecting their operations in Venezuela, for instance, Shell and several American companies established their refining facilities on Aruba, a Dutch island, in 1928.

and resorted to private security firms, another factor that further strained their relations with a sovereign state (Amunwa 2011: 55–56).

Despite the suspension of extraction activities here and there, however, few people believed that some majors would eventually withdraw. Indeed, exploration in the Niger Delta appeared to be so promising that it seemed possible to maintain some sort of status quo. This assumption was no doubt justified so long as oil operators and investors continued to earn huge profits despite the prevailing insecurity and corruption. It took quite some time before successive shocks finally eroded the industry's margins, first with the Ogoni crisis of the 1990s, which cast a long shadow over Shell's public image, then with the Ijaw's armed struggle of the 2000s and the economic recession caused by the COVID-19 pandemic in the late 2010s, together with the requirement to achieve carbon neutrality by 2050.

In fact, as early as 2003, some experts had predicted that, given the rising violence, Shell would abandon its plans to operate onshore by 2008 (Nyheim, Zandvliet & Morrissey 2003: 6). The disengagement of international oil companies actually began slightly later, during the 2010s. In the meantime, investors shunned Nigeria. A 2005 government tender, one of the last of its kind, attracted little competition. Most blocks (57%) drew just one bid, and nearly half of all the OMLs granted never went into operation, especially those held by domestic firms (Ribadu 2012: 107). From 2007 onward, aborted discussions over the PIB also deterred investors because of the uncertainty it created around the industry's taxation.

At the time, some analysts believed that Asian firms would take over if Western oil companies opted to cut back their operations. But the example of China, which had invested significantly in Angola, was not to be repeated in Nigeria. Beijing lacked the experience, the trust, and the connections of the majors. Despite their promises to help the Nigerian government boost infrastructure in areas such as refineries, railroads, and power plants, the Chinese were unable to make inroads, while two licenses granted to KNOC (Korea National Oil Corporation) were revoked in 2008 (Vines et al. 2009).

At the national level, the oil industry thus suffered an investment freeze in the offshore sector and a gradual disengagement from onshore fields. Ashland, an American chemical company that saw its assets seized by the government and put up for sale in 1997, was the first to exit, followed by the Texan and Brazilian firms ConocoPhillips and Petrobras. Norway's Statoil, which became Equinor in 2007, also abandoned its plans to expand in Nigeria. As for Shell, Chevron, and Total, they sold their operating rights to significant onshore blocks. The sums involved were considerable, reaching billions of dollars in some cases. Such a dynamic highlighted the scale of the dissension between the Nigerian state and international oil companies based on relations that were ultimately no more fluid or peaceful than with the so-called civil society.

References

Aaron, Kiikpoye. 2012. "New Corporate Social Responsibility Models for Oil Companies in Nigeria's Delta Region: What Challenges for Sustainability?" *Progress in Development Studies* 12 (4): 259–273.

Amunwa, Ben. 2011. *Counting the Cost: Corporations and Human Rights Abuses in the Niger Delta*. London: Platform.

Azaiki, Steve. 2007. *Inequities in Nigerian Politics: The Niger Delta, Resources Control, Underdevelopment and Youth Restiveness*. Ibadan: Y-Books.

Daly, Samuel Fury Childs. 2022. *A History of the Republic of Biafra: Law, Crime, and the Nigerian Civil War*. Cambridge, Cambridge University Press.

Financial Mail. 28 April 2016. Johannesburg: 30–31.

Frederick, William. 1991. "The Moral Authority of Transnational Corporate Codes", *Journal of Business Ethics* 10 (3): 165–177.

Frynas, Jedrzej George. 2009. *Beyond Corporate Social Responsibility: Oil Multinationals and Social Challenges*. Cambridge: Cambridge University Press.

Heap, Simon. 2000. *NGOs Engaging with Business. A World of Difference and a Difference to the World*. Oxford: INTRAC (International NGO Training and Research Centre).

Ite, Uwem. 2004. "Multinationals and Corporate Social Responsibility in Developing Countries: A Case Study of Nigeria". *Corporate Social Responsibility and Environmental Management* 11 (1): 1–11.

Klieman, Kairn. 2012. "U.S. Oil Companies, the Nigerian Civil War, and the Origins of Opacity in the Nigerian Oil Industry", *Journal of American History* 99 (1): 155–165.

LeVine, Steve. 2007. *The Oil and the Glory: The Pursuit of Empire and Fortune on the Caspian Sea*. New York: Random House.

Madujibeya, Sylvanus Azuwueze. 1976. "Oil and Nigeria's Economic Development". *African Affairs* 75 (300): 284–316.

Naanen, Ben. 2012. "The Nigerian State, Multinational Oil Corporations, and the Indigenous Communities of the Niger Delta". In *The Politics of Resource Extraction: Indigenous Peoples, Multinational Corporations, and the State*, edited by Suzana Sawyer and Edmund Terence Gomez, Houndmills, Hampshire: Palgrave Macmillan: 153–179.

Ngomba-Roth, Rose. 2007. *Multinational Companies and Conflicts in Africa: The Case of the Niger Delta, Nigeria*. Berlin: Lit Verlag.

Nyheim, David, Luc Zandvliet & Lockton Morrissey (eds). 2003. *Peace and Security in the Niger Delta: Conflict Expert Group Baseline Report for Shell*. London: WAC Services.

Okonta, Ike & Oronto Douglas. 2001. *Where Vultures Feast: Shell, Human Rights, and Oil in the Niger Delta*. San Francisco: Sierra Club Books.

Omoweh, Daniel. 2007. *Shell Petroleum Development Company, the State, and Underdevelopment of the Nigeria's Niger Delta: A Study in Environmental Degradation*. Trenton (NJ): Africa World Press.

Onuoha, Austin. 2005. *From Conflict to Collaboration: Building Peace in Nigeria's Oil-Producing Communities*. London: Adonis & Abbey Publishers.

OPTS. 2018. *Memorandum on the Petroleum Industry Fiscal Bill*. Lagos: Oil Producers Trade Section.

Ottoway, Marina. 2001. "Reluctant Missionaries". *Foreign Policy*: 44–55.

Ovadia, Jesse Salah. 2016. *The Petro-Developmental State in Africa: Making Oil Work in Angola, Nigeria and the Gulf of Guinea*. London: Hurst.

Pendleton, Andrew (ed.). 2004. *Behind the Mask. The Real Face of Corporate Social Responsibility*. London: Christian Aid.

Pérouse de Montclos, Marc-Antoine. 2014. "The Politics and Crisis of the Petroleum Industry Bill in Nigeria". *Journal of Modern African Studies* 52 (3): 403–424.

Pérouse de Montclos, Marc-Antoine. 2019. *Au-delà des stéréotypes: la culture politique du pétrole et l'État en Afrique*. Bordeaux : LAM (Les Afriques dans le Monde).

Pérouse de Montclos, Marc-Antoine. 16 November 2020. "Pourquoi la Petroleum Industry Bill ne résoudra pas les problèmes du Nigeria et du delta". Paris: *Jeune Afrique*.

Ribadu, Mallam Nuhu. 2012. *Report of the Petroleum Revenue Special Task Force*. Abuja: Federal Ministry of Petroleum Resources.

Thurber, Mark, Ifeyinwa Emelife & Patrick Heller. 2012. "NNPC and Nigeria's Oil Patronage Ecosystem". In *Oil and Governance. State-Owned Enterprises and the World Energy Supply*, edited by David Victor, David Hults & Mark Thurber: 701–752. Cambridge: Cambridge University Press.

Vines, Alex *et al.* 2009. *Thirst for African Oil: Asian National Oil Companies in Nigeria and Angola*. London: Chatham House.

Zalik, Anna. 2004. "Niger Delta: 'Petro Violence' and 'Partnership Development'". *Review of African Political Economy* 31 (101): 401–424.

Zalik, Anna. 2011. "Labelling Oil, Contesting Governance". In *Oil and Insurgency in the Niger Delta: Managing the Complex Politics of Petroviolence*, edited by Cyril Obi & Siri Aas Rustad: 184–199. London: Zed.

CHAPTER 13

The Leviathan of the Mangroves

A Deficient, Predatory, and Contested State

Ann-Kio Briggs is a well-known militant in the Niger Delta. With close ties to the rebels, she is active on both the environmental and political fronts. We have agreed to meet in the car park of a Port Harcourt hotel. She arrives in a gleaming four-wheel drive worth around €100,000. The vehicle has a federal government registration plate and tinted windows, a privilege that Nigerian law reserves only for officials. Ann-Kio Briggs also benefits from close protection provided by special policemen, the MOPOL, who have their own pick-up. She gets out of her black four-wheel drive as if she were a queen, stepping out of a horse-drawn carriage, and I am somewhat disconcerted. Exactly whose side is she on?

The militant in her soon comes out. She speaks vehemently against the misdeeds of the federal government—a government that has obligingly provided her with a luxury car. She exclaims:

> Local communities should control resources onshore … and even offshore. Pipeline terminals on the coast can help determine whose community is the owner of a well in the ocean. It's not fair that only the federal government should earn royalties on offshore production.[1]

With her smart four-wheel drive, Ann-Kio Briggs is, in fact, one of the benefactors of the generosity of President Goodluck Jonathan—an Ijaw, like her. Her opposition to the federal government is quite ambivalent in this regard. It shows that the interactions between so-called civil society and the ruling class are no less ambiguous than those between oil companies and the state. These relations take many different forms at different political levels. Niger Delta communities feel naturally closer to the local authorities. By contrast, the federal government in Abuja seems very far away. In the creeks, the Nigerian state is seen as a kind of predatory monster reminiscent of Thomas Hobbes's Leviathan. Its structural deficiencies are admittedly not specific to the Niger Delta. However, in the region, the failures of the state have clearly fed into the

---

1 Interview with the author in Port Harcourt in October 2012.

FIGURE 42   Slums in Port Harcourt (1994)

resentment felt against a federal government accused of hijacking oil revenue, abusing its citizens, and robbing natives of their rights.

1   A Sense of Alienation

The Land Use Act of 1978 powerfully captures the tensions within the Niger Delta. While the military federal government seized control of all natural resources, it indeed authorized state governors to expropriate and acquire both private and public lands necessary for engaging in mining activities. In the specific case of oil, companies were left to compensate residents evicted from production zones. But the rates set by the government remained extremely low insofar as they took no account of inflation and the loss of farming and fishing income resulting from the industry's activities. In addition, oil companies were not required to relocate displaced residents, a prescription that even the Nigerian state did not apply.[2]

---

2   For example, as part of the construction of the federal capital in Abuja from 1977 onward, the government planned to relocate natives who had been expelled from their homes. Housing estates were developed for this purpose in Usuma, Kubwa, Kuje, Giri, Karu, and

Admittedly, prospectors had to comply with customary land rights when demarcating production zones. Therefore, they continued to pay rents to traditional authorities despite the government's attempt to nationalize land under the 1978 military decree. Oil companies also gave money to appease the "gods" of once polytheistic societies, especially when sacred trees were damaged. However, the process of identifying beneficiaries caused many disputes. In the absence of any land registers or property deeds, compensations were often paid out through the medium of urban chiefs, notaries, or usurpers who cheated rural people, leading to numerous legal complaints. In 2021, a new Petroleum Industry Act (PIA) even restricted the scope of procedures in cases of damages (Amaduobogha, Subai, Mazzi & Akhigbe 2021).

The sense of dispossession felt by host communities was further reinforced by the practice of naming oil wells without any reference to the local toponymy. For example, the hamlet of Dere in Ogoniland was renamed Bomu by Shell (Agbonifo 2018: 35). Similarly, among the Ijaw Ogbia of Bayelsa State, Shell gave the name Kolo Creek to a deposit located at the site of three villages: Imiringi, Otuasega, and Elebele. Disputes over toponymy were not merely symbolic; they also involved requests for land compensation. In Bayelsa State, the Nembe of Oluasiri claimed that their village of Ijaw-Kiri, established in 1901, was the closest to the Soku gas deposit operated by Shell. However, their Kalabari rivals retorted that the company's plant was named after one of their communities, Soku. As a result, the Nembe asked Shell to rename the site Oluasiri (Nyheim, Zandvliet & Morrissey 2003: 55).

In some cases, disputes turned violent. For example, in the Degema LGA to the south of Port Harcourt, the Bille claimed customary ownership of wells operated by Shell in Emupele near the Cawthorne Channel (Von Kemedi 2003: 16). In 1995, this small minority sued the Ke clan of the Kalabari Ijaw. The Bille requested that the Shell flow station continue to bear the name Awoba, after one of their goddesses. But the Ke wanted to have it renamed Opuso, after one of their own gods. The dispute eventually took a nastier turn. The Ke, who were ultimately unsuccessful, accused Shell of siding with the Bille. The two communities came to blows during clashes that resulted in several deaths in

---

Ushafa. However, between 1985 and 1991, only 500 new homes were completed, before being resold by their owners because they were poorly equipped and too small. In practice, the vast majority of displaced residents received no compensation and were left to fend for themselves in neighboring Plateau, Kwara, and Niger states. Damages were paid to only a handful of villagers who bribed officials or had the necessary connections to have their claims relayed to the government (Dauda, 2002: 139).

early 2001 and that led to the Nigerian navy setting up permanent bases in the sub-region.

The amount of compensation claimed from oil companies undoubtedly contributed to exacerbate tensions. However, disputes over matters of toponymy also involved people outside production zones. For example, after the end of the Biafran War in 1970, the Ikwerre of Rivers State set about changing the name of their villages to integrate the power networks of coastal communities and to distinguish themselves from the Ibo of the hinterland, who had been defeated. Umuokoro thus became Rumuokoro (Uchendu 2018).[3] Likewise, further south, the Ibibio of present-day Akwa Ibom wanted to use the vernacular name Ibekwe for Opobo Island. Yet, they were ultimately unable to prevent it being renamed Ikot Abasi when it was granted to Rivers State by the military governor of Cross River, Captain Tunde Elegbede, in 1979 (Udoma 1987: 252–257).

In this respect, it is not certain that the expropriations associated with the development of oil activities were the major factor contributing to tensions in the Niger Delta. Nigeria's most densely populated regions are to be found elsewhere. For example, according to the 1991 and 2006 censuses, most of the LGAs in Bayelsa and Delta states are rural and have fewer than 200 inhabitants per square kilometer, such as in Southern Ijaw, Nembe, Brass, Ekeremor, Sagbama, and Akuku Toru (Alagoa, Tamuno & Clark 2009: 31). Admittedly, it is difficult to estimate population densities in the green labyrinth of a delta. Statistics contain errors and the land mass varies from year to year, depending on the season, the reconfiguration of creeks, and the water levels in the tributaries of the Niger River. Outside towns and cities, however, LGAs with the highest number of people per square kilometer are mostly on the coast, in Okrika, Andoni, and Asari Toru, or in semi-urban areas further north, in Ogu-Bolo, Gokana and Yenagoa. As for the Ogbia, Kolokuma, Abua, Bonny, and Degema LGAs, they have intermediate levels of population density.

In other words, population distribution in the Niger Delta does not mirror the location of extractive activities. Although the oil boom led to an influx of migrants toward the cities of Port Harcourt and Warri, the industry's footprint is not as significant as is sometimes assumed. Production per se covers a smaller area than sectors such as agro-forestry and open-pit mining.[4] It is also important not to overstate the scale of oil spills, which have sometimes been artificially inflated to obtain more compensation and to secure contracts to

---

3 See also Bersselaar 1998: 69–70, 200–201, Afigbo 1987: 14–17.
4 For example, during the colonial period, tin mining in the Jos area covered 40% of the land of the Birom in 1935, rising to 59% by 1950 (Goshit 2002: 383).

FIGURE 43   Aerial view of the Niger Delta (2011)

clean up the affected sites. For example, based on calculations performed in Delta State, oil wells, processing plants, and pipelines covered 0.8% of the surface of the Isoko homeland, representing 881 hectares out of a total of 104,800, while the resulting pollution impacted 1.7% of the territory, or 1,800 hectares (Omoweh 2007: 224). This pattern is not unique. In general, the industry operates in rural and sparsely populated areas. Consequently, its activities tend not to generate displacements on a large scale, unlike public government projects in urban areas.[5]

Within the Niger Delta, there is also no evidence of any systemic correlation between population density and violence, including clashes that do not involve oil companies and that take place outside production areas. Based on press reports, data collected by the NigeriaWatch project testify to this. Covering a fifteen-year period (2006–2021), they provide no basis for identifying any conclusive proof of links with land pressure, except possibly in Port Harcourt and Warri, where conflicts are more visible in the media.[6] Taking into account the

---

5   For example, the construction of a new capital in Abuja resulted in the eviction of over 20% of the area's natives, or 5,412 out of a total of 26,328 households, according to the 1991 census (Dauda 2002: 139).

6   http://www.nigeriawatch.org/.

magnifier effect associated with urban areas, the mapping of lethal incidents highlights a wide range of cases. For example, the most densely populated rural government in Rivers, Asari Toru, had a lower homicide rate than the average for the state. Conversely, despite being the least populated areas in Bayelsa, Nembe and Southern Ijaw recorded higher levels of fatalities than the regional average. Except for Port Harcourt, the hypothesis of a positive link between the two variables was evidenced only in two Rivers State LGAs: Gokana and Bonny, which recorded higher violent death rates than the sub-region's average. Situated in Ogoniland, Gokana was the state's second-most densely populated rural area, while Bonny recorded the highest population growth rate after Eleme and Opobo, with its population increasing threefold between the 1991 and 2006 censuses.

Another important finding is that land conflicts in the Niger Delta are not restricted to oil and community disputes. As in other regions of Nigeria, they also involve local and state governments over contested administrative boundaries and, sometimes, international borders—for instance, over the Bakassi peninsula during a war with Cameroon, which continued until the signing of a peace agreement in 2006. In addition, land conflicts typically oppose tenants and owners, or families laying claim to the same parcel of land.[7] Some scholars have thus shown that the most common disputes in the area concern fraudulent sales of plots to several individuals at once (Ebiede, Bassey & Asuni 2021: 112).

2   Land as a Key Bone of Contention

Conflicts over oil fields, however, are different. The stakes are higher and opposition to the Land Use Act of 1978 has been a primary focus of Niger Delta militants, because it reflected a strong sense of political frustration, cultural alienation, territorial dispossession, and social injustice. Moreover, it fueled protests aimed at changing the formula governing the redistribution of oil and gas revenue. "Resource control" and "true federalism" became a leitmotiv of Niger Delta militants to secure a larger slice of the so-called national cake. After the Biafran War, the military had indeed dismantled the "derivation" system put in place by the British to ensure that the budget of each of Nigeria's three administrative regions would be self-funded. The governments in power

---

7   It is not certain in this respect that private ownership of oil deposits would have brought more stability than the nationalization process undertaken as part of the 1978 Land Use Act. For a different point of view, see Weinthal & Luong 2006.

opted instead to centralize oil revenue to develop the country's poorest areas in the north. To do so, they supported an "equalization" logic against a "derivation" system that rewarded Nigeria's wealthiest regions in the south based on their contribution to the federal government's budget. It was not until the end of the Abacha dictatorship in 1999 that the share of onshore oil revenue was increased to 13% in favor of producing states.[8]

The return to a more democratic regime did little to appease Niger Delta militants in this regard. Corruption and fraudulent elections maintained a sense of distrust toward deficient, predatory, and brutal governments that often dealt with land and community disputes through repression. For example, surveys conducted in 2000 showed that a majority of people in Bayelsa, Delta, and Akwa Ibom saw little value in sending delegations to local, state, or federal authorities in a bid to improve their situation.[9] Defense and security forces were not trusted either. On the contrary, they were widely perceived as a threat rather than a means of maintaining law and order against organized crime. According to surveys conducted in 2017, the populations of Bayelsa, Delta, and Rivers states reported fearing attacks by gangs of "cultists" or "militants" just as much as retaliation and indiscriminate repression by the army (SDN 2017). Locals placed more trust in traditional chiefs and self-defense militias.

In the same vein, many people do not expect the government to help them settle their disputes with oil companies. The Nigerian judicial system is handicapped by corruption, especially at the local level. State courts in particular are very vulnerable to political interference, since they depend financially on the goodwill of governors (Ukata 2018: 306). Unlike federal courts, which receive recurrent funding, state courts are not supervised by a National Judicial Council and face conflicts of interest that sometimes take a personal turn. For example, judges at the High Court of Rivers State have included the wives of incumbent governors Peter Odili and Ezenwo Wike.

Admittedly, federal courts are not spared from problems either. The Supreme Court in Abuja is relatively independent and, in 2007, it refused to give in to pressure from President Olusegun Obasanjo to exclude one of his main opponents, Atiku Abubakar, from the electoral race. However, it does not have the power to compel the federal government to apply its rulings. At the end of the military dictatorship in 1999, it was unable to prevent President Olusegun Obasanjo from flouting judgments ordering him to release the payment of budget allocations owed to LGAs in the hands of the opposition, especially

---

8   For an overview, see Pérouse de Montclos 2017.

9   Out of the 284 people surveyed at the time, the proportions ranged from 70% to 92% depending on the state (Ukeje 2002: 29).

in Lagos (Suberu 2008: 482). In addition, the Supreme Court has not always been immune from conflicts of interest. For example, having been appointed by President Goodluck Jonathan in 2011, one of its judges, the wife of former Rivers State governor Peter Odili, has been suspected of concealing electoral fraud and of dismissing various charges brought against her husband, ranging from embezzlement to political assassinations.

3   A Deficient Judicial System

In such a system, demands for justice from Niger Delta communities are unlikely to be satisfied. To bury land disputes, military regimes often set up commissions of inquiry whose findings were never published or enforced. For example, the government tasked a federal judge, Ephraim Akpata, with investigating clashes between the Ibeno and the Eket over the Mobil oil terminal in Akwa Ibom State in 1993. But his report was not published because he was accused of being biased in favor of the Eket. A similar scenario arose regarding the recurrent conflicts that opposed the Itsekiri, the Ijaw, and the Urhobo in the city of Warri. Led by judges Philip Nnaemeka-Agu in 1993 and Hassan Idoko in 1997, and later by General Bashir Salihi Magashi in 1999, various commissions of inquiry recommended creating LGAs to satisfy the demands of all three parties. However, the Ijaw and the Urhobo requested in vain that the reports be made public. As for the Itsekiri, they refused to participate in the hearings held by Judge Hassan Idoko, whom they accused of bias.

In 1999, the return to civilian rule also failed to satisfy the calls for justice from Niger Delta communities. Established to investigate human rights violations committed between 1984 and 1998, when the military were in power, the so-called Oputa Panel, named after its chairman Chukwudifu Oputa (1924–2014), received more than 10,000 complaints from Ogoni citizens, a national record for Nigeria (Aaron 2005). Unlike South Africa's Truth and Reconciliation Commission, however, it was not allowed to initiate trials or grant amnesties. Moreover, after the hearings, the federal government blocked the publication of its White Book, ten voluminous reports that were finally leaked by activists in 2005. The African Commission on Human and Peoples' Rights was no more successful in this regard. The complaint lodged by Ogoni organizations in 1996 against General Sani Abacha was not dealt with until 2001 and resulted only in an admonition that President Olusegun Obasanjo, a former putschist and a victim of the dictator, quickly endorsed to portray himself as a democrat (Coomans 2003).

After 1999, the various commissions put in place by oil-producing states were just as disappointing. For example, Bayelsa Governor Diepreye Alamieyeseigha tasked Judge Moore Adumein with conducting an investigation into the involvement of the Iseinasawo, a Nembe secret society, in the assassination of twelve people, including four local councillors, near Brass in February 2005. However, no report was released, and no charges were ever brought. Similarly, in November 2007, the Rivers State Governor, Rotimi Amaechi, launched a Truth and Reconciliation Commission to investigate the root causes of violence in the region since the end of the military dictatorship in May 1999. Led by a retired Supreme Court judge, Kayode Eso, the body received 215 complaints, and its hearings were broadcast live on Nigerian television, as had been the case with the Oputa Panel. The former governor of the state, Peter Odili, agreed to testify but denied having provided support to armed gangs to win elections, while his successor and collaborator, Rotimi Amaechi, did nothing to exert further pressure on him. As a result, the commission's findings made little impact after an official report was handed over to the authorities in March 2009 (Omotola 2010).

Unsurprisingly, such impediments cause much frustration. In the creeks of the Niger Delta, the Nigerian judicial system is seen as beyond reach, procedure-driven, incomprehensible, slow, expensive, and useless. Trials drag on without any prospect of conclusion and seem to serve the interests only of the wealthy. Some militants thus justify the use of violence as an alternative and far more effective means of resolving disputes. Cases against oil companies in particular are perceived as having little chance of being heard. Despite their technical complexity, the burden of proof falls on complainants who, in order to gain access to the courts, must first demonstrate that they have suffered a wrong as a result of prospection or production activities (Damfebo 2009). The challenge is considerable for a humble fisherman who might, for example, have seen his nets destroyed at sea by a ship carrying supplies to an offshore platform. Farmers face similar challenges when seeking to demonstrate the long-term impact of oil pollution. According to Nigeria's Criminal Procedure Code, a claim is no longer admissible in court after six years. In 2021, the PIA even reduced the period for appeals against government decisions related to land requisitions.

A further dissuasive factor is the slow speed of proceedings. Rivers State holds a national record in this regard, with cases taking an average of five years to run their course (*Guardian* 2020). Even if judges sometimes pass sentences at the end of a trial, the outcome is hardly ever satisfactory, since rulings are seldom applied. In the case of air pollution, the Nigerian state often does little more than levy fines without paying compensation to those directly affected by the toxic emissions of gas flares. Judges too are usually careful not to order the suspension of oil production to avoid any adverse impact on government revenue. As for appeals, they are generally beyond the reach of complainants because, since 1999, they have to be referred to the federal level.

As a result, cases are often settled out of court. Nigeria's Criminal Procedure Code encourages complainants to favor negotiation through alternative dispute resolution channels. However, this system does not motivate oil companies to properly compensate the victims of their activities. Moreover, the decisions resulting from such arrangements are not always enforced. For instance, a commission of inquiry established by Rivers State and chaired by Judge Opubo Inko-Tariah requested that Shell and the federal government compensate the victims of the deadly repression of a peaceful demonstration held in Umuechem in 1990. Local councils were expected to pay the beneficiaries. However, thirty years on, the residents of Umuechem have yet to receive the earmarked funds, which were either embezzled or never released (Naagbanton 2017).

These failures are not only embarrassing; they also shed doubt on the capacity of grassroots organizations to play an informal mediation role. During the Abacha dictatorship, the Ogoni crisis stimulated a proliferation of NGOs that received substantial international backing until 1999, when it was widely assumed that the return to civilian rule would help to appease the situation (Ibeanu 2006: 47). For example, aside from Action Aid and Christian Aid, which are both British, the Church of England supported peace-making initiatives in the Niger Delta with Reverend Nicky Gumbel from the Holy Trinity Brompton Church in London and Canon Stephen Davis from the Reconciliation Ministry of Coventry Cathedral. As for the American MacArthur Foundation, it funded the peace education programs of a group, AAPW (Academic Associates Peace Works), established in Warri in 1988 to help with the demobilization of armed militants after 2003.

Some commentators have thus argued that international and local NGOs have done much to push the federal government to take into account the needs of the Niger Delta people and to reform the system governing the redistribution of oil revenues. However, grassroots organizations have not been immune from the ills of violence and corruption affecting the Nigerian state (Ikelegbe 2001a, 2001b, Adekson 2004).[10] As for foreign NGOs, they have not been perceived as neutral when they took side with the authorities. For example, the International Centre for Reconciliation at Coventry Cathedral awarded

---

10   For a positive view of grassroots organizations, see Akinola 2008.

a peace prize to President Olusegun Obasanjo in 2005, while Reverend Nicky Gumbel, a lawyer, worked with the governor of Bayelsa State, Timipre Sylva. Criticisms have also been leveled at the American director of AAPW, Judith Asuni, for accepting funds from US oil companies.

Nigerian organizations are no better in this regard and have often defended ethnic interests at the risk of further fueling community conflicts. It is important, therefore, not to idealize them. For example, IYC hardly reflected the description given by Darren Kew (2016: 293), who saw it as a "representative" and "democratically structured NGO" with a "moderating influence". Likewise, MOSOP and IYC were not organizations dedicated to mediation or the defense of human rights, contrary to the claims made by Claude Welch (1995) and Okechukwu Ibeanu (2006). Rather, they were direct stakeholders in the Niger Delta's conflicts. From the very beginning, they were designed to mobilize people on an ethnic basis. It was only at a later stage that they launched special branches such as the ORAREF (Ogoni Relief and Rehabilitation Fund), a body founded by MOSOP in 1993 to provide aid to victims of military repression. As for IYC, it used two NGOs established in 1993 and 1995, ERA (Environmental Rights Action) and ND-HERO (Niger Delta Human and Environmental Rescue Organization), to provide "intellectual" and "scientific" substance to its claims against oil pollution (Ukeje 2001: 30).

In the same vein, some associations were created by militants to confer on themselves a degree of respectability. For example, a nephew of Ateke Tom, Richard Akinaka, established a platform called Grassroots Initiative for Peace and Democracy. Similarly, in 1998, the spokesperson for the Ijaw Republican Assembly, Ann-Kio Briggs, founded her own feminist NGO, Agape Birthright, while continuing to take part in the activities of the Niger Delta Women for Justice (NDWJ). Politicians have also sought to consolidate their social base through the non-profit sector. A chair of the presidential amnesty program, Kingsley Kuku, thus established a charity named after his mother, the Keketobou Care Foundation. Likewise, the Foundation for Ethnic Harmony was officially tasked with training and reintegrating demobilized militants in 2009, although its main objective was to promote Peremobowei Ebebi, the deputy governor of Bayelsa State and a rival to Timipre Sylva, who had been elected in 2008.

4   When Crime Pays: The Reign of Impunity

As further evidence of their failure to play a mediation role, none of these initiatives succeeded in achieving peace talks at the regional level. Rather than NGOs, it was envoys of the Nigerian government who negotiated with the rebels when, in April 2008, MEND announced its intention to lay down its weapons if Abuja agreed to declare a ceasefire, release Henry Okah, withdraw its troops, and replace them with a more professional and less brutal police force while engaging in discussions on the redistribution of oil revenue. As noted in Chapter 6, however, the implementation of the June 2009 amnesty was ultimately unsuccessful in addressing the fundamental problems afflicting the region. For one thing, the authorities failed to make provision for any framework to support mediation, dialogue, and reconciliation. In addition, the amnesty confirmed the impunity enjoyed by both the rebels and corrupt governors. Despite the scale of embezzlement, financial scandals remained unpunished. Of all the governors elected in the main oil-producing states after 1999, only James Ibori from Delta State served time in prison; Diepreye Alamieyeseigha in Bayelsa was pardoned, while Peter Odili in Rivers was never sued.

Heading up Nigeria's largest oil-producing state, Peter Odili was nonetheless among the first to benefit from soaring oil prices and the increase in the "derivation" percentage granted to the Niger Delta in the early 2000s. Coming from one of Rivers' smallest minorities, he used this wealth to buy the loyalty of voters and his political cronies. In overseeing ever increasing revenues, he was also careful to reward himself in the process. For example, a year before the end of his second term in 2007, his office was spending an amount equivalent to three times the budget of the Rivers State health ministry, theoretically earmarked as a priority. Estimated at $60,000 a day, the item posted for Odili's travel expenses even exceeded that of President Olusegun Obasanjo and was greater than the amount granted to development programs in the region (Albin-Lackey 2007).

In other words, there is ample evidence to charge Niger Delta political leaders. For example, in Akwa Ibom, the opposition paid for an insert in a *Newswatch* issue dated 20 March 2006, to list all the fraudulent contracts signed by Governor Victor Attah. Occasionally, honest civil servants and security operatives—or those keen to settle scores—also leaked information to denounce corrupt officials. In a secret report dated 7 November 2007 and published by Sahara Reporters three years later, a copy of which is held by the author, military intelligence thus revealed that governors James Ibori and Diepreye Alamieyeseigha had facilitated the sale of weapons stolen from the Nigerian Army to MEND and Henry Okah's brother.

With disconcerting brazenness, even corrupt officials have sometimes publicly acknowledged that so much pressure was weighed on them that they had no choice but to take liberties with ethics and the law. For example, when he testified before the Senate on 22 October 2015, prior to being appointed as federal minister, Peter Odili's successor in Rivers, Rotimi Amaechi, claimed that he had never accepted a bribe but that corruption was a somewhat vague concept, implying that he would not rule out sleeping with a woman prepared to have sex in return for a job (Umoru & Erunke 2015). As for Timipre Sylva, Diepreye Alamieyeseigha's successor in Bayelsa, he once admitted in an interview, published on 6 September 2010, that he could not afford to turn down favors. As he put it: "If a chief walks into my office, he expects me to take care of his problems. That's what he's used to. If I don't, I've got a very big political enemy ... You will read that as corruption, but me, I probably will read that as political survival, because I have to survive before I become incorruptible". He went on to note that "the whole system might just blow up and implode" if the struggle against corruption was not gradual (*Financial Times* 2010).

The examples of Diepreye Alamieyeseigha and James Ibori speak volumes in this respect. The former was elected governor of Delta State twice, in January 1999 and again in April 2003, despite having a criminal record. In the United Kingdom, he had been found guilty of theft, fraud, and the use of a fake identity card (Walker 2012). In Nigeria, he was also convicted for breach of trust in a small court in Bwari, a small town near Abuja, in September 1995. At the time, Ibori was close to General Sani Abacha, for whom he worked. He argued that such protection meant that he could not possibly be sentenced for merely stealing zinc roofing sheets. If we are to believe him, he was only implicated in the case by rivals seeking to tarnish his reputation. The person charged in Bwari was, in fact, a homonymous truck driver, or someone by the name of Shuaibu Anyebe. As evidence of this, the judge who passed the sentence was briefly arrested and questioned by the police. His testimony was full of contradictions, and he was unable to remember key details. He also allegedly reduced the amount of the stolen goods, from ₦110 million to ₦110,000, to ensure that the case remained within his jurisdiction (Akiri 2006: 68–83, 214).

Once elected governor, Ibori was then suspected of maintaining links with armed groups involved in kidnapping, piracy, and bunkering in the Niger Delta. He often offered his services to secure the release of hostages and was so close to the rebels that he faced the risk of being deposed by Abuja and replaced by a military administrator, as happened in Plateau State, where his counterpart, Governor Joshua Dariye, was taken to court and threatened with impeachment in January 2004 (Davis 2009: 70). After completing his second term, Ibori eventually lost his parliamentary immunity and was arrested in December 2007 by the Economic and Financial Crimes Commission (EFCC). However, as a major donor to the PDP, the Delta State governor had supported the election of President Umaru Yar Adua in April 2007 and the appointment of Michael Aondoakaa as justice minister in July. The investment proved wise. Ibori was quickly pardoned, while the director of the EFCC, Nuhu Ribadu, lost his job and was dismissed from the police (Smith 2018: 297).

Ultimately, it was the British judicial system that convicted the former governor of Delta State. On the run in Nigeria and then Dubai, from where he was extradited to London, Ibori was sentenced in April 2012 to thirteen years in prison for, among other things, money laundering, misuse of corporate assets, and embezzlement. However, he was released for good behavior just four years into his sentence in December 2016 and placed under house arrest in Britain (Easton 2016). As for his counterpart in Bayelsa, Diepreye Alamieyeseigha, he was able to escape the British courts by posting bail and fleeing the country while disguised as a woman after his arrest in London with a suitcase full of cash in December 2005. A supporter of the Ijaw National Congress, he was just as implicated as Ibori in the financing of armed groups and the misappropriation of public funds—for instance, to build the campus of Niger Delta University in his home village, Amassoma.

On his return to Nigeria, Diepreye Alamieyeseigha agreed in July 2007 to plead guilty and to return his fraudulently acquired assets to the federal government. Despite being sentenced to two years in jail, he was immediately released, having already spent that time behind bars. He was subsequently pardoned by President Umara Ya'Adua to avoid hampering negotiations with Ijaw armed groups before the June 2009 amnesty. If Diepreye Alamieyeseigha were to fall ill and die in prison, the fear was that his death would reignite hostilities and destabilize the entire region. He was finally pardoned in March 2013 by his former deputy Goodluck Jonathan, who in the meantime had been elected President of Nigeria (Bolaji 2017: 338).

These various cases plainly show that the judicial system of Africa's most populous country is incapable of dealing with financial scandals that contribute to delegitimizing the state. Ultimately, it was only through the courts of the former colonial power that Diepreye Alamieyeseigha and James Ibori ended up behind bars. Similarly, it was British and American judges who were able to punish oil majors such as Shell and Chevron by forcing them to pay compensation to complainants living far away in the Niger Delta. By contrast, the Nigerian judicial system has mostly served the interests of the rich and failed to meet the expectations of ordinary people.

Significantly, sentences handed down overseas against multinationals accused of bribing officials to secure contracts, such as Halliburton in the United States and Siemens in Germany, have spared politicians in Abuja and the Niger Delta. The recipients of kickbacks have seldom been taken to court, let alone identified and summoned to account for their actions. Matters are even worse in the interior of the Niger Delta far from the prying eyes of the media and the international community. The degree of impunity of the ruling class increases in line with the distance from Abuja. This is especially true at the local government level, the most corrupt tier of the Nigerian federal system.

References

Aaron, Kiikpoye. 2005. "Truth without Reconciliation: The Niger Delta and the Continuing Challenge of National Reconciliation". In *The Crisis of the State and Regionalism in West Africa*, edited by Alada Fawole & Charles Ukeje: 127–137. Dakar: Codesria.

Adekson, Adedayo Oluwakayode. 2004. *The "Civil Society" Problematique: Deconstructing Civility and Southern Nigeria's Ethnic Radicalization*. London: Routledge.

Afigbo, Adiele Eberechukwu. 1987. *The Igbo and their Neighbours: Inter-Group Relations in Southeastern Nigeria to 1953*. Ibadan: Ibadan University Press.

Agbonifo, John. 2018. *Environment and Conflict: Place and the Logic of Collective Action in the Niger Delta*. London: Routledge.

Akinola, Shittu. 2008. "Coping with Social Deprivation through Self-Governing Institutions in Oil Communities of Nigeria". *Africa Today* 55 (1): 89–107.

Akiri, Chris. 2006. *The Way It Is*. Lagos: Bertie-John.

Alagoa, Ebiegberie Joe, Tekena Tamuno & John Pepper Clark (eds). 2009. *The Izon of the Niger Delta*. Port Harcourt: Onyoma.

Albin-Lackey, Chris. 2007. *Chop Fine. The Human Rights Impact of Local Government Corruption and Mismanagement in Rivers State, Nigeria*. New York: Human Rights Watch.

Amaduobogha, Simon, Pereowei Subai, Peter Mazzi & Lillian Akhigbe. 2021. *The Petroleum Industry Bill 2020: Briefing*. Port Harcourt: Stakeholder Democracy Network.

Bersselaar, Dmitri van den. 1998. *In Search of Igbo Identity. Language, Culture and Politics in Nigeria, 1900–1966*. Leiden, University of Leiden.

Bolaji, Mohammed. 2017. *On a Platter of Gold: How Jonathan Won and Lost Nigeria*. Lagos: Kachifo.

Coomans, Fons. 2003. "The Ogoni Case before the African Commission on Human and Peoples' rights". *International and Comparative Law Quarterly* 52 (3): 749–760.

Damfebo, Derri. 2009. "Litigation Problems in Compensation Claims for Oil and Gas Operations in Nigeria". In *Law and Petroleum Industry In Nigeria: Current Challenges*, edited by Festus Emiri & Gowon Deinduomo: 11–34. Lagos: Malthouse.

Dauda, Saleh. 2002. "The Establishment of a New Federal Capital in Abuja, Central Nigeria Area: An Appraisal". In *Studies in the History of Central Nigeria Area, vol. 1*, edited by Aliyu Idrees & Yakubu Ochefu: 133–142. Lagos: CSS Ltd.

Davis, Stephen. 2009. *The Potential for Peace and Reconciliation in the Niger Delta.* Coventry: Coventry Cathedral.

Easton, Mark. 21 Dec. 2016. "Nigerian Ex-Governor James Ibori Released from UK Jail". Lagos: *BBC News.* https://www.bbc.com/news/uk-38395396 (accessed 23 january 2017).

Ebiede, Tarila Marclint, Celestine Oyom Bassey & Judith Burdin Asuni (eds). 2021. *Insecurity in the Niger Delta. A Report on Emerging Threats in Akwa Ibom, Bayelsa, Cross River, Delta, Edo and Rivers States.* London: Adonis & Abbey Publishers.

Financial Times. 6 September 2010. Johannesburg.

Goshit, Zakariya Damina. 2002. "Food Crisis in the Plateau Area during the Second World War, 1939–45", In *Studies in the History of Central Nigeria Area, vol. 1*, edited by Aliyu Idrees & Yakubu Ochefu: 367–386. Lagos: CSS Ltd.

Guardian. 5 March 2020. Lagos: 45.

Ibeanu, Okechukwu. 2006. *Civil Society and Conflict Management in the Niger Delta: Scoping Gaps for Policy and Advocacy.* Lagos: Cleen Foundation, Monograph Series no. 2.

Ikelegbe, Augustine. 2001a. "Civil Society, Oil and Conflict in the Niger Delta Region of Nigeria: Ramifications of Civil Society for a Regional Resource Struggle". *Journal of Modern African Studies* 39 (3): 437–469.

Ikelegbe, Augustine. 2001b. "The Perverse Manifestation of Civil Society: Evidence from Nigeria". *Journal of Modern African Studies* 39 (1): 1–24.

Kew, Darren. 2016. *Civil Society, Conflict Resolution, and Democracy in Nigeria.* New York: Syracuse University Press.

Naagbanton, Patrick. 2017. *Conflicts, IOCs and Community Rising in the Niger Delta.* Port Harcourt: Social Action.: https://saction.org/social-action-joins-umuechem-community-in-27th-year-remembrance-of-shells-massacre/ (accessed 18 march 2018).

Nyheim, David, Luc Zandvliet & Lockton Morrissey (eds). 2003. *Peace and Security in the Niger Delta: Conflict Expert Group Baseline Report for Shell.* London: WAC Services.

Omotola, Shola. 2010. "Rivers State's Truth and Reconciliation Commission: Between Hope and Despair". In *Dynamics of Peace Processes*, edited by Isaac Olawale Albert & Is-haq Olanrewaju Oloyede: 139–155. University of Ilorin: Centre for Peace and Strategic Studies.

Omoweh, Daniel. 2007. *Shell Petroleum Development Company, the State, and Underdevelopment of the Nigeria's Niger Delta: A Study in Environmental Degradation.* Trenton (NJ): Africa World Press.

Pérouse de Montclos, Marc-Antoine. 2017. "Rebellion and the Sharing of Oil Wealth in Nigeria". Ibadan: IFRA-Nigeria.

SDN. 2017. *Public Perceptions of Security Dynamics and Stabilisation Interventions in the Niger Delta*. Port Harcourt: Stakeholder Democracy Network.

Smith, Daniel Jordan. 2018. "Progress and Setbacks in Nigeria's Anti-Corruption Efforts". In In *The Oxford Handbook of Nigerian Politics*, edited by Carl LeVan & Patrick Ukata: 288–301. Oxford: OUP.

Suberu, Rotimi. 2008. "The Supreme Court and Federalism in Nigeria". *Journal of Modern African Studies* 46 (3): 451–485.

Uchendu, Egodi. 2018. *Islam in the Niger Delta, 1890—2017. A Synthesis of the Accounts of Indigenes and Migrants*. Berlin: Studien zum Modernen Orient, Klaus Schwarz Verlag.

Udoma, Udo. 1987. *The Story of the Ibibio Union*. Ibadan: Spectrum.

Ukata, Patrick. 2018. "The Judiciary in Nigeria Since 1999". In *The Oxford Handbook of Nigerian Politics*, edited by Carl LeVan & Patrick Ukata: 302–318. Oxford: OUP.

Ukeje, Charles. 2001. "Oil Communities and Political Violence: The Case of Ethnic Ijaws in Nigeria's Delta Region". *Terrorism and Political Violence* 13 (4): 15–36.

Ukeje, Charles *et al.* 2002. *Oil and Violent Conflicts in the Niger Delta*. Ile-Ife: Obafemi Awolowo University Press.

Umoru, Henry & Joseph Erunke. 25 Oct. 2015. "Ministerial Nomination Impasse: My Story, by Amaechi". Lagos: *Vanguard*. https://www.vanguardngr.com/2015/10/ministerial-nomination-impasse-my-story-by-amaechi/ (accessed 17 november 2017).

Von Kemedi, Dimieari. 2003. *Community Conflicts in the Niger Delta: Petro-Weapon or Policy Failure?* Berkeley: University of California, Workshop on Environmental Politics Working Paper.

Walker, Andrew. 28 Feb. 2012. "James Ibori: How a Thief Almost Became Nigeria's President". London: BBC News. https://www.bbc.com/news/world-africa-17184075 (accessed 23 april 2019).

Weinthal, Erika & Pauline Jones Luong. 2006. "Combating the Resource Curse: An Alternative Solution to Managing Mineral Wealth". *Perspectives on Politics* 4 (1): 35–53.

Welch, Claude Emerson. 1995. *Protecting Human Rights in Africa: Roles and Strategies of Non-Governmental Organizations*. Philadelphia: University of Pennsylvania Press.

"Authority Stealing"

Corruption as a System of Government

Benin City is the capital of Edo State.[1] Situated halfway between Lagos and Port Harcourt, it is removed from the turbulence of the main oil-producing areas. Yet some Niger Delta activists use it as a base. One of them, Godwin Ojo, works for ERA (Environmental Rights Action). Established in Benin City in 1993, this NGO became famous because of its mobilization against Shell during the Ogoni crisis.[2] Ojo receives me in his office and we talk about the many issues facing the Niger Delta. The solution he proposes is to increase the share of oil revenue automatically allocated to producing states. According to him, this "derivation" would help foster a sense of responsibility and accountability in host communities. By being directly associated with the industry's output and performance, residents would have no interest in sabotaging production and would have good reason to prevent oil revenue from being misappropriated by the ruling class.[3]

Others do not share Ojo's view. As one Nigerian academic put it (Ifeka 2001: 465), "most rural people do not expect that decentralization will generate more accountable local government and better services; they find that

---

1 "Authority Stealing" refers to the title of a song released in 1980 by famous musician and political activist Fela Anikulapo Kuti. The lyrics criticize the ruling class for abusing power and acquiring wealth at the expense of the people, comparing Nigerian authorities to armed robbers.
2 The organization was initially set up to campaign against a dam construction project in Yobe in the north and against the development of a Michelin rubber tree plantation near the Okumu Forest Reserve along the River Osse in Ondo State to the south. ERA's original mission was not to focus specifically on oil pollution. However, its three founders hailed from the Niger Delta: Oronto Douglas was an Ijaw lawyer from Bayelsa State; Nnimmo Bassey, an Ibibio architect from Akwa Ibom; and Godwin Ojo, a Bini pastor from Edo State. In the mid-1990s, ERA got involved in the Ogoni struggle and rose to prominence thanks to funding from the Ford Foundation and Oxfam in Holland. It also developed international connections by joining the network of Friends of the Earth rather than Greenpeace, whose headquarters in the Netherlands had a highly centralized approach to communications, leaving little autonomy to its affiliates. At the end of the military dictatorship, ERA returned to its original mission, launching, for example, a campaign against Michelin and the expulsion of residents from Iguobazuwa village in Edo State in 2008.
3 Interview with the author in Benin City, November 2010.

FIGURE 44   Portrait of Ken Saro-Wiwa in the offices of
Environmental Rights Action (2011)

donor driven and funded dream rather a joke". Indeed, corruption would still
be rampant. In an interview granted in 2005, the president of the country's
largest union (the Nigeria Labour Congress), Adams Oshiomhole, said it quite
bluntly: the people of the Niger Delta who demand more "derivation" just
"prefer their own people to steal their money than outsiders".[4] Three years
later, Oshiomhole was himself elected Governor of Edo State—and accused
of embezzlement when he completed his second term in 2016, lost his parliamentary immunity, and fell out with his successor (Nnochiri 2020).

---

4   *This Day*, 15 April 2005, cited in Eberlein 2006: 573.

The problem of corruption is, in fact, a multifaceted and multidimensional issue at international, national, and regional levels. It is important to place the matter into some perspective to understand how the misappropriation of oil revenue became a system of government in Nigeria. In the Niger Delta in particular, logic dictates that widespread embezzlement should give rise to protest insofar as it significantly hampers the region's development and contributes to impoverishing its people. However, the misappropriation of public funds also feeds into power networks that benefit local communities. In practice, the moral condemnation of corruption thus stops where economic interest in sharing the spoils of the state begins (Adebanwi & Obadare 2011: 185). Political contestation arises when the wealth generated by oil is no longer redistributed informally among the population (Frank 1984: 305).

1   A Model of Maladministration

Schools without teachers, clinics without doctors, dilapidated or unfinished buildings, potholed roads, electricity supply failures—the damaging effects of corruption in the Niger Delta are clear to see. The provision of basic services is defective or non-existent for the simple reason that public funds disappear before they can be put to good use. The easy money earned from oil has undoubtedly contributed to the problem, destabilizing the tax base of a state that once lived off agricultural exports. Nigeria's huge size and its federal structure have also been a factor, if we are to believe the findings of studies showing that more centralized regimes minimize the risk of embezzlement and misappropriation of public funds at the local level (Treisman 2000). In Abuja, regional lobbies fight over their share of the national cake. However, there are no such counterpowers at the state and LGA levels, where local councilors are subject to less scrutiny.

A former President of the Senate in 2007, David Mark, once publicly acknowledged the scale of the disaster: "The Niger Delta problem, he said, is not about military presence or militancy. One of the biggest problems is that no local government in this country is working ... More often than not, what you discover is that [local councilors] only visit Abuja and collect the allocation after which they go into a hotel and share the money" (*National Mirror* 2007). One might add that federal and state governments also contribute to the problem. In principle, LGAs receive 20% of the revenue collected by Abuja and are tasked with paying primary school teachers. But the federal government knows all too well how corrupt local councilors tend to be. As a result, it generally prefers to oversee the management of public schools itself, meaning

FIGURE 45   A school in Akwa Ibom State (2009)

that it typically deducts up to a third of a LGA's budget to ensure that teachers' salaries are paid.

The rest goes to joint accounts managed at a state level.[5] Governors find it easy to dip into these accounts since they often appoint loyal followers as caretaker chairpersons to head up LGAs, either because local elections could not be held or because their results were contested and annulled. The federal system leaves much room for embezzlement and political interference in this regard. Indeed, governors control the state's tribunals that preside over local election disputes … and that can justify delaying elections further. Moreover, the organization of local polls is no longer under the responsibility of the federal electoral body since 2004. SIECs (State Independent Electoral Commissions) are now in charge and they help to rig the vote and alter results. For example, governors can disqualify candidates and discourage opposition participation by charging high, non-refundable registration fees. Moreover, they can withhold

---

5   This system was supposed to be abolished in 2019. But in early 2023, the Local Government Autonomy Bill was finally abandoned in the National Assembly because it did not secure enough buy-in from state legislative bodies. Interestingly, it was rejected by Rivers and Bayelsa despite positive votes from Edo, Delta, Akwa Ibom, and Cross River. As a result, the bill failed to be officially accepted by 24 State Houses of Assembly to go to the next stage and be signed by the President.

voting materials from opposition strongholds and schedule or postpone election dates at short notice. From the bottom up, finally, they can deploy security agents to suppress turnout, hire thugs to intimidate voters, and stuff ballot boxes. According to Matthew Page and Abdul Wando (2021), their growing confidence of winning local polls thus explains why they became less likely to appoint caretaker chairpersons.

On some occasions, governors may also dismiss elected local officials. For example, in Rivers State in 2011, Rotimi Amaechi used allegations of embezzlement to dissolve the Obio-Akpor local government council and depose his rival Nyesom Wike, who had presided over the LGA since 1998 (LeVan 2018). The conflict had a national dimension too. Amaechi had recently been suspended by the PDP and was about to join the opposition, while Wike was to support Goodluck Jonathan's presidential bid in 2011. The political game in Abuja nonetheless confirmed the fragility of local governments in Rivers State. Wike's successor at the head of Obio-Akpor from 2008 was dismissed by Amaechi despite legal injunctions ordering that the council be reinstated in late 2013. Over the course of its thirty-year existence since its creation in 1989, Obio-Akpor has been led by just seven elected chairpersons—compared with thirteen appointed by civilian or military regimes.[6]

Local governments are also littered with numerous instances of internal embezzlement. For example, in the early 2000s, again in Rivers State, the chairman of the Opobo-Nkoro LGA, Christopher Ogolo, was dismissed for depositing public funds into bank accounts controlled by his own company, bypassing tender procedures, signing dubious contracts, and pocketing commissions by inflating invoices charged for the diesel used to fuel his office's generator. In the same vein, he hired well-paid staff, incurred "miscellaneous" and "unexpected" expenses without ever justifying them, granted himself a travel budget twice as large as that allocated to Opobo-Nkoro health workers, and set up a slush fund, the infamous "security vote", equivalent to the LGA's entire education budget. Despite this, Ogolo was never taken to court. According to witnesses, he was eventually deposed because he refused to redistribute the spoils of his looting to local councilors, and not because he had embezzled public funds (Albin-Lackey 2007: 36–38).

Similar problems can also be found within states and federal institutions specifically dedicated to the region. Established at the end of the military dictatorship, the NDDC (Niger Delta Development Commission) and the Ministry

---

6 List of chairmen and caretaker committee chairmen of Obio-Akpor. Available at: https://en .wikipedia.org/wiki/List_of_chairmen_and_caretaker_committee_chairmen_of_Obio-Akpor.

of Niger Delta Affairs are worthy of note in this regard since they were set up to meet militants' expectations. Both achieved very little and proved incapable of supporting the maintenance of basic public services. For example, the Ministry of Niger Delta Affairs did not complete more than 12% of the projects it had undertaken, according to an audit of a total accumulated budget of ₦423 billion between 2009 and 2015 (*Premium Times* 2017). The picture was no rosier in the case of the NDDC, an institution described by Asari Dokubo as a "mere signboard" (Pérouse de Montclos 2018: 35). Over a twenty-year period since its inception in 2000, the commission received more than \$40 billion to support the region's development. But it executed less than 13% of its projects and it never published the names of the defaulting contractors (Social Action 2022: 7, Udoh & Isaac 2023).

Headed by Niger Delta politicians, the NDDC got involved in numerous financial scandals. For example, its first director, Ndutimi Alaibe, was an Ijaw from Opokuma-Kolokuma, a Bayelsa LGA that did not produce oil, and he was charged with embezzling funds in pursuit of his political ambitions in the 2007 elections (Sahara Reporters 2008). As usual, the matter was quietly forgotten about and eventually dropped by the courts. Such impunity only served to consolidate the impunity of other senior NDDC figures who also used the commission's resources to stand in elections, such as Onyema Ugochukwu in Abia, Emmanuel Aguariavwodo in Delta, and Nsima Ekere in Akwa Ibom in 2019.

2   The Merits and Drawbacks of Cronyism

In general, however, the misappropriation of public funds is not only geared toward enriching a select group of powerful individuals; embezzlement is also designed to maintain cronies, entertain the youth and buy social peace, especially during electoral campaigns, weddings, and traditional ceremonies when "big men" are expected to hand out large sums of money to reinforce their standing. While they are not unique to the people of the Niger Delta, these practices have reached an unprecedented scale in the region because of the wealth generated by oil.

Undoubtedly, the problem of corruption touches on social problems that extend beyond the relationship between users and civil servants. Gifts, bribes, commissions, tips, and tolls are characteristic features of officials abusing their powers to profit from selling services that are technically free. In return for payment in cash or in kind, civil servants can thus facilitate an administrative procedure, fast-track an application, secure special favors, pull strings for a job, or illegally exonerate an individual liable for a fine or tax. In Nigeria, many

FIGURE 46   Most people in the Niger
Delta depend on the informal
economy: A hat seller in
Yenagoa (2011)

public officers also extort money by force—for instance, at police checkpoints. Other widespread practices involve dipping into public accounts, pirating, falsifying or reselling official documents, and stealing public goods or using them temporarily for personal gain, a phenomenon known in France as "*la perruque*" (Blundo & Olivier de Sardan 2001).

Nonetheless, corruption, defined as an abuse of power and a form of deviance, is not the sole preserve of public officials and civil servants, let alone of the oil industry (Nye 1967: 419). At a local level, it also involves communities through mutual obligations sometimes derived from ancient systems of vassalage. Corruption is a complex matter. It is both an obstacle to development and an informal mode of resource redistribution and conflict regulation that can occasionally benefit the majority. For instance, it serves to stabilize the political arena, consolidate patronage networks, and defuse tensions by "feeding" opponents. As Steven Pierce aptly notes (2006: 900), "the history of Nigerian corruption is also a history of Nigerian state formation". In the Niger Delta, many people benefit from a system based on sharing the spoils of oil wealth. But arrangements between allies within the ruling class are hardly conducive to reforming the region's governance. On the contrary, impunity encourages the misappropriation of revenue, allowing those in power to enrich themselves, finance their cronies, and consolidate their power, popularity, and prestige.

Corruption is, admittedly, a double-edged sword. The implication of politicians in financial scandals can stand in the way of electoral ambitions, as it provides opposition groups with handy weapons for attack. In 2007, James Ibori and Peter Odili were thus sidelined from the presidential race because of their poor reputation and their involvement in shady deals. The former had his eyes set on becoming Vice-President, while the latter aspired to become President of Nigeria. They were confident about their chances of success given that they had largely contributed to financing the PDP. However, the evidence compiled against them played into the hands of their challengers within the ruling party. As for President Olusegun Obasanjo, he used the EFCC to neutralize key figures supporting PDP rival factions, such as Diepreye Alamieyeseigha in Bayelsa.[7] On occasion, incriminating evidence also forced politicians to switch camps to renegotiate their immunity, as was the case of the former governor of Akwa Ibom State, Godswill Akpabio, who left the PDP to join the APC in 2018.

At the international level, finally, corruption scandals further tarnish the image of Nigeria abroad. For example, while they remained popular in the Niger Delta, Diepreye Alamieyeseigha and James Ibori were widely ridiculed when the former fled London disguised as a woman, while the latter was extradited to England as a vulgar common law criminal. The United Kingdom often played an interesting role in this regard. Following the nationalization of BP in 1979 and the suspension of diplomatic relations with Lagos in 1984, Margaret Thatcher thus threatened to publicly reveal the names of corrupt Nigerian politicians whose bank accounts in London held sufficient funds to repay all the foreign loans contracted by Nigeria. Once again, financial scandals served as leverage that weakened the beneficiaries of embezzlement.[8]

---

7   The head of the EFCC, Nuhu Ribadu, was thus accused of double standards because he targeted perceived enemies of his boss. The end ultimately justified the means. For example, he summoned some governors to appear in federal court to circumvent the judicial system at state level, where judges were paid and promoted by the same governors. In the same vein, the entourage of President Olusegun Obasanjo was suspected of bribing local officials to initiate impeachment proceedings and strip opponents of their immunity in order to sue them.

8   At the time, corruption stories also involved opponents exiled in Britain, notably General Yakubu Gowon, who had been deposed in 1975 and whom London had refused to extradite in 1976, and Umaru Dikko, a former transport minister that the military junta of Muhammadu Buhari attempted to kidnap in 1984.

3   Flexible Perceptions

Obviously, perceptions of corruption vary widely depending on one's point of view. While they can easily take a diplomatic dimension at the international level, they are embedded in a complex game of social obligations and cronyism within the Niger Delta. For example, when Diepreye Alamieyeseigha returned in secret from London, where he had been arrested on charges of money laundering while carrying large amounts of cash, he was welcomed as a hero in his home state of Bayelsa. Even if his embezzlement contributed to local poverty, he enjoyed huge levels of popularity as a champion of the Ijaw cause and as a victim of both Abuja and the former colonial power. His case was not specific to the Niger Delta in this respect. At the time of independence, Yoruba and Ibo leaders Nnamdi Azikiwe and Obafemi Awolowo also claimed to have been framed by the colonial master when they were found guilty of financial irregularities and fraud in 1962 and 1956 respectively (Pierce 2016: 95).

It is, of course, easier for the people of the Niger Delta to criticize corruption at the federal level. The system governing the misappropriation of oil wealth is run at a distance from Abuja, which centralizes the industry's royalties and taxes. A large proportion of the revenue then "evaporates" in foreign bank accounts before it can be redistributed to producing states, while the revenue of offshore deposits goes directly to the federal government and circumvents the principle of "derivation". At the end of the military dictatorship, IYC militants thus denounced the "looting of the national treasury by the Abacha junta" in the Kaiama Declaration of 1998. Despite the establishment in 2007 of a Nigerian Extractive Industries Transparency Initiative (NEITI), the return to civilian rule was somewhat disappointing in this regard since the presidential terms of Olusegun Obasanjo, Umaru Yar Adua, and Goodluck Jonathan continued to be marred by countless financial scandals.

In practice, Nigeria has remained well below the standards of oil-producing developing countries such as Ghana. The federal government has proved incapable of improving the sector. While it may not reach the levels of opacity seen in Gabon and Congo, which have no petroleum codes, Nigeria still relies on operators to estimate its production and the losses resulting from pipeline attacks. Despite obvious conflicts of interest, the figures provided are not verified independently and involve significant discrepancies depending on whether they are calculated at wellheads or at export terminals. In many cases, attempts to quantify thefts of crude have also led to confusion by combining the volumes of stolen oil and the loss of income caused by production interruptions, two figures estimated respectively at 40,000 and 200,000 barrels a day in the mid-2010s. Such a system has paved the way for smugglers and

fraudsters to underestimate actual exports to sell a portion of crude oil as contraband (NEITI 2019).

Muhammadu Buhari's election in 2015 did little to change this. Despite
his personal reputation for integrity, the president was never genuinely committed to improving the industry's accountability. As a military man, he had
refused to appear before a tribunal led by Judge Ayo Irikife, who, following a
brief return to civilian rule in 1979, had been tasked with investigating embezzlement by the previous junta. At the time, Buhari was Minister for Oil and
$3.4 billion had disappeared from the accounts of NNPC. As a civilian in 2015,
the president-elect was also unable to explain how Nigeria's hydrocarbon revenue had halved within the space of just one year, a decrease not consistent
with the falling levels of production or the drop in the price per barrel (*La
Tribune Afrique* 2018). To escape criticism, he opted to put the blame on his
Ijaw predecessor Goodluck Jonathan and was accused by the NDA (Niger Delta
Avengers) of using the fight against corruption for political gain (Oriola &
Adeakin 2018: 140).

From one regime to another, militants have generally held the view that it
is primarily the federal government that steals their resources by siphoning
off oil revenues. Armed groups such as the NDA and MEND have sometimes
acknowledged that the local ruling class is also partly to blame. For example,
in a communiqué dated March 2010, MEND portrayed the region's governors
as "shameless and visionless stooges who are more concerned with looting
the state treasuries and seeking a second term in office" (Oriola & Adeakin
2018: 141). However, the blame has generally tended to fall on the ruling class in
power in Abuja, while overlooking the venality of local officials on the grounds
that they are natives.

In calling for an increase in the share of oil revenue automatically allocated
to producing areas, Niger Delta militants have thus given the impression of
promoting a kind of "decentralization" or "derivation" of corruption at the state
level. While recognizing that local politicians are part of the problem, many
Nigerian researchers have also suggested that the federal system should be
reformed to allow host communities to manage mineral resources themselves
(Akani 2002). However, they have failed to explain how an increase in the derivation percentage, from 3% to 13% in accordance with the 1999 Constitution,
would help improve governance in the Niger Delta (Pérouse de Montclos 2017).
Historically, for example, this percentage was far higher, standing at 20% until
1979. Despite this, it did little to contain embezzlement in a region where local
politicians played a central role in the misappropriation of oil revenue.

4   The Contradictions of the "Marginalization" Argument

The poor governance of the Niger Delta undoubtedly lies at the heart of the matter. Although militants like to portray themselves as victims of "marginalization", several factors point to the need for a more nuanced view of the situation. First, at a national level, the fluidity of ethnic groups undermines claims about alleged community-based discrimination policies. In addition, no official document has ever confirmed anything like a deliberate attempt to exclude certain sections of the population on racial, ethnic, religious, or social grounds, unlike in South Africa and the United States. As Adedayo Adekson notes (2004: 152), the notion of "marginalization" is impossible to quantify, making it all the more difficult to prove. David Pratten (2013: 251) rather sees it as a narrative and political resource.

Of course, this is not to deny that tensions exist and that, in some cases, repressive policies have been used to crush rebel groups. For example, the military in the north did little to conceal their distrust of Niger Delta officers suspected of having had a hand in the putsch of Gideon Orkar in 1990, in a mysterious explosion at the Ikeja barracks in Lagos in 2001, or in various thefts of weapons in Kaduna and Jaji to supply armed militants in oil-producing areas from 2003 onward.[9] However, these hard feelings cannot be said to be indicative of a systematic policy of exclusion and persecution against the so-called South-South, one of Nigeria's six geopolitical zones. The federal system statutorily guarantees the protection of minorities and the rotation of power. Hence the Niger Delta supplied six of Nigeria's fifteen oil ministers over a period of fifty years since the first appointment to this post in 1971, with the region's ministers holding the position for a total of ten years (see Table 1).

Regional differences in the level of development are not evidence of discriminatory policies either. In any case, Nigeria's poorest areas are not located in the South-South but in the north, where the standards of living are much lower (NBS 2020: 7, Abidde 2017: 41). Attempts to explain the Niger Delta crisis based on poverty rather than the influx of wealth are hardly persuasive in this regard. For example, researchers have attempted to correlate the number of acts of sabotage carried out on pipelines with standards of living to predict the likelihood of conflict (Anifowose, Lawler, Van der Horst & Chapman 2012). From a methodological perspective, they relied on official records and somewhat arbitrarily assumed that oil leaks and explosions invariably resulted

---

9 See, for example, the analysis conducted by the Nigerian army's intelligence services in a report dated 7 November 2007, released by Sahara Reporters and in the author's possession.

TABLE 1   The regional origin of oil ministers and advisers (1971–2021)

Term	Name	State of origin	Geopolitical zone
1971–1975	Alhaji Shettima Ali Mungono	Borno (Kanuri)	North-East
1975–1979	General Muhammadu Buhari[a]	Katsina (Hausa-Fulani, Daura)	North-West
1979–1983	Alhaji Engineer Yahaya Dikko	Kaduna (Hausa, Zaria)	Center-North
1984–1986	Professor Tamunoemi David-West	Rivers (Ijaw, Kalabari)	South-South
1986–1990	Dr. Rilwanu Lukman[b]	Kaduna (Zaria)	North-West
1990–1992	Professor Jibril Aminu	Adamawa (Fulani)	North-East
1992–1993	Dr. Chu Okongwu[c]	Anambra (Ibo, Nnewi)	South-East
1993–1994	Chief Phillip Asiodu[d]	Delta (Ibo, Asaba)	South-South
1994–1995	Chief Donald Dick Etiebet	Akwa Ibom (Annang)	South-South
1995–1998	Chief Dan Etete[e]	Bayelsa (Ijaw, Kolokuma-Opokuma)	South-South
1999–2007	Olusegun Obasanjo[f]	Ogun (Yorouba)	South-West
2005–2007	Edmund Maduabebe Daukoru	Bayelsa (Ijaw, Nembe)	South-South
2008–2010	Rilwanu Lukman[b]	Kaduna (Hausa, Zaria)	North-West
2011–2014	Diezani Allison-Madueke	Rivers (Port Harcourt)	South-South
2015–2021	Muhammadu Buhari[a]	Katsina (Hausa-Fulani, Daura)	North-West

a   Head of the junta in 1983–1985 and subsequently elected President of Nigeria in 2015
b   Secretary General of OPEC from 1995 to 2000.
c   Resigned following embezzlement allegations.
d   Permanent Secretary in the oil ministry, 1971–1975.
e   Also known as Dauzia Loya, sentenced in abstentia in France in 2007 and again in 2009 for money laundering.
f   Combined terms as President of Nigeria from 1999 to 2007.

from attacks rather than accidents caused by poor maintenance. While their study focused on five vast regions of Nigeria with widely different economic and demographic profiles, the researchers also failed to consider the fact that the route of pipelines carrying crude and refined oil is primarily determined by the location of deposits, factories, and cities, meaning that it is not a good indicator for understanding the role of poverty in the use of violence.

Interregional comparisons have not always been very helpful either. A number of very poor areas are not traversed by pipelines, while others are sparsely populated, as in Bayelsa State, meaning that they are less likely to suffer attacks. According to the study cited above, acts of sabotage on pipelines have actually focused on "wealthy" areas. Based on police data from Rivers State, other studies have also shown that there is no link between lack of infrastructure and the frequency of community conflicts. Most clashes occur in the northern part of the state rather than in the marshy and less populated areas located along the coast, a logical pattern from a demographic point of view (Arokoyu & Ochulor 2016).

Attacks on pipelines rely in fact on the systemic embezzlement of oil revenue. Poverty is not the main driver, since bunkering thrives on high-level protection, particularly when it comes to exporting crude oil on a large scale. The Nigerian army and navy have generally tended to overlook trafficking in exchange for bribes, which allegedly reached ₦300,000 (approximately €600) a day near Bodo in the Ogoni homeland in 2020 (Ebiede, Bassey & Asuni 2021: 375). In the same vein, their rare offensives are generally a response to specific circumstances, such as when officers are attacked, pirates stop paying protection fees, or rivals try to take their place. In some cases, they are also driven by communication objectives to incite militants to negotiate when Abuja announces yet another plan to resolve the crisis.

In this system, bunkering is no proof that Niger Deltans are discriminated against, or that they are poorer than Muslims in the semi-arid Sahelian areas of northern Nigeria. By contrast, thefts of crude or refined oil speak volumes about the region's political economy. Acts of sabotage on pipelines can be driven by a wide range of objectives, from stealing and exporting crude oil to supplying illegal refineries, securing repair contracts, or sending threats to extort money from foreign companies. Different types of motivation also contribute to determining the profile of attackers. For example, the cartels that siphon off pipelines for export tend to be more professional than the gangs engaged in refining crude oil in collusion with local communities. It can even happen that the two groups end up competing.

Illegal refineries in the Niger Delta serve a genuine social purpose. While they typically use less oil (perhaps 20% of stolen volumes) than criminal organizations involved in smuggling crude for export, they provide a means of subsistence for many people in the creeks. According to some studies, they employ as many as 19,000 men, women, and children, as well as 7,000 sub-contractors, welders, canteens, messengers, guards, transporters, and retailers selling *asari*, a type of oil named after the Rivers State LGA of Asari Toru, the location of the Soku deposits and one of the region's main sources of supply.[10] In total, some 100,000 people are said to depend either directly or indirectly on bunkering, including the families of production site workers and owners. The amounts involved are significant. For example, with $1000 a month, an employee of an illegal refinery often earns more than a graduate working in the local or federal civil service (Ugor 2013). In addition, given the levels of corruption in the police, he is very unlikely to be arrested and taken to court. Studies show that of the 25 sentences secured by the EFCC against 103 individuals involved in bunkering activities, just one resulted in a prison sentence, with the others receiving insignificant fines (NEITI 2019).

As a result, this informal economy is deeply embedded in the population simply because it pays well and generates revenues estimated at some $3 billion a year through smuggling, illegal crude exports, and services associated with the maintenance of camp infrastructures, the running of clandestine warehouses, the transportation of oil by truck or by boat, payments made to the security forces and local militias, and so on. Another "advantage" is that local refineries require very little investment. They generally operate with cheap and rudimentary technology inspired by traditional gin distilling. In local pidgin, bunkerers are said to *cook* crude oil in vats that burn wood, coal, or tar recycled from production waste. The temperature is controlled by artisanal cooling mechanisms called *okpuroku*, while boxes of Omo washing detergent are left nearby to be used as fire extinguishers in the event of an explosion. The pumps feeding the system take water from the surrounding creeks and get their electricity supply from generators, which themselves run on illegally refined oil.

Depending on the season and the level of demand, a refinery can produce up to fifty barrels of diesel a day, which are sold for around $100 per unit, sometimes less (Ugor 2013). Since there are no taxes or royalties to be paid, profits remain high, even at half the official price in town. This is also the case in the creeks of the Niger Delta, where supply is deficient. In 2006, NNPC announced plans to build a dozen floating gas stations for riverine communities. However,

---

10   These calculations are based on information reported by the army, which claimed to have destroyed more than 4,300 illegal refineries in 2012, and on field surveys indicating an average of 9 workers per production unit: from 6 in Rivers to 15 in Bayelsa (Naanen & Tolani 2014).

the project never went ahead. Speedboat transporters therefore continued to buy contraband oil rather than having to pay a higher price for fuel "imported" from the mainland.

References

Abidde, Sabella Ogbobode. 2017. *Nigeria's Niger Delta: Militancy, Amnesty, and the Post-amnesty Environment*. Lanham (MD): Lexington Books.

Adebanwi, Wale & Ebenezer Obadare. 2011. "When Corruption Fights Back: Democracy and Elite Interest in Nigeria's Anti-Corruption War". *The Journal of Modern African Studies* 49 (2): 185–213.

Adekson, Adedayo Oluwakayode. 2004. *The "Civil Society" Problematique: Deconstructing Civility and Southern Nigeria's Ethnic Radicalization*. London: Routledge.

Akani, Christian (ed.). 2002. *Corruption in Nigeria: The Niger Delta Experience*. Enugu: Fourth Dimension.

Albin-Lackey, Chris. 2007. *Chop Fine. The Human Rights Impact of Local Government Corruption and Mismanagement in Rivers State, Nigeria*. New York: Human Rights Watch.

Anifowose, Babatunde, Damian Lawler, Dan van der Horst & Lee Chapman. 2012. "Attacks on Oil Transport Pipelines in Nigeria: A Quantitative Exploration and Possible Explanation of Observed Patterns". *Applied Geography* 32 (2): 636–651.

Arokoyu, Samuel Bankole & Evangeline Nkiruka Ochulor. 2016. "Spatial Patterns of Community Conflicts (1990–2015) and Its Implication to Rural Development in Rivers State". *World Rural Observations* 8 (1): 27–37.

Blundo, Giorgio & Jean-Pierre Olivier de Sardan. 2001. "La corruption quotidienne en Afrique de l'Ouest". *Politique Africaine* 83 : 8–37.

Eberlein, Ruben. 2006. "On the Road to the State's Perdition? Authority and Sovereignty in the Niger Delta, Nigeria". *Journal of Modern African Studies* 44 (4): 573–596.

Ebiede, Tarila Marclint, Celestine Oyom Bassey & Judith Burdin Asuni (eds). 2021. *Insecurity in the Niger Delta. A Report on Emerging Threats in Akwa Ibom, Bayelsa, Cross River, Delta, Edo and Rivers States*. London: Adonis & Abbey Publishers.

Frank, Lawrence. 1984. "Two Responses to the Oil Boom: Iranian and Nigerian Politics after 1973". *Comparative Politics* 16 (3): 295–314.

Ifeka, Caroline. 2001. "Playing Civil Society Tunes: Corruption and Misunderstanding Nigeria's 'Real' Political Institutions". *Review of African Political Economy* 89: 461–465.

LeVan, Carl. 2018. "Linkage: Federalism as an Instrument of Opposition Organizing in Nigeria". *African Affairs* 117 (466): 1–20.

Naanen, Ben & Patrick Tolani. 2014. *Private Gain, Public Disaster: Social Context of Illegal Oil Bunkering and Artisanal Refining in the Niger Delta*. Port Harcourt: Niger Delta Environment and Relief Foundation.

National Mirror. 2 Nov. 2007. Lagos: 3.

NBS. 2020. *2019 Poverty and Inequality in Nigeria*. Abuja: National Bureau of Statistics.

NEITI. 2019. *Stemming the Increasing Cost of Oil Theft to Nigeria*. Abuja: Nigeria Extractive Industries Transparency Initiative.

Nnochiri, Ikechukwu. 17 June 2020. "Corruption Allegation: Court Extends Order Stopping Obaseki from Arresting Oshiomhole". Lagos: *Vanguard*. https://www.vanguardngr.com/2020/06/court-extends-order-stopping-obaseki-from-arresting-oshiomhole/ (accessed 30 July 2020).

Nye, Joseph. 1967. "Corruption and Political Development: A Cost-Benefit Analysis". *American Political Science Review* 56 (2): 417–427.

Oriola, Temitope & Ibikunle Adeakin. 2018. "The Framing Strategies of the Niger Delta Avengers". In *The Unfinished Revolution in Nigeria's Niger Delta: Prospects for Socio-Economic and Environmental Justice and Peace*, edited by Cyril Obi & Temitope Oriola: 138–158. London: Routledge.

Page, Matthew & Abdul Wando. 2021. *Halting the Kleptocratic Capture of Local Government in Nigeria*. Washington DC: Carnegie Endowment for International Peace.

Pérouse de Montclos, Marc-Antoine. 2017. "Rebellion and the Sharing of Oil Wealth in Nigeria". Ibadan: IFRA-Nigeria.

Pérouse de Montclos, Marc-Antoine. 2018. *Oil rent and corruption: the case of Nigeria*. Paris: Etudes de l'IFRI.

Pierce, Steven. 2006. "Looking Like a State: Colonialism and the Discourse of Corruption in Northern Nigeria". *Comparative Studies in Society and History* 48: 887–914.

Pierce, Steven. 2016. *Moral Economies of Corruption: State formation and Political Culture in Nigeria*. Durham: Duke University Press.

Pratten, David. 2013. "The Precariousness of Prebendalism". In *Democracy and Prebendalism in Nigeria: Critical Interpretations*, edited by Wale Adebanwi & Ebenezer Obadare: 243–258. New York: Palgrave Macmillan.

Premium Times. 31 May 2017. Abuja. https://www.premiumtimesng.com/news/headlines/232723-despite-spending-n423-billion-in-6-years-niger-delta-ministry-had-only-12-per-cent-project-execution.html (accessed 12 sept. 2023).

Sahara Reporters. 29 December 2008. "NDDC MD, Mr. Alaibe, Accused of Massive Corruption". http://saharareporters.com/2008/12/29/nddc-md-mr-alaibe-accused-massive-corruption (accessed 13 january 2019).

Social Action. 2022. *Pond of Crocodiles: Citizens Report on Budgets and Projects of the Niger Delta Development Commission*. Port Harcourt: Social Action.

Treisman, Daniel. 2000. "The Causes of Corruption: A Cross-National Study". *Journal of Public Economics* 76 (3): 399-457.

Tribune Afrique (La). 10 January 2018. "Nigeria: le rapport accablant de la NEITI sur la gestion du secteur des hydrocarbures". Paris. https://afrique.latribune.fr/finan ces/commodities/2018-01-10/nigeria-le-rapport-accablant-de-la-neiti-sur-la-gest ion-du-secteur-des-hydrocarbures-764134.html (accessed 12 september 2023).

Udoh, Harry & Botti Isaac. 2023. *Policy Brief on Policy Options for Addressing the Failure of the Niger Delta Development Commission.* Abuja: MacArthur Foundation.

Ugor, Paul. 2013. "Survival Strategies and Citizenship Claims: Youth and the Underground Oil Economy in Post-Amnesty Niger Delta". *Africa* 83 (2): 270–292.

CHAPTER 15

Pollution

Who Is to Blame?

If there is a hell on earth, then it is right here in front of me, not far from Gbaramatu in Delta State. I am wading through foul-smelling, slippery, sticky sludge. The toxic fumes are constricting my throat. The combined effect of the heat, humidity, smoke, burned vegetation, and earth blackened by the constant oil spills all point to the fact that I am getting close to the continually burning fire of Gehenna.

Fueled by the crude stolen from pipelines, the illegal artisanal refinery I am visiting nonetheless has a reputation for being a highly efficient production site. One of its "managers" tells me that it produces up to 10,000 liters of petrol, diesel, and lamp oil every day. The workers operating the site are relatively well paid and work bare-chested in the open air. Their skin is covered in burns, and I am told that they typically last no more than two years before succumbing to incurable respiratory problems. And for good reason: one of them has no hesitation dipping his hand into the liquid coming out of the makeshift tank that "cooks" the oil. This is how he tests the viscosity of the products that are then transported in buckets and distributed between various types of barrels used to store petrol, kerosene, and diesel.

The landscape around me has been ravaged by fires, oil leaks, and the evacuation of residue. The wooden barges that transport the precious cargo leak from all over the place, with estimates suggesting that up to 50% of all the crude illegally refined in the Niger Delta is lost as waste (Naanen & Tolani 2014). The Warri region is not the only area affected. At the other end of the Niger Delta, Ogoniland is just as badly impacted by activities associated with bunkering, a technical term that originally meant the trans-shipment of fuel between two vessels but that now refers to the siphoning of pipelines and artisanal oil refining.

With his habitual verve, Ijaw militant Asari Dokubo, whom I meet not long after in Warri, is quick to condemn the criminals polluting the region. He reserves particular ire for the Ogoni. "They are the ones who pollute their own land, not Shell", he claims. The company stopped producing oil in Ogoniland after leaving the area in 1993. Criminal gangs have filled the gap and now plunder unprotected wells with complete impunity.

As Asari Dokubo explains:

FIGURE 47   An illegal refinery near Gbaramatu in Delta State (2011)

It has nothing to do with Shell. [...]. These are criminal elements: people destroying our environment. Oil thieves who are desperate to make money at the expense of our environment and the lives of our people. [Bunkerers] don't give a damn. They just want to make a few penny. They cook crude, they pour it into the sea. It kills marine life and it destroys everything. So whatever pollution is going on in Ogoniland today has nothing to do with Shell. And we must admit it. Anywhere, not only in Ogoniland, everywhere in the Delta. Those types of pollution have nothing to do with oil companies. These [illegal] products are also dangerous for consumption. We have kerosene explosions. People are burnt to death. MOSOP as a group must go out against these people. [They should stop looking for] some cheap international publicity stunt by saying it is Shell.[1]

Dokubo's views are anything but politically correct. His position highlights the fact that, on the ground, some host communities play an important role in the environmental damage caused to the region. First, because they distrust

---

1   Interview with the author in Warri, February 2011.

the security forces, they tend not to report oil spills to the police for fear of being accused of sabotage and having to pay a bribe to secure their release. Others are actively involved in bunkering as a means of livelihood, or they deliberately build their homes close to production sites to ensure that they will receive compensation in the event of an incident. Following pipeline explosions, some have even sought to aggravate spillages with the aim of securing clean-up contracts. For example, among the Ijaw of Ogbia to the south of Yenagoa, residents of Kolo Creek dispersed the oil spilled into the environment before collecting it with buckets in the hope of getting the bulk of the compensation at the expense of neighboring villages (Nwajiaku 2005: 490).

Such contributions to pollution go against the narratives of Niger Delta militants who claim that bunkering and illegal refining represent forms of civil resistance against oil companies and a predatory state. According to the most radical activists, stealing crude is a legitimate endeavor since the natives are simply recovering by force what is theirs by right. To them, bunkering is equivalent to the artisanal mines operated illegally by private individuals in the north and the Middle Belt. However, it is difficult to detect a political or social strategy at work in this process. Niger Delta militants have never sought to make up for the state's failures by funding schools or clinics with the gains derived from smuggling contraband oil.

The main driver of bunkering is crime; hence, it does not follow the major sequences of the conflict with oil companies and the government since the 1994 Ogoni uprising. For example, the number of acts of sabotage committed against pipelines rose at the end of the Abacha dictatorship, just when the derivation percentage granted to producing states was increased. Before 1999, military repression probably deterred people from bunkering. Conversely, pipeline sabotage became more visible and widely reported in the media following the return to civilian rule, with seven attacks recorded in 1993, 33 in 1998, 497 in 1999 and 600 in 2000 (Ghazvinian 2007: 17ff). Subsequent events have not, however, confirmed the political dimension of bunkering. According to available (albeit debatable) figures, the frequency of attacks on pipelines declined in 2006 when MEND took over from Asari Dokubo's NDPVF, before increasing again at the time of the 2009 amnesty and President Goodluck Jonathan's unsuccessful bid for re-election in 2015, especially in 2013 and 2016 (Anifowose, Lawler, Van der Horst & Chapman 2012: 644).

It is, in fact, impossible to draw any political conclusions from these erratic and contradictory variations. Some researchers have argued that the increase in bunkering after the 2009 amnesty reflected efforts by demobilized militants to make up for the loss of revenue previously derived from racketeering and kidnapping. However, the same analysts have also reported that more thefts of crude oil occurred during the most intense periods of conflict, particularly in 2001–2005, when the insurgents were in desperate need of funds to purchase weapons, while the authorities were too busy fighting them and had no time to combat traffickers (Naanen & Tolani 2014: 31, 34).

From a political point of view, bunkering actually highlights the incoherence of pseudo-militants who claim to be combating pollution while actively contributing to devastating their own environment. This paradox challenges common wisdom on the social repercussions of the damage caused by the oil industry. According to many Nigerian researchers, oil spills, combined with land requisitions, have not only impoverished communities but also exacerbated tensions by destroying fishing and farming areas, thereby reducing access to increasingly scarce resources (Okoh 1996, Von Kemedi 2003). Some have even gone as far as to argue that pollution became the main cause of violence in the region because it contributed to driving unemployment and the influx of rural migrants to shanty towns, a breeding ground for juvenile delinquency (Jike 2004).

However, opinions differ. First, the role of oil pollution in violence is debatable, as many cities also saw a sharp rise in criminality in non-producing regions. In addition, Nigerian researchers have noted that environmental degradation should not serve to conceal the deep causes of conflicts, which are primarily of a political and economic nature (Idemudia & Ite 2006). Others have cast doubt on the actual impact of oil spills. In their view, the resulting damage is not irreparable, and the causal links are impossible to prove scientifically, given the multiple factors that are likely to have contributed to the long-term evolution of the fauna and flora in oil-producing areas (Moffat & Linde 1995). It is also worth noting that dominant narratives around increasing resource scarcity are largely a political construct designed to advance specific causes (Scoones *et al.* 2019).

1 A Degraded Environment

Amid all the controversy, one thing is certain: the Niger Delta is a severely polluted region. The damage to the environment comes in many forms, from the oil spills ravaging the creeks to the exhaust fumes emanating from the poorly maintained cars stuck in the traffic jams of Port Harcourt or Warri. In the oil industry specifically, there are risks at every stage of production (Frynas 2003: 107–108). First, prospectors use explosives that leave craters at the surface of the land. Moreover, they require clearing the bush and felling trees, some of which take more than thirty years to grow back in the mangroves. Second, drilling needs chemical additives that are released into the environment. Road and pipeline construction can also result in waterways being rerouted, creeks being obstructed and blocked, and fish populations being unable to move around and reproduce. Production itself sometimes leads to oil spills that are made worse during periods of flood in the rainy season.

In this regard, a distinction must be made between the damage caused by the industry on land, in the sea, and in the air. For example, gas flares have a devastating impact since they emit carbon dioxide and methane, both of which contribute to the greenhouse gas effect and cause acid rainfall. In this particular area, Nigeria was reported to be the world's first or second-largest polluter alongside Russia and ahead of Iran and Algeria in the late 2000s (D'Armagnac 2012). Shortly before his death in a mysterious plane crash in 1996, the renowned Nigerian economist Claude Ake, a native of Port Harcourt, even went as far as to argue that his country contributed more to global warming than the rest of the planet combined.[2] Since then, the situation appears to have improved a little. Nigeria's contribution to the total volume of flared gas globally fell from 16% in 2008 to less than 7% ten years later (PWC 2019: 3, Ariweriokuma 2008: 177). According to official statistics, it also fell from 99% of the country's production in 1970 to 75% in 1990, 54% in 2000, and 10% in 2018.[3]

In the meantime, onshore oil spills have continued unabated, in contrast to the situation offshore. It seems quite likely that they may even have increased as bunkering became routine through "hot" or "cold" tapping—that is, "siphoning oil from a functioning pipeline or blowing up the pipe and carting off the crude that spills out" (Burgis 2015: 176). In the absence of reliable independent sources, the available figures are disputed. Environmental lobbies often exaggerate actual trends. For example, according to the World Wide Fund for Nature (WWF) and the International Union for Conservation of Nature (IUCN), oil production resulted in the spilling of somewhere between 9 and 13 million barrels in the Niger Delta between 1956 and 2006, fifty times more than the notorious oil spill caused by the shipwreck of the Exxon Valdez off the coast of Alaska in 1989 (NCF 2006: 1). The comparison drew significant attention and was widely relayed by media outlets and activists, who never questioned how the figures were obtained.[4] While acknowledging that it was difficult to accurately measure the volumes poured into the environment, Amnesty

---

2   Interview in *Tell*, 29 January 1996, cited by Cayford 1996: 185.

3   It is worth noting, however, that this decrease reflected the development of gas production instead of a reduction in the volumes flared (Singh *et al.* 1995: 4, Dan Kikile *et al.* 2009, PWC 2019: 3).

4   See, for example, Montanyà 2012: 31.

FIGURE 48   An oil spill caused by the rupture of an Agip pipeline in Bayelsa State (2011)

International (2009: 15) thus argued that the annual level of oil pollution in the Niger Delta was equivalent to one Exxon Valdez spill.

However, the figures reported by the WWF and the IUCN would have merited corroboration and discussion. They were obtained from focus groups and meetings held with Nigerian environmentalists during a week-long visit to the Niger Delta. In the absence of any site survey, the "experts" from the WWF and IUCN simply extrapolated the incomplete official figures released by NNPC and its DPR (Department of Petroleum Resources), to which they arbitrarily added a few million barrels to allow for the omission of an oil spill. They also applied the same average from one year to the next and made no effort to adjust the figures in line with production levels, which were very low in the late 1950s and during the Biafran War. Moreover, their estimates contradicted the findings of other environmental lobbies.[5] Finally, they proved to be invariably higher than the assessments provided by the US government and the United Nations, which reported between 1.5 and 3 million barrels of crude oil spilt into

---

5   For example, the Nigerian Environmental Society reported a loss of some 1.7 million barrels from oil spills at sea and on the continent between 1970 and 1983. This more sensible estimate roughly reflects the figures provided by the NNPC, at around 1.8 million barrels of oil over the period 1976–1996 (Azaiki 2007a: 147, Orubu, Odusola & Ehwarieme 2004: 206).

the Niger Delta over forty years of production between 1960 and 2000 (Kew & Phillips 2007: 159, UNDP 2006: 76).

In fact, Nigeria is not among the world's worst affected countries when it comes to large-scale oil spills (Le Hir 2010). Soil contamination in the Niger Delta is primarily the result of continuous infiltration and spillage. Pollution figures have often been manipulated to serve as a political argument against multinationals and the federal government. However, quantification attempts are generally lacking in rigor, and, as things stand, it remains difficult to identify trends, whether upwards or downwards. Within the state apparatus itself, different government bodies have often released conflicting figures, with the DPR reporting a loss of 9,718 barrels in 2018 compared with 25,308 in the case of the NOSDRA and 76,150 in the case of NNPC (SDN 2020).

Inconsistencies are also apparent in different interpretations of the trends. Some analysts have estimated that the intensity of oil spills decreased following the return to civilian rule during the Second Republic, from 1979 to 1983. For example, according to Augustine Ikein, the volumes lost in Rivers State, which at the time included Bayelsa, fell from 311,000 barrels in 1980 to 12,100 in 1981 and from 206,000 to 8,400 in neighboring Bendel State, which included present-day Delta State. However, the number of barrels lost each year was, on average, higher than the levels recorded during the previous military dictatorships, with 9,100 barrels having been reported in Rivers State between 1981 and 1984, compared with 8,097 between 1970 and 1980, with the equivalent figures for Bendel standing at 5,300 and 4,320 respectively (Ikein 1990: 171–173).

Not without contradiction, other analysts have reckoned on a decrease in the scale of oil spills over the following decade, with an annual average of 50,000 barrels lost in the whole of the Niger Delta between 1991 and 1996 (Azaiki 2009: 47). At the same time, some researchers have acknowledged that rising violence made it more difficult to intervene in conflict areas to mitigate environmental disasters. In their view, the proportion of oil spills that were stopped without the surrounding area being cleaned up rose from 72% in 1976 to 97% in 1996 (Orubu, Odusola & Ehwarieme 2004: 206). However, their environmental impact also had to be related to the levels of oil production, which collapsed during the 1980s. Moreover, the number of attacks on pipelines was not necessarily indicative of the evolution in the volumes of oil spilt into the environment and never recovered.[6] Indeed, part of this oil has been stolen for smuggling and export.

---

6   For example, between 2012 and 2013, a lower number of pipeline attacks was recorded whereas production increased, but the number of barrels lost doubled (Adibe, Nwagwu & Albert 2018: 348–349).

Figures are still contested today. Since the end of the military dictatorship, most researchers have reckoned on a substantial increase in onshore pollution levels because of the development of bunkering activities, while the quantification of the volumes of stolen oil has improved (Katsouris & Sayne 2013). However, the siphoning of pipelines or fuel depots is not new. It already existed during the Biafran War, and it continued over the following decades when the police arrested sailors implicated in misappropriating crude oil on board supertankers such as the *Shanghai Express*, a Korean vessel, in 1983. Attacks on pipelines were also recorded during the military dictatorship of Muhammadu Buhari, who imposed the death penalty on perpetrators under two decrees enacted in 1984 and 1985.

2   Multinationals in the Eye of the Storm

Meanwhile, oil companies have played an important role in pollution. As early as July 1970, just a few months on from the end of the Biafran War, a Shell oil well exploded in Bomu near Dere, a village inhabited by the Ogoni clan of the Gokana in Rivers State. Ten years later, in January 1980, near Sangana in present-day Bayelsa State, a Texaco well called Funiwa 5 or North Apoi 20 blew up and killed 180 people in what was probably the industry's worst disaster ever seen in Nigeria in terms of human cost. Yet such accidents were not the only cause of pollution and environmental devastation. For example, in 1975, at the border of present-day Delta and Ondo states, Gulf Oil (later Chevron) dug a canal in Opuekeba Creek to facilitate the transfer of its production to the ocean. In the absence of any prior assessment of its environmental impact, the project resulted in saltwater entering and ravaging the mangrove of the villages of Tsekelewu and Opuoma. Nearby, Chevron abandoned several drilling sites that had not been correctly filled in.

It was the Ogoni revolt of the mid-1990s that forced the majors to pay more attention to environmental preservation. For example, since 1995, Shell has stopped opening new oil wells without making provision for the treatment and recycling of the associated gas to avoid flaring and global warming. The majors continued nonetheless to experience incidents increasingly at sea as the industry's center of gravity moved offshore. For example, in January 1998, the rupture of a Mobil pipeline connecting the Idoho platform to land contaminated the coastline by spilling 40,000 barrels of Qua-Iboe light crude oil. In December 2011, again, leaks from a vessel and a hose on the Shell platform in Bonga caused another oil spill some 120 kilometers off the coast of Nigeria.

However, these industrial accidents are just the tip of the iceberg. On a daily basis, oil spills result from acts of sabotage, design problems, engineering errors, lack of maintenance, or obstructions caused by moving sandbanks. For example, corrosion caused 80% of recorded leaks over the period 1976–1980 according to NNPC (Omoweh 2007: 146). The situation then changed with the rise in protests and violence. Between 2000 and 2010, more than 97% of 16,083 leaks recorded by NNPC were caused by malicious attacks on oil pipelines (Anifowose, Lawler, Van der Horst & Chapman 2012: 640). Confirmed by the federal government, the trend continued over the following decade (Ribadu 2012: 19). According to the National Oil Spill Detection and Response Agency (NOSDRA), three quarters of the leaks recorded in 2018 were due to third party interference (SDN 2020: 47). By comparison, incidents resulting from human error or accidents appear to have become negligible.

Official figures have, admittedly, been rejected by environmental lobbies. Activists have denounced conflicts of interest as the federal government tasked oil companies with reporting incidents and funding the travel expenses of its inspectors when visiting impacted sites. In general, local militants and international NGOs have assigned responsibility for pollution in the Niger Delta solely to the majors.[7] For example, Friends of the Earth pointed to the role of Shell in 2,976 leaks recorded between 1976 and 1991, an average of four per week (Rimmer et al. 2003). The NGO did not mention the fact that NNPC, a majority stakeholder in all joint ventures in Nigeria, was also responsible for failing to maintain the equipment used. Similarly, environmentalists placed responsibility for the 2012 Niger Delta floods squarely on the shoulders of the oil industry and climate change. They made no mention of the government's failures, despite the fact that the authorities had neither dredged the Niger River nor maintained the irrigation canals, which would have helped to evacuate the excess rainwater stagnating on land toward the sea.

3   Shared Responsibilities

A major study conducted in 2010 by the United Nations Environment Programme (UNEP) on pollution in Ogoniland is significant in this regard. Few people have taken the time to closely read what is in fact a highly technical report that has been cited indiscriminately to pour scorn on Shell. However, the UNEP experts clearly highlighted the damage associated with bunkering

---

7   See, for instance, Azaiki 2007b.

(*kpofire* in the Ogoni language) after the sudden departure of the company in 1993. As nature took over, the abandoned equipment rusted, and local residents took advantage of Shell's absence to occupy the space. Meanwhile, oil workers could no longer access the sites to seal the wells properly and maintain the pipelines that continued to traverse Ogoniland by carrying crude extracted elsewhere in the Niger Delta, not to mention the repairs required to fix leaks caused by acts of sabotage.

Somewhat paradoxically, the UNEP experts actually blamed Shell for having left. Indeed, the company's inability to clean up spills after 1993 exacerbated the impact of pollution, while satellite images revealed an impressive proliferation of illegal refineries between 2009 and 2011 in the wake of the amnesty granted to Niger Delta militants. The UNEP experts also criticized Shell for failing to apply its own environmental standards. The management made no effort to select professional subcontractors and verify that their funds were directed toward cleaning up areas affected by oil spills. In the same vein, it paid little attention to technical competence and was more interested in obtaining official completion certificates as soon as possible (UNEP 2011: 9, 148).

It is worth noting, however, that Shell was the only oil company that agreed to open its archives and answer the questions of UNEP experts, probably to exonerate itself from international pressure. The report is quite clear in this regard: NNPC did not cooperate and refused to let foreigners investigate and assess its responsibility in the repeated leaks recorded on pipelines shared with Shell (UNEP 2011: 10, 93, 127). As a result, the UNEP experts had to seek information from local villagers to uncover what proved to be the worst oil spill ever seen in the region. This ecological disaster, which occurred in 2005, came from a pipeline carrying refined NNPC products that contaminated the drinking water wells of Nissioken Ogale, a community near Eleme and Port Harcourt. Another significant source of pollution identified by the UNEP experts was the presence of illegal deposits of toxic residues. As Shell no longer extracted oil in Ogoniland, the residues originated from the production sites of other companies that rented out the land to unscrupulous owners, especially near the port of Onne.

It is important to clarify the role of majors in this regard. Given their critical mass, Nigeria's largest producers, including NNPC, have been implicated in the majority of oil spills and toxic gas emissions affecting the Niger Delta. Relatively speaking, however, small domestic companies adhere to a far lesser extent to environmental standards. Although they claim to be closer to local communities, they emit, for example, more greenhouse gases per barrel produced. By contrast, Shell seeks to apply international standards and was ranked third in the sector in a 2018 rating produced by an independent NGO of good reputation in Port Harcourt (SDN 2020).

Such findings go against conventional views on the misdeeds of the majors. For marketing reasons, environmental lobbies and human rights activists generally find it easier to criticize the oil giants in order to have a greater impact on public opinion globally. Yet UNEP experts refrained from assigning responsibility for pollution in the Niger Delta to a specific company, arguing instead that their mandate solely consisted in assessing the impact of environmental damage in Ogoniland. Scientifically, it would, at any rate, have been impossible for them, after so many years, to identify the cause of an oil spill on account of erosion, lack of maintenance, or sabotage. Diplomatically, the UNEP experts were also reluctant to address more fundamental political problems such as corruption, the structural deficiencies of NNPC, and collusion between the army and bunkerers (UNEP 2011: 204, 207). Their report was somewhat disappointing in this regard since it recommended cleaning up contaminated areas before even stopping the sources of pollution.

Therefore, the question remains: who is responsible for the ecological disaster in the Niger Delta? Oil companies, the Nigerian state, or the thieves siphoning pipelines? Magnifier effects around majors should not obscure the role of other stakeholders. Oil multinationals are, first and foremost, capitalist enterprises. They have no interest in losing part of their production in the mangroves of the Niger Delta or in the depths of the Bight of Bonny, just as they are keen not to tarnish their reputation when it comes to the environment and global warming. Bunkering and sabotage force them to suspend their activities and, in some cases, to definitively close down certain wells. As mining leases are not indefinite, such losses also impact future profits, and there is no reason to assume that majors would prefer to speculate on a resumption of production when prices are on the increase. On the contrary, thefts of crude oil diminish extraction capabilities at a given point in time and accordingly reduce the profitability of a deposit before operating rights expire.

4   Between Impotence and Conflicts of Interest: The Role of the State

Bunkering also means a net loss for the Nigerian state. Besides the cost of repairs, the damage to the environment impacts the revenue of fish farming and agriculture, which normally provide jobs to peoples of the Niger Delta. In addition, interruptions in oil production result in a loss of income that diminishes the state's redistribution capacity through formal or informal channels, such as the financing of development projects or the allocation of fraudulent contracts to political cronies. In short, the persistence of bunkering highlights the impotence of the authorities, who are not even capable of banning the construction of houses near pipelines.

From a logistical perspective, the challenge is immense insofar as the oil transport system is extensive, with, respectively, 5,120 and 4,441 kilometers of pipelines carrying refined products and crude oil across Nigeria (NEITI 2019: 4). From a geographical point of view, the thick canopy of the Niger Delta also hinders attempts to monitor such a network. Some pipelines are completely submerged underground or in shallow waters and are therefore not visible to drones, but are accessible to bunkerers. From a security perspective, finally, government forces and their "private" auxiliaries have shown their limits. Following the demobilization of militants as part of the 2009 amnesty, the contracts granted to pirates failed to stop bunkering. As for the army, it has either covered up thefts of oil by accepting kickbacks or actively contributed to pollution through the use of disproportionate force. By bombing illegal refineries, the military have, for example, caused huge fires that ravaged surrounding areas and destroyed barges whose cargo spread to neighboring creeks. As an alternative, the authorities only proposed to support the development of small, "clean" modular refineries designed to replace bunkering activities that could not be legalized.

More fundamentally, the environmental crisis raises political structural issues. Indeed, the Nigerian state does not separate its roles in oil production and the regulation of the industry. Conflicts of interest have abounded since the ministry of petroleum resources merged with the Nigerian National Oil Corporation (NNOC) to form the NNPC in 1977. In practice, the federal government has always prioritized revenue maximization over adherence to environmental standards. With a majority stake in all JVs, NNPC has, for example, consistently sought to avoid paying its share of the cost of maintaining pipelines and production facilities. As a result, the majors were forced into advancing funds to ensure a minimum level of repairs. They also suffered delays caused by corrupt officials under JOAs that forced them to await approval from various NNPC technical, operational, and development committees (DevCom, Tecom and Opcom) to be authorized to release funds.

The issue of greenhouse gas emissions speaks volume about the shortcomings of the Nigerian state. As early as November 1969, during the Biafran War, the federal government imposed a five-year moratorium to stop the use of flares. In September 1979, the Associated Gas Re-injection Act No.99 then postponed the ban to January 1984, with further extensions to January 2010 and December 2012. In January 2021, finally, the PIB allowed for derogations for gas flaring. While cracking down a little more severely on companies responsible for methane leaks, lawmakers made no provision for any compensation to the victims of air pollution and did not define a minimum amount of fines, which were treated as royalties. Even more surprisingly, the PIB specified no deadline to definitively ban gas flaring (Amaduobogha, Subai, Mazzi & Akhigbe 2021).

In practice, the Nigerian state has been very lenient. And for good reason: the government would have to pay itself if it really wanted to impose fines on the JVS in which NNPC holds a majority stake. Moreover, it did not want to bear the costs of the treatment or the re-injection of gas associated with the extraction of oil. Finally, it was reluctant to put in place a tax framework that would have pushed multinationals to stop flaring and allow them to develop production to export gas. Indeed, such a policy would have committed NNPC to investing significantly to supply the local market below international prices. As a result, the fines for gas flaring were seldom enforced, and the amounts involved were often negligible.

The state has also been lax with the old oil wells that were not closed to meet OPEC quotas and maintain production levels. The government has taken the view that the industry should apply corporate social responsibility and comply with environmental standards on a voluntary basis, unlike countries such as Norway, which has taken a far more coercive approach (Frynas 2009: 53). Decreed in 1992, Nigeria's norms were aligned to minimal requirements. In the event of a spill, the authorities left it to oil companies to complete the clean-up process and resume production prior to decontaminating the soil and checking that the situation allowed for a return to normal life for the fauna and flora (UNEP 2011: 142).

In other words, the bodies established to regulate the industry failed to put an end to pollution following the creation of a Federal Environmental Protection Agency (FEPA) in 1988, a dedicated ministry in 1999, and a National Oil Spill Detection and Response Agency (NOSDRA) in 2006. The missions of federal and regional departments responsible for managing ecological disasters overlapped and produced confusion. As for NOSDRA, it competed with the DPR, which operated with a different understanding of the standards decreed in 1992. It lacked the personnel, expertise, and resources required to intervene on the ground and had to rely on NGOS and the industry to obtain information on oil spills. In addition, NOSDRA staff depended entirely on the logistics of companies to travel to affected sites by boat or helicopter. Furthermore, its most competent executives were attracted by higher pay and often chose to end their career in the oil industry. Finally, NOSDRA struggled to allocate staff to the Niger Delta, as its agents in Abuja preferred to stay in the capital (UNEP 2011: 12, 139–140).

Following debates in the National Assembly in early 2021, the PIB offered no significant improvements in this regard (Amaduobogha, Subai, Mazzi & Akhigbe 2021). Keen to revitalize production and attract investors during a period of declining oil prices, lawmakers granted little importance to the protection of the environment and reduced the powers once devolved to NOSDRA. To avoid conflicts of interest with NNPC, which was earmarked for privatization, two authorities were now due to take over to regulate the entire industry, but without any provisions being made for combating pollution. Similarly, the PIB did not specify any clean-up obligations in the event of a spill and did not impose compliance with environmental standards on companies that responded to tenders to obtain oil blocks. Sanctions remained vague, and the responsibility of operating firms primarily consisted in paying a discretionary flat-rate contribution to a federal fund earmarked for the fight against pollution.

As for bunkering, the only provision was for host communities to take charge of policing pipelines by having a greater stake in the industry's profits. This approach seemed somewhat incongruous given the power of a simple fisherman against heavily armed gangs.[8] In practice, the PIB failed to put in place effective mechanisms to combat bunkering. Both oil thieves and companies were thus able to continue business as usual.

References

Adibe, Raymond, Ejikeme Nwagwu & Okorie Albert. 2018. "Rentierism and Security Privatisation in the Nigerian Petroleum Industry: Assessment of Oil Pipeline Surveillance and Protection Contracts". *Review of African Political Economy* 45 (156): 345–353.

Amaduobogha, Simon, Pereowei Subai, Peter Mazzi & Lillian Akhigbe. 2021. *The Petroleum Industry Bill 2020: Briefing*. Port Harcourt: Stakeholder Democracy Network.

Amnesty International. 2009. *Nigeria: Petroleum, Pollution and Poverty in the Niger Delta*. London: Amnesty International.

---

8 According to the law passed in 2022, people living near oil wells are supposed to benefit from projects funded by Host Community Development Trusts, with huge amounts of resources, between 500 and 800 million dollars a year, as much as the NDDC's budget and much more than the sums earmarked for CSR. The problem is that the management of this money remains obscure. In exchange, host communities would have to reimburse operational costs and the loss of income in case of sabotage (Pérouse de Montclos 2020).

Anifowose, Babatunde, Damian Lawler, Dan van der Horst & Lee Chapman. 2012. "Attacks on Oil Transport Pipelines in Nigeria: A Quantitative Exploration and Possible Explanation of Observed Patterns". *Applied Geography* 32 (2): 636–651.

Ariweriokuma, Soala. 2008. *The Political Economy of Oil and Gas in Africa: The Case of Nigeria*. London: Routledge.

Azaiki, Steve. 2007a. *Oil, Gas and Life in Nigeria*. Ibadan: Y-Books.

Azaiki, Steve. 2007b. *Oil, Politics and Blood*. Ibadan: Y-Books.

Azaiki, Steve. 2009. *The Evil of Oil*. Ibadan: Y-Books.

Burgis, Tom. 2015. *The Looting Machine: Warlords, Tycoons, Smugglers and the Systematic Theft of Africa's Wealth*. London: William Collins.

Cayford, Steven. 1996. "The Ogoni Uprising: Oil, Human Rights, and the Democratic Alternative". *Africa Today* 43 (2): 183–198.

D'Armagnac, Bertrand. 10 February 2012. "Le grand gâchis du 'torchage' des pétroliers" : 7. Paris : *Le Monde*.

Dan Kikile, Esueme *et al.* 2009. "Analysis of the Petroleum Industry Bill from the Perspective of Communities". In *Communities and the Petroleum Industry Bill*, edited by Fidelis Allen: 10–18. Port Harcourt: Social Action.

Frynas, Jedrzej Georg. 2003. "The Oil Industry in Nigeria: Conflict between Oil Companies and Local People". In *Transnational Corporations and Human Rights*, edited by Jedrzej Georg Frynas & Scott Pegg: 99–114. London: Palgrave Macmillan.

Frynas, Jedrzej George. 2009. *Beyond Corporate Social Responsibility: Oil Multinationals and Social Challenges*. Cambridge: Cambridge University Press.

Ghazvinian, John. 2007. *Untapped: The Scramble for Africa's Oil*. London: Harcourt.

Idemudia, Uwafiokun & Uwem Ite. 2006. "Demystifying the Niger Delta Conflict: Towards an Integrated Explanation". *Review of African Political Economy* 109: 391–406.

Ikein, Augustine. 1990. *The Impact of Oil on a Developing Country: The Case of Nigeria*. New York: Praeger.

Jike, Victor Teddy. 2004. "Environmental Degradation, Social Disequilibrium, and the Dilemma of Sustainable Development in the Niger Delta of Nigeria". *Journal of Black Studies* 34 (5): 686–701.

Katsouris, Christina & Aaron Sayne. 2013. *Nigeria's Criminal Crude: International Options to Combat the Export of Stolen Oil*. London: Chatham House.

Kew, Darren & David Phillips. 2007. "Seeking Peace in the Niger Delta: Oil, Natural Gas, and Other Vital Resources". *New England Journal of Public Policy* 21 (2): 154–170.

Le Hir, Pierre. 6 August 2010. "La marée noire s'estompe, la polémique persiste": 4. Paris: *Le Monde*.

Moffat, David & Olof Linde. 1995. "Perception and Reality: Assessing Priorities for Sustainable Development in the Niger River Delta". *Ambio: Journal of Human Environment*, 24: 527–538.

Montanyà, Xavier. 2012. *L'or noir du Nigeria: Pillages, ravages écologiques et résistances*. Marseille: Editions Agone.

Naanen, Ben & Patrick Tolani. 2014. *Private Gain, Public Disaster: Social Context of Illegal Oil Bunkering and Artisanal Refining in the Niger Delta*. Port Harcourt: Niger Delta Environment and Relief Foundation.

NCF. 2006. *Niger Delta Natural Resource Damage Assessment and Restoration Project*. Lagos: Nigerian Conservation Foundation.

NEITI. 2019. *Stemming the Increasing Cost of Oil Theft to Nigeria*. Abuja: Nigeria Extractive Industries Transparency Initiative.

Nwajiaku, Kathryn. 2005. "Between Discourse and Reality: The Politics of Oil and Ijaw Ethnic Nationalism in the Niger Delta". *Cahiers d'études africaines* 45 (2): 457–496.

Okoh, Peter. 1996. "Environmental Degradation, Conflicts and Peaceful Resolution in Nigeria and Between Nigeria and Neighbouring States". In *Environmental Degradation as a Cause of War*, edited by Günther Bächler & Kurt Spillmann: 183–245. Zurich: Rüegger.

Omoweh, Daniel. 2007. *Shell Petroleum Development Company, the State, and Underdevelopment of the Nigeria's Niger Delta: A Study in Environmental Degradation*. Trenton (NJ): Africa World Press.

Orubu, Christopher, Ayodele Odusola & William Ehwarieme. 2004. "The Nigerian Oil Industry: Environmental Diseconomies, Management Strategies and the Need for Community Involvement". *Journal of Human Ecology* 16 (3): 203–214.

Pérouse de Montclos, Marc-Antoine. 16 November 2020. "Pourquoi la Petroleum Industry Bill ne résoudra pas les problèmes du Nigeria et du delta". Paris: *Jeune Afrique*.

PWC. 2019. *Assessing the Impact of Gas Flaring on the Nigerian Economy*. Lagos: Price Waterhouse Coopers.

Ribadu, Mallam Nuhu. 2012. *Report of the Petroleum Revenue Special Task Force*. Abuja: Federal Ministry of Petroleum Resources.

Rimmer, Lisa *et al.* 2003. *Failing the Challenge. The Other Shell Report 2002*. London: Friends of the Earth.

Scoones, Ian *et al.* 2019. "Narratives of Scarcity: Framing the Global Land Rush". *Geoforum*, 101: 231–241.

SDN. 2020. *2018 Nigerian Oil Industry Environmental Performance Index*. Port Harcourt: Stakeholder Democracy Network.

Singh, Jasdip *et al.* 1995. *Nigeria: Defining an Environmental Development Strategy for the Niger Delta. Vol. 1.* New York: World Bank.

UNDP. 2006. *Niger Delta Human Development Report.* Abuja: United Nations Development Programme.

UNEP. 2011. *Environmental Assessment of Ogoniland.* Nairobi: United Nations Environment Programme.

Von Kemedi, Dimieari. 2003. "The Changing Predatory Styles of International Oil Companies in Nigeria". *Review of African Political Economy* 30 (95): 134–139.

Incoherence and Fantasy

A Versatile Elite

To ensure my safety while traveling in the Niger Delta, I am told I should be escorted by an officer from the Nigerian Mobile Police force (MOPOL). However, the security operative I am assigned comes from a different region of Nigeria and he is unable to provide my driver with any guidance. Moreover, with his Kalashnikov clearly in view, he causes fear among locals and draws unwanted attention to me. His only use is getting us through the various police checkpoints along the road without wasting time to negotiate the payment of a *dash*. When we arrive in Warri, I decide to leave him at a barracks before picking him up on our way back to Port Harcourt.

In the meantime, I have a meeting arranged with INC (Ijaw National Council) militants. We meet in a dilapidated building that is either in the process of being built or restored or has been abandoned—a common sight in Nigeria. The militants I speak to gesticulate dramatically when we start talking about the conflicts opposing the Ijaw and the Itsekiri of Warri. I get the distinct impression that they are under the influence of drugs. After a while, I realize that one of them is, in fact, a police commissioner. I am taken aback to find him siding with a militant organization that is openly defiant of the state.

However, no one seems surprised when I mention the matter. And for good reason: in the Niger Delta, the Nigerian state, oil companies, and so-called civil society do not form monolithic blocks. Furthermore, the relationships between them are constantly evolving and are anything but fixed. Local politicians cultivate the ambivalence, whether out of conviction, to seduce voters, or to approach rebels to negotiate peace. For example, Isaac Boro is officially celebrated as a hero in Rivers State, where he gave his name to a public park in Port Harcourt. As for Tom Polo and MEND, they convinced the government to establish a federal university for the Nigerian navy in Okerenkoko, near Gbaramatu; the building was inaugurated in 2018 and counts as one of Delta State's few successfully completed projects.

© MARC-ANTOINE PÉROUSE DE MONTCLOS, 2024 | DOI:10.1163/9789004697911_018

FIGURE 49   Emblem of Bayelsa State (2005)

1   On Collusion with Rebels

The self-proclaimed "Governor General of the Ijaw", Diepreye Alamieyeseigha, is a good example of collusion with rebels. While in power in Bayelsa State from 1999 to 2005, he made no secret of his sympathy for militants and openly supported the Ijaw Youth Council (IYC), which was chaired by his cousin Oyeinfie Jonjon in 2004. Alamieyeseigha's successors continued this policy and financed the construction of the IYC headquarters in Yenagoa, Izonwari House. In power from 2012 to 2020, Henry Seriake Dickson inaugurated an "Ijaw National Academy" in Kaiama, Isaac Boro's native village, the site of the IYC's founding declaration and one of the few completed projects in the state (Social Action 2018: 29). In 2012, during ceremonies held to commemorate Nigeria's independence, Dickson again undertook to consolidate the region's ethno-nationalist project by providing Bayelsa with its own official anthem and a blue, red, and green flag in the colors of INC, each bearing a white star. The state's emblem was also designed to represent the agility and dynamism of the Ijaw by depicting a leopard, a crocodile, a shark, a palm tree, a sun, a canoe, a couple of fishermen … and a gas flare in the background. In 2020, finally, Dickson's successor, Douye Diri, renamed the Ijaw National Academy after the late Captain Samuel Timinipre Owonaro (1944–2020), one of the heroes of the "12-day Revolution" of Isaac Boro in 1966.

Meanwhile, young militants have consistently sought to maintain relations based on collusion and complicity with the authorities. Some have even accepted official positions or stood at elections. The careers of former IYC presidents are telling in this regard. For example, Felix Tuodolo became commissioner for Ijaw affairs in Bayelsa State, while Udenz Eradiri and Elvis Donkemezuo made a bid for the National Assembly but lost at the 2018 primaries of the Peoples Democratic Party (PDP) and of a small opposition party, respectively. In neighboring Delta State, IYC president Chris Ekiyor also had to resign from his position to stand for the PDP in the 2011 elections.

In most cases, the careers of Niger Delta militants have, in fact, oscillated between power and extra-parliamentary opposition, thereby underlining the porous boundaries between the state and so-called civil society. For example, NDPVF's leader Asari Dokubo initially worked for the Rivers PDP governor, Peter Odili, before opting for armed struggle, until he was eventually appointed to a federal commission tasked with organizing the pilgrimage to Mecca. In Nigeria, political games of this kind are actually not specific to oil-producing areas. In the southwest, the leader of the Yoruba militia OPC (Oodua People's Congress), Ganiyu Adams, also mixed with the democratic opposition to General Sani Abacha before wreaking havoc on Lagos—and eventually settling down when traditional chiefs granted him an honorific title. As for the founder of MASSOB, Ralph Uwazuruike, he joined the PDP and supported President Olusegun Obasanjo in 1999 before breaking ranks to defend the Ibo separatist cause.

The leader of MOSOP is a case in point. After graduating from the University of Ibadan in 1965, Ken Saro-Wiwa applied for a job with Shell and failed to secure a position in the company, which nonetheless offered him a scholarship to continue his studies in Britain. A member of the military government of Rivers State between 1969 and 1973, the Ogoni writer then lived off various official contracts during the 1970s and 1980s. In 1989, he agreed to become the director of the propaganda arm of Ibrahim Babangida's junta, the MAMSER (Mass Mobilization for Self Reliance, Social Justice, and Economic Recover). According to his own son, General Sani Abacha even put him forward as Minister of State for Petroleum Resources in late 1993 (Maja-Pearce 2005: 22). However, Saro-Wiwa declined the offer ... before being hanged by the military two years later.

His execution stands as an exception in this regard. Armed militants in the Niger Delta were generally able to reconvert to business following the 2009 amnesty. Unless they lost their lives in gunfights with the military or rival gangs, many also played a double game to continually renegotiate benefits with the authorities by threatening to resume hostilities in the creeks. The versatility of the ruling class was conducive to this pattern: like the militants, state governors often changed sides by moving from the opposition to the ruling party, as with Rotimi Amaechi in Rivers, Timipre Sylva in Bayelsa, and Godswill Akpabio in Akwa Ibom when they left the PDP and joined the ACN and then the APC.

Such opportunism also underlines the extent to which politicians tend to put their own personal interests first. For example, just as the UNEP experts were publishing their recommendations at the time of the 2011 general elections, President Goodluck Jonathan allegedly delayed clean-up operations in Ogoniland as a form of revenge on Saro-Wiwa, who had refused to grant him a scholarship when he was a commissioner for education in Rivers in 1970–1973. Rotimi Amaechi, who became a member of the Muhammadu Buhari administration in 2015, also reportedly abused his position as transport minister to settle scores with his rival and successor in Rivers, Nyesom Wike, by blocking subsidies earmarked to renovate Port Harcourt's international airport.

Local residents thus find themselves caught between a rock and a hard place. They distrust both the ruling class and the militants. Therefore, it is difficult to know what the silent majority really thinks in the Niger Delta. Turnout at elections is very often low and, sometimes, below the national average, probably also because citizens are fearful of intimidation and political violence, such as in Rivers State during the 2019 and 2023 presidential elections.[1] At the same time, polls conducted in rural communities appear to indicate higher turnouts than in urban areas, perhaps because villagers are more likely to obey instructions from community leaders. For example, according to some surveys, more than 80% of residents of Onelga in Rivers and Eastern Obolo in Akwa Ibom regularly participated in elections at federal and regional levels (Renouard *et al.* 2008: 30). In the same vein, many Niger Delta states do not have the highest voter abstention rates in Nigeria (Taiwo & Ahmed 2015).

By contrast, so-called civil society organizations appear to be unrepresentative of the people. Some are used to promote personal interests. For example, Robert Azibaola set up an advocacy NGO, ND-HERO (Niger-Delta Human and Environmental Rescue Organization), which helped him to secure funding from Agip to manage community affairs from 2005 onward (Adunbi 2015). The owner of a construction company, he also used his close relations with his

---

1   In 2023, technological difficulties excluded many from voting. In Rivers State, the official turnout was just 15.6% of registered voters, the lowest in the country (Akinpelu 2020).

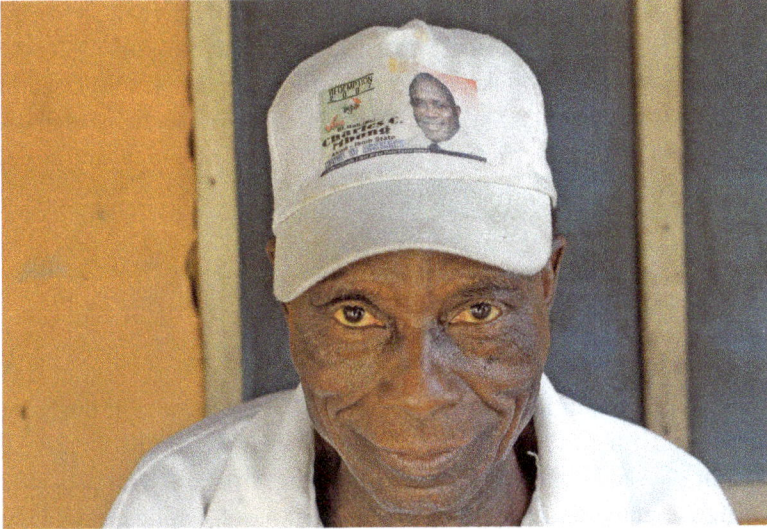

FIGURE 50   A PDP supporter in Akwa Ibom State (2009)

cousin, President Goodluck Jonathan, to secure a contract to build Bayelsa's "international" airport in 2012. In 2019, however, he was finally taken to court by the EFCC (Economic and Financial Crimes Commission) on charges of fraud and money laundering (Ogune 2019).

It is important in this regard not to idealize the grassroots initiatives of so-called civil society. Many NGOs are, in fact, very small. Eleven of the fifteen organizations examined by Okechukwu Ibeanu in the Niger Delta included fewer than twenty members, and just two—MOSOP and IYC—had more than 150 (Ibeanu 2006: 47). Moreover, civic NGOs usually rely heavily on foreign support and public subsidies, unlike the tribal unions of the 1930s, which were based on self-help. For example, when it was launched in September 1990, MOSOP was essentially an ethno-political lobby for a small English-speaking elite that most Ogoni peasants did not understand (Okonta 2008: 193–205). Like INC, however, the organization was keen to present itself as a mass movement. It claimed that any Ogoni was automatically a member by birthright and, in January 1993, its charter incorporated youth and women's committees in an effort driven by Ken Saro-Wiwa to obtain the resignation of conservative figures such as Garrick Leton and Edward Kobani.

Armed movements that emerged in Ijawland were not representative of Niger Delta communities and subalterns either. Established in 1997, 2003, and 2005 respectively, FNDIC, NDPVF, and MEND competed against each other. Despite their strong media presence, they had few members and remained deeply divided. Their hierarchies were highly fluid and their chains of command very fragile. As for their leaders, they often found themselves disowned by their base, as with Bello Oboko, the FNDIC's founder, who was replaced in 2007 by Dennis Otuaro because he had refused in 2006 to boycott peace negotiations and had agreed to participate to an Abuja-based economic and social council for the development of the region.

2   Independence, Autonomy, Regionalism, Federalism: An à la Carte Menu

In other words, there is little evidence to suggest that the peoples of the Niger Delta are favorable to … or opposed to independence. According to surveys conducted in Bayelsa, Delta, and Akwa Ibom states in 2000, less than 30% of the region's inhabitants supported greater levels of self-determination. However, the vast majority (71%) wanted to negotiate with the federal government a greater share of oil and gas revenue.[2] The local elites in particular cited cultural and economic arguments in calling for an increase in the derivation percentage for oil-producing states. Decentralization and "true federalism", so they said, fitted the characteristics of acephalous societies in which traditional powers used to rotate between different clans, as with today's zoning system.

Following this logic, many activists did not claim for independence. They rather supported the creation of states and local governments because the proliferation of administrative entities was to lead mathematically to additional budgets being granted. From Asari Dokubo to John Togo, armed rebels also took up these demands and steered clear of proclaiming independence to avoid repeating Isaac Boro's mistake in 1966. For example, in the early 2000s, NDPVF called for three new states and 120 LGAs for the Ijaw (Kalu 2008: 178).

Actually, such demands are nothing new. They have their roots in the constitutional negotiations that led to the independence of Nigeria in 1960, and they never stopped during the military regimes that followed the proclamation of the short-lived Niger Delta Republic in 1966. For example, the Ijaw called for the creation of new LGAs and a state known as Abayelsa and then Bayelsa in the late 1980s, and again at a constitutional conference in 1995. In 1991, they also established a lobby, INC, to relay these demands.

---

2   In the absence of a referendum, these surveys are not formal polls and they involved only 284 respondents, without any sampling (Ukeje *et al.* 2002: 32).

After 1999, the return to a parliamentary regime made these claims more visible. For example, in 2002, during hearings before the human rights commission chaired by Judge Chukwudifu Oputa, INC reiterated the demands for more LGAs. Supported by John Pepper Clark, a renowned writer, and two Ijaw veterans of politics—Harold Dappa-Biriye and Edwin Clark—a petition also called for the creation of two new states to the west and east of the Niger Delta. Known as Itoru-Ibe, Toro-Ebe, or Toru-Ebe, the first was to be centered around Bomadi, at the heart of present-day Delta State and would have included the "lost tribes" of the Ijaw in Ondo and Edo. With Port Harcourt as its capital, the second would have been named Oil Rivers and would have incorporated the Ijaw of Rivers and Akwa Ibom.[3] As for the governor of Bayelsa, Diepreye Alamieyeseigha, he created new LGAs that had no formal legal existence and were never recognized by Abuja.[4]

Since then, there has been a constant flow of similar demands. Taking advantage of the election of an Ijaw president, Goodluck Jonathan, petitions from the South-South geopolitical zone called on the National Assembly in Abuja to create additional states, including Ogoja in Cross River, Ahoada, Bori, Minji-Se, and Oil Rivers in Rivers State, and Ado, Anioma, Ethiope, New Delta, Toru-Ebe, Urhobo, Warri, and Orimile in Delta State (Wakili 2012). Interestingly, the proposed entities overlapped with some of the projects discussed at the 1995 Constitutional Conference, one year before Nigeria's latest major administrative review, which saw the creation of six new states in 1996. Examples include demands for states such as Toru-Ebe in Bomadi, Orashi in Ahoada, Ogoni in Bori, and New Rivers in Okrika.

3   Everyday Arrangements: The Obolo between the Ocean and the Niger Delta

However, these calls have, for the most part, remained the affair of the ruling class at a national level. On a day-to-day basis, local demands have typically

---

3   Aside from Bomadi, Toru-Ebe was theoretically meant to include the LGAs of Burutu, Ogulagha, Warri North, Warri South, Ayakoromo, Kiagbodo, Ezebiri, Seimbiri, Tuomo, Ndoro, Torugbene, Patani, and Kumbokiri (Alagoa, Tamuno & Clark 2009: 732, Kukah 2011: 371).

4   Under his term, the state acquired 33 "development committees" overlaid on the 8 LGAs listed in the 1999 constitution: Brass, Ekeremor-Operemo, Ogbia, Sagbama, Kolokuma, Opokuma, Nembe, Nembe West, Oporoma, Yenagoa, Akassa, Kaiko-Ibeawo, Aleibiri, Alabini, Oporomor West, Opuokede, Kolo Creek, Anyama, Odi, Tarakiri, Toru-Abobou, Mein-Oyiakiri, Mini-Ikensi, Okoroma-Tereke, Apoi-Olodiama, Bomo East, Bomo West, Bassan-Koluama, Ogboin North, Ogboin South, Gbaraun-Ekpetiama, Okordia-Buseni, and Zarama.

centered around subtle changes to administrative boundaries or names. For example, the Obolo-Andoni in Rivers and Akwa Ibom never took up arms to call for a state of their own. They live in rural areas, far from the turbulence of Port Harcourt and the oil-producing areas of Bayelsa State, and their voice is barely heard in the media. Their recriminations have focused instead on the negligence of the government and their administrative division on either side of the mouth of the Imo River, at the border between two states. To assert their cultural unity, some inhabitants of Eastern Obolo in Akwa Ibom thus called for Andoni LGA in Rivers State to be renamed Western Obolo.

Historically, the Obolo-Andoni formed a single ethno-linguistic community, originally ruled from Calabar province until the creation of Rivers State at the start of the Biafran War in 1967. Later, however, they were separated by the major local government reform of 1976 that changed Nigeria's administrative boundaries, following the recommendations of a commission chaired by Judge Mamman Nasir. As a result, the Obolo-Andoni on the right and left banks of the Imo River were placed under the authority of, respectively, Port Harcourt to the west and Calabar to the east, and later Uyo when Akwa Ibom was carved out of Cross River State in 1987.

The top-down redrawing of administrative boundaries was not the only factor responsible for such divisions. As early as 1975, a petition signed by Eastern

FIGURE 51   Edowin beach in Eastern Obolo in Akwa Ibom State (2009)

Obolo leaders had requested incorporation into Cross River State, which was safer and calmer compared with Port Harcourt. One argument was that they had traditionally traded with the Efik of Calabar. The Obolo also felt culturally closer to the Ibibio in the hinterland than to the Ogoni and the Ibani in Rivers, communities into which they married less. However, their position went against the affinities maintained with the Andoni of Opobo on the other side of the Imo River. The 1975 petition did not reflect the general opinion of the Eastern Obolo, whose various clans had different inclinations, with the Okoroinyong favoring inclusion in Rivers and the Iko and Emereoke preferring to side with the Ibibio of Ikpa Ibom and Ukpum Ete in Akwa Ibom State.

Today, the Eastern Obolo continue to waver in their preference for being in one or the other state. Rivers is the region's wealthiest oil-producing state, an advantage for the Western Obolo (i.e. the Andoni), who have more resources to share with other minorities. By contrast, the Eastern Obolo of Akwa Ibom have fewer political connections because they live in a more homogeneous state dominated by the Ibibio of Uyo, alongside the Oron, the Annang and the Ibeno. For example, their LGA was created in 1996. However, its status as an electoral district during the Second and Third Republics, in 1979 and 1992, was removed in 1999. To assert their rights, some citizens have therefore called for the number of wards in Eastern Obolo to be doubled from ten to twenty, while asking for the creation of an electoral district with their neighbors in Ikot Abasi and Mkpat Enin LGAs to the north, rather than with Ibeno LGA to the east.

Furthermore, the Akwa Ibom State government in Uyo has recognized only two of their clans, compared with four for the Andoni in Rivers, who are more numerous and united, making it easier for them to make their demands heard in Port Harcourt. The difference is significant since it partly determines access to public funding, with 5% of LGA budgets being earmarked for traditional rulers. Some Eastern Obolo argue that they were marginalized because the government in Uyo was reluctant to formalize the customary rights of a non-Ibibio minority, while their paramount ruler had no interest in multiplying the number of clans because he wanted to continue monopolizing state resources.

However, it would be difficult to prove that the Western Obolo of Andoni LGA were really favored by the Rivers State government. According to the 2006 census, their community was three times larger than their "cousins" in Akwa Ibom (211,099 and 65,543 inhabitants respectively). Therefore, it stands to reason that they should have received more public funding. Moreover, their administrative structures were different. Unlike Akwa Ibom, Rivers State does not grant the title of paramount ruler to top-ranking chiefs. For many years, the Andoni had also to make do with a regent considered as a second-class traditional leader. It was not until 2016 that they acquired two first-class rulers in Ikuru and Ngo—namely, Aaron Miller Ikuru ("Ikwut VII") and Job Williams Okuruket ("Nnabiget XIV"). Conversely, the creation of the Eastern Obolo LGA in 1996 enabled Owen Sylvanus Ukafia (1933–2016) to be promoted to the rank of paramount ruler and crowned in 1997 as "Ede VI".

To sum up a long story, the Obolo-Andoni thus quietly lobbied the administration to demand changes in the local government. But they neither organized demonstrations nor took up arms to call for the creation of new states. As a result, their experience has been largely neglected; researchers and journalists have generally focused their attention on the Ogoni and the Ijaw crisis. This is unfortunate because, by contrast, the case of the Obolo-Andoni has highlighted the contradictions and incoherencies of Niger Delta activists campaigning for greater autonomy at a regional level. Demands for new states have indeed revealed high levels of competition and division between and within rival groups.

4 The Balkanization of the Niger Delta

For example, calls for an Ogoni State from 1990 onward were first thwarted by the Eleme, who wanted their own administrative entity known as Nchia, and then by the Ibo-speaking minorities of Oyigbo LGA, who formed part of Imo State until 1976 and who requested to be included in Abia State in 2005. Coveted by many, the capital of Rivers State, Port Harcourt, was also the subject of competing initiatives among the Ikwerre of the northern outskirts and the Ijaw to the south. Each group called for its own entity, but with the same administrative seat. The Ijaw themselves were focused on a range of different projects. Some requested the formation of an Abaji State that would have included Port Harcourt City as well as the communities of Obolo, Bolo, Ogu, Okrika, Ogoloma, Isaka, Bonny, Kalaibiama, Iniasiri, Opobo, Nkoro, Agbo, Amaiba, Amajaaba, Oka, Okoromita, Okosun, Okuba, Okwaan-Aja, Okwaan-Okuka, Oru, and Ujama. Meanwhile, a little further west, the Ijaw of Degema campaigned in favor of a Kengema State that would have incorporated the subregions of Abisse, Aguda Toru, Akilama Toru, Akuku Toru, Asari Toru, Kalabari Toru, Ke, Kula, Obu-Kula, Obilo, Ololo Toru, Owuanga Toru, Old-Kalabari Toru, Sombreiro, Sankrama, and Tobu.

The many twists and turns that eventually led to the creation of Delta State in 1990 and Bayelsa State in 1996 are significant in this regard. In the late 1980s, attempts to form a state called Abayelsa initially failed as a result of opposition from the Ahoada, the Ogbia, the Egbema, the Ndoni, and the Ekpeye in the hinterland, who feared the domination of the Ijaw on the coast (Okoko & Lazarus

1999). In the south, the Ogbia and the Nembe preferred to support the idea of a state called Oloibiri, in reference to the first oil well operated in Nigeria. Carved out of Bendel State in 1990, Delta State also experienced many challenges. At the end of the military dictatorship in 1999, the Urhobo of Ughelli in the center and the Ibo of Asaba in the north demanded new states, to be named Anioma or Orimile, that would have annexed parts of Anambra and Imo (Onokerhoraye 2011: 567). As for the Ijaw further west toward present-day Edo and Ondo states, they called for the creation of another entity, Beni-Ebe, which was to be centered around Arogbo and which would have included the communities of Ukparamo, Adogba, Adoloseimoh, Ajakpata, Apoi, Awodikuro, Egbema, Furupagha, Gbekebo, Ofunama-Opuama, Okomu, and Olodiama.

Throughout the Niger Delta, these demands have concerned ever smaller territories. They have generally resulted from marriages of convenience between groups that were themselves deeply fragmented and who sometimes called for the creation of administrative entities with artificial names such as Bayelsa, an acronym derived from Brass, Yenagoa, and Sagbama LGAs, or Onelga, an LGA that incorporated the communities of Ogba, Ndoni, and Egbema in Rivers State. The proliferation of competing demands clearly went against the narratives of militants who accused the federal government and oil companies of seeking to divide and rule the Niger Delta people. However, the contradictions were endorsed by many activists and local politicians. For example, a technical committee set up at the federal level in 2008 and chaired by the president of MOSOP recommended multiplying local governments to avoid the "balkanization and marginalization" of the Niger Delta's least developed areas (Mitee 2008: 129).

One of the members of the committee, Professor Omafume Onoge (1938–2009), went even further. In one of his very last interviews before his death and the 2009 amnesty, he emphasized the need to remain united and the importance of tackling problems at a regional level to solve the crisis. He blamed the federal government for fomenting division, by its thinking "in terms of states only" and playing up the "differences in languages and customs" between different communities in the Niger Delta (Amurun 2009). At the same time, Onoge requested additional states and LGAs to foster development and bring the administration closer to the people. For example, he called for the creation of a state for his own group, the Urhobo, to ensure that his own community would not be accused of seeking to dominate others in Delta State.

Such contradictions speak volumes about the limits of militancy and the fragmentation of the struggle in the region. Political conflicts mainly opposed a ruling class that mobilized the youth as footsoldiers. So-called militants were often instrumentalized by state governors, "godfathers", elders and traditional

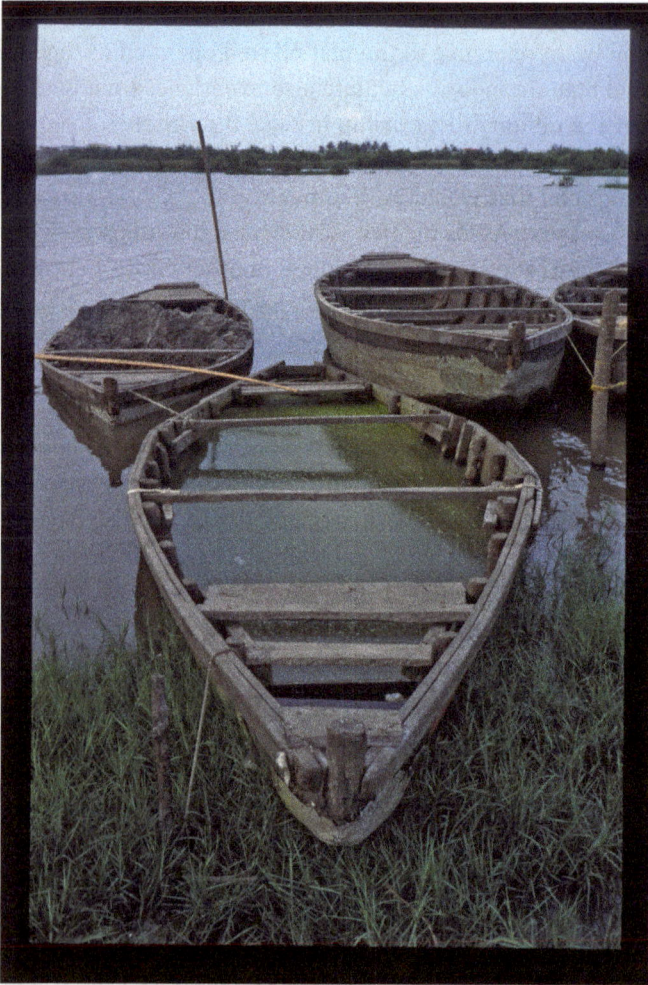

FIGURE 52   Canoes in the lagoon (2000)

chiefs. Their armed struggle was thus used to press the federal government
to give more stipends to the Niger Delta. But it did not open new avenues for
development, social change and political reform. Quite on the contrary, the
rebellion of some segments of the youth reproduced old patterns of domination. This situation brings a sense of despair, even if all hope is not lost in the
next generations.

References

Adunbi, Omolade. 2015. *Oil Wealth and Insurgency in Nigeria*. Bloomington: Indiana University Press.

Akinpelu, Yusuf. 8 November 2020. "Nigeria Spending More on Elections, But Voter Turnout Keeps Reducing". Abuja: *Premium Times*. https://www.premium timesng.com/investigationspecial-reports/425122-special-report-nigeria-spend ing-more-on-elections-but-voter-turnout-keeps-reducing.html (accessed 12 september 2023).

Alagoa, Ebiegberie Joe, Tekena Tamuno & John Pepper Clark (eds). 2009. *The Izon of the Niger Delta*. Port Harcourt: Onyoma.

Amurun, Omafume. 31 January 2009. "Why Other Regions Do Not Want a United Niger Delta": 32–33. Port Harcourt: *Niger Delta Standard*.

Ibeanu, Okechukwu. 2006. *Civil Society and Conflict Management in the Niger Delta: Scoping Gaps for Policy and Advocacy*. Lagos: Cleen Foundation, Monograph Series no. 2.

Kalu, Kalu. 2008. *State Power, Autarchy, and Political Conquest in Nigerian Federalism*. Lanham (MD): Lexington.

Kukah, Matthew. 2011. *Witness to Justice: An Insider's Account of Nigeria's Truth Commission*. Ibadan: BookCraft.

Maja-Pearce, Adewale. 2005. *Remembering Ken Saro-Wiwa and Other Essays*. Lagos: The New Gong.

Mitee, Ledum. 2008. *Report of the Technical Committee on the Niger Delta*. Port Harcourt, PDF File.

Ogune, Matthew. 30 March 2019. "Alleged $40m Fraud: Jonathan's Cousin, Azibaola, Knows Fate May 27". Lagos: *Guardian*.

Okonta, Ike. 2008. *When Citizens Revolt: Nigerian Elites, Big Oil and the Ogoni Struggle for Self-determination*. Trenton (NJ): Africa World Press.

Okoko, Kimse & Lazarus, Abonor 1999. "The Creation of Bayelsa State". In *The Land and People of Bayelsa State*, edited by Alagoa, Ebiegberi Joe: 251–257. Port Harcourt: Onyoma Research Publications.

Onokerhoraye, Andrew Godwin. 2011. "Urhobo Unity in Contemporary Times". In *The Urhobo People*, edited by Onigu Otite: 531–588. Ibadan: Gold Press Ltd.

Renouard, Cécile *et al.* 2008. *L'impact de l'activité pétrolière sur le développement local au Nigeria: enquêtes dans les zones d'Onelga (Rivers State) et d'Eastern Obolo (Akwa Ibom State)*. Paris: Manuscript.

Social Action. 2018. *Abandoned Projects: Citizens' Report on Budget of Selected States of Nigeria, 2017*. Port Harcourt: MacArthur Foundation.

Taiwo, Olalekan John & Fethi Ahmed. 2015. "Geographical Analysis of Voter Apathy in Presidential Elections between 1999 and 2011 in Nigeria". *African Geographical Review* 34 (3): 250–268.

Ukeje, Charles *et al.* 2002. *Oil and Violent Conflicts in the Niger Delta.* Ile-Ife: Obafemi Awolowo University Press.

Wakili, Isiaka. 14 May 2012. "Niger Delta Demands 14 More States". Abuja: *Daily Trust.*

Conclusion

Since the proclamation of a short-lived Niger Delta Republic in 1966, Nigeria's oil-producing areas have never really been at peace. Initially, conflicts concerned mainly the Ibo of the hinterland, who dominated the Eastern Region, before shifting to so-called host communities when oil production began to expand along the coast following the end of the Biafran War in 1970. The Ogoni uprising and the Ijaw's armed rebellion later set ablaze the entire Niger Delta. Since then, the end of the military dictatorship and the return to a parliamentary regime under the Fourth Republic have legitimized the impunity of corrupt leaders, the rise of militias, and the proliferation of armed youth gangs. The 2009 presidential amnesty, in particular, did little to help resolve the crisis. It even had the opposite effect, because the payment of stipends and the attribution of contracts to militants have consolidated and institutionalized their power. The rebels were able to penetrate the state and sometimes stood successfully for political office in Abuja. Such a system forced the government to endlessly continue paying subsidies to avoid a resumption of hostilities.

From one political regime to another, however, the youth never took the lead to emerge as a class in itself. The notion of age-group is indeed a bit confusing in the Niger Delta, as well as in Iboland. In the context of population pressure and extended family patriarchal structures, the so-called "youth" include many men in their forties and mainly refer to a generation which is more exposed to the modernity of a global world, by contrast to the tradition of elders (Bersselaar 1998: 262). Some militants thus contested the power and the abuses of corrupt warrant chiefs and officials. But they did not really challenge social reproduction and they eventually became family men and women once they benefited from the oil wealth and the 2009 presidential amnesty. Even the initation rites of cult societies confirmed the domination of older leaders on subalterns.

The aim of this book was thus to demonstrate that violence in the Niger Delta cannot be reduced to ethnic uprisings or to a struggle against oil companies. The structural political, social, and economic factors of conflicts are rooted in a long history that began well before Nigeria gained independence and Shell ever set foot in the region. In the long term, oil was mainly a trigger that exacerbated latent tensions. For example, the economic boom of the 1970s, together with rapid urbanization, attracted many migrants from all over Nigeria and accelerated the dissolution of traditional community ties. At the same time, the competition for oil wealth has intensified ethnic nationalism, notably among the Ogoni and the Ijaw. From this point of view, the Niger Delta

FIGURE 53   A fishing boat off the coast of Bayelsa State (2011)

rebellion fits the pattern of insurrections that, in mining areas, are typically driven by a strong sense of marginalization, sometimes combined with a feeling of religious discrimination, and that demand political autonomy to secure a greater share of revenues and better compensation for indigenous people impacted by expropriations, pollution, and unemployment as a result of workers migrating from other regions (Ross 2003: 7).

Today, disputes over the appropriation of oil revenues transcend all levels of the Nigerian state, the industry, and local communities. Parties to the conflict are bound by complex relationships. The multinationals pay taxes to the state that are used to fund political cronies and that ultimately serve to unite key players around a common interest: profit maximization. In other words, the tendency of many analysts to focus only on the oil industry is reductive, insofar as it conceals the central role played by the federal government and the Niger Delta's ruling class.

Human rights organizations, environmental lobbies, and the media routinely denounce the misdeeds of mining companies. The latter undeniably play a crucial role in the many problems facing the Niger Delta. However, the so-called resource curse is, first of all, a symptom of bad governance rather than the other way around. In Nigeria, the state continues to be of primordial importance despite its weakness. In addition, the sociocultural dynamics of conflicts cannot be ignored or minimized. The "cargo cult" and resource curse narratives of Nigerian and Western scholars often serve to obscure the responsibility of the local ruling class. Focusing too much on the role of international oil companies can even lead to misguided public policies.

For example, the Nigeria Extractive Industries Transparency Initiative (NEITI), established in 2007, performs financial audits to monitor money transfers between multinationals and the central bank. However, it pays no attention to embezzlement within the state-owned NNPC, a corporation founded in 1977 that only began publishing its accounts in 2020 as part of its bid to become a listed company. In the same vein, NEITI does not investigate capital flight and the misappropriation of oil revenue by corrupt leaders. To respect Nigeria's sovereignty, it also does not monitor federal and regional budgets. It was only in 2019 that NEITI began to question the industry's taxation levels, making public policy recommendations and conducting audits of physical flows to measure the scale of bunkering.

A thorough analysis of the situation should, however, lead to a self-evident conclusion: the solution to the Niger Delta crisis lies, first and foremost, with the Nigerian people, especially the youth. Put bluntly, there is no alternative. For example, a researcher from the Niger Delta once noted that the three main communities in competition in Warri had lived in the region for centuries; all claimed to be the original settlers and they had nowhere else to go (Courson 2007: 10). Therefore, it was up to them to find common ground if they wanted to avoid self-destruction. By contrast, oil companies always had the option of leaving, which is precisely what they did when they began to disinvest and sell their onshore mining leases in the 2010s.

A peaceful Niger Delta is possible in the long term. The case of Calabar testifies to this. As Ukoha Ukiwo (2009) pointed out in a remarkable and little-known article, the city has been spared the unrests thanks to the social capital of its inhabitants and their capacity to regulate conflicts without resorting to violence. Unlike the three main competing groups in Warri, the Efik, the Qua, and the Efut of Calabar indeed originate from the same territory. As a result, the Efik, who traditionally dominate Calabar, see themselves as "senior brothers" charged with protecting other communities. They do not follow the pattern of the Itsekiri, who claim to be the "overlords" of Warri and who ask the Urhobo and the Ijaw to "go back" to the "land of their ancestors" in rural areas. Unlike the Itsekiri, also, the Efik were more than just slave merchants and colonial political officers. As school teachers and catechists, they rather helped develop surrounding rural areas.

Moreover, the Calabar townspeople forged a common identity by fighting together against the preeminence of the much more numerous Ibo and Ibibio in the hinterland. While the Itsekiri elite would have preferred to remain under a Yoruba domination within a vast Western Region at independence, the Efik struggled to obtain the creation of a Cross River State, whose first governor after the military dictatorship in 1999, Donald Duke, was of Efik father and Qua mother. In fact, the three original groups of Calabar still intermarry and live peacefully in the same neighborhoods. In this regard, they are quite different from the Itsekiri who avoid mixing with Urhobo or Ijaw families. Last but not least, each group has a traditional chief recognized by the authorities and all of them share the same urban, linguistic, symbolic, and touristic heritage.

Such characteristics, as we can see, have little to do with oil production, which is more intensive in Warri than in Calabar. Yet advocacy organizations usually prefer to focus on the role played by international companies, to explain the Niger Delta crisis. For communication purposes, oil majors indeed represent choice targets because Shell, ExxonMobil, Chevron, and Total are known worldwide. Also, listed multinationals are more responsive to diplomatic, media, and economic pressures than a state entity such as NNPC. By contrast, indigenous companies or groups unfamiliar to anyone outside the Niger Delta are less likely to mobilize global public opinion. Few people are prepared to devote time and attention to the social intricacies of the Urhobo, the Itsekiri, the Ijaw, or the Ogoni. Therefore, my main purpose in writing this book was to provide keys for understanding a very complex situation.

The Niger Delta's protracted crisis is set to last, as Nigeria's oil production is stagnating or falling because of persistent insecurity, bunkering, endemic corruption, investor fatigue, and the countdown to corporate net-zero carbon emissions by 2050. In late 2021, less than a third of the NNPC's revenue ended up in state coffers. The remaining two-thirds were used to pay for the subsidies that finance imports of refined product to keep pump prices artificially low. This state of affairs is a good indication of the prospects facing the youth of the Niger Delta. The challenge now is to manage the shortage, rather than the abundance, of mineral resources.

References

Bersselaar, Dmitri van den. 1998. *In Search of Igbo Identity. Language, Culture and Politics in Nigeria, 1900–1966.* Leiden, University of Leiden.

Courson, Elias. 2007. *The Burden of Oil: Social Deprivation and Political Militancy in Gbaramatu Clan, Warri South West LGA, Delta State, Nigeria.* Berkeley: University of California, Institute of International Studies.

FIGURE 54   Mile 2 Diobu Market in Port Harcourt: Umbrellas provide shelter from both the
rain and the sun (2011)

Ross, Michael. 2003. *Nigeria's Oil Sector and the Poor*. London: UK Department for
International Development.

Ukiwo, Ukoha. 2009. "Between 'Senior Brother' and 'Overlord': Competing Versions of
Horizontal Inequalities and Ethnic Conflict in Calabar and Warri, Nigeria". *Journal
of International Development* 21 (4): 495–506.

Overview of "Cult" Societies in Nigeria

From Students' Fraternities to Street Gangs

Main name / other names	Symbol & color	Date & place of creation on a campus	Comments
Pyrates Confraternity (PC) / National Association of Seadogs (NAS)	-Skull and crossbones -Red beret or scarf with a long-sleeved white shirt and black trousers	1953, Ibadan (officially established as NAS in 1980)	-Nigeria's oldest students' fraternity. Its banning from campuses in 1984 marked the beginning of its criminalization. -No armed branch.
Buccaneers Association of Nigeria (BAN) / Alora, Sea Lords Association of Nigeria	-Skull and crossbones with the motto: "No Price No Pay" -Green beret or scarf with a long-sleeved white shirt and black trousers -Color: yellow	1972, Ibadan; 1975, Nsukka; 1980, Calabar	-Dissident faction of the Pyrates, registered in 1982 and sometimes spelt Baccaneers
Black Axe / Neo Black Movement of Africa (NBM/NBA), Black Axe Movement (BAM)	-Axe and white sword with the motto: "Ayei! Axemen" -Black beret with a yellow ribbon, long-sleeved white shirt and black trousers	1977, Benin City; 1979, Ibadan; 1984, Ekpoma LGA (Ambrose Ali State University)	-Dissident faction of the Eiye and Buccaneers, with strong Edo ethnic roots in Benin City. It expanded to Port Harcourt under the leadership of Atemie Pepple. -NBM was officially registered as an association in 1994. Inspired by the Black Panthers in America, it claims to be pan-Africanist, to fight against racism and oppression and to fund student scholarships, provide equipment to the police, and offer legal assistance to prisoners.

Main name / other names	Symbol & color	Date & place of creation on a campus	Comments
	-Magic number: 7.7.77, in reference to the date of its creation, on 7 July 1977		-Armed branch off campus: Black Axe. Named after the NBMA's quarterly magazine, which adopted a new name, *Uhuru* (Liberation), after splitting from BAM in 1985. -Its colours are black for blackness, white for peace and yellow for intellect.
Klansmen Konfraternity (KK) / EFOLC or EFOLK (Eternal Fraternal Order of the Legion Consortium, or Konsortium)	-Two crisscrossed swords and a skull adorned with a scarf -Motto: "Ave", "Debt na debt", "Deebam" (or "Degbam") (lit. "to be strong", in pidgin) -Black beret with a white ribbon, long-sleeved white shirt and black trousers	1983, Calabar; 1991, Port Harcourt	-An armed branch, Deebam (or Dey-Gbam), was established in Port Harcourt in 1991 and mobilized youths who were not students. Its founder, Onengiye-Ofori Terika (a.k.a. "Occasion Boy"), hailed from Buguma and also formed a gang called Okomera in 1999 in Tombia, where he was killed in October 2003 by the Deewell, a group supporting Ateke Tom. A new leader from Omoku in the Ogba/Egbema/Ndoni LGA, Kingsley Akogu "King", took over but was soon arrested and executed by the security forces. His successor, Ichechi Owaka (a.k.a. "Angel"), therefore moved the gang's general headquarters from Tombia to Ogbakiri in Emohua LGA. He was also killed by the army in June 2004, while trying to take control of Ogoni villages with the support of the leader of Gokona LGA, Fred Barivale Kpakol, and the Rivers State finance commissioner, Kenneth Kobani. Prince Glad Igodo (a.k.a. "Gibson Kaka") then took over the Deebam to stand in elections in his native town of Tombia in May 2007, earning him

Main name / other names	Symbol & color	Date & place of creation on a campus	Comments
			the hostility of another PDP candidate, Celestine Omehia, who supported the rival faction of the Deewell of Soboma George. Despite the departure of dissident factions such as D-12, G-12 and the Titians, Deebam remained the largest gang in Rivers State in terms of membership and territories, which included the Ogbia and Yenagoa LGAs in Bayelsa State.
Supreme Vikings Confraternity (SVC) / Sea Robbers, National Association of Adventurers, De Norsemen Club of Nigeria	-Skull and crossbones topped with a vampire bat and the letter v -Black beret or scarf with a red ribbon, long-sleeved white shirt and black trousers	1981, Port Harcourt; 1986, Calabar	-Dissident faction of BAN; no initiation; recruitment on an ad hoc basis. Members do not know each other and sometimes end up fighting against each other without knowing it. -To combat the Deebam of the KK, the Vikings sponsored the creation of two gangs in 2000: Deewell, a group based in Port Harcourt's Mile 111 Diobu; and the Icelanders (a.k.a. the Germans or Malaysians) under Ateke Tom in the Okrika suburb, which formed a militia for PDP's governor of Rivers State, Peter Odili. Before the April 2007 elections, Deewell controlled the Ken-Khana, Degema, and Emuoha LGAs. Its members were allied to the Outlaws of Marine Base in Port Harcourt and received support from local politicians such as Gabriel Pidomson, an Ogoni member of the Regional Assembly, and Rotimi Amaechi against his rival Celestine Omehia. With its stronghold in Harry's Town near Degema, the group also fought against a self-defense

Main name / other names	Symbol & color	Date & place of creation on a campus	Comments
			militia, Elegemface, which was established in 2003 by Endurance Orlu and the residents of Nkpolu Oroworukwo to repel attacks by Deebam and Deewell in Mile III Diobu, before being absorbed by Ateke Tom's men. As for the Outlaws, they left the Icelanders when their leader, Soboma George, was betrayed by Ateke Tom and handed over to the police for murdering a fighter close to Asari Dokubo in 2004.
Eiye Supreme Confraternity / The Bird, National Association of Air Lords, Supreme Eiye Confraternity (SEC)	-"Eiye" (Yoruba word meaning sorcerer) -Red eagle -Color: blue	1965, Ibadan; 1992, Calabar	-Mostly composed of Yoruba members, it started developing after the Biafran War in 1970. -Armed branch off campus: Black Axe (see above)
Black Berets / Brotherhood of Blood, Two-Two	-Black beret	Around 1995, Enugu State University of Science and Technology	-Ibo membership; supplied with weapons from Akwa blacksmiths in Anambra
Mafia / Campus Mafia, Family		Around 1991, Ile-Ife (Obafemi Awolowo University)	-N.a.

Main name / other names	Symbol & color	Date & place of creation on a campus	Comments
Maphite	-Green beret	1978, Benin City	-Sometimes spelled Maphlate or Marphite, the brotherhood does not make the political claims of its Black Axe rivals. Its initiation rites refer to a sacred book, the Great Book, or Green Bible, and to an imaginary god, Gudphada. -Maphite is supposed to be an acronym that means: Maximum Academic Performance Highly Intellectuals Train Executioner. -To get around a 2001 law banning cults, the brotherhood set up a legal front in 2002 with a "charity" called GCA (Green Circuit Association).
Jurists		1991, Auchi Polytechnic (Edo State)	In 1992, the society allegedly set up a legal organization, the PLIJ (Patriotic Lords Initiative for Justice). It is also called Juris' National Association of Grand Lords.

NB: Other "cult" societies include the Corsairs, Pirats, Green Berets, Fregates, Barracudas, Musketeers, Walrus, Temple of Eden, Trojan Horse, MgbaMgba Brothers, Black Cats, Bats, Dragons, King Cobras, Scorpions, and Gentlemen. In Rivers State alone, the Secret Cult and Similar Activities Prohibition Law passed in June 2004 officially listed a hundred organizations, among them the Agbaye, Airwords, Amazon, Barracuda, Bas, Bees International, Big 20, Black Axe, Black Beret Fraternity, Black Brasserie, Black Brothers, Black Cats, Black Cross, Black Ladies, Black Ofals, Black Scorpions, Black Sword, Blanchers, Blood Hunters, Blood Suckers, Brotherhood of Blood, Burkina Faso: Revolution Fraternity, Canary, Cappa Vandetto, Daughters of Jezebel, Dey Gbam, Dey Well, Dolphins, Dragons, Dreaded Friends of Friends, Eagle Club, Egbe Dudu, Eiye of Air Lords Fraternity, Elegemface, Executioners, Fangs, FF, Fliers, Frigates, Gentlemen's Club, Green Berets Fraternity, Hard Candies, Hell's Angels, Hepos, Himalayas, Icelanders, Jaggare Confederation, KGB, King Cobra, Klam Konfraternity Klansman, Ku Klux Klan, Knite Cade, Mafia Lords, Mafioso Fraternity, Malcolm x, Maphites/Maphlate, Mgba Mgba Brothers, Mob Stab, Musketeers Fraternity, National Association of Adventurers, National Association of Sea Dogs, Neo-Black Movement, Night Mates, Nite Hawks, Nite Rovers, Odu Cofraternity, Osiri, Ostrich Fraternity, Panama Pyrate, Phoenix, Predators, Red Devils, Red Fishes, Red Sea Horse, Royal House of Peace, Royal Queens, Sailors, Scavengers, Scorpion, Scorpion Fraternity, Sea Vipers, Soiree Fraternity, Soko, Sunmen, Temple of Eden Fraternity, Thomas Sankara Boys, Tikan Giants, Trojan Horses Fraternity, Truth Seekers, Twin mate, Vikings, Vipers, Vultures, Walrus, and White Bishops.

References

Best, Shedrack Gaya and Dimieari Von Kemedi. 2005. "Armed Groups and Conflict in Rivers and Plateau States, Nigeria". In *Armed and Aimless: Armed Groups, Guns, and Human Security in the ECOWAS Region*, edited by Nicolas Florquin & Eric Berman: 22. Geneva: Small Arms.

Offiong, Daniel. 2003. *Secret Cults in Nigerian Tertiary Institutions*. Enugu: Fourth Dimension.

Pérouse de Montclos, Marc-Antoine. 2012. "Rebelles, gangsters et cadets sociaux dans le delta du Niger: les jeunes au défi de la politique". In *L'Afrique des générations. Entre tensions et négociations*, edited by Muriel Gomez-Perez & Marie Nathalie Leblanc : 617–644. Paris: Karthala.

Pérouse de Montclos, Marc-Antoine. 1997. *Violence et sécurité urbaines en Afrique du Sud et au Nigeria, un essai de privatisation: Durban, Johannesburg, Kano, Lagos et Port Harcourt*. Paris: L'Harmattan. Various articles in the local press.

Three Examples of Domestic Companies

The domestic oil industry is a highly diverse sector. Three examples provide a good illustration of its variety: Conoil, the only Nigerian company to be active in both the upstream and downstream sectors; Sapetro, which operates abroad; and Seplat, a success story of mixed fortunes.

1   The Veteran: Conoil

Founded by Mike Adenuga in 1984, Conoil (Consolidated Oil Limited) is a veteran of the domestic oil industry. It drilled its first wells in 1991 at OML 103 and became active in both the upstream and downstream sectors. Conoil is also one of the few Nigerian firms to operate offshore, at OML 59 near the coast, as well as in Block 4 of the JDZ (Joint Development Zone) with São Tomé. According to its own estimates, it sits on reserves of a billion barrels of oil and 7 billion cubic feet of gas, potentially making it one of Africa's largest oil companies. For example, in 2013 it drilled a 6,000-meter deep well onshore called Ango with its technical partner CONOG (Continental Oil and Gas Limited) at OML 59.

However, Conoil is handicapped by major structural weaknesses. First, it is not a listed company. It does not adhere to international standards, and it has never attracted foreign investors. It also has a reputation for paying its subcontractors, employees, and taxes with much delay, despite regular cash flows from its oil production. According to many observers, the mismanagement of the company has a lot to do with its Yoruba founder. In his autobiography, the official in charge of privatization programs under President Olusegun Obasanjo, Nasir Ahmad El-Rufai (2014), reported how Mike Adenuga attempted to bribe him to lay his hands on Shell's distribution network, nationalized as NOLCHEM (National Oil and Chemical Marketing Company) and resold by the state in 2000. At the time, the CEO of ConPetro (later Conoil) was able to secure the support of General Ibrahim Babangida and Vice-President Atiku Abubakar to bypass public market regulations and oust the former head of the junta, General Yakubu Gowon, from the board of NOLCHEM.

2   Sapetro, or the Call of the Sea

Sapetro (South Atlantic Petroleum) reflects a somewhat different model insofar as it does not operate in Nigeria. Founded in 1995 by General Theophilus Danjuma, the then chairman of the Nigerian subsidiary of ENI, the company was initially very close to the military junta of Sani Abacha. In 1998, Sapetro secured an OPL (Oil Prospecting License) in a block where huge offshore deposits were discovered at Akpo, Egina, Preowei, and Kuro in the 2000s. Through Gilbert Chagoury, a Lebanese-Nigerian billionaire and a close associate of General Sani Abacha, a joint venture was established with Total and Petrobras's local subsidiary, Brasoil, to develop highly promising fields that included condensates not subject to OPEC quotas, making exports easier.

However, Sapetro had neither the funds nor the technical capabilities to exploit OPL 256, which later became OML 130 in 2005. The company was entirely dependent on Total in this regard. Moreover, its early political connections backfired. A member of the military junta with Olusegun Obasanjo from 1975 to 1979, Theophilus Danjuma fell out with his former brother in arms after criticizing him for seeking to amend the constitution in an attempt to run for a third term in 2007. In retaliation, the government seized half of Sapetro's share in OML 130 in 2006, prompting Danjuma to accept a production sharing agreement with NNPC, while CNOOC (China National Offshore Oil Corporation) financed 95% of its contribution.

This reversal of fortune highlighted Sapetro's structural vulnerabilities. The company had fewer than thirty employees in 2009 and no operations in Nigeria. Sapetro nonetheless survived by selling OML 130, a block purchased for very little that had gained considerably in value following the discovery of the Akpo and Egina fields. The company was even able to grow its activities after the second wife of the ageing Theophilus Danjuma, Daisy, took over. She was well connected and was elected to the Nigerian Senate in 2003. Under her supervision, Sapetro became the first Nigerian company to operate wells abroad. In 2004, it acquired an offshore field abandoned since 1997 in the Republic of Benin, Seme, and it began in 2013 to extract crude oil consisting of a third of water. Incidentally, it is worth noting that Sapetro also acquired offshore licenses in Madagascar, Mozambique, and even France—specifically, at Juan de Nova in the exclusive economic zone of the Scattered Islands in the Indian Ocean.

3   Seplat: A Success Story of Mixed Fortunes

Formed in 2009 through a partnership between Shebah Petroleum Development Company Limited and Platform Petroleum Joint Ventures Limited specifically to pursue upstream oil and gas opportunities in Nigeria, Seplat (Shebah Exploration Platform) has been operating at OMLs 4, 38, and 41 since 2010. It is often described as a success story because the production of its onshore wells at Oben, Amukpe, Ovhor, Okporhuru, and Sapele increased from 18,000 barrels a day in 2011 to around 70,000 barrels in 2013. At OML 53, the company was nonetheless taken to court in 2013 by Britannia-U, which claimed primacy of rights but was unable to raise the funds needed to purchase the block from Chevron. Moreover, Seplat has not been spared the political constraints that have also affected Conoil and Sapetro.

This is highlighted by the two entities that formed the company. Operating without expatriates and foreign capital, Platform was established in June 2001 by a Kalabari chief from Rivers State, Dumo Lulu Briggs, its chairman and the son of Olu Benson Lulu-Briggs, the founder of another domestic company, Moni Pulo. In November 2004, it began to exploit onshore fields (Umutu/Asuokpu) at OML 38 in Delta State. Dumo Lulu Briggs, a former manager of Moni Pulo, soon became involved in local politics. In 2013, he supported President Goodluck Jonathan against the governor of Rivers, Rotimi Amaechi, and was one of the front-running PDP candidates in the state gubernatorial race in 2015 and 2023.

As for Shebah, it was established in May 2004 to purchase a 40% stake from ConocoPhillips at OML 108 in shallow waters where it operated a field, Ukpokiti, with Express Petroleum & Gas, one of the many businesses owned by Aminu Dantata, a well-known billionaire from Kano. Unlike Platform, Shebah had foreign investors and political connections in northern Nigeria. Also known as SEPCOL (Shebah Exploration & Production Company Limited), it was based in Minna in Niger State, with offices in Lagos. Its main shareholders included Nasiru Ado Bayero, a prince of Kano and a cousin of Sanusi Lamido Sanusi, the head of the Central Bank under President Goodluck Jonathan. The founder of Shebah, "ABC" Ambrosie Bryant Chukwueloka Orjiakor, was a surgeon who also owned Zebbra Energy and OPL 248 in the deep offshore through his connections with the head of the military junta in the 1990s. It was therefore no coincidence that SEPCOL had its head office in Minna, the hometown of General Ibrahim Babangida.

4   Conclusion

All three domestic companies are deeply embedded in the political games surrounding the appropriation of oil revenue. Sapetro is a product of the military dictatorship, while Conoil and Seplat are ready to make deals with "Any Government In Power", hence their nickname AGIP. However, despite their diversity, they face relatively similar challenges in seeking to raise funds, free themselves from political interference, limit the damage from bunkering, and develop their operational capabilities (see Table 2).

TABLE 2   Conoil, Sapetro and Seplat: Common challenges

	Conoil	Sapetro	Seplat
Capacity to raise own funds	Limited	Yes	Yes
Nigerian management and ownership	Yes	Yes	Yes
Political autonomy	"AGIP"	In progress	"AGIP"
Quality of relations with host communities in the Niger Delta	Poor	Not applicable	Unknown
Capacity to limit bunkering	Poor	Poor	Poor
Potential for operational development	Yes	Yes	Yes
Main strength	Resilience; operational upstream and downstream	Resilience; internationalization of activities	Industrial performance and increase in production
Main weakness	Mismanagement; poor relations with subcontractors	Not operational in Nigeria; declining political network	Uncertainties over tax reforms and scale of bunkering

Reference

El-Rufai, Nasir Ahmad. 2014. *The Accidental Public Servant*. Ibadan: Safari Books.

Index

Abacha, Sani   54, 57, 59–63, 65, 67, 91, 98,
    101, 103, 113, 118, 138, 150–2, 155, 174–5,
    181–2, 184, 189, 190, 216–7, 219, 222, 235,
    246, 263, 289
ACN: Action Congress of Nigeria   264
AD: Alliance for Democracy   118, 186
Ada George, Rufus   59, 76, 91, 198
ADEF: Ateke, Dokubo, Egberipapa &
    Farah (private security firm in
    Rivers)   97, 99
Adenuga, Mike   150, 154–6, 288
Afren   149, 151–2, 156
Agip: *Azienda generale italiana petroli* (Italian
    oil company)   16, 31, 33, 47, 78, 97, 131,
    146, 148–9, 152, 155, 190, 249, 264
AGIP: 'Any Government In Power'
    (nickname)   290–1
Ahoada   XIV, 45, 55, 133, 142, 267, 270
Akassa   1, 14, 152, 171, 178–9, 203, 267
Akwa Ibom State   3, 7, 27, 43, 45, 55, 122, 134,
    148, 159, 160, 163–5, 168, 171, 185, 186, 188,
    198, 213, 216–7, 221, 227, 230, 232, 234,
    238, 264–9
Alamieyeseigha, Diepreye   77–8, 90, 92,
    101, 103, 111, 133, 171, 218, 221–3, 234–5,
    262, 267
Alison-Madueke, Diezani   154, 156, 199
Amaechi, Rotimi   93, 99, 101, 104, 149, 170,
    218, 222, 231, 264, 284, 290
Amanyananbo   164
Amnesty International   53
Andoni   54–5, 57–9, 75, 163–4, 167, 169, 189,
    213, 268–70
Annang   45, 130, 238, 269
ANPP: All Nigeria People's Party   76
APC: All Progressives Congress   93, 99,
    234, 264
APP: All People's Party   101, 118
Azikiwe, Nnamdi   44, 57, 180, 182, 235

Babangida, Ibrahim   19, 50, 59, 90, 111, 113,
    119, 143, 146, 150–2, 172, 263, 288, 290
Bakassi   81, 215
Bayelsa State   3, 15, 18, 20, 45, 63, 66–7, 76–8,
    81, 83–5, 89–93, 97, 100–3, 109–11, 122–3,

130, 133–4, 137, 144, 147, 152–4, 163, 170–
    1, 178, 180–6, 189, 203–4, 212–3, 215–6,
    218, 220, 227, 230, 232, 234–5, 238–40,
    249–51, 262–8, 270–1, 276, 284
Bendel: Benin-Delta (State)   45, 49, 98,
    250, 271
Benin City   43, 47, 63, 161, 227, 282, 286
Bini   43–4, 163, 165, 227
Bonny   11, 21, 31–3, 42, 50, 55, 58, 99, 103, 129,
    146, 161, 163–4, 166, 168, 178, 180, 186,
    213, 215, 254, 270
Bori   46, 53, 55, 58, 61, 161, 167, 267
Boro, Isaac   16–20, 42, 57, 75, 79, 96, 181, 184,
    261, 263
BP: British Petroleum   18, 28–31, 33, 47–8,
    142, 200, 234
Brass   1, 11, 13, 29, 45, 97, 109–10, 131, 136, 146–
    7, 165, 171, 179, 186, 213, 218, 267, 271
Briggs, Ann-Kio   211, 220
Buhari, Muhammadu   93–5, 98–9, 102, 104,
    136, 155, 234, 236, 238, 251, 264
Bunkering   3, 32, 64, 95–6, 98, 122–3, 190–1,
    222, 239–40, 244, 246–8, 251–2, 254–5,
    257, 277–8, 290–1
Burutu   15, 30, 44, 100, 113, 173–4, 185, 267

Calabar   21, 43–5, 55, 75, 97, 122, 130, 152, 161,
    167–8, 172, 190, 268–9, 277–8
Chevron   15, 29, 51, 96, 98, 100, 131–2, 137, 139,
    146, 148, 150, 175, 185, 188, 191, 202–4,
    207, 223, 251, 278, 290
Clark, Edwin   91, 267
CLO: Civil Liberties Organisation   112
Comey   13, 117, 168
Conoil: Consolidated Oil Limited   149–50,
    151, 154–7, 288, 290–1
Cross River State   20–1, 43–4, 81, 84, 112,
    122–3, 152, 168, 171, 181, 190, 203, 213, 230,
    267–9, 278
CSR: Corporate social responsibility   96, 134,
    139, 146, 197, 201, 203–5, 256–7
Cult societies, Cultist   3, 104, 128–31, 275,
    277, 281–6

Dangote, Aliko   142, 144, 199

Dappa-Biriye, Harold   2, 40, 43–4, 66, 267
Dash   117, 128, 261
Delta State   3, 47, 50, 66, 76, 78, 80, 84–5,
        89, 96–101, 103, 112–3, 122–3, 131–2, 137,
        144, 146, 152, 164, 169–75, 182, 185, 188,
        190, 202–4, 213–4, 216, 221–3, 230, 232,
        238, 244–5, 250–1, 261, 263–4, 266–7,
        270–1, 290
Derivation   215–6, 221, 227–8, 235–6,
        246, 266
Dickson, Henry Seriake   66, 102, 181, 262
Diete-Spiff, Alfred   45
Dokubo, Asari   2–3, 66, 71–7, 80, 82, 86, 95–
        7, 99, 103, 183–5, 232, 244, 263, 266, 285
Douglas, Oronto   63, 92, 111–2, 186, 227
DPR: Department of Petroleum
        Resources   197, 249–50, 256

Edo (State)   77, 83, 98, 134, 150, 171, 174, 227–
        8, 230, 267, 271, 286
Edo (ethnic group)   43–4, 161, 163, 165,
        186, 282
EFCC: Economic and Financial Crimes
        Commission   83, 222–4, 240, 265
Efik   20, 43–5, 122, 161, 167, 172, 269, 277–8
Egbesu   1, 14, 64, 71–3, 78, 111, 130
Eleme   15, 46, 55, 57–8, 97, 163, 215, 253, 270
Elf   16, 28–31, 47, 100, 137, 197, 202, 204
Ellah, Francis   21
ENI: *Ente Nazionale Idrocarburi*   16, 142, 289
Enugu (Town and State)   17, 43–4, 84,
        138, 285
ERA: Environmental Rights Action   63,
        220, 227
Escravos   30, 51, 100, 146, 175, 188, 203
Etete, Dan   150, 155–6, 190, 238

FNDIC: Federated Niger Delta Ijaw
        Communities   66, 99–100, 123, 137, 185
Forcados   18, 30–2, 85, 146, 152, 161, 166, 204
FPSO: Floating Production Storage and
        Offloading   152, 201

Gbaramatu   1, 51, 76, 89, 96, 164, 166, 173–5,
        244–5, 261
Godfather, Godfatherism   89, 98, 155
Gowon, Yakubu   20–2, 28, 30–1, 33–6, 40, 43,
        45–7, 60, 145, 181–2, 234, 288

Greenpeace   58, 111, 115, 227
Gulf Oil   15, 29–31, 47, 145, 200, 251

Hausa   17, 55, 116, 151, 182, 186, 238

Ibani   55, 57, 75, 129, 161, 180, 269
Ibibio   20, 43–5, 55, 57, 122, 130, 161, 172, 185–
        6, 189, 213, 227, 269, 278
Ibo   11–2, 15, 17, 19–23, 26, 29–30, 32–3, 35–7,
        40–5, 55, 57, 59–60, 63, 67–8, 116, 130,
        159, 163–5, 168–70, 172, 179–83, 185–6,
        189, 205, 213, 235, 238, 263, 270–1, 275,
        277, 285
Ibori, James Onanefe   78, 100, 103, 170, 172,
        221–3, 234
Ijaw   1, 2, 4, 12, 14, 15, 17–21, 23, 42–5, 50–1, 53,
        57, 59, 63–8, 71, 74–7, 79, 83, 85, 89–93,
        99, 101–3, 114, 122, 130, 133–4, 149–50,
        161, 163–7, 169–75, 178–86, 190, 198, 203,
        207, 210, 212–3, 215, 217, 220, 223, 226,
        232, 235–6, 238, 244, 246, 261–7, 270–1,
        275, 277–8
Ikwerre   21, 45, 64, 170, 213, 270
Imo River   58, 163–4, 167, 268–9
Imo State   136, 152, 168, 270–1
INC: Ijaw National Council   66, 261–2, 265–7
Ironsi, Johnson Aguiyi   25, 36, 45
Itsekiri   12, 42–3, 51, 59, 66–7, 100, 122, 161,
        163, 165, 167, 170, 172–5, 180, 188, 202,
        217, 261, 277–8
IYC: Ijaw Youth Council   66, 74–6, 78–9,
        81, 83, 101–3, 112, 184–5, 198, 220, 235,
        262–3, 265

Jonathan, Goodluck   63, 76, 79, 85, 89–93,
        98, 101, 111, 144, 154, 156, 183, 186, 199,
        210, 217, 223, 235–6, 264–5, 267, 290
JV: Joint-Ventures   5, 46–7, 136, 144–6, 150,
        152, 157, 199–200, 205–6, 252, 255–
        6, 289

Kaiama   64, 66–7, 79, 85, 184, 198, 235, 262
Kalabari   43, 75, 90, 122, 131, 149, 161, 163, 168–
        70, 184, 190, 204, 212, 238, 270, 290
Khana   55, 57–8, 65, 284
Kobani, Edward   60, 62, 181, 265

Land Use Act   48, 211, 215

LGA: Local Government Area 64–5, 136, 148, 163, 168–9, 171, 173–5, 213, 215–7, 229–31, 266–71

MAMSER: Mass Mobilization for Self Reliance, Social Justice, and Economic Recover 61, 263
MASSOB: Movement for the Actualisation of the Sovereign State of Biafra 63, 183, 263
MEND: Movement for the Emancipation of the Niger Delta 73, 76–84, 86, 91, 95–6, 99, 100, 112, 130, 133, 137, 183, 185, 189, 190, 221, 236, 246, 261, 265
Mitee, Ledum 63, 65, 97, 112
Mobil, ExxonMobil 30, 47–8, 132, 146, 148, 188, 200, 217, 251, 278
Mohammed, Murtala 41, 48
Moni Pulo 150, 152, 154, 157, 190, 290
Mopol (Mobile Police) 132, 210, 261
MOSOP: Movement for the Survival of the Ogoni People 53–4, 57–60, 62–6, 68, 97, 112, 133, 139, 181, 183, 186, 189, 220, 245, 263, 265, 271

NCNC: National Council of Nigeria and the Cameroons 21, 44, 57, 168, 180, 186
NDA: Niger Delta Avengers 85, 185, 189, 236
NDC: Niger Delta Congress 17, 180
NDPVF: Niger Delta Volunteer People's Force 66, 71–8, 80–2, 91, 103, 133, 183–5, 246, 265–6
NDV: Niger Delta Vigilantes 103
NDVF: Niger Delta Volunteer Force 17, 66
NEITI: Nigerian Extractive Industries Transparency Initiative 63, 156, 235, 277
Nembe 13–4, 100, 114, 122, 131, 133, 137, 153, 161, 165–6, 168, 171, 178, 189, 204, 212–3, 215, 218, 238, 267, 271
NigeriaWatch 64, 120, 123, 131, 147, 214
NIMASA: Nigerian Maritime Administration and Safety Agency 80, 97–9
NNOC: Nigerian National Oil Corporation 47, 255
NNPC: Nigerian National Petroleum Corporation 5, 47, 51, 97, 99, 122, 136, 143–7, 149–50, 175, 185, 199, 200, 206, 236, 240, 249–50, 252–7, 277–8, 289
NPDC: Nigerian Petroleum Development Company 47, 144, 152, 155, 190, 203
NOSDRA: National Oil Spill Detection and Response Agency 250, 252, 256–7
NUPENG: Nigeria Union of Petroleum and Natural Gas Workers 138–9
NYCOP: National Youth Council of Ogoni People 60–2, 65, 68

Oando 152, 154, 156
Obasanjo, Olusegun 14, 48, 67, 71, 75, 78, 80, 90–1, 93, 152, 154–5, 186, 189, 199, 216–7, 220–1, 234–5, 263, 288–9
Obolo 1, 134, 159–60, 163–5, 167, 169, 189, 264, 267–70
Odi 67–8, 14–5, 18, 80, 267
Odili, Peter 75–6, 82, 84, 91, 103, 130, 168, 170, 216–8, 221, 234, 263, 284
Ogoja 43–4, 267
Ogoni 2–3, 11, 15, 21, 42, 45, 49, 109, 119, 122, 130, 132, 161, 163, 167, 169, 181–6, 189–90, 203, 207, 217, 219–20, 227, 239, 244, 246, 251, 253, 263, 265, 267, 269–70, 275, 278, 283–4
Ojukwu, Odumegwu 19–21, 28, 32–6
Okah, Henry 78–80, 86, 91, 97, 112, 221
Okilo, Melford 45, 186
Okrika 1, 14, 55, 59, 75–6, 93, 96, 103, 163–4, 166, 169–70, 184–5, 189, 213, 267, 270, 284
Oloibiri 15–6, 18, 47, 271
Olu 165, 167, 172–5
ONELGA: Ogba-Ndoni-Egbema Local Government Area (Rivers) 264, 271
Onitsha 33, 42–3, 168, 179
Opobo 11, 13, 55, 57–8, 75, 163–4, 166–8, 186, 189, 213, 215, 231, 269–70
OPC: Oodua People's Congress 67, 91, 96, 175, 182, 263
OPEC: Organisation of Petroleum Exporting Countries 47, 145, 200, 206, 238, 256, 289
Oputa Panel 41, 53, 217–8, 267
Orkar, Gideon Gwarzo 49–50, 237
Oron 45, 269
Owerri 15, 33, 43, 55

PDP: People's Democratic Party   75–6, 78,
    89–91, 93–4, 99–104, 118, 131, 133, 171,
    182, 222, 231, 234, 263–5, 284, 290
PENGASSAN: Petroleum and Natural
    Gas Senior Staff Association of
    Nigeria   138–9
Pere   89, 164, 166
Phillips (oil company)   29, 145
PIB: Petroleum Industry Bill   144, 157,
    201, 212
Polo, Tom   77–80, 86, 96–7, 99–100, 137, 185,
    190, 261
Port Harcourt   1, 11–12, 14–5, 17–8, 21–2, 30,
    32–4, 37, 40, 42–8, 53–4, 57, 62, 65–8, 71,
    76, 78, 82, 84, 90–1, 93, 97, 99, 101, 103–
    4, 128–30, 132, 142, 161, 163–4, 169–70,
    178, 180, 184, 187, 197, 202, 205, 210–5,
    227, 238, 247–8, 253–4, 261, 267–70,
    279, 282–4
PSA: Production Sharing Agreement   150,
    157, 199–200, 289

Rivers (State, Province)   2, 3, 13, 18, 21, 40–5,
    50, 55, 58–9, 62, 64–6, 75–8, 82–5, 90–1,
    93, 97, 99–101, 103–4, 122–3, 129–34, 142,
    149, 167, 168, 170, 182, 184–6, 190, 199,
    213, 215–9, 221–2, 230–1, 238–40, 250–1,
    261, 263–4, 267–71, 283–4, 286, 290

São Tomé   29–30, 288
SAFRAP   16, 28–31, 145, 202
Sapetro: South Atlantic Petroleum   152, 154,
    157, 190, 288–91
Saro-Wiwa, Ken   2, 11, 21, 42, 45, 53, 57–63,
    65, 112, 181, 183, 228, 263–5
SDP: Social Democratic Party   60, 75
Security vote   95, 100, 231
SEPCOL: Shebah Exploration & Production
    Company Limited   289–90
Seplat: Shebah Exploration Platform   152,
    154–6, 288–91
Shell   15–6, 18, 27–34, 42, 47–8, 50, 53, 57–8,
    60, 62–4, 66, 79, 85, 93, 96, 98, 111, 115,

130–5, 137, 139, 142, 144–6, 148–9, 154–7,
    190–1, 198–200, 202–4, 206–7, 212, 219,
    223, 227, 244–5, 251–3, 263, 275, 278
Statoil   203, 207
Sylva, Timipre   83–4, 101–2, 189, 220, 222, 264

Tenneco: Tennessee Gas Transmission
    Company   29, 145
Texaco   29, 51, 146, 251
Togo, John   2, 82, 89–90, 95, 266
Total   134–5, 142, 146, 149, 190, 197, 199, 202–
    3, 205, 207, 278, 289
Tuodola, Felix   102–3, 112, 184

Uduaghan, Emmanuel Eweta   100, 170
Ughelli   15, 43, 122, 161, 172, 202, 271
UNEP: United Nations Environment
    Programme   252–4, 264
Urhobo   43, 50–1, 98, 113, 122, 161, 163, 165,
    167, 170, 172–5, 180, 186–8, 217, 267,
    271, 277–8
Uyo   43–4, 55, 161, 268–9

Victor-Ben, Ebikabowei ('Boyloaf')   2, 77, 79,
    84, 91, 96–7, 101, 137
Vikings   101, 104, 129, 284, 286

Warrant chief   159, 166–7, 169, 188, 275
Warri   1, 12, 16, 42–3, 48, 51, 59, 66–7, 74, 76,
    82, 89, 98–101, 142, 161, 163–7, 172–6,
    180, 184–6, 188–9, 202–3, 213–4, 217, 219,
    244–5, 247, 261, 267, 277–8
Wike, Ezenwo Nyesom   99, 104, 170, 216,
    231, 264
Willink, Henry   18, 44
WWF: World Wide Fund for Nature   248–9

Yar'Adua, Umaru   90–1
Yenagoa   64, 81, 90, 101–2, 130, 133, 171, 178–
    80, 213, 233, 246, 262, 267, 271, 284
Yoruba   17, 57, 67, 80, 91, 93, 96, 116, 118, 149–
    50, 171, 173, 175, 182, 185–6, 189, 235, 263,
    278, 285, 288

www.ingramcontent.com/pod-product-compliance
Lightning Source LLC
Chambersburg PA
CBHW070601270326
41926CB00013B/2391